The Quest for Love

The Quest for Love

DAVID HOLBROOK

UNIVERSITY OF ALABAMA PRESS
UNIVERSITY, ALABAMA

Copyright © 1965 by
UNIVERSITY OF ALABAMA PRESS
Library of Congress Catalog Card Number: 65-24879
Manufactured in the United States of America

The lyf so short, the craft so long to lerne,
Th'assay so hard, so sharp the conquerynge,
The dredful joye, that alwey slit so yerne:
All this mene I by Love . . .

Geoffrey Chaucer,
The Parlement of Foules, opening lines

AUTHOR'S NOTE

The completion of this book was made possible by the extension of my Fellowship in 1963 by King's College. I should like to express my gratitude for this. The figure on p. 48 is from a sixteenth-century woodcut by Bernard Salomon and is reproduced from the Nonesuch Press Bible 1963, by kind permission of the Nonesuch Press.

Contents

Preface

In this book I try to make connections between recent findings of psychoanalysis about love and our dealings with reality, and the poet's preoccupation with these.

The conscious practice of psychotherapy as a healing art and medical science is leading to fresh perceptions of human nature, and postulating new truths. These may yet need much more corroboration to establish. But literary criticism and artistic creativity have so far largely failed to take them enough into account. Yet these aspects of our experience have been understood by great artists of the past intuitively, and expressed in their poetic vision. Of course, their intuition has often been mixed with error. But we can no longer ignore the illuminations offered by psychotherapy, where these vindicate the poetic vision in new and exciting ways.

Psychoanalysis is a conscious practice, and is an attempt to make a rational approach to the nature of being, a use of reason and intelligence in exploring the spirit. It has the advantage of some empirical basis in its dealings with human truth, since what it learns from practice it employs in future clinical work. But, as it mellows, this medical science seems to be breaking away from its more deterministic and mechanistic origins in nineteenth-century biology, and to be recognizing more and more the power of love. It has developed a more hopeful attitude to human nature and its creative and constructive potentialities, and it has come to recognize the phantasy as integral to all conscious powers.

It has come to terms more and more with the subtlety and complexity of human nature, and has become resigned to the infinity of ways in which our motives are formed and our actions conditioned. In its clinical work psychoanalysis is increasingly inclined to co-operate in awe with the natural creative power of the psyche, while related social theories – as on child care, such as those derived from the work of John Bowlby – are increasingly based on the recognition of love and creative phantasy as primary. In many ways psychoanalysis has come to accept its need to collaborate with those processes that belong to creative art, and to insist that poetry and love are fundamental human needs. That is, the former preoccupation with explaining human nature in merely functional terms of the 'survival' of the 'organism' has given way to something more humane, and closer to the view of life of those concerned with creativity and art. Psychoanalytical practice has learnt to accept the reality of the immense creativity of the human spirit – so that papers on quite medical topics may contain such phrases as 'union with body and soul' and the late Melanie Klein could talk about the 'good influence of one character on another', and 'hopefulness about the world', in quite old-fashioned 'liberal' ways. This has come about with a crucial change in attitudes, from Ian D. Suttie to more recent psychoanalytical writers such as D. W. Winnicott, who have come to believe that Freud was wrong to suppose that hate was innate, self-interest predominant, and the death-instinct a primal drive. They see hate rather as the consequence of frustrated or thwarted love.[1]

[1] This book was complete before the present writer was able to make use of a further study *Personality Structure and Human Interaction*, by Dr Harry Guntrip of Leeds University Department of Psychiatry (Hogarth Press, 1961). Dr Guntrip makes a far more radical reassessment of Freud's theories than it was possible for Suttie to do in 1935, and he examines the deeper implications of the work of Melanie Klein, W. R. D. Fairbairn and Winnicott. Through the work of these later psychoanalytical writers a more dynamic picture of the inward structure of the personality has emerged, to replace Freud's over-simple structural theory which tended to cling too mechanically to psychobiology. This development has made it necessary to reconsider many assumptions which have found their way into common thought – concepts, for instance, of the nature of instinct, and its 'conflict' with society. Guntrip makes a meticulous rejection of Freudian instinct theory, and its implication that civilization is inimical to mental health. In the light of recent British psychoanalytical theory the creative processes of phantasy and metaphor are seen as essential means to the growth of the capacity for object-relationships, a sense of identity, and for love, from the moment of birth. Culture and social patterns are a positive means to maturation and fulfilment, while mental disorder is seen as a manifestation of inward processes failing to complete themselves, rather than a consequence of innate drives which society has 'inhibited'. This more hopeful attitude to human nature may well make it possible for many

Psychoanalytical philosophy and practice, certainly, it seems, are vindicating poetry once again, as once science was supposed to have dislodged it. A patient's dreams or poetic ramblings are part of his cure: his whole culture is crucial. In vindicating poetry with the sick mind, and with the growing mind, in healing practice and child care, psychoanalytical work has demonstrated the importance of such creative processes in all.

So we may find a meeting place, between rational and empirical studies of human nature, and the exploration of our inner reality by the creative imagination. In our apprehension of the growth of love – which is essentially bound up with the growth of our capacities to deal with reality – we may find a meeting place between science and art. Certainly the new truths of psychiatry would seem to have cultural and moral implications to which the literary critic and writer must now pay attention. We can no longer ignore these fresh lights. Indeed, if we can understand them, we may perhaps find in them the basis for better criticism of works of literature, for fresh creation, better methods of education, and a new (and more real) morality.

Meanwhile there is much in contemporary culture, by way of attitudes to love, to art, and to moral issues in life, which seeks to deny these truths. In popular culture, in 'avant garde' art, and in popular concepts at the level of 'serious' journalism (at, say, the level of the *New Statesman*), many mistaken 'psychoanalytical' notions are employed to justify pessimism and negative attitudes to behaviour – for instance, at the crudest level, that all that is wrong with us is that our 'instincts' are' repressed' and that if only 'society' would remove its restrictions, all would be well, because we would be 'uninhibited'. With this unreal kind of enlightenment goes a cult of futility in art (as in Italian films and the *film noir*), and a fashion for 'playing it cool' in emotional life and leisure pursuits. Culture and academic education manifest at all levels

_____

to accept psychoanalytical theories who have previously (like the present writer) found Freudian pessimism unconvincing, and unreal. It is hoped to relate the deeper implications of the work of Guntrip and Fairbairn to literary criticism in a later work.

today in various ways a disregard for, or an actual inhibition on, deep and committed feelings. A mistaken Freudianism is often employed by bright journalists in the 'quality' papers to undermine conscience in moral debate and to deny the potentialities for good in human nature. Their negative attitude to human nature is not only cynicism masquerading as 'emancipated' but really (as Suttie suggested) a kind of sickness itself. In fact this cynical and suspect misuse of psychoanalytical theories is now confronted with discomforting evidence to refute it in the work of post-Freudian psychologists, and much debate since Ian D. Suttie's telling critique of Freud in *The Origins of Love and Hate* (1935). Many prevalent attitudes which suppose themselves based on psychoanalytical theory have remained to a strange degree out of date. Those holding them seem extravagantly unwilling to accept the implications of more recent developments in psychoanalysis. The reasons are hinted at in Suttie. He showed that some of Freud's own more pessimistic attitudes – depressively neurotic as they were – have suited the modern world, in some of its more destructive trends, well. They suit 'free' commerce, which depends largely upon vindications of that self-interest which exploits others. They justify commercial and cultural irresponsibility and amorality and seem to vindicate those who seek to avoid life's exigencies by disguising or fleeing from the more positive aspects of life – not least the reality of human good. To point out such weaknesses in Freud, of course, as Suttie does, is not to deny Freud's greatness, nor the altruism inherent in his work. But there is, in fact, nothing rational nor proven behind the prevalent contempt (which supposes itself based on Freud and biological 'realism') for such values as goodness, integrity and altruism, nor behind the disparagement of positive moral concern.[1] The *oeuvre* of Freud himself is answer enough – itself a great altruistic effort, in his life's work, and in those who follow him. Moreover, whereas Freud and the whole of psychoanalytical theory is based on compassionate and painstaking work for human good, the 'intellectual world' which purveys the more negative interpretations of Freudianism is, alas,

[1] See my discussion of Suttie's comments on Freud's 'negative ethical theory' in *The Secret Places*, pp. 179–80.

too much cut off from that struggle with suffering in human common life – in which man's capacities for goodness and love are always to be found, as realities themselves.

That human nature is predominantly altruistic and capable of love is not a naïve statement, for these are now biologically and psychologically established truths. Without such virtues, indeed, human consciousness and human society could never have evolved and endured, as Suttie argues. In each personal life the growth of love is the root of our personal stability and is interwoven with the growth of our capacity to deal with reality. Since society is composed of individuals the growth of love is thus the basis of the stability and effective vitality of all human societies. Love is, indeed, the basis of human evolution and civilization: in this sense it is truly love that makes the world go round.

For decades some have been excited by the apparent revelation that love was a mere manifestation of self-interest and really no more than sex, as a ruthless element in the struggle of the animal organism merely to survive. Hate, lust, and destructiveness were innate instincts, and unless 'sublimated' or curbed would drive us to destroy ourselves. 'Social activities . . . [were] . . . defence reactions . . . or guilt expiations' (Suttie). Now we may accept that such a view was false, and reject it as pessimistic and depressive. The truth as seen by later psychoanalytical theory is rather more as it was seen by writers such as Shakespeare and Dickens who valued human ideals, creativity, and 'good' feelings in sincere relationship, by intuition, as our greatest reality. Where there is hate and destructiveness it is likely that there has been a failure of the feelings to flow – as between lovers or parents, so that the mother was not able to give the child that intuitive flux of her love and care that guarantees wholeness and sanity. The adult who is hate-filled, or whose feelings are inhibited, is the child of a not-good-enough environment. Our intellectual world has tended to elevate this latter kind of deficiency to a norm. In this it has made a comment on itself.

Dickens' comment on Lady Dedlock may therefore be taken as a very modern statement, most relevant to our predicament, as psychoanalytical philosophy now would seem to see it:

In truth she is not a hard lady naturally; and the time has been when the sight of the venerable figure sueing to her with such strong earnestness would have moved her to great compassion. But, so long accustomed to suppress emotion, and keep down reality, so long schooled for her own purposes, in that destructive school which shuts up the natural feelings of the heart, like flies in amber, and spreads one dreary gloss over the good and bad, the feeling and unfeeling, the sensible and the senseless; she had subdued even her wonder until now.

Dickens' marvellous story *Bleak House* enacts, as does much of his work, the deadly effects of such denial of our primal feelings, and celebrates (as the same author does elsewhere as in *Little Dorrit*) our need to love, and to give in love.

My purpose in writing this book is to urge that we are unlikely to have new writing of any consequence, minority or popular, unless the writer-as-artist makes his own positive quest for insight into such profound human truths as have to do with love and our dealings with reality, such as are being revealed by our increased insight into the mind, through recent psychoanalytical philosophy and practice. The question is not only one of writing: it has to do with our attitudes to life at large, our acceptance of possibilities of new growths in living power, based on hopefulness about the future, a belief in the continuity of life, creative attitudes, and positive values. There can be aims and values in our living, even in the absence of religious faith, if we listen to our deepest inward needs. The writer, teacher and critic who has to do with fiction, drama and poetry inevitably has to do with such aims and values, and such visions and concepts as we develop to help us to come at them. The writer is inevitably concerned with promoting (or obscuring) insight and understanding. There is no way of escaping this responsibility – one's literary work inevitably touches life thus.

In the first part of this book I try to explore some of the relevant truths of psychoanalytical philosophy. They concern the growth of consciousness in the infant, and his capacity to love, and to develop a sense of his own reality, in complex with the world's reality 'outside'. I discuss the bearing of these on adult culture.

It may be pointed out that here I am dealing with ideas very much at second-hand and this is so. But as I shall explain, this is inevitable. In the face of those who deny the effectiveness of psychoanalysis altogether, such as Professor Eysenck, I can only suggest that in asking for measurement of 'cure', in changed individual lives, they are asking for a surety they know to be impossible. From the one life things look very different, and my interest in psychoanalytical theories has been impelled by the experience of being presented with the inescapable truth of at least some of psychoanalytical theory and practice, first-hand enough in terms of actual living, since I have been in love with and married to the subject of treatment.

But the psychic areas we need to explore – the very earliest stages in the formation of consciousness – *can only be known at second-hand.* In the memory of anyone trying to remember them 'at first hand' they are deeply hidden and inaccessible, though we can all have intuitive glimpses. Objective observation, such as the excellent work of John Bowlby, is valuable as offering confirmation. But the way in which the earliest processes of the life of the psyche-soma have come to be re-experienced is in the psychoanalytical clinical situation, in which the analyst is wholly involved in, while still able to study with some detachment, the re-enactment of very early stages and situations in patients in a state of regression – 'living through' infantile experiences. The more severe the illness, speaking generally, the earlier its origins. A few post-Kleinian psychoanalysts such as D. W. Winnicott have even taken on severe psychotics, and have found that these patients have needed to 'return' to very early states of existence, in order to live through the first infantile situations during which 'things had gone wrong', or during which significant and necessary developments had failed to happen or to complete themselves. The patients were, by regression, thereby re-enacting successfully (often over and over again) developments which they had not survived without severe dissociation, at the actual time. Or they may even have been 'becoming a self' for the first time ever, in terms of the 'shell and the kernel' relationship between mother and child (see pp. 34-5).

This work inevitably began to throw more light on the earliest periods of life and their significance in the adult's sense of identity and his dealings with reality. Not even in being psychoanalysed oneself would one be likely to experience such early stages of being. One simply has to take accounts of them on trust from those psychoanalysts who have had the courage to encounter and live in these terrible areas of primaeval spirit – too terrible for the adult (though every baby suffers them) because the adult is aware of the risks involved in a way the baby cannot be. The degree of exigency may be judged from the fact that at times in the analysis of psychotics the strain is so immense that the analyst himself needs to resort to further psychoanalytical treatment from another doctor, from time to time, in order to be helped to cope with the deeper disturbances evoked in himself by such work.

An additional problem for us is that it is difficult to judge these theories, since we have no actual experience we can remember with which to compare them. For this, and for other unconscious reasons, we tend to either resist them altogether, or attach an undue loyalty to them – as we are inclined to do by, say, inventing the myth of the 'perfect analyst', or an unreal concept of a psychotherapy that can do everything for us. I have no doubt I have suffered from such lapses in my enthusiastic use of the work of psychoanalytical writers.[1]

But the more one explores psychoanalytical theory, the more one begins to locate the focus of morality, and the cruces of our creative explorations of reality, which are in the early life of the child and its immediate environment. The child needs the experience of 'the rainbow' – to walk under the arch of security of its parents' togetherness, for nearly twenty years, during which the first five or six years are critical and the first six months are crucial. This parental security in marriage is as intangible as the image of the rainbow suggests: yet it is as significant as is the rainbow in human myth – a guarantee of continuity and an earnest that the world will not be destroyed. For only if men and women can offer the rainbow-security to each generation can each subsequent

---

[1] Here I should perhaps take the opportunity of expressing a heavy debt to Dr D. W. Winnicott and to others in this field and to say that where my account is garbled or wrong it will be my fault, and no responsibility is theirs.

generation develop sanity and stability, and this demands of each of us a continual quest for love.

Our communal life nowadays needs desperately to find stability again, after the cataclysmic disruptions caused by the industrial revolution, the abrupt changes in social and family life which accompanied this and followed it,[1] accelerating with the invention rate, and finally culminating in the terrible wars into which machine society has plunged. Even the good things brought by these changes – such as increased wealth and leisure – so far, have, it seems, if anything, made it more difficult for the psyche to find stability. Yet it should be more possible now for all to find love, fulfilment and stability, because of the easier conditions of life made possible by material progress, medicine, and such inventions as contraception. So the recreation of this stability depends upon conscious effort, and this requires that we work to free and deepen feeling and to keep alive such positive values as are embodied in literature, in the other arts, culture at large, and in the poetry and ceremony of religion, if we believe.

The tremendous influence of mass entertainments, such as television and periodical publishing, has become on the whole destructive of creative attitudes to life, distractive and trivializing because it has no responsibility, except to 'hold' an audience for cash returns. These things may, indeed, be contributing to greater dissociation from reality. Nearly all our culture nowadays is linked with selling, and so with urging 'wants'. Linked with advertising and commerce, our entertainments mostly present false, acquisitive ideals, and are both sensational (to 'hold' the audience) and amoral (to exploit it). They mostly offer kinds of hallucination that tend to weaken our capacities to deal with actuality. The promotion of respect for real feelings, and for more positive values, by education and culture, inevitably conflicts today with dominant commercial influences into whose hands we have given a power over heart and mind which they misuse. (More complex is the problem of the effect of those who disguise their attack on life as 'enlightened'.) In this situation only a more creative education and a better and more sound culture can restore at root

[1] See E. P. Thompson, *The Making of the English Working Class*, Gollancz, 1963.

adequate concepts in love, marriage, family life, parenthood and child care, and help us all at large to develop more adequate capacities to deal with inner and outer reality. Our first cultural problem is to keep 'good' feelings flowing, and hope viable.

Secondly, from psychoanalysis, as from our knowledge of children and our educational experience, we may recognize phantasy to be a vital part of our psychic growth. Phantasy is intimately linked with processes of learning to deal with reality, and with the growth of intelligence. Certainly it is a fundamental element in the capacity of the child to grow to love and self-possession under the arch of parental security. Phantasy is, too, the medium in which our concepts, such as help us direct and fulfil our lives as far as we may, are grown. In this process verbal imaginative processes are crucial. So we must accept the need for the conscious cultivation, fostering and nourishment of imagination and phantasy, as fluxes and inward activities integral to all human growth and cultural activity including reasoning powers, scientific capacity, effectiveness in social living and a sense of aims and significance – in the adult as well as the child. This need is real and must be provided for, by conscious public development of a rich cultural life at the popular level. The starved imagination is the cause of much of our prevalent discontent, frustration and waste of human potential. The roots of such cultural restoration can only be in a more creative education, and deliberate provision for a better live culture at large.

Thirdly, from the early capacity to identify as children with the 'good mother', to our capacities to respond to high tragedy, moral discrimination is also a means to self-respect and self-fulfilment, the release of our sympathy and energy in community, and our dealings with reality. Discrimination has its roots in what D. W. Winnicott calls 'true guilt' – that natural and necessary urge to seek the 'good' and to make creative 'reparation'. This does not mean that art need be didactic, nor does it mean that education must be morally propagandist – but that both must be responsible to such values as human civilization has established, even though the values require constant challenging and re-creation. We need the recurrent experience of constructive imaginative experiences that leave us possessed of 'good' concepts and attitudes to life. Art criticism and education have an inevitable responsibility in the imaginative formation of concepts and the contribution creativity can make to our sense of reality, and our capacities to deal with it.

'The essential function of art is moral' – in the light of what we now know of the growth of human consciousness, this precept of D. H. Lawrence's needs to be upheld more than ever before. This sense of the relevance of art to actual living needs still to be exerted, in the face of mandarinism, in resistance to a new shrinking from moral energy and deep committed feeling among the literati. It is also most urgent for us to discriminate against the moral duplicity of the writer with one foot in the commercial words of advertising and mass journalism, and the other in sentimental cynicism and the exploitation of depressive attitudes. He weakens our reality sense, and he threatens our sanity by undermining our capacity for discrimination.[1]

We do mould ourselves on others and are influenced by the character and quality of others, from childhood onwards, and our culture continues this process with effect on our moral choices. We do and can gain guiding concepts from our culture: the connection is as direct as that though it is never obvious. However complex its processes, it is only craven to deny that some real connection exists.

To make fine moral discriminations and to seek the 'good' is a primary and natural activity of the human spirit, fundamental to the growth of consciousness, and to 'healthy social development', in both child and man. Altruistic, compassionate activity – the release of energy in community such as great art sets aflow – these activities are a primary human need and a prime basis of human evolution. To deny the quest for 'the good' and to disparage altruism are but a further extension of the neurotic denial of life's better potentialities, as first diagnosed by Suttie. There are many pressures in a commercial economy which seek to justify and enlarge certain areas of irresponsibility (e.g. 'development' that destroys the environment, tobacco advertising, the reckless use of

[1] Cf. the remark at the Cheltenham Literary Festival of 1962 by Kingsley Amis, that he was 'all for pornography'.

drugs and chemicals, and so forth). So there is an impulse in commercial culture to disarm the critical minority in terms of 'non-commitment', or assent in quietude. Our kind of commerce works best if criticism is disarmed, and irresponsibility fostered. If the value of human nature can be depressed, people may be more easily exploited. These trends must be consciously resisted, but by true understanding of the dangers, not by mere 'protest' behaviour by the enlightened minority, which can be but a form of ineffective 'opting out', if it takes the form of merely fashionable rebelliousness. We need a sterner and more effective cohesion among those who care.

Altogether, then, I would justify my interest in psychoanalytical theories by saying that they suggest deep reasons why it is true to say that to learn to live well we have to learn to discriminate and choose, in our dealings with inner and outer reality, and that we do this according to concepts derived from our imaginative life which illumine the sum of our remembered experience. Our ways of doing these things have much to do with our phantasy life: the creative arts are a chief source of nourishment for this life, being the means to establish bridges between inward and outward life. For this reason the central discipline in our education must be the creative arts, and their place in adult life needs to be as central.

Such concerns are questioned or at worst derided by many present day littérateurs, and by the fashions and trends established by journalism, as it becomes increasingly dependent upon advertising and commerce. Much academic criticism, too, is anti-life.[1] There is supposed to be a possible position of 'non-commitment', and an art which is 'anti-art'. For a concern for art as 'criticism of life' has been substituted a sterile aestheticism, or the claim, for instance, that literature is not really to do with life at all,

---

[1] The late Professor C. S. Lewis, for instance, coined the word 'biolatry' in a comment on D. H. Lawrence in *An Experiment in Criticism*. Lewis spoke angrily and distastefully of how the lovers in *Sons and Lovers* felt themselves, in making love, 'grains' of life. But Lewis in giving the account used the cold word 'copulate', typically – for it is life that he hated, rather than the art which 'worships' it. It is disturbing to find in academic criticism so many such clues to sensibilities which are thereby shown to be filled with suppressed hatred.

but is really a form of 'play' – a point of view which seems to forget how serious 'play' is for the child and his growth. Such abrogations, in so far as they are anything more than empty postures or sail-trimming to popular acclaim, are surely disastrous, when so much needs to be done, to establish a better culture. They seem to me an aspect of the prevalent schizoid weakness of the whole sensibility in our time – a dissociation from reality related to the 'taboo' on tender feelings diagnosed by Suttie. For such reasons we seem to be increasingly less able to see what kind of cultural problem we have, and why it matters that we should try to solve it. More could be done if it were not for the increasing deficiency of sound periodical criticism and the absence of any concensus of attitudes and opinion. These are so much in abeyance as to allow charlatanism to take over much of the field of minority culture.[1] This absence of values, again, marks a larger weakness of our reality-sense: we can no longer see 'the object as in itself it truly is' because there is an increasing deficiency in our culture of disinterested opinion and thought. These are more and more in the service of Mammon, and, so, compromised.

Meanwhile, many of those who resist the essential creativity of literature in living are now gaining control of areas of cultural influence, as in our university English departments, from whence they may, for instance, control and determine the grammar school syllabuses through examinations. This is happening possibly because those who are most insecure – that is, those with the weakest reality-sense themselves, and perhaps the most anaemic feelings – tend to substitute the indulgences of ambition, organization, and power for that teaching and writing in which long-term satisfactions can be found, and where the deeper contest with experience is made. Power and administration become substitutes for the true disciplines of emotional growth, education, learning and research – a typical danger in a time of 'expansion'.

The effect of such trends in journalism and higher education –

[1] Cf. Colin Wilson, 'I've always been certain that my influence will be of the kind of Plato's and the Buddha's'. Ours is a time in which such intellectual impudence is not even ridiculed, let alone condemned. That anything 'sells' silences criticism at once, as may be observed in Sunday newspaper reviewing, with its intellectual pretensions so closely bound up with the ethos of commercial success.

as I suggested in *Llareggub Revisited* – is that a good deal of our intellectual energy at large seems to go into inhibiting and resisting the deeper feelings and those painful but often necessary disturbances that go with the pursuit of inward truth. The intellect can be an enemy to our whole psychesomatic reality and come to defend us against the disturbances caused by good, tender, discriminating feelings, and even come to resist and inhibit growth in the soul. It is possible (see below, pp. 44–6) that precocious development of the intellect may be a consequence of certain very early forms of psychic damage originating in homes deficient in emotional warmth, and this may be related to the tendency for the intellectual milieu to be so aligned against feeling and committed relationship. But even if arid intellectualism derives from early impingements and environmental deficiencies, this mental defence against wholeness of feeling is also fostered by later failures of the environment to foster the intuitive life. It is, for instance a feature of the typical English Grammar School exam-bound education to leave the culture of the emotions largely to chance. This neglect of the intuitive faculties of being among intelligent girls (shown often by the way they write about their distaste for their functions as women) may mean that they are likely to reproduce this fault in their infants by bad child management which lacks intuitive warmth – because their own education and culture have encouraged them to despise motherhood, and, with motherhood, 'mere' *being*.[1] Lawrence diagnosed the problem in a different way as a failure of 'touch'. This intellectual defence against wholeness seems to be an increasing feature of our periodical journalism, university English schools, academic education, and 'enlightened' culture generally. This minority would certainly seem to be becoming (despite its frequent claims to the contrary) more energetically anti-creative, as one may judge, for example, from the poets and novelists it admires.

[1] We may contrast the impression gained by an American research team among women of the Yoruba tribe in Nigeria: '*Our world as women centres on children.*' 'Time and time again women told us that the most important thing in their lives is children. The pinnacle of a woman's desires lies in the sense of repeatedly being pregnant and having a baby to suckle.' *Psychiatric Disorder Among the Yoruba*, Cornell University Press, 1963, p. 47ff.

This is why criticism is worth writing – because, one hopes, it may help shift resistances to the disturbances to art, by sustained explicit arguments which open the mind to allow and accept the full effect of the poetry and fiction on the feelings. Criticism is even more necessary at a time when our education neglects the feelings and wholeness of sensibility, to concentrate on a limited range of intellectual capacities – such as the acquisition of facts to unload in examinations, or on a dull and irrelevant 'scholarship'. We have to labour to clear the way for the sensibility, inhibited by an arid education and mandarin, intellectualized, or emotionally illiterate attitudes to culture, to begin to respond, and to help readers find a whole delight in literature as a companion in our quest for insight, for understanding – and for love.

Where the art of writing has fulfilled its creative task with due responsibility it has inevitably pursued, among other themes, the quest for love, closely linked with the exploration of inner and outer reality. To show what I mean by 'the quest for love' in a great artist, to show the relevance of his exploration of guiding concept and human truths to our living today, I shall go back to Chaucer. After writing my essay below I was glad to see a psychoanalytical writer call Chaucer a 'great analyst': certainly he offers us profound and discomforting truths – truths that can help us grow – in his understanding of human reality and of the nature of love. For instance, we assume we are 'frank' about sex: but we are in fact no 'franker' than Chaucer, while we have yet to begin to understand *love* as Chaucer explores it. He sees the reality of love: we take the reality, erroneously, to be in sex. He explores territories of human experience, where we are, still, faltering. But if we possess his poetry we may possess a little of his fineness of civilized awareness, and may ourselves be refined, in our feelings, in our guiding concepts, and thus in our living. (From my discussion of the complexities of the psyche below however, it should be obvious how and why there is no direct relationship, as between 'good reading' and 'good living'.)

With the great writer the creative power is properly regarded with awe and with devotion:

> The lyf so shorte, the crafte so long to lerne . . .

To Chaucer, the 'crafte' was the striving, all his life, to make the best combination of words, in order to discover, place, and illuminate as much of human experience as he could, for the sake of common humanity. In his craft, as Shakespeare did later (though it was surely a formidable and original task for the man who lived earlier?), Chaucer gave habits, inflexions, modes, terms, forms of metaphor, ways of construction, dramatic forms, varieties of irony, comedy and social satire to the language, to poetry, and thus by giving these to the language, gave them to the modes of thinking and feeling of those who belonged and belong to that one continuous civilization which has been ours in England for six hundred years.

To write as Chaucer did requires opening oneself to the inexorable tragic conditions of human life. This is resisted in much modern writing – certainly in that which becomes most popular – by the defensive use of the intellect to disguise, hide, and defend the self against painful disturbances, awarenesses and acceptances at the level of feeling and intuitive life.

But this resistance may be found even in the greatest artist, and so there is some excuse even for the scribblers of the literary world. 'Human kind cannot bear very much reality', and even the bravest spirit may be overcome, because we are all flawed, and the flaws of the great are great flaws. So I end this volume with a long essay in which I seek to demonstrate that Lawrence's fate in setting out to write his bravest book was to produce his greatest falsification, in *Lady Chatterley's Lover*. This book is both a courageous assault upon our problems in dealing with reality – and yet at one with them. Its very nature made it inevitable that it would be absorbed into the universal epidemic. The unfortunate trial and the vast sale of this book indeed virtually demonstrated the success of his offer of false comfort – success in terms of fortifying our defences against the urgency of our needs to deal with reality or perish – needs not to be met in any sensual pursuit, but in the quest for love.

Between Chaucer and Lawrence I write on one of Shakespeare's later plays, *The Winter's Tale*. In this, I consider, Shakespeare finds, in that love which is 'an ever-fixèd mark', the clue to a belief in the

continuity of life, and a resignation to reality which is full of hope –
a hope which offers an enduring value in human experience.

It requires considerable efforts of adjustment and painful exertion to understand oneself, human nature and reality better, and to
grow to be able to love. It is to these capacities that such writers as
Chaucer, Shakespeare and Lawrence at his best lead us. From the
contemplation of the actual personal relationship in time a sense of
creative significance may be distilled as a universal concept of love
and its transcending reality that is outside time.[1] Moreover, this
needs to be achieved in terms of actual living, in contentment that
not all need be at the highest level of the transcendant ideal.
Florizel and Perdita, Dorigen and Averagus, are but symbols of
the best there can be in us, in terms of loyalty, total acceptance,
mutual respect, compassion and love. So the writers I write about
here are some who have made as artists a relentless quest for meaning, in exploring the subtle complexity of shared experience and
devotion which love between two human beings may bring. They
explore love as an aspect of civilization, capable of yielding great
stability, strength and creative potential, as factors in the evolution
of individual fulfilment and of society.

So much is devoted at present in our literature to denigrating,
reviling, and making trivial this greatest gift of our existence that
I am glad to offer even these struggling essays in the hope of
affirming its value and truth. My readers will recognize, I hope,
from their own courtship, their own walks by the Salley Gardens,
their love-beds – and their sick-beds, child-beds and death-beds –
what this tender and continually mysterious quest can yield, not
only as a means to escape isolation, or to find the self by finding
the 'other', but even in giving point to the brevity of human life.
Of course, as we know from *King Lear*, love does not only exist
in the man-woman relationship – it is a whole human capacity.
Of course, the relationship between man and woman is not the
only means of self-realization, or the only source of love, or source
of a sense of significance in life: but I choose it because of its

---

[1] This is Thomas Hardy's poignant quest in *Veteris Vestigia Flammae,* his
Poems of 1912–13 in which he seeks to find a meaning in the early years of his
marriage, after his wife's death.

importance to me, and many like me, who find in such love their deepest and most illuminating mystery. And I chose love between man and woman as a theme because it seems to have been assailed and disparaged by so many writers since D. H. Lawrence died, at a time when we need its creative gift to the community more than ever, when we have lost our way.

A last personal point: I hope this book will explain to the puzzled critics why I write so much in my poems and other creative writing about love – 'and married love at that' as one of them exclaimed, as if this were an idiosyncrasy.

ONE

The Quest for Love and Our Sense of Reality

Recent Psychoanalytical Theories of the Origins of Consciousness

For some time he lay gasping on a little flock mattress, rather un-equally poised between this world and the next: the balance being decidedly in favour of the latter. Now, if, during this brief period, Oliver had been surrounded by careful grandmothers, anxious aunts, experienced nurses, and doctors of profound wisdom, he would most inevitably and indubitably have been killed in no time. There being nobody by, however, but a pauper old woman, who was rendered rather misty by an unwonted allowance of beer; and a parish surgeon who did such matters by contract; Oliver and Nature fought out the point between them. The result was, that, after a few struggles, Oliver breathed, sneezed, and proceeded to advertise to the inmates of the workhouse the fact of a new burden having been imposed upon the parish, by setting up as loud a cry as could reason-ably have been expected from a male infant who had not been pos-sessed of that very useful appendage, a voice, for a much longer space of time than three minutes and a quarter.

Charles Dickens, *Oliver Twist*

The psychoanalytical theories about the origins and growth of human consciousness which I am going to discuss are largely based on experiences we can never have, and could not tolerate if we had them. They are, that is, largely worked out from the clinical experience the psychoanalyst has of the insane or mentally sick patient in regression, when the latter is living again through remembered states of infancy, and re-enacts infant experiences. Of course, to these experiences the psychoanalytical writer adds his own intuitive perceptions, aspects he remembers of his own infancy, and what he has worked out from his own theoretical study of psychopathology, and of childhood.

Because of their origins, psychoanalytical theories are possibly distorted through excessive attention to disbalance and insanity, rather than to natural growth. But because the origins of these theories are in such strange experiences, they inevitably have an air of being suffused with aspects of being which we try hard to forget or ignore. Indeed, we have a natural impulse to suppress many memories of this whole area of experience, our infantile, tormented past. In this tendency, which protects us from intolerable pain, lie the mechanisms of severe repression, and in these are the roots of some mental illnesses. That is, where certain aspects of these troubled psychic processes have gone wrong, we have hidden the fault, and lived the less because of it. Where this hiding or dissociation is severe there is mental disorder.

So we have a natural resistance to psychoanalytical theories, because they seek to open up for rational examination those areas of our experience which, sometimes for very survival, the human 'organism' naturally seeks to keep closed and hidden. Whenever we feel an 'impulse to keep hidden' this 'reminds' us of those areas where we have kept cloaked away our own flaws and traumatic wounds – the places in the soul where we have failed to grow up, and are thereby inhibited in our living. Because we are darkly aware of the clandestine existence of these suppressed areas of pain, we fear disbalance or madness. So, when we first encounter a psychoanalytical concept, we resist it, because we feel 'that way madness lies' – certainly discomfort.

Such responses are immediately evoked in us all, as soon as we hear or read such words as 'psychiatry', 'madness', 'infantile', 'analyst', 'baby' – and the anxiety surrounding any approach to our 'unknown' self explains the endless jokes about psychoanalysis which are a manifestation of that anxiety. It also explains the mystique with which psychoanalysis sometimes surrounds itself; the protective severity, as of a closed monastic order, of the strict Freudians. Fear explains the hysterical prejudice and misrepresentation with which the subject is often greeted or attacked.

Fortunately this latter kind of reaction is gradually yielding as a more rational approach to psychic illness and psychoanalytical theory becomes more familiar, and the concepts become common currency (though many of these current popular concepts are misleading).[1]

But these opening paragraphs will convey my apprehension that a layman's stumbling account of psychoanalytical theories of the growth of consciousness, on his way to discuss works of literature, will not be easily received. One problem is the termin-ology – not so much the terminology of mental illness, with which we are more or less familiar – for example, words such as 'de-pressive' or 'schizoid' – but the simpler words such as 'infantile' or 'nursing couple' or even 'baby' which at first seem so out of place in a literary critical work – until we recall Traherne, Wordsworth and Blake's easy transition from the infant to the man. The words and the area of experience they deal with evoke such painful resistance that it will be a long time before psychoanalytical theories are assimilated into art criticism.

However, it now seems apparent to me that before we can understand adult behaviour as we need to understand it nowadays, including the complexities of our culture, and before we can ad-vance discriminating connections between these and living, we need to study the origins of consciousness, in the baby. Not only is 'child psychology' part of human psychology, and a natural way to come to the study of the human mind, beginning, as it were at the beginning. But we must now accept that in the growth of consciousness in the embryo and baby we may find the character-

---

[1] At the simplest and worst level is the common belief that the trouble with us all is that 'society' causes us to 'repress' our 'instinctual drives' – and that all that is needed is for all restraints to be abandoned whereupon there will be no 'guilt'. In a writer such as Alex Comfort the inability to accept the larger reality of human adult love is expressed in terms of urging the 'emancipated' toleration of modes of behaviour such as promiscuity and adultery. Not only do these recommendations ignore such realities of our emotional life as jealousy, but, in failing to accept the reality of love, they suggest as norms modes of behaviour which a psychoanalyst would see as symptoms of failure to mature, and of dissociation from reality. 'En-lightened' proposals are often rationalizations of a refusal to accept adult reality – at their most ridiculous they may be represented by the claim in an undergraduate paper (*Isis*) that 'chastity' was 'a weapon of the Establishment'.

istics of all human thought, like the shape of a leaf in bud, or the
form and markings of a flower from its first swelling growing
point, to its unfolding. We may also find there, as we may in the
growth of plants, tendencies towards those inevitable departures
from the postulated norm, which may be called weaknesses or
shortcomings, distortions or flaws. These may range from a fear of
heights, or slight shyness, to such distortions of the personality as
compulsive ambition, through neuroses such as character disorders,
to psychosis (or insanity). But we shall also find that, since every
living thing is flawed to some degree, and none is perfect, we are
all psychically imperfect. Together with all living things we are in
continual contest – each an imperfect organism in a never-quite-
good-enough environment. Out of this contest is born all human
civilization, and our long spiritual and cultural evolution. The
contest *is* real growth, real living, a creative relationship with experience, seeking to make what we can of it. But his inevitable
weaknesses threaten each individual's prowess and survival, and
so these tend to be hidden away – repressed, because in that area of
his make-up growth and development are too painful. There, a
growth process has failed to complete itself. To maintain their
concealment, to deny their existence, to avoid contest with these,
an individual may virtually 'split off' aspects of his personality –
and so must seek to preserve certain distorted views of himself, and
of the reality of his life, so that he may remain (apparently) comfortably unaware of the ways in which he comes short of adequate
living. This is the first source of distorted attitudes. Processes we
develop which are necessary to our psychic growth, such as projection and introjection, and their accompanying forms of identification, can in their development become capacities which can be
used by us to deceive ourselves. This tendency to deny, distort,
and deceive oneself by illusion is not only a personal trait: in many
ways it becomes a cultural manifestation, as powerful as the true
cultural effort we also make to come closer to the reality of ourselves and our world. Most people combine both kinds of activity
– sometimes pondering their experience with great sincerity and
courage, and making choices or taking action with effectiveness:
then, even in the same week, being dishonest or deceiving them-

selves about some other aspect of life with equal force. In extreme cases we have a Jekyll and Hyde life. But all of us are ambivalent and inconsistent to a degree. Most adults are to some extent involved in a complex of such living processes, and alternate between saint and sinner. While we can all gain insight by efforts of one kind or another no one can take into account motives or prejudices which are unconscious – and we all have these.

The artist has the additional problem of trying to distinguish between his honest or 'healthy' and his dishonest, or 'neurotic' work. Culture consists of a complex mixture of forms of activity, some of which help us to understand ourselves and the outside world better, and to deal with it effectively. Some of them may offer comfort or temporary relief, but probably do not help us to deal with reality at all – and may place distortions and illusions between us and the world we live in, and even between us and ourselves – our sense of our own identity. In examining the differences between that which contributes to our 'reality' sense, and that which hinders it, we may begin to find the basis for kinds of criticism, as of literature, which may justify such terms as 'life-promoting' or 'anti-life', and enable us to distinguish between enlightenment and hallucination. This is not an easy problem, because some 'deranged' works (like Blake's prophetic works, which, as R. D. Laing[1] suggests, convey the existential nature of a schizoid state) may have some value in helping us to understand deranged states in others, and thus help us to understand human nature's inner reality, since we all have elements of such derangements.

But in order to discover how we may judge between that culture which helps the 'real contest' and that which 'fosters the illusion' we must look at the way in which this inevitable division of human perception develops, as consciousness itself originates in each human being.

Firstly, however, it will be as well to accept thoroughly that, as I have already said, each individual *is* 'flawed' and imperfect in all his complexity of being. This explains why there is never a direct connection between 'the quality of a man's life' and 'what he reads', as Matthew Arnold suggested there must be. A psycho-

[1] R. D. Laing, *The Divided Self*, Tavistock, 1960.

path with a tendency to homicide could read all the books in the British Museum, and his emotions would not be refined and deepened to the extent necessary to restrain him from murder. At a more common level, painful to accept, we have to accept that to be 'cultured' individuals will not prevent us being childish boors to our wives at times, or lechers, or suicidal – if these happen to be prompted in us by weaknesses which we have, as imperfect creatures, taken in from a not-good-enough environment. Therefore, while there is everything to be said for a rich cultural life for child and adult, as a means to assist the development of maturity and refinement, culture alone cannot make a silk purse out of a sow's ear. All creative experiences are good: but they cannot do everything for us. Experience may reform; the influence of others, and, as a last resort, psychotherapy *perhaps* can – though there will be some who cannot be made good, fine, or even tolerable individuals by any human means.

This is the first painful fact we must take in – that of, say, a hundred individuals – such as members of a school or college – though a rich cultural life will offer all of them possibilities for greater insight, understanding, self-realization and for becoming civilized and well-mannered (in the deepest sense), each will only be able to make use of the liberal and humane opportunity *to a degree limited by the imperfections of his make-up*, and a few perhaps not at all, because they are so gravely flawed. To accept this reality, of course, in life, while it should never prevent our striving to help people fulfil themselves, may help us to avoid the frustrations of idealizing ('I've done everything for that young man, and then he lets me down') and of failing to accept some inevitable failure ('That woman was going to be my most brilliant teacher – now she's thrown herself away on a middle-aged blackguard'). It will also help us to tolerate our own shortcomings – as when we are ashamed that a man who has read *King Lear* can yet make pompous demands on his loved ones that they demonstrate their love in return. Disturbing too is the recognition we need to make, that disbalance of the mind bears no relation to intelligence. We fear 'dim witted' people, and we fear 'mad' people (see my comments on this problem in *English for the Rejected*). We do so, because we also know and fear that they are not made of different stuff from us – and have a disturbing realization that the line that divides 'them' from 'us' is tenuous.

In accepting this principle that 'all are flawed' we may be accepting also, to begin with, one of the most recent of psychoanalytical concepts. As one writer says:

> If I am right, psychoanalysis is about to develop a new conception which may be called 'basic illness' or perhaps *'basic fault' in the biological structure of the individual, involving in varying degrees both his mind and his body.* The origin of this basic fault may be traced back to a considerable discrepancy between the needs of the individual in his early formative years (or possibly months) and the care and nursing available at the relevant times. This creates a state of deficiency the consequences of which are only partly reversible. Although the individual may achieve a good, or even very good, adjustment, the vestiges of his early experiences remain, and contribute to what is called his constitution, his individuality, or his character make-up, both in the psychological and in the biological sense. The cause of this early discrepancy may be congenital – i.e. the infant's needs may be too exacting – or environmental, such as insufficient, careless, haphazard, over-anxious, over-protective, or only not-understanding care . . . 'clinical illnesses' . . . have to be considered symptoms or exacerbations of the 'basic illness' brought about by the various crises in the individual's development, both external and internal, psychological and biological . . .
>
> Michael Balint, M.D.,
> *The Doctor, His Patient and the Illness*, Pitman, 1957

How everybody's early development 'goes wrong', and how we are 'all traumatized' may be seen as we follow the stages of the growth of consciousness. In this I shall follow four sources, hoping to make their combination coherent. One is a more popular account intended for child welfare workers, of the growth of perception in the infant, *Feeling and Perception in Young Children* (1963) by Mrs Len Chaloner (Tavistock Press). Another is an essay which I suppose is a classical one in Freudian psychoanalytical literature, *The Problem of Acceptance of Unpleasant Ideas – Advances in Knowledge of the Sense of Reality* (1926) by Sandor

Ferenczi.[1] And I shall quote from *Collected Papers* (1958) by D. W. Winnicott, and also from papers by Melanie Klein.

We may begin with some remarks from Winnicott, from an essay on *Anxiety Associated with Insecurity* (1952. *Collected Papers*, p. 97) in children who have grown up in a damagingly not-good-enough environment. These remarks will serve here to introduce us to the concepts necessary to understand the early stages of consciousness. Our first difficulty is to take in the enormousness, the totality, of those things which happen to the new infant in the first weeks of life, and their crucial effect on his whole being for ever afterwards.

One first concept we need to grasp is that of 'object relationship' – that is, the sense the child develops of there being something other than itself and its feelings, 'out there' – a 'not-me' reality, an 'other', with which it may have a relationship. But we need first to conceive of a state *before this has happened*.

What then precedes [asks Winnicott] the first object relationship? . . .

He then goes on to say that after struggling for a long time with this problem he came to pronounce, *'There is no such thing as a baby'*.

. . . if you show me a baby you certainly show me also someone caring for the baby, or at least a pram with someone's eyes and ears glued to it. One sees a 'nursing couple'.

The first process we must think of then, is the formation of consciousness in the context of a 'two-body' relationship, after which the capacity for a 'one-body' relationship follows 'through the introjection of the object' – that is by the infant seeming to himself to be 'taking the mother into himself'.

But this process is a crucial and tremendous one: before object relationships (that is before the baby has any sense at all of a relationship between itself and another, or other things) the state of affairs is this: that the unit is not the individual, the unit is an environmental-

[1] In *Further Contributions to the Theory and Technique of Psycho-Analysis*, The Hogarth Press and the Institute of Psychoanalysis, 1960 edition.

individual set up. The centre of gravity of the being does not start off in the individual. It is in the total set up. By good-enough child care, technique, holding, and general management the shell becomes gradually taken over and the kernel (which has looked all the time like a human baby to us) can begin to be an individual. The beginning is potentially terrible because of the anxieties I have mentioned [i.e. anxieties caused by failures in technique of child care] and because of the paranoid state that follows closely on the first integration [that is, the baby attributes 'bad' feelings in himself, by projection, to external forces which 'persecute' him], and also on the first instinctual moments, bringing to the baby, as they do, a quite new meaning to object relationships. The good-enough infant care technique neutralizes the external persecutions, and prevents the feelings of disintegration and loss of contact between psyche and soma.

IN OTHER WORDS, WITHOUT A GOOD-ENOUGH TECHNIQUE OF CHILD CARE THE NEW HUMAN BEING HAS NO CHANCE WHATEVER ...

Collected Papers, p. 99
(Interpolations in square brackets and small capitals mine, D.H.)

Fortunately, as Winnicott himself points out, women naturally tend to do the right thing for their babies, unless they are prevented by their own grave psychic disabilities, or by interfering, perhaps unconsciously anti-creative, people.

Why should the first awareness of reality in a baby produce terrible anxiety and ('paranoid') feelings of persecution?

Here we need to go back earlier, and consider the baby – or perhaps rather the 'nursing couple' – in the first stages of his life, before he is even aware of his separate existence. Having tried to grasp a state in which the self is aware of nothing other than itself, we now have to try to enter into the condition of the unborn organism.

Babies have strong feelings from the beginning, and these feelings are linked with biological processes. From psychoanalysis of psychotic patients who seem to experience intra-uterine states it would seem that the unborn infant has feelings and awarenesses linked with biological reactions. In the womb the baby will make respiratory movements in response to a lack of oxygen as early as the third month of pregnancy: 'quickening' takes place at about four or five months – vigorous and generalized movements. The heart rate of the foetus can reflect a mother's agitation. Such manifestations of life in the unborn child seem to show that it would respond positively to oxygen lack (as in a protracted labour) and to anxiety – that, indeed, the human infant has an innate predisposition to anxiety. (But this word will be qualified later.) At the biological level, then, we already have in pregnancy a link between the child's capacities for being, and the mother's capacities for love and care: and these in their turn depend to some extent upon love between the adult partners, as well as the mother's own make-up, as determined in her infancy. In these complexes of the inter-dependence of one generation on another we can see the child's absolute need for the 'rainbow' of security, love and stability, over its head, protecting, without which its life may be forfeit, its potentialities or even its sanity impaired. In this lies the basis of a sexual morality based on biological truth, and a vindication of marriage which does not depend upon reference to ancient Hebrew writ.

Very little, however, is yet known about the intra-uterine experience of the baby, or about our birth experience. D. W. Winnicott, who has written a fascinating paper on the subject of *Birth Memories, Birth Trauma, and Anxiety*, confesses that he does not know whether one can postulate a 'normal' birth experience which is non-traumatic. What he does know from clinical experience is that there seem to be definite disturbances of the psyche which may be traced to birth traumata, and that these take two forms:

> I . . . have invented two grades of traumatic birth, the one being common, and largely annulled as to its effects by subsequent good management, and the other being definitely traumatic, difficult to counteract by most careful nursing, and leaving its permanent mark on the individual.
>
> *Collected Papers*, p. 190

While it is a truism, the following statement should be present in the mind of all who wish to consider and deal effectively with aspects of human consciousness: *we have all been born*, and the few hours in which this takes place are crucial to our basic make-up.

From this brief and immense experience we may inherit, by no 'fault' of persons and by no circumstances that can be amended, a condition of being flawed, even gravely flawed. This is a tragic aspect of human life, and a difficult one to come to terms with – in the sense that whatever we do, to improve conditions of living, attitudes to birth and preparedness for parturition (as through the marvellous work of Dr Grantley Dick Reid), according to all the best ideals of social reformers, there will always be a proportion of people left with traumatic birth experiences which affect their lives deeply.[1]

In all of us there is thus a continuity between intra-uterine and extra-uterine life: Winnicott found that some of his patients were able to regress in psychoanalytical sessions and re-enact an intra-uterine state, before birth, while others were able to re-experience birth itself.

The 'cultural' problem in our consideration of this large experience in our existence is this – what is the relation between the experiences of the foetus and baby (who is a completely narcissistic creature, knowing no 'not-me') and the problems of the ego – the personality of the adult which exists in its relationship with others and the external world, where we have the 'me' in relationship with the 'not-me'? Answers would seem to be suggested by the character of certain manifestations in psychoanalytical patients. These are virtually poetic or phantasy manifestations which symbolize anxieties belonging to the period before, during and immediately after birth – symbolizing even biological conditions, such as a dangerous shortage of oxygen – the main source of that anxiety in the baby which compensates in reaction by increased lung activity.

The earliest anxieties, we may deduce, are not those of separation from the mother, as we shall find later ones to be, but such as are experienced by a creature, which since it does not know a

---

[1] Many sociological theories and ideals ignore such truths, as they ignore later difficulties by equating happiness with improvement of material conditions, and 'well-being'. This is a sentimental weakness in 'progressive' social theories.

'not-me', cannot indeed know a sense of loss or deprivation. The anxiety caused by being born is not the anxiety of awareness of 'leaving' the mother, but has a character derived from more primal biological processes. Winnicott records the behaviour of one child patient who needed to re-experience being born:

> He would get inside my coat and turn upside down and slide to the ground between my legs; this he repeated over and over again.
>
> *Collected Papers*, p. 178

Of another patient's re-experience of birth Dr Winnicott speaks of its 'terrific intensity'.

> She had suddenly to go to bed with what she called a 'blackout'. She had lain absolutely rigid and curled right up tight on her side, unable to do anything at all, and as near unconscious as may be. A doctor was called in who said he could find nothing wrong with her body . . .
>
> ibid., p. 129

The immediate cause of this experience was the attempt by this patient to demonstrate to a mentally ill child with a fear of the Underground Railway in London that the Underground was 'all right': by identifying with the child who was also re-approaching birth anxieties, the woman came to re-experience the intra-uterine state, the 'Tubes' being symbolic of the birth-passage. Of 'birth-play' in analytical sessions Winnicott adds:

> The feeling one gets is . . . *that the child's body knows about being born.*
>
> ibid., p. 180 (My italics)

If the child's 'body' knows about being born, then this knowledge remains for ever in the memory and conditions all later life. This 'body knowledge' is of the kind D. H. Lawrence insists on in *Apropos of Lady Chatterley's Lover* (see below, pp. 224–5). But our thought at large has yet to take into account the immense bearing on our attitudes to experience of the ('archetypal') 'body-memory' of the womb and of birth. It affects all our attitudes to achievement, to delay, and being at the mercy of forces we cannot control.

A sense of confidence, sequence, stability and security in a person may (Winnicott says) have begun in a birth experience which was natural and untroubled, triumphantly survived by the baby, and therefore a source of enrichment of its natural way of life. In this the birth experience itself may contribute positively to the adult's make-up. So, a woman who can give herself intuitively to the experience of birth is helping to ensure a creative child.

What kind of reaction can difficulties in birth generate? Not knowing a 'not-me' the baby cannot experience anxiety in the common sense of the word, since this involves a sense of 'the expectation of danger, preparedness for it, even if it be an unknown one'.[1] But the baby has feelings and body reactions; as we have seen, he responds to oxygen deficiency. Yet his feelings do not include our kind of awareness, nor any awareness of being a separate being. What he does experience is what Winnicott calls 'intercourse with the environment', in which the environment is all-important: the only thing he knows is 'environmental impingement'.

> In health the infant is prepared before birth for some environmental impingement, and already has had the experience of a natural return from reacting to a state of not having to react, which is the only state in which the self can begin to be . . . [the birth experience] is a temporary phase of reaction and therefore of loss of identity, a major example, for which the infant has been prepared, of interference with the personal 'going along', not so powerful or so prolonged as to snap the thread of the infant's continuous personal process.
>
> *Collected Papers,* p. 183

The temporary loss of identity as the environment impinges, if it goes on long enough to become traumatic, gives an extreme sense of insecurity, and can lead to an expectation of further examples of loss of continuity of self, and even a 'congenital (but not inherited) hopelessness in respect of the attainment of a personal life'.

In adult patients under psychoanalysis the 'snapping of the thread' caused by birth traumata is expressed as the feeling of 'being in the grip of something external, so that one is helpless'

[1] Freud, *Beyond the Pleasure Principle,* 1920.

An allied intolerable feeling is that of experiencing something *without any knowledge of when it will end*. These experiences Winnicott connects with the forms of art: in music form is important because in this the end is 'in sight from the beginning'. Positive directions in works of art, and a positive attitude to the function of art itself in living, would seem to belong to that confidence which comes from more natural and non-traumatic birth. The strange appeal of 'anti-art', present day cults of futility in art, and that aestheticism which seeks to deny the influence of art in living, would seem to have some connection with that 'hopelessness in respect of the attainment of a personal life' such as is found in those who are mentally ill through severe birth traumata. Such cultural manifestations might be the consequence of inhibiting traditions and conditions in mothers of the previous generation. Winnicott finds that some severe impingements of the environment at birth can virtually generate a kind of paranoia, as of a hostile environment. The connection between this dream (by a woman of twenty-eight with schizophrenia with paranoid features) and the way the human predicament is symbolized by Beckett's plays, such as *Happy Days*, will be obvious:

> She dreamed that she was under a pile of gravel. Her whole body at the surface was extremely sensitive to a degree which it is hardly possible to imagine. Her skin was burned, which seemed to her to be a way of saying that it was extremely sensitive and vulnerable. She was burned all over. She knew that if anyone came and did anything at all to her, the pain would be impossible to bear, both physical and mental pain. She knew of the danger that people would come and take the gravel off and do things to her in order to cure her, and the situation was intolerable. She emphasized that with this were intolerable feelings comparable to those which belonged to her suicide attempt. 'You just can't bear anything any longer. It's the awfulness of having a body at all, and the mind that's just had too much. It was the entirety of it, the completeness of the job that made it so impossible. If only people would leave me alone. If only people wouldn't keep getting at me.'
>
> *Collected Papers*, p. 185

Our problem as literary critics is to seek to judge whether, when such a paranoiac reaction to an 'impingement' of reality, as it were, in terms of remembered birth traumata, is rendered into a literary work, such as a work of drama, the record is of value as communicated experience. It may be that a very disordered attitude to reality – really an attitude to experience emanating from a wounded psyche – is elevated into a statement that 'all human experience is like this' (as I think it is in Beckett). If it is, then it must be rejected, despite the partial truth (that things look like that to *some* people). Or the aspect may be exploited by a writer who is unconsciously aware that we, because of our own flaws, will be deeply affected by his use of such material. But he may be content *merely* to affect and disturb us (as is Pinter), and not to involve us in any contest against the vision of futility or hopelessness, or to include in his work other creative aspects of reality – such as the individual's capacity to overcome the effects of birth traumata, except where the damage caused has been gravely psychopathological. That is, such writing may be unreal because it ignores the successful end – of being born, and so we must reject it again, as the attempt to involve us too wholly in what is only a partial truth.

Of course, the mere rendering of dissociated states of psyche may be valuable for the light they cast on other – extremely 'other' – lives (as of mad people), and for the light they cast on our own tinges of their disorders. But Clare's poem *I Am* and Crabbe's poetry of contest with despair (for instance) are more valuable than the rambling 'poetry' of a schizophrenic patient, despite common origins in madness, because their beauty lies much in elements of courage and brave awareness – in the wrestle with distress, towards 'self-esteem'. Clare's line:

> The vast ship-wreck of my life's esteems

is a noble line, conveying a poignant awareness of his suffering, from the point of view of one who regards his lost self-esteem (this is implicit in the imagery) as a buoyant ship, carrying before the wind, trimmed and impressive: the name of the ship is the title of the poem, *I Am*. It is a tribute to that confident state of being which he has known, and which he has lost: the greatness of the poem is in its positive commendation of effective normality, despite the ruin, and it is at the furthest remove from mere existential rendering of dissociated states, or the elevation of them into a norm, as in much twentieth century fashionable art.

Even the movements of birth itself would seem, from Winnicott's account, to be significant in many adult activities. He quotes the word 'reptation' from speleological accounts of movements in holes in cave-exploration done without movement of either arms or legs. Experience of delay in birth may make for a feeling of helplessness associated with such movements which we know a foetus to make. Then comes the 'crowning', and this may be re-experienced in disturbed adults as headaches which feel like 'a band round the head' – again often associated with an environmental impingement that has no foreseeable end. All kinds of 'head feelings' in adults seem to originate in the experience of crowning, and in analytical work Dr Winnicott finds phantasy themes of scalping, helmets, discharge through the top of the head, horns and unicorns related to the 'extension of the personality' in this birth process whereby the body propels itself 'along the birth channel'.

The next stage in the baby's emergence is for him to cry and to begin breathing. Here the normal process is for a significant and clear change to happen. In abnormal circumstances the baby has to react, instead of 'going on being' in its physical function. Delay and difficulty in birth produce confusion, which may later become 'confusion about anger and its expression'. Yet, of course, the cry is also the baby's first expression of itself in the new environment, and so a first stage of establishing a lively vitality. But an additional danger at birth is connected with the immediate need to breathe – and trouble here can lie at the root of anxieties which focus on suffocation. Winnicott here points to the manifestations of this suffocation anxiety in adult life derived from this moment. These include those perversions which involve breathing obstruction; masturbation phantasies which express the desire to be suffocated (sometimes acted out even to suicide in those who had no suicidal intention); in inverted suicide 'which is commonly called murder' – that is in active suffocation as a perverted kindness ('the active person feeling the passive one must be longing to be suffocated'). The latter, he says, is of course an element too in the healthy passionate sexual relationship. And finally Winnicott associates the Eastern mystic's attempt to suspend breathing with his denial of the difference between internal and external reality.

Our first breath, and our first cry, are therefore significant, not only in going on living physically, but also in our psychic patterns throughout life. In culture these experiences are recognized, as they are remembered by each of us. The feather which King Lear holds to Cordelia's nose, and Othello's pillow which quenches Desdemona's light are poetical expressions of aspects of existential reality which have their origin in the moment of the first wail, so exquisitely and agonizingly recorded for us by Tolstoy in *War and Peace*.

> Piteous, helpless, animal groans came from the next room. Prince Andrey got up, went to the door, and would have opened it. Someone was holding the door.
>
> 'Can't come in, can't!' a frightened voice said from within. He began walking about the room. The screams ceased; several seconds passed. Suddenly a fearful scream – not her scream, could she scream like that? – came from the room. Prince Andrey ran to the door; the scream ceased; he heard the cry of a baby.
>
> 'What have they taken a baby in there for?' Prince Andrey wondered for the first second. 'A baby? What baby? . . . Why a baby there? Or is the baby born?'
>
> When he suddenly realized all the joyful significance of that cry, tears choked him, and leaning both elbows on the windowsill he cried, sobbing as children cry . . .
>
> *War and Peace*, Part IV, IX

This first experience of birth may be linked with the later processes of individual human development, in which 'bad' experiences tend to affect weak areas of our make-up, in contest with the process by which 'good' experiences built up a confident vitality, resisting 'bad' experiences, and overcoming the weaknesses. Thus, a 'normal' pregnancy and birth contribute to a quality of lively viability in the baby, which sends it well on the road to stability, confidence and security. A baby can be born

unviable, as we know, and will simply die. But bad experiences –
such as severe birth traumas – will not of themselves, Winnicott
points out, cause – say – paranoia: it merely 'places on the infant
a pattern of expected interference with basic "being" '.

For one thing, the baby is, before birth, prepared for it by his
phases of reaction to impingement, and Winnicott believes that
the self begins to include rudimentary memories of limited phases
of such impingement, disturbing the continuity of experiencing.
When it is born the baby finds birth but another impingement, and
if the reaction to it does not exceed what the infant is prepared for,
then it will not be traumatic, and cause anxiety or tendency to
paranoia. But at this stage, he says, the intellect can be forced into
a precocious activity, recording intolerable reactions, defending
the psyche by, as it were, recognizing and collecting them, for
hiding away in the memory and holding on to, there. This is
possibly one origin of our capacity to develop an intellectual
defence against whole experience. Two possible cultural implications may follow. First, the mother's capacity to give herself to the
birth experience, by intuitive bodily co-operation, such as is enhanced by ante-natal relaxation, is a primary contribution to the
new individual's whole capacity to deal with experience. While
we can never eliminate difficult births, and while it is also true
that infants can triumph successfully over the scars of a hard birth,
obviously it is of importance to do all we can to foster 'natural
childbirth' and that security and happiness in which it can happen
most richly. Here love is a real creative force – and at the other
extreme is the 'unwanted' or illegitimate birth, consequent upon a
lapse perhaps exacerbated by a cult of sexual irresponsibility, in
which the new life may have little or no chance of sanity, from the
beginning.[1]

Secondly, where we find intellectual defence against feeling, or
futility and hopelessness expressed in forms of art, the origin may

[1] I think not enough is yet known about the unconscious motives which prompt
people to have 'unwanted' children. There is some belief among psychoanalysts,
I believe, that girls who become pregnant often do so as an act of hostility or
revenge, etc. But, of course, this suggests once more a whole 'reality problem'–
and this may be made worse by cultural influences which undermine natural good
sense.

be in the birth traumata in the individual who promotes these attitudes – traumata which left him with a hopeless feeling about experience. Again, while the expression of such hopelessness may fascinate us, it would be wrong for us to accept it as a whole view of the human predicament.

However, our baby is now born, and henceforward must necessarily begin to come to terms with external reality, and with its own inner reality, both of body and mind. It is separated from its mother's body, and the word 'separation' will from now on take a central place on our discussion. Birth imposes tremendous biological changes from the foetus' existence up to now, and makes great demands on his constitutional powers of adjustment to his new environment – and, of course, on his mother, as part of that 'nursing couple'.

In this crucial process many things can go wrong – the situation tests both the baby's congenital condition, and his mother's whole capacity as a being – her power to love, her relationship with reality, her stability and security, and her capacity to function as a natural maternal creature. In the 'nursing couple' situation is to be tested everything that the mother's world has given her, from the love and care of her own parents, to her own growth to consciousness, love and creativity, her love relationship with her husband (and with her other children if she has a family already) – and her education and culture, which will contribute a good deal to her attitudes to herself as a mother, to her child, and to her ability to function as a natural being intuitively. Every human being's sanity and fulfilment depends on things being viable and sound in this process at the time of absolute dependence, particularly during the first few months when the relationship between the members of the 'nursing couple' are so intense as to be a particular and unique psychic state, in which the mother is deeply involved, and a very different creature from her normal self, being 'gone' into the baby's psychic atmosphere, and complementing his needs within this sphere. We owe a great deal to Lawrence and Tolstoy for rendering something of this state in fiction: it is also symbolized in a million paintings of the virgin and child. Yet, considering it is the most important area of all life, there is really surprisingly little in art about this condition of maternal devotion, explicitly. In fact, it is so disturbing a condition that it seems we may repress our memory, and suppress our awareness of it.

Winnicott calls this state 'primary maternal preoccupation', which has the following characteristics:

> It gradually develops and becomes a state of heightened sensitivity during, and especially towards the end of, the pregnancy.
>
> It lasts for a few weeks after the birth of the child. It is not easily remembered by mothers once they have recovered from it.
>
> I would go further and say that the memory mothers have of this state tends to become repressed.
>
> *Collected Papers*, p. 302

We have here a clue to the difficulties some 'intellectual' women, or women with an inability to accept their femininity, or women who find it difficult to let their feelings flow, have, over mothering – they find it impossible to tolerate the lapse of their whole beings, into a state which is virtually a psychic 'illness':

> This organized state (that would be an illness were it not for the fact of the pregnancy) could be compared with a withdrawn state, or a dissociated state, or a fugue, or even with a disturbance at a deeper level such as a schizoid episode in which some aspect of the personality takes over temporarily . . . I do not believe that it is possible to understand the functioning of the mother at the very beginning of the infant's life without seeing that she must be able to reach this state of heightened sensitivity, almost an illness, and to recover from it. (I bring in the word 'illness' because a woman must be healthy in order both to develop this state and to recover from it as the infant releases her. If the infant should die, the mother's state suddenly shows up as illness. The mother takes this risk.)
>
> ibid., p. 302

This natural function in a woman is of course inevitably affected by her upbringing and culture. It will be very little helped by the philistine education offered her by her grammar school, for instance, in which such creativity as there may be struggles unequally against intellectual denial of the intuitive life, often in an atmosphere that suppresses femininity. And, of course, her concepts of herself and her femininity will count – and so will her love-relationship with her husband. When people write to the papers saying they cannot fulfil themselves in marriage *if* they have children, or say they can't see why sex should involve procreativity, they are possibly rationalizing a fear of the realities of bodily life. They sense they could not tolerate the 'cow-like' state of entering into the baby's psychic world, and risking the 'illness' involved. On the other hand, an adequate mature development of capacities to love, and to enter into the sexual life, will lead towards the capacity to 'give' in this state, to a degree that guarantees sanity in the child. Interestingly enough, the development of 'relaxation' classes for pregnant women was intended to have the effect of enabling them to enter into a whole awareness of their bodies, and to prepare them, in terms of the whole 'psyche-soma' for parturition. It might be almost considered a discipline of being something like that of Yoga. The relaxation is not only a preparation for physical collaboration with the natural events of birth, but also a means of contemplating the whole state of pregnancy, its meaning, and preparing at the intuitive level for the psychic changes involved. No amount of lecturing, intellectual knowledge. or even 'imaginative' experience would have done the same for the thousands of women who have benefited from these courses in relaxation. They have experienced a kind of 'body-awareness' which our civilization neglects, and so it has to be deliberately given them by the hospitals. The implications for schools are, I think important – that girls should have some experience of handling live babies, and much of contemplating their creativity, as in imaginative work, at a deeper level than biological information. For adult culture, the implications are that in order to guarantee psychic health in the nursing couple and sanity in the child, the security of marriage and of the mother-child relationship needs to be recognized and celebrated to a significant degree. Yet, as we know, our entertainment culture pays a hundred times more attention to depersonalized sex, prostitution, homosexuality, adultery and mental pornography than it does to the celebration of the deeply satisfying and courageous ordeal of motherhood.

But our pursuit of the growth of consciousness in the baby

must first begin with biological processes, and their links with the origins of consciousness.

The first problem of the new-born baby is a biological one characteristic of human beings – because their nervous organization and their brain have developed to such a degree of fineness

and complexity. From these initial problems, to those of the late stages of development in our capacities consciously to deal with reality, those things which can and do go 'wrong' with us all in some degree are 'the curse of Adam'. Interestingly enough, this truth is symbolized by the poetic myth of Adam and Eve. Eden before the Fall is a poetic statement of the bliss we apparently remember, of the intra-uterine state, in which existence was 'monistic' or completely narcissistic, a closed circle (as of a garden) on which no environment impinged.[1] This is the state of innocence, from which we all 'fall' almost literally at birth (the baby's fear of falling is one of its greatest, after the surrounding

[1] A child of mine at two would ask for the garden gate to be opened, so she could go into 'the other garden' – meaning the world outside. Mrs Sibyl Marshall points out in *An Experiment in Education* that the child's first 'ideogram' in painting is a circle or spiral. This surely is the enclosed 'self', and children are (as she points out) afraid of the edges and corners of the paper because there are areas of unknown experience (where, as it were, one might 'fall off the edge of the world'). Later this circle is filled with dots (eyes, nose, etc.) and has parallel lines added outside – the extremities, arms and legs – and, implicitly, all those sensations and contacts that extend perception of the 'not-me'.

confinement of the womb is left behind). The symbol of the 'occasion' of the Fall, or its focus, is the 'apple' of knowledge of good or evil. That this is a symbol of the mother's breast is born out by the way in which it has been unconsciously made plain by many artists who have illustrated the myth, and have made Eve hold the apple in one hand and her breast in the other.

As we shall soon see, the mother's breast *is* the focus of our loss of innocence – of the beginnings of our knowledge of 'evil' within ourselves, in terms of the rage we feel when the nursing mother takes her self away. This rage we project on to the world, to avoid the pain of accepting that it is in ourselves – and conceive it paranoically as a persecuting force of evil in the world (i.e. the serpent[1]). But the knowledge of good also comes from the 'apple', from the way in which, as the mother continues to offer it to us, at the right moment, we begin to form phantasy concepts of good things ('the apple of my eye'), and concepts in continuity, of goodness and the mother. This knowledge of good and evil brings also the need to accept painfully the realness of reality – even that 'in the sweat of thy face shalt thou eat bread'.

The 'curse of Adam' is therefore the inevitable flaw in each of us, not least our always limited capacity to distinguish between the real and the unreal, the good and the evil, the right and the wrong – to which capacity we are continually driven to add, by our culture, in order to survive. But this flaw is also the means by which we enter the contest with the real world outside Eden. There is, even as we read the Book of Genesis, a sense of relief after the Fall, because we then come into our recognizable environment, in which there are woes, difficulties and death – in the

[1] Why should the projected persecutor take the form of a serpent (often shown in ancient pictures as having female breasts)? Since it is a projection of the newly born self's badness, perhaps its armless shape is the felt shape of the self which thrust through the birth passage so by reptation. It is also now mixed with the 'bad', persecuting, side of mother and so has breasts. Its aggressiveness is also phallic, perhaps because as in adults, as Winnicott says, the body that thrust through the birth passage can, in deviant individuals, become identified with the male genital: see above on horns and unicorns, p. 42. As male phallus, of course, the serpent is symbol of procreativity, and thus of sexual life which follows the loss of innocence, from the infant's genital feelings to adult libidinousness, associated with aggression.

contest with which real satisfactions and achievements are to be found. 'Disobedience' – the first expression of hate and rage directed against the mother as inevitably she is felt to behave as an independent creature – is the focus of a much richer complex of human interest than 'innocence' or 'heavenly bliss'. Paradise 're-gained', in which all contests with experience were solved, would be insufferably tedious and unreal: we say 'we would go mad with boredom' – and this is true, since sanity exists in our continuing and effectual dealings with an imperfect and trouble-filled reality. Eternal happiness is a maddening concept.

In the Book of Genesis, then, we find a very beautiful poetic statement of that painful, but satisfying, contest with reality – the means to growth and development, of all human civilized powers and self-realization – which the baby enters soon after birth, through his experience of the mother, coming to discover reality:

> . . . in sorrow shalt thou eat of it all the days of thy life;
> Thorns also and thistles shall it bring forth to thee, and thou shalt eat the herb of the field.
> In the sweat of thy face shalt thou eat bread, till thou return unto the ground; for out of it wast thou taken: for dust thou art, and unto dust shalt thou return.
>
> *Genesis* 3, 17–19

The reality into which we enter is that with which we can only come to terms and live effectively in, inasfar as we accept the tragic meaning of those verses. For the long and tormented path towards consciousness must also be a consciousness of pain that must be endured, separation and absolute loss which must be accepted, and the agonizing toleration of our inescapable mortality.

But to return to the biology of the new-born baby. As an American medical research worker says:

> The baby is by its very incompleteness of brain and nervous system continually in potential danger of functional disorganization . . . because the young infant's breathing mechanisms are not well enough developed to work adequately with the increased demand caused by the rapid forebrain development.

Dr Margaret Ribble on Infantile Experience in *Personality and the Behaviour Disorders,* New York, Ronald Press, 1949. (See also John Bowlby in *Child Care and the Growth of Love.*)

The baby's first need is to *feel,* and to feel strongly enough through the stimulus of his mother's body – being held and fed and tended by her. By this body-stimulus the feelings are kept viable, and in their turn this keeps the reflex mechanisms of breathing going, and keeps the sensory nervous system active.

From the observations of such medical research as that of Dr Ribble and John Bowlby we find confirmation of the significance of 'touch' between human beings, and the primary significance of bodily life such as D. H. Lawrence insisted on. (See below, Mrs Bolton on 'the touch of a man' and a quotation on the body's 'real feelings' from *Apropos of Lady Chatterley's Lover,* pp. 224–5.) Lawrence's preoccupation, however, was with 'touch' and 'body' in adult sex, often at the expense of attention to the kind of creative contact necessary between mother and child, of which aspect of procreativity Lawrence seemed to be unconsciously jealous to a destructive degree (see pp. 224–71 below passim). But, of course, a recognition of the richness and significance in the adult life of love, of 'touch', contact, and the full life of the body will make its own contribution to the 'nursing couple' of which the baby is part. In common language, a woman who is sexually happy and fulfilled is likely to make a mother who finds richness in tender contact with the baby, and give him intuitively the 'touch' he needs. It is of course also possible for a woman who is not sexually fulfilled yet to find fulfilment in the love-contact with her child, and also for a woman who is apparently sexually fulfilled to be an over-anxious or not-tender-enough mother – though the latter seems less likely. I don't want to suggest any direct and automatic connections between such complex aspects of behaviour. What one can say, I think, is that every positive experience of love, 'touch', and enrichment of body life adds to one's capacities to enjoy others and to give richness and satisfaction to others, including one's children. Positive culture – that which makes for tenderness, and 'going out' in sympathy – assists the development of this capacity to flow. Culture which promotes depressive attitudes,

negativism and the 'taboo on tenderness' – which urges 'playing
it cool' – has an inhibiting effect, especially on those already prone
to these disabilities.

Insufficient oxygen consumption, possibly due to a lack of
sufficient attention and 'warmth' from the mother, can cause
actual brain damage. The breathing of the newly born is precari-
ous even (according to Dr Ribble) for as much as the first three
months. Crying during this period is an 'emergency reaction',
stimulated by a partial suffocation from lack of oxygen to the
brain.

This biological explanation of the baby's needs justifies recent
insistence on the need to feed a baby 'on demand', and of the
mother's loving care. Mechanical and cold methods ('letting the
baby cry out') are even dangerous to the organism. The baby also
needs such things as warm and closely wrapped bed-clothes, the
movement of cradles with rockers, to have his hand held in dress-
ing and undressing, to be sung and murmured to, and to be
handled with confidence. All these help to overcome the terrors
of his awareness that he is no longer in the womb-environment
which hugged him close, swayed and pulsated, was warm and
embracing, a contact of living flesh, embracing and secure. Many
deep disorganizations in adults have been traced to their excessive
feelings of insecurity as new-born babies who felt they were falling
through space, because they were supported on one side only,
insecurely held, or unclothed. Anyone who has bathed a baby
will have felt the involuntary movements of terror (rather like
those of a cat which has fallen out of a tree) which subside when
the child is in the warm supporting embrace of a warm bath – and
enjoys his happy return to an experience like that of being immersed in the amn otic fluid. Of course, many babies have to
survive, and do happily survive, insecurities of handling at this
stage. But we must be conscious of the immense changes in a
new-born baby's environment, and of the immensity of the effect
of these on our own adult feelings of security or insecurity. Good
handling at this stage would seem to contribute, as does a trouble-
free birth, to successful dealings with later developments in our
relationship with reality. At the same time, from inevitable mis-

haps and failures of our imperfect mothers, we are also all flawed by this period of great change – from intra-uterine seclusion, to living in light and air, breathing, feeding by our mouth and excreting, all for the first time. The mother's continuous care is life's creative means by which we survive this revolution.

The baby knows nothing at this stage of his parents' care and love. He experiences only his own feelings – including anxiety and distress, against which, utterly helpless, he can only utter a cry. Perhaps the most significant contribution this period may make to our adult personality, and to culture, is the sense of loneliness. A deficiency of contact, as in babies who are rigidly placed in immobile cots in separate rooms in hospitals and 'left to cry it out', and the individual may suffer later incapacities to give and receive contact, may be less capable than others of bearing isolation and loneliness, and may be less self-reliant, especially if things go wrong later, when further separation must needs be borne. In the adult world we may find it possible to make connections between 'touch' and the lack of it, and various kinds of ability and disability in living in the community – the unconscious desire to be in prison, for instance, or the capacity to stand enforced isolation and such brainwashing techniques which exploit the confusion and break-down of mind after solitary confinement. Since we unconsciously symbolize the ground as 'Mother earth' such manifestations as the astronauts' 'earth-sickness' (according to Mrs Len Chaloner) may be attributed to the dissociations we all feel, because of the inevitable anxieties of this period. Fear of heights, and some forms of travel sickness may have the same origin. On the more positive side, a devotion to the earth as in good farming, and a sense of 'at-oneness' with the natural world may be promoted by the loving care a mother gives to her child at this stage.

If this is so, it may be that where we find desecration of the landscape, ugliness and erosion, the huddled crowding together of megalopolis, the breakdown of local community, and an incapacity to find remoteness tolerable in the dispersed locality, we may find a possible psychological cause. If we find depopulation of huge areas such as the Western Highlands of Scotland, going with too great dependence on crowded conurbations, we may deduce that something has gone wrong in our society with love and care in the raising of babies, and that this is an index of a larger failure in 'touch', love, tenderness and satisfaction between man and woman, the adult parents – and in our relationship with reality altogether. It may indicate a kind of psychomatic philosophical breakdown, in felt and thought attitudes to life – that people are losing self-reliance, and so cannot bear to be separated from a herd. Lawrence pursued this theme, from the desecration of the Nottingham countryside, and his parents' sad life, to the need for man and woman to learn to love well enough to provide the 'rainbow' of security and richness for each next generation. Alas, as I try to show below, what is said of the truth about this in *The Rainbow* is thrown away in the denial in *Lady Chatterley* of procreative love, and Lawrence's exploration of reality ends in the sterility of narcissistic hallucination.[1]

But the clues to the origin of our disabilities in love may be found in the next stage of the child's growth. Another aspect of Adam's curse is his tendency to seek to avoid pain and effort and thus avoid both the satisfaction and the reality of the world after the 'Fall'. The growth to love has as enemy not only the hate and destructiveness which come from love's frustration, but the urge to seek hallucination and a superficial temporary gratification, rather than the deep lasting one – 'fobbing off', rather than enrichment and achievement. As Bunyan knew, we have other enemies than those who confront us directly. As Genesis puts it, 'the serpent was more subtil than any beast of the field'. As the human organism is the most complex, so it has a capacity such as no other creature has, to cheat and deceive itself. But even this aptitude is but an aspect of that capacity for illusion and phantasy, without which there could be no consciousness to be deceived or undeceived.

[1] It is possible that those who have suffered a lack of mother love in early infancy, because of 'frigid' methods of child care, are not only those who care most about warmth of personal relationships culturally, and about 'the face of the land', but also those who are most likely to come to grief in wrestling with these very themes, as Lawrence did, because they are so dear to them, and at the centre of urgent psychic preoccupations.

The discovery of the reality of the self and the reality of the outside world, as separate things, goes inseparably with the development of love in the place of narcissism. Psychoanalytical theory calls this love of another one 'object-love' because it is the love of a being whose separate existence is recognized. So object-love may be distinguished from, say, that love of an image projected over another being which is still subjective and narcissistic, self-love, in deep and complicated senses. Probably the distinction between these kinds of love is never clear-cut, and often confused. But it is important for us to take in this association between the growth of love and the growth of our perception of reality, as going hand in hand, for when we come to examine poetic explorations of love such as those by Chaucer in the Debate on Marriage or Shakespeare's *The Winter's Tale* we shall find that the major preoccupation of these great minds is not with sex or even loving, but rather with the problem of our whole relationship with reality of which love and sex are a part. That is, they are concerned with such themes as illusion and reality, time and the consequence of actions, death and mutability, memory, and the sense of continuity:

> when you do dance, I wish you
> A wave o' the sea, that you might ever do
> Nothing but that; move still, still so ...

The child's growth of love is intimately bound up with its dealings with reality.

A new baby, while he feels even in his enclosed first state the impingements causing reactive 'breaks in continuity' such as I have referred to above, lacks the perception, during his first few months of acute helplessness, to know he is separate from his mother. So, he does not mind being left alone, though, as we have seen, he does need the touch of his mother at feeding time, and the stimulus of her care, to maintain viability, and a continuous thread of being. On the whole, however, he can, when satisfied, be put down without anxiety, and will go quietly to sleep. He is protected by his lack of perception from becoming aware, in his total dependence, that he is separate from the mother, and that therefore she could possibly leave him for ever. The pain of awareness of this would be intolerable at this stage, and so to keep him immune from such pain 'the whole of existence must appear to be a unity – monistic, so to speak'. (Sandor Ferenczi, op. cit. p. 366.)

The baby has strong feelings, and there comes a time when increased perception leads to an awareness that the mother has a separate existence – and when we say 'mother' here we are really meaning the whole of the 'other than me' or 'not-me', since a baby, having lived in a monistic world, and actually having been part of the mother, has hitherto assumed[1] that he *is* everything, and everything, including the mother, is him, in complete omnipotence and narcissism. Having felt only impingements from the surrounding environment, which have caused reactions (such as breathing movements, the heart beating faster, movements down the birth passage, the head pressure of crowning, a loss of support after being born and when undressed, reflex crying to amend oxygen deficiency), he has been sustained only by a sense of his thread of continuous being, fostered by the mother's presence and continuous existence and care (unknown to him as such of course), which have sustained his viability and his 'going on being'.

When perception increases there begins to come to him a rudimentary memory, a sense of sequence and time, and a capacity to anticipate by hallucination. His feelings are the gateway to perception (as Mrs Chaloner says), *and phantasy is its mode*. Without the phantasy generated by powerful feelings, as of hunger and the instinctual will to survive, there could be no consciousness.

The first stage of development comes through instinctual feelings, of hunger and the need for the stimulus of 'touch' and care. The baby begins to respond to his mother's smile, and when she approaches he opens his mouth in anticipation and holds up his arms. Her approach means so much to him, because he is aware that he depends upon her for survival. All his pleasure and security are bound up with his mother, and the love and food she gives

---

[1] Terms of cognition and knowledge are all virtually impossible to use in talking about such states of being and apprehension. Here 'can know nothing else but' is nearer, but clumsier.

him. So he comes to feel that he absorbs into himself her love and care with his food.[1]

In terms of his earliest dealings with reality this means that the baby feels he is 'taking in goodness' from the life-sustaining mother. This process as a phantasy process is a significant one in all psychic development, and is called by the psychoanalytical writer 'introjection'. In children and adults this 'taking in of goodness' is a continual means to growth and enrichment, and it has a significant role in the effect upon us of positive creativity (as the record of successful contests with experience) and in our 'taking in' the good influence of others. I will discuss later some remarks by Melanie Klein on these cultural processes of introjection. We may delineate a continual process of 'tasting' and 'taking in' reality, from the baby's feelings around and putting things in its mouth, the child's exploration of this area and then that area of experience (as in play-acting and painting) to the adult's pursuits and explorations of themes and areas of perception through art and science.

However, as the baby comes to anticipate his feed, and to recognize his mother as a separate being, and to feel need and pleasure that she satisfies, he comes to the first tremendous crisis of object relationships. From his intense feelings, his rudimentary sense of time and memory, and his capacity for phantasy, he develops at a particular stage (about four months) a capacity for increased perception, which brings with it conflicts which have the intensity of a life-or-death struggle – a struggle from which no one emerges unscathed, and from which, in a sense, no one ever emerges, since our bridges between subjective and objective can never be complete.

The major elements of the crisis are as follows. There is the attempt by the hungry baby to hallucinate his feed, in order to try to obtain satisfaction, and thus relieve the pain of hunger. Inevitably must come his discovery that this fails, with consequent pain. But the situation under good management will be remedied

[1] Mrs Chaloner quotes a little boy of four who was left at a kindergarten and said, 'I felt very empty when you left me this morning.' He was still equating love and food: in adult life the connection reappears when, in early love, the lover loses interest in food, because he is 'too full of love'.

by his mother's capacity to 'present' the breast[1] to him at the naturally right moment, so that his phantasy may meet a comple- ment in reality which gives the infant the *illusion* that there is an external reality that corresponds to the infant's own capacity to create.

Winnicott (whom I am quoting) goes on:

> In other words, there is an overlap between what the mother supplies and what the child might conceive of. To the observer the child per- ceives what the mother actually presents, but this is not the whole truth. The infant perceives the breast only in so far as a breast could be created just there and then. There is no interchange between the mother and the infant. Psychologically the infant takes from a breast that is part of the infant, and the mother gives milk to a child that is part of herself. . . . In psychology, the idea of interchange is based on an illusion.
>
> *Collected Papers,* p. 239

To put it crudely, the baby thinks he makes the mother, though at first he is in the perplexing situation of not knowing what to make since his concepts are so rudimentary. In his progress to- wards weaning, of course, a child must be disillusioned – and must come to accept the breast as a 'real' breast. But at the begin- ning, because of her deep natural entering into the baby's psychic envelope, as it were, or 'adapting' to his early needs, the good mother meets him half way, in these early stages, by her 'primary maternal preoccupation'. He conceives at an early stage the idea of something which would 'meet the growing need which arises out of instinctual tension'. But as yet he doesn't know *what it is that has to be created*. 'At this point in time the mother presents her- self' – and allows the infant to suppose he has created her. Cultural manifestations, and crises of adult consciousness, with their origins here, are obvious, from Dante's Beatrice to Pygmalion and the Fata Morgana. (We may also note here how impossible it always must be to talk about 'instincts' with human beings, since from the beginning complexities of consciousness are integral with primal needs.)

[1] The word 'breast' in this discussion includes not only his source of food and 'touch', but the whole 'mother environment'.

Winnicott insists on the importance in these stages of the child's first cultural artefact – a 'transitional object' around which the disillusionment takes place. In this object, which may be a piece of wool or cloth, a teddy bear, or a ritual, mouth movements or words – we have the origins of all creative culture, that assists our passage towards a whole reality-sense. But here, at this premature stage, we may find the origins of flaws, of many of our later difficulties in approaching reality, not least in personal relationships, since no mother *is* good enough and no infant is completely able to make use of her adaptation. The baby also has a 'standard' – in the 'ideal' image he has spun out of hallucination and his memory of intra-uterine bliss. There are situations and occasions in which we are dealing not with the actual person who 'presents' herself to us, but an illusion which is part of ourselves, narcissistic, and thrown over their reality. In adult life we may still be living with such a projected image, unaware that we are signally failing both to find interchange with the real person behind the illusion, or, when we do find her, find she clashes with the narcissistic image we had created. In sexual relationships particularly these capacities for hallucination and projection reassert themselves. In these we enter again into the baby's capacity to 'create' his illusion, anticipating the pleasure of his feed, which, when it comes, satisfies both the created image and the hunger. The progress of desire in adult sex follows similar patterns. This process is of great importance, and to understand it may help us again to establish a link with cultural influences. For instance, images of women which are close to reality, and yet full of joy and beauty, will help us towards a creative image in desire, which meets reality happily and is enriched by it. A false image (such as that more-than-perfect one promoted by advertising or the erotic cinema) will inhibit our capacity to make the illusion accord with the reality of our own love-object and sexual life. Relevant disabilities are fear of satisfaction, because it dissipates the desire-created illusion, and will seem thereby to annihilate the love-object. Failures to relate desire and reality may generate a cynicism about sexual reality such as we find often in modern poetry. For instance, in a little magazine, a modern poet recently said:

'After possession the woman is as humdrum as yesterday's break-fast.' This expresses a form of fear of satisfaction (sometimes found in medical case-histories), of created illusion being destroyed by gratification, bringing disillusionment. Such consequences of a breakdown in the mother's toleration and fostering of the baby's phantasy processes may give rise to forms of 'unreality feelings' in her child's adult sexual living – anxieties often manifested as a 'craving for the new', that is, the pursuit of fresh images in promiscuity or adultery, because of an inability to accept any real partner.

'*Partir, c'est mourir un peu*': the baby's increased perception now brings him suddenly to realize that if this good caring mother is a separate being, then she can go away, taking all his goodness and security with her – and with these his life. As Mrs Chaloner says, 'this discovery, at five or six months, [is] a staggering blow to their security and *an almost irreconcilable loss*, so that they may cry inconsolably when left outside a shop in a pram, or in the cot at night'.

These separation fears, and their accompanying perceptions of 'almost irreconcilable loss' are crucial to all adult consciousness, and the origin of our progress towards accepting – or failing to accept – the tragic awareness of the conditions of our life, and reality. They are of profound cultural importance.

It will help us to follow the increasing relevance of psycho-analytical ideas to culture if we follow the growth of these theories themselves at this point. The early and 'classical' account of the origins of our dealings with reality is given in Ferenczi's essay mentioned above. The first distresses of the baby, between hal-lucinations, hunger, the pain of deprival, and satisfaction, are very great: significantly, the way out of these distresses is by the development of 'concrete ideas' – and a sense of continuity derived indivisibly from love.

Ferenczi quotes Freud, who says that a hungry baby 'tries at first to procure satisfaction by a kind of hallucination; and only when this fails does it make those manifestations of "pain" that lead to a real satisfaction as a result'. In this we may find the begin-nings of our dealings with reality – how we may come to accept painful aspects of an indifferent universe. 'The recognition of the hostile environment is unpleasant, but at the moment non-recognition of it is still more painful; consequently the less painful becomes relatively pleasurable.'

The situation of being between two evils and choosing the lesser, as it were – either the hallucination which does not allay, or the real hunger – may be escaped in various ways. According to Winnicott it is overcome by the positive contribution of the mother, meeting the child half-way, filling in its concepts, and providing a sense of continuity. This is the beginning of what may be called 'creative attitudes to experience' – the ability to triumph over difficulties and to make things 'come good' – to use the appropriate phrase of Huckleberry Finn.

But in the meantime the primaeval infant mind takes other ways out of the dilemma. 'In its primal, narcissistic self-assurance', as we have seen, 'it has hitherto known nothing of the existence of objects outside itself . . . and so has no feelings towards them, friendly or hostile'. But as the mother begins to offer her breast (which in the beginning, as Winnicott suggests, is still to the baby a part of himself, that he has 'made') it becomes, because of his waiting, his hunger, his choice between pains, '*an object of love and hate*'. It is an object of hate because of its having been temporarily unobtainable, and of love because after its loss it offers a still more intense satisfaction. But 'it certainly becomes . . . the subject of a "concrete idea"'.

Our first concrete idea, then, is formed directly around nourishment, intense 'touch' feelings powerfully sexual, in care and love, and in relation to something intensely needed *that is taken away and returns*. The bearing of this on our ideas of rhythm, periodicity, time and continuity are obvious, and these may be found expressed in poetry such as folksong and love poetry, and these themes are eminently present in such a work as *The Winter's Tale*. The way forward from the painful primal conflict is by the developing sense of continuity – and a growing security, that joy will return. This 'separation' problem is a crucial one in an adult sexual relationship. We often find that trouble here is caused by our not being able to bear the 'in-betweens', the periods when 'desire fails'. Such difficulties give rise to overdependency and destructive idealizing. These may be found in D. H. Lawrence, sometimes seen and 'placed', as in some of the poems in *Look! We Have Come Through!*, sometimes not, while as we shall see, the whole of *Lady Chatterley* is virtually a hallucination in which overdependency and false idealizing are accepted as normative. The root of such adult woes in love are in a lack of confident conviction that satisfaction and joy will return. This again may be linked with the fear of satisfaction which is also common – because it is the beginning of a period of such uncertainty. At a deeper level the anxiety marks a fear even of annihilation. Winnicott also argues that it is 'the aggressive component' in adult love relationships which needs to find 'the object' and take in her continuity, thereby reassuring lovers of their existence. This I discuss below, at a stage in my discussion of Lawrence (pp. 217–22).

Ferenczi quotes Freud on that 'testing' of reality which is a means to gradually overcoming the anxiety of the 'in betweens' – those periods when there is a sense of 'flop' in any relationship: 'The first and foremost aim of testing the reality of things is not to find in reality an object corresponding to the thing represented, but to find it *again*, to be convinced that it is still there', and 'we recognize as a condition for the testing of reality that objects which formerly had brought satisfaction must have been lost'. Erotic reality, says Ferenczi, can be traced back to 'finding *again* and recognizing *again*'. This no doubt lies at the root of the continuing and recurring sense of significance we find in making love. In cultural terms this may be linked with the general aspect of universality. When we recognize the portrayal of some experience as exact ('Yes – that is *it!*') we recognize that this is an experience we have had, and may have again – and that someone else has had it, and lived through it. Children are sometimes astonished at the way in which their creativity has 'caught' some aspect of life, in poetry or painting (indeed, they can even disbelieve later that they were capable of doing what they did – Marjorie Hourd records a girl disclaiming a poem altogether, because it was so full of unconscious sexual awareness[1]). But they also delight in their work

[1] See *Coming Into Their Own*, pp. 44–45.

as 'artefact', whether it is a troubling poem, or a painting which 'gloats' on a delightful experience. The satisfaction is not only in the 'ordering' of experience – giving it form and pattern – but in the continuity – 'this comes round again and I recognize it'. The satisfaction associates with an assurance that we are real. A 'sad' or difficult poem tells us not only that the experience was painful or terrible, but that the poet survived and triumphed over it – for one cannot write a poem while in a depression or withdrawal state (nor, of course, if one ceases to exist). To have lived to write the poem is part of the emergence from and triumph over difficulty, and to have gone on existing.[1]

The re-experience of the delight or the triumph over difficulty as we read poems and stories of others (or re-read our own expression) has an effect similar to the long sequence of feeding times and moments of love and care by the mother. That is, the effects accrue, in a gathering sense of nourishment, a reinforcing of constructive feelings and attitudes, and a confidence in continuing to exist despite impingement. In this we have a recognition that casts light on the whole value of imaginative culture – that it provides a fostering sequence of positive recognitions, such as we follow in infancy as we are cared for by the mother. As her recurrent love and care are integral with our powers of phantasy, our growth of concepts, our dealings with reality, our first sense of time and periodicity, so the arts continue our pursuit of these aspects of experience, as a means to extending our exploration of the relationship between external reality and our inward understanding of it. Because our most intimate personal relationships follow the same progress and are a matter of building from moments of contact a creative sense of continuity in love that triumphs over time and death – so the quest for love is always intimately bound up with imaginative culture.

[1] We easily forget how evanescent is the child's sense of reality and his continuing identity. Children fear the dark because they fear that when the light is extinguished they may cease to exist. A degree of such fears persists in adults, too and our inward culture is one means to overcome them, as it provides resources which, when we fall back on them, reassure us that we are continuing to exist. In a lower way, a transistor radio or a television set will do the same, as a substitute for true resources.

Conversely, in some writers in whom the chief impulse is to disguise their own dissociation from reality, and to vindicate their own inability to construct an apprehension of continuity from recurrent moments of satisfaction, the cultural effort becomes an attempt to disrupt and reverse these processes with destructive and negative force. A typical example is Kingsley Amis, the effect of whose work is to depersonalize sex and to deny human decency. Such a writer springs traps under moments of expected triumph, and mocks at creativity, love and committed feeling. Many of our more fashionable writers thus undermine confidence. One common theme of frustrated creativity in their stories is drunkenness or some other inward weakness that robs the protagonist of his success – he sets the bed on fire, falls off the platform, rambles instead of giving a lucid lecture, is frightened by tortoises while fornicating, and so on. These are incidents symbolic of fears of impotence, and fears of satisfaction or achievement: they manifest a schizoid shrinking from those achieved and committed dealings with reality which, as having behind them a good relationship with the mother, enable a stable growth towards maturity, and a confidence in going on existing. Concomitants are an exclusive attention to the 'reality' of sensual sex which is empty of tender feeling and is associated with no concept-formation and so devoid of the realities of love, courtesy, self-respect and mutual regard. This is particularly true of the American novel in which 'reality' is sought in 'sexual reality' – as in Henry Miller or Mary Macarthy. The absence of the reality of love and goodness in such books suggests a dissociation which may have its origins in forms of untender and mechanical handling in infancy – i.e. feeding without tenderness, satisfaction without the mother's contribution to creative concept-formation by 'meeting the baby halfway', and separation becomes a break in the love circuit. An infant who is deprived of the contribution to his capacity for object relations, love and his dealings with reality, by a not-loving-enough mother (though he was no doubt fed well enough in terms of mere substance) may become an adult who can only 'hurl himself at the breast' to try to seek in desperation that more whole reality of which he unconsciously feels deprived – to recapture thus those achievements he never had, and to convince himself he still exists. Here the 'breast' means 'woman's body': significantly, it tends often to be one woman after another (both in life as well as books), and done rather more in hostility and hate (e.g. by seducing friends' wives), because the self really knows the original love-lack can never be remedied by mere further sensual satisfaction, and so, in bewilderment, hates and turns destructive in envy. The 'reality'-seeking sensuality is merely symbolic of poignant deprivation, not a true quest to love and reality. Indeed the original trouble was that the infant's gratification was too merely sensual – that way madness lies, still. The negative quality of the cultural output of people who are driven by such forces is often concealed by the intellectual brightness and the anxious clowning, often used to make positive and tender impulses – and creative and reality-seeking impulses – seem ridiculous. With the merely sensational crime best-seller, such as Fleming, the imaginative use of 'cool' seduction and blasé killing associates in a similar way with a reduction of the sense of reality – the dream indulgence reassures us that mortal reality is not real. A fare of this kind of culture can in time weaken living power, obviously, by fostering dissociation.

The popularity of such destructive expression can perhaps be explained by the prevalence in our society of a large minority of those who suffer the same predicament – a taboo on tender feeling, and a dissociation from reality, caused by an inhibition of love in their nursing mothers, and the failure of the 'meeting-half-way' period of psychic incubation towards disillusion. From this they have not been able to recover, nor have they been helped to wrestle with the deficiency by an imaginative culture and education, to help restore the development, as by a continuity of creative achievements. The prevalence of such schizoid 'art' marks a prevalence of dissociation in the intellectual community, and its whole capacity for living. It also seems to be an inevitable aspect of an acquisitive society whose impulse is to denigrate human nature for commercial purposes: significantly, the writer who 'does dirt' on human nature becomes respectable if his sales are large enough.

It should be emphasized, however, that one's objections to such writers is not just to their pornography (though they often are that, and the effect of this is in itself disabling enough). The objection is rather to their destructiveness, which spreads abroad and involves others (as it is intended to do) in their own incapacities to accept reality in a mature way. Their essential problem is fear of annihilation. Henry Miller, significantly, does not believe he will ever die: in such ways these apparently 'sternly realistic' writers are psychically close to *Peter Pan*, and to Barrie's kind of disastrous infantilism.[1] Amis's compulsive obsession with 'looking' and sex in terms of 'the act' that 'ends up in children' suggests a schizoid terror of adult relationship. The cheerful promiscuity he commends by implication is both a denial of deep psychic truth, and an attempt to involve others in forms of an anxious self-deception, whose roots are perhaps in some personal failure at the stage of primal formation of object relationships. His preoccupations with flatus and facial deceptiveness are infantile too.

While no writer can be blamed for his own personal inadequacies, he can be blamed for exploiting and fostering destructive attitudes at large, and must be resisted if he seeks to elevate his partial view of life as a universal picture of the human condition. The disastrous fact is, culturally, that such dangerously disparaging attitudes to life's possibilities are too often found to be endorsed at large, in university, journalistic and critical milieus. The appeal of the psychic negativism in such works has overcome the common readers' decency and sense of respect for the positive elements in human nature, which these books so abominably attack and deny.

In Ferenczi's essay now follows an important paragraph which I feel I must quote in full, because of its poetic implications:

> Things that always love us, i.e. that constantly satisfy all our needs, we do not notice as such, we simply reckon them as part of our subjective ego; things which are and always have been hostile to us, we

---

[1] See the superb essay on Barrie by Edgell Rickword in *Scrutinies I*, Wishart, 1928. That Miller's boastful exhibition of his inabilities to enter into adult relationship is pitiful makes it no less objectionable. See p. 289.

simply deny: but to those things which do not yield unconditionally to our desires, which we love because they bring us satisfaction, and hate because they do not submit to us in everything, we attach special mental marks, memory traces with the quality of objectivity, and we are glad when we find them again in reality, i.e. when we are able to love them once more. And when we hate an object but cannot suppress it so completely as to be able to deny it permanently, our taking notice of its existence shows that we really want to love it, but are prevented from doing so only by the 'maliciousness of the object'.

op. cit., p. 371

This, he says, explains an aspect of murder: 'why should I not destroy the thing I love?' As Ferenczi says, 'the savage is therefore only logical when after killing his enemy he shows him the greatest love and honour'. This attitude may be linked too, with sexual murder and the final act of auto-eroticism that is suicide.

But we may ponder the quotation over aspects of dealings with reality which seem closer at home to us. Dorigen in *The Franklin's Tale*, in wishing the rocks away, implicitly denies the existence of the inevitable flaws and faults in external reality that threaten her love for Averagus. From this impulse towards unreality her perplexity begins. Her husband's acceptance of the reality of the destructive adultery aimed at her, and of her fault, completes the progress of the poem towards 'finding again' and love. The rocks are not only the real rocks beneath all living experience, threatening and indifferent – they are also a projection of Dorigen's weakness, in not being able to bear separation from her husband, and not being able to bear his mortality. The hallucination of their disappearance (a denial of hostile elements), offered by the would-be adulterer, combines with the hallucination of a perfect relationship in which such threatening realities would not exist – 'it seemed'. Her triumph is to return to painful contest with truth and the realities: it is this that moves us so deeply.

Again, in *The Winter's Tale* Leontes, unable to bear the more disquietening aspects of sexual reality, and its inherent treacherousness in mortality, projects these 'malicious' elements over his courtiers ('You're liars all'). The baby who is exposed is the supposedly 'malicious' object: continuity is established by the symbolic 'finding again' of what was lost (Perdita). Florizel 'replaces' the Mamillius destroyed by Leontes' hate: Hermione, the mother, is restored at the end. The seasonal element in the play expresses the triumph of 'the continuity of life' over the torments of our dealings with reality which are a life and death struggle for the infant – and which remain so at the heart of our cultural and spiritual progress, in time. Both Chaucer and Shakespeare show themselves aware of our tendency to project our inward conflicts thus (as with the denial of an internal 'bad object') over the external world, and of the psychic progress by which such problems may be solved.

Ferenczi admits a platitude when he expresses this progress as

> the capacity for objective judgment and action is thus essentially a capacity for the tendencies of loving and hating for neutralizing each other.

op. cit., p. 372

But this platitude is one which is continually being stated in various forms by creative art, as a manifestation of our lifetime's quest for love and truth.

The baby's feelings are 'the gateway to perception' says Mrs Chaloner. And these feelings are at this time engaged in the intensity of a life and death struggle, beginning in terms of introjection and projection. The baby feels he takes in 'good' with his mother's food and care: the negative feelings in himself he projects on to the mother who leaves him to suffer the pangs of hunger and separation. He cannot escape the pain of this intensely conflicting situation of separation without 'forgoing some of his happiness and security' (*Feeling and Perception in Young Children*, p. 19). In this he makes a great step forward, towards his dealings with reality, but he also loses something for ever – and this leaves in all of us a damaging nostalgia for a state that certainly was, but which is also forever coloured by hallucinations as of a 'perfect' union that certainly never was, though our concept of it is coloured by memories of intrauterine states. This nostalgia can be damaging, not only because it is a yearning for a state that never was *in a separate being* but because to live in the state before disillusion would mean to forfeit the growth to consciousness and maturity. Pain and loss are inevitable if we are to grow up, but we seek to avoid these by clinging to illusions of omnipotence, in ourselves and others.

These attempts to avoid this pain and loss take many forms, which again are manifest in all human culture. They are not only negative, for they make for concepts which urge and promote the human search for meaning – as for the concept of a God who planned the universe, or a sense of harmony in experience such as may be expressed in music whether religious or 'secular'. But they may also make for concepts which obstruct our closer approach to reality, and stand in the way of our scientific progress, such as that of a God who is lowered to the status of a magical tribal deity (in wartime, at the level of the Army chaplain's sermon, or nowadays, when bishops bless nuclear submarines), or the vestigal belief in magic as expressed in many adult activities (Führer-worship, astrology, cigarette filter-tips, prayers for rain, pharmaceutical preparations containing no effective ingredient, gambling, the use of clergy to exorcize ghosts, belief in 'racial purity', space fiction and so forth). Grave psychopathic cases will manifest compulsive 'magic' rituals and incantations as we know. There are also many magical and irrational beliefs attached to the sexual life, such as the African woman's belief that Reckitt's Blue is a charm against conception, and that rhinoceros horn is an aphrodisiac.

These activities may be traced to an element of projection in that the infant's belief in his own omnipotence as it becomes 'disillusioned' is projected as a belief in the existence of omnipotent powers. Herein is the origin of the Gods.

The totally narcissistic baby, as we have seen, exists in a world which is monistic and all 'him'. At first his mother is also 'him' and, as Winnicott has suggested, his mother at first plays his game, and allows him to believe that the breast from which he takes sustenance has been 'made' by him, and is part of him, rather than part of her. (She can 'allow' this because she still feels he is part of her.) Despite the failure of his hallucinations it still seems to him that vivid wishing *creates* his gratification, and his noises and gestures are magical in the sense that they bring this.

As the necessary disillusionment progresses he becomes aware that his mother is a separate being, and his appeals need to be modified if he is to be successful. He could not yet bear the reality of recognizing the whole imperfect reality of his environment – and, indeed, in this sense 'human kind' can never 'bear very much reality'. So, the infant makes his mother omnipotent – and projects this later over father, nurses and over gods, fairies, or God as he grows up. (For an 'enlightened' parent to tell a child such things don't exist is, of course, destructive, since his stage of consciousness cannot do without such myths for the time being.)

Freud suggested that this corresponded to the religious period in human history, from Magog to Christ, and that the final surrender of omnipotence, by that insight derived from painful experience and the recognition of reality, represented by scientific empiricism, was an emergence into a higher stage. Later writers would, I think, accept the projection of our sense of omnipotence on to the gods as an important stage in the poetic symbolizing of the truths of our inward conflict. The growth of human consciousness, power and stature obviously derives a great deal from the great myths by which we share concepts of courage and heroism, in the contest with inward and external reality, as in protagonists from Odysseus to Birkin. As with all cultural manifestations of our psychic development, projection, magic and the sense of omnipotence can go 'wrong' and become obstructive or debilitating instead of 'life-promoting'. All children believe in magic and play ritual games, and these are an important 'living through' of the primitive stages of relationship with reality, of great poetic significance.[1] But paranoid children will live in a world of magical omnipotence in which any psychoanalyst who is brave enough to seek to cure them is the subject of their attempts at 'control'. 'It is a world of magic, and one feels mad in it. All of us who have treated psychotic children of this kind know how mad we have to be to inhabit this world, and yet we must be there, and must be able to stay there for long periods in order to do any therapeusis.' (Winnicott, Collected Papers, p. 227.)

[1] See the present author's Children's Games and the works of I. and P. Opie.

Religion is one way in which man expresses his need for relationship and meaning, at its greatest in culture in creative artists such as Bach, George Herbert, Handel, T. S. Eliot, Gerard Manley Hopkins, and Igor Stravinsky. In other directions – from the philosophy of Bishop Berkeley (a total denial of reality which might seem to have its origins in an unconscious infantile fear of being poisoned internally by 'matter'[1]) to some of the extremest of evangelical sects, and the immense attack on the rational intelligence that was (and is) Fascism, we find this impulse towards magical omnipotence at its most negative. Another modern example is the Marxist denial of inner reality as explored by psychoanalytical philosophy and their 'magical' attempt 'not to see' this aspect of human study. This is much like a child who magically extinguishes the existence of a visitor with whose presence she cannot deal by covering her eyes with her pinafore. Another obvious example is racial prejudice, as expressed in Apartheid, by which unconscious hostilities and fears of the 'bad' in ourselves and external reality are projected over all those with different coloured skins. These are then 'magically' divested of their existence by being divested of recognition of their rights – and the threat represented by their actual existence is 'denied' by acts of hostility and violence. The danger of Apartheid at its deepest is that it manifests a group disability in dealings with all reality (as in Nazi Germany) as much as in the local danger of conflict, and the terrible suffering and inhumanity caused.[2]

[1] See J. O. Wisdom, *The Unconscious Origins of Berkeley's Philosophy*, Hogarth, 1953.

[2] Ferenczi would describe 'ultra-idealistic solipsism' in philosophy as 'a relapse into egocentric infantilism', while 'the purely materialistic psycho-phobic standpoint' – i.e. Marxism, and the related attitudes of sociology and fabian socialism, represent 'regression to the exaggerations of the projection-phase'. Belief in the efficacy of making a good environment which will bring happiness is a false belief which belongs to an infantile attempt to escape realities both of human nature and of the imperfect outer world. Materialist socialist thought must therefore necessarily defend this projected hallucination by refusing to 'see' psychoanalytical truth, which is closer to expressing the poetic and tragic truth, that, despite 'progress' we shall always be imperfect creatures struggling with our imperfect environment – and that our greatest happiness and good are in the struggle.

We find now in Ferenczi's accounts a paragraph very relevant to our study of the growth of love:

> The first painful step towards recognition of the external world is certainly the knowledge that some of the 'good things' do not belong to the ego, and must be distinguished from it as the 'outer world'.

(That is, the mother, her nourishing body, her love and care, the 'concept of continuity' she is helping to establish.)

> Almost at the same time a human being has to learn that something unpleasant, that is, 'bad', can take place within him (in the ego itself, so to speak) which cannot be shaken off either by hallucination or in any other way.

(That is hunger, thirst, and also the anger, rage and frustration associated with these.)

> A further advance is made when he learns to endure absolute depriv-ation from without, i.e. when he recognizes that there are also things that must be relinquished for good and all; the process parallel to this is the recognition of repressed wishes while realization of them is at the same time renounced. Since, as we know now, a quota of Eros, i.e. of love, is necessary for this recognition, and since this addition is inconceivable without introjection, i.e. identification, we are forced to say that the recognition of the surrounding world is actually a partial realization of the Christian imperative, 'love your enemies'.
>
> p. 374

That is, to become capable of love we must needs come to love and embrace the bad in ourselves, and to come to terms with the bad in the world and in others. And to relinquish for ever certain desires to be omnipotent, to possess an idealized perfection, and to control what cannot be controlled.

Melanie Klein puts the process in slightly different terms. With her the inward phantasy life is of more importance, as between the inner reality of the child and his cultural environment.

> Introjection and projection . . . are part of the infant's phantasies, which in my view also operate from the beginning and help to mould his impression of his surroundings; and by introjection this changed picture of the external world influences what goes on in his

mind. Thus an inner world is built up which is partly a reflection of the external one. That is to say the double process of introjection and projection contributes to the interaction between external and internal factors. This interaction continues through every stage of life . . . even in the adult . . .

Our Adult Society and Its Roots in Infancy, p. 6

The ego develops round the 'good object', says Melanie Klein – that is the 'introjected' mother, and her influence helps establish a balance between introjection and projection. Also,

> . . . a strong identification with the good mother makes it easier for the child to identify also with a good father and later on with other friendly figures. As a result his inner world comes to contain predominantly good objects and feelings, and these good objects are felt to respond to the infant's love. All this contributes to a stable personality and makes it possible to extend sympathy and friendly feelings to other people. It is clear that a good relation of the parents to each other and to the child, and a happy home atmosphere, play a vital role in the success of this process.
>
> ibid., p. 7

Projection differs from introjection and the kind of identification associated with it, though projection involves a kind of identification too – in which we attribute to others some of our own qualities. (If we feel persecuted we will throw the mask of a persecutor over the other.) Projection can have good effects if it helps us to understand the feelings, needs and satisfactions of others, by 'putting ourselves in their shoes', or even 'losing ourselves in someone else'.[1] While 'excessive introjection endangers the strength of the ego . . .' 'if projection is predominantly hostile, real empathy and understanding of others is impaired'. But,

> if the interplay between introjection and projection is not dominated by hostility or over-dependence, and is well-balanced, the inner world is enriched and relations with the external world are improved.
>
> ibid., p. 7

[1] That this may be a sign of weakness and a danger is seen when one person's influence over another is used for criminal ends, or the satisfaction of hostile impulses, as when a prostitute said of a society pimp, 'he had control of my mind'.

'Object love,' says Ferenczi, 'takes place at the expense of narcissism', and his earlier quotation shows that advances – such as towards taking in good from the outer world, and coming to terms with the bad one seeks to project away from oneself – are inevitably mixed up with losses of benign innocence, as if 'loved portions of the ego are given up'. In giving up loved portions of the self and loved states of being, even though this might appear to be self-destructive (as with some animal organisms that lose part of themselves to survive crises) such 'adaptation . . . does in actual fact become the "cause of being" ' – that is, the beginning of a true reality sense.

It is this acceptance and 'love' of the imperfections of the world and of introjected others that Ferenczi links with the Christian injunction, 'love your enemies'. Again, this process is one which, though it has to be solved by every child as he grows to stability and sanity, yet goes on all our lives, in our search to come to terms with imperfect selves in an imperfect world.

Our reaction to inevitable forms of loss in the growth of consciousness has been explored by Melanie Klein and D. W. Winnicott to a much more complex and deeper degree, and we shall now need to cover some of Ferenczi's ground over again. We shall then find a significant difference – that whereas to Freud hate was innate and inevitably there to be reckoned with, later writers (Suttie, Klein and Winnicott) see hate as frustrated love – and this leads to a philosophical outcome that is far more hopeful.

There comes now a significant crisis related to the processes just described in the infant's development, to which Melanie Klein gave the somewhat confusing term 'the depressive position'. (Winnicott says he would prefer the name 'the *Stage of Concern*'.)

Winnicott describes the depressive position as *an achievement*. This stage occurs at weaning, and 'if all goes well' occurs sometime in the second half of the first year.

To reach the depressive position a baby must have become established as a whole person, and to be related to whole persons as a whole person.

Collected Papers, p. 264

(Some babies who have 'not become whole persons' at this stage 'just get on without it'.)

The term does not mean that the healthy infant has to 'pass through a stage of depression'. Winnicott characterizes it as having to do with the passage from being ruthless to 'having ruth' (that is, remorse or pity):

> At first the infant (from our point of view) is ruthless; there is no concern yet as to results of instinctual love.

This 'stage of concern' or 'depressive position' comes in an infant's life between the first stages of its awareness of a 'not-me', and the next stage of psychic growth, which is enacted round the triangle of mother, father and child, in what has come to be called the Oedipus situation.

It is a crucial stage in development, which is never reached by some. Schizoids, and all those in mental hospitals who have never reached 'a true self-life or self-expression', do not know it, and for them it is 'not the thing that matters' – as Winnicott says, 'it must remain for them like colour to the colour-blind'. He goes on:

> For the whole manic-depressive group that comprises the majority of so-called normal people the subject of the depressive position in normal development is one that cannot be left aside; it is and it remains *the problem of life* except in so far as it is reached.

Collected Papers, p. 277

Culturally this stage is important, since it introduces the question of the urge to make reparation. The infant may have felt loved and loving, and from this will be able to devote himself as an adult to causes and pursuits that are felt to be good and valuable. Now to this capacity to love is added the wish to make reparation that merges with our natural altruism.

Melanie Klein says:

> Constructive activities gain more impetus because the child unconsciously feels that in this way he is restoring loved people whom he has damaged . . . none of us is ever entirely free from guilt . . . it implies the never fully exhausted wish to make reparation and to create in whatever way we can.

All forms of social service benefit by this urge . . .

Our Adult Society, p. 12

In extreme cases, Mrs Klein says, feelings of guilt drive people to sacrifice themselves completely, or they become fanatics. But the motives of all who risk their lives for others are not necessarily rooted in guilt, but rather in 'the capacity for love, generosity, and an identification with the endangered fellow being'. Ian D. Suttie would probably attribute such acts much more to the natural capacity for good and for altruism which have made human beings what they are – 'love, not "selfish appetite" ', he says, 'is the mainspring of social life'. Suttie criticizes Freud for 'accepting hatred and violence as inevitable and even as instinctual'. As we shall see, D. W. Winnicott's account of the depressive position suggests that the origin of guilt is not so much in an instinctual hate and destructiveness as an excess of love.

We have seen how the baby is first totally narcissistic, then begins to form within the shell of his mother's care and love. She adapts to his needs, and her 'technique' of care, including her pattern of moods and behaviour, becomes the object of his love. (Later, as we have seen, the infant transfers these qualities to a 'transitional object' – a piece of cloth or a doll – and exercises his object love on this. This is both his first 'cultural' act, and the origin of much cultural activity.) We have also seen how he both takes aspects of the mother into himself and projects aspects of himself over her and others. He knows something of the mother both as a 'good' satisfying aspect of his environment, and as a 'bad' frustrating one, who 'becomes the object of assault during phases of instinctual tension'.

There comes a stage, inevitably, when, as it were, the baby's mind begins to put two and two together. As he becomes aware to some degree of the actual existence of a mother 'out there' who is a separate being, so he becomes aware that there has been a connection (as we have seen) between his phantasy wishes and her actuality – indeed, the mother herself has adapted to 'filling this in'. by offering herself at the right moment. But – to put things in our terms – how can the baby accept that the mother who is good and 'quiet' is the same as the mother who is 'bad', and the subject of assault? If she were, he concludes, may she not even be destroyed by my phantasies? These, as the baby is beginning to be aware, have some bearing on her actuality, since his phantasy has seemed to him to actually 'create' the breast and virtually to 'make' the mother.

In this perplexity perhaps we may trace the origins of the fear of feeling, of phantasy, and of the imaginative life itself, as manifest in many forms of anti-creativity, from Philistinism to aestheticism? As all must have sometime feared possible damage to the loved and creating environment by assault in phantasy, those who have never resolved this infant problem must inevitably have deep fears associated with all phantasy life, and its effects on the world of reality. To avoid this fear they must either deny or suppress imagination and fancy, or assert that these things must be cultivated separately, each in its own right – creative art for aesthetic reasons, and life as a separate autonomous reality from which art is kept away (and its irrelevance rationalized as being 'fancy' or 'mere enjoyment' or 'a frill'). Indeed, perhaps the very Philistinism of our era may have its origins in failures of 'the stage of concern'.

But to return to Winnicott on the nature of this stage:

> The human infant cannot accept the fact that this mother who is so valued in the quiet phases is the person who has been and will be ruthlessly attacked in the excited phases.
>
> The infant, being a whole person, is able to identify with the mother, but there is no clear distinction yet between what is intended and what really happens. Functions and their imaginative elaborations are not yet clearly distinguished as fact and fantasy. It is astonishing what the baby has to accomplish at just this time.

'The Depressive Position in Normal Emotional Development', in *Collected Papers*, pp. 266–7

One of the 'astonishing' things is not only the perception of the 'two' mothers, but

> the beginning of the recognition of the existence of ideas, phantasy, imaginative elaboration of function, the acceptance of ideas and phantasy related to fact but not to be confused with fact.

ibid., p. 276

This immense cultural development cannot take place without a good-enough environment, and here the continuance and survival of the mother (despite phantasy attacks on her) is crucial. From the 'nameless acts of kindness and of love' the infant 'collects' 'memory material'. Wordsworth would be wrong in supposing these to be 'unremembered': they *are* remembered, and they establish a concept by which we solve 'the problem of life'.

The baby has moments of instinctual tension, in which it hallucinates a ferocious cannibalistic attack, seeking to devour the mother's breast. Eventually it comes to see that the mother on whom it depends is also the object of 'instinctual (biologically driven) love'. The *concern* comes from his fear that the one will destroy the other – that he will destroy her, and with her, himself. With this concern may go a moment of existential 'flop' in which it almost seems something of the kind has happened: a feed often fails to absorb the energy, with its tension mounting to a climax, which was inherent in the gathering aggression. Physical satisfaction will rob the infant of zest for life for a time, and *the infant does not know it will return*. He may fear that neither he nor the mother (who has been involved in the full flood of instinctual tension) will revive. He fears annihilation. Only, as time goes on, and the 'quiet' mother remains 'there', can he develop a confidence that these conflicts will be survived.

> This is repeated day after day, and adds up eventually to the baby's dawning recognition of the difference between what is called fact and phantasy, or outer and inner reality.
>
> Winnicott, ibid., p. 268

I have mentioned above the bearing of this kind of experience in the infant, on adult sexual experience. It perhaps accounts for distress when an urge of desire fails to be satisfied by sexual intercourse, or when even that satisfaction is feared which may unconsciously seem to have the power of destroying a zest for life. If this zest goes, we may unconsciously fear it may never return. This probably accounts too for the common experience of postcoital depression, outward causes for which are untraceable, and the sense – often recorded in poetry and fiction – in which the satisfaction of desire seems to bring one closer to a sense of mortality, death and oblivion. The melancholy of 'not knowing the zest will return' is overcome by that mutuality in love which establishes continuity, as by the 'quiet' mother, and by a closer approach to reality. As we shall see, this problem is one of Lawrence's deepest (pp. 217ff. below).

As the infant develops more complex ideas, more complicated forms of distress now trouble it.

The cannibalistic attack on the mother's breast, a breast (we may remember) for some time thought by the infant to be part of itself, makes it feel that the consequence of its assault may be an 'emptiness' in the mother – Winnicott calls it 'a hole', where 'once was a body of richness'. It also feels, since it was taking in good from this source, that now in its own inside it contains both good and 'self-supportive' things, and, in conflict with these, bad and persecutory things – which return to attack it, as it were, in consequence of its attacks on the mother. The 'hole' is also felt to be within itself. This complex situation of conflicting impulses and fears the infant has to 'work through' while the mother 'holds the situation': in the mother's care he can 'surrender to what is going on inside' and wait for the outcome. The 'hole' is repaired within itself, by constructive activity of the growing awareness:

> In health this personal inner world becomes the infinitely rich core of the self.
> *ibid.*, p. 269

In this, as we have seen, there are many processes involved, of being able to accept the good and bad in oneself, and in the mother, and loving both bad and good. Besides learning to love, the baby is also learning to give – for him a matter of gestures through its bowel-movements, as well as its gestures in terms of clutching, smiling and moving its body:

> Towards the end of this day in the life of any healthy infant as a result of inner work done, the infant has good and bad to offer. The mother takes the good and bad, and she is supposed to know what is offered as good and what is offered as bad. Here is the first giving, and without this giving there is no true receiving.
> *ibid.*, p. 269

This process is obviously crucial to the beginnings of identity and personal relationship. And Winnicott's account (drawing, too, a good deal from the work of Anna Freud and W. R. D. Fairbairn) is full of the experience of re-enacting these processes in patients who failed to accomplish them in life as infants, and need to do so in regression in the course of psychoanalysis.

As an outcome of this situation by sorting out the good and bad within, the child becomes able to tolerate its apprehension of that 'hole', that 'emptiness' in the mother, which is a 'consequence of instinctual love' and to repair this wound in itself.[1]

In this originates our 'true guilt': so the 'hole' might be said to be the bite taken from the apple of the knowledge of good and evil, since it is the basis of our subsequent reparative quest for love and the good and the consequence of our first knowledge of object-relationships.

> This is the only true guilt, since implanted guilt is false to the self. Guilt starts through the bringing together of the two mothers, and of quiet and excited love, and of love and hate, and this feeling gradually grows to be a healthy and normal source of activity in relationships. Here is one source of potency and of social contribution, and of artistic performance – (but not of art itelf which has its roots at a deeper level).
>
> ibid., p. 270

Winnicott's great value as a psychoanalytical philosopher is that he portrays this development as positive and triumphant, and he attributes great importance to Melanie Klein's account of the depressive position (or 'stage of concern'), as a contribution to child care and education.

> *The healthy child has a personal sense of guilt,* and need not be taught to be guilty or concerned.

– at least, those who have attained the depressive position (others, who haven't, have to be taught). But this true guilt leads to the positive and creative urge, to seek the good, and to make repara-

---

[1] I think it is possible that, in the poetic symbolism of the Christian myth, the wounds of Christ represent those in the mother and the self believed to be caused by us at the "stage of concern", and that atonement and resurrection are symbolic of our consequent reparative effort.

tion, naturally.[1] As the mediaeval carol puts it, 'Blessèd be the time that apple taken was!'

The child learns to tolerate 'concern', because it comes to see that it is possible to 'restore' the mother's damaged body by reparation. As it does so, its 'instincts become freer and greater risks are taken'. There is yet more guilt, but also 'an intensification of instinctual experience with its imaginative exploration'. As Winnicott says, this process can go on outside early infancy and outside the analytical situation. (A good deal of this kind of development in 'backward' and unstable children is described by the present author in *English for the Rejected*.)

As the memories of experiences felt to be good, and the 'holding' mother, are taken into the self, so the child finds increasingly that the mother becomes less and less necessary. 'The individual acquires an internal environment' – that is, he acquires his first culture.

Of course, many things can go wrong in such a complex stage of development. For instance, a loss of the situation-holding mother, or her inadequacy in child care, can lead to the loss of the capacity for the true sense of guilt. Without guilt and the need for 'giving' and reparation, the child can continue with sensual gratifications, but may even lose the capacity for affectionate feelings. He will not learn to love and give. This disaster one may link with the condition Suttie diagnoses as 'the taboo on tenderness' as a personal and cultural manifestation:

'. . . . It is in this field of feeling or meaning-interplay as well as that of direct personal cordial appreciation that the taboo on tenderness manifests itself. It is not a definite lack of feeling (as in idiocy) not a withdrawal (as in *Dementia Praecox*) as much as an *inhibition* which dulls the social responsiveness of the individual and may come to

---

[1] The 'falsity' of 'implanted guilt' may be studied, e.g., in Methodism and its place in English history. It possibly manifests a 'false solution' to the problem of successfully completing 'the stage of concern'. See E. P. Thompson, op cit., esp. Chapter XI. Thompson is wrong, of course, to attribute the origins of such excessive guilt to 'masturbation'! The more likely explanation of the morbidity and submissive element in Methodism is that good and loving mothering was undermined by that 'immiseration' brought about by the Industrial Revolution which Thompson himself so poignantly reveals.

be *known* and deplored by him. He cannot tolerate 'warm' or demonstrative relationship; he gives all his friends the 'frozen mitt'; he takes refuge in formal relationships, abstract interests, and sensuality, and usually he does not like 'good' music or 'good' literature – yet he knows, dimly or clearly, his lack. He is an uncomfortable friend or relative and an unhappy man . . .'

The Origins of Love and Hate

There are no doubt other explanations of the complex developments of human consciousness, guilt, and 'reparative drives' at this period of life, and the reader will no doubt prefer to turn to the sources of the theories I discuss. But the theories of Melanie Klein and D. W. Winnicott seem to me to offer much to our understanding of art. The cultural relevance of the 'stage of concern' is that it is, like earlier crises of the growth of consciousness, a constructive stage in which love fosters the creative outcome. In normal development the depressive position is (Winnicott stresses) 'an achievement' – a constructive stage in the growth of consciousness. It is a further stage of triumph over disturbing apprehensions (of loss and pain) consequent upon a more adequate coming-to-terms with the reality of the outside world and the reality of the self. It marks an advance in personal identity, and of the ability to develop a sense of hopefulness, of good, and of the 'continuity of life' out of a series of contests with experience, in which the mother is a crucial presence – 'holding the ring' as it were, and 'continuing to exist'. (Of course as the nature of my account indicates, these stages overlap in their complexity, and nothing is as straightforward as it might appear in anyone's summary of life-processes, which happen only in each individual, and differently in each one.) In these elements of this postulated stage in the growth of consciousness we may see, once more, features which inevitably become expressed in child and adult culture – not least the sense of guilt (sin) for which reparation (atonement) must be made. That atonement is good, and that we find a relief from it, related to constructive effort, is a basis even for works of art that are painful – and this may even account at the unconscious level for the elation that follows the experience of a painful work such as *Oedipus Rex* or *King Lear*. Here we may have the inward explanation of Aristotle's *katharsis*: a purging of guilt by the imaginative indulgence in the woe and destruction we once unconsciously wished to wreak on our dearest one. But the art experience harms no one, actually: and this alone reassures us. We may afterwards feel that the pain of the re-experienced terror and woe such as we experienced in our moments of hate and ruthlessness has been sufficient reparation. Certainly, if this is accompanied by such an expression of totally accepting love, and total acceptance of the imperfect self, as at the end of *King Lear* ('And so I am, I am'), then we may re-experience a triumphant feeling of having survived 'the worst that sorrow ever bore', with all its threats of dissociation. We fear annihilation less, and have a greater hold on life. In Shakespeare's tragedies this sense of survival is reinforced by the emphasis on continuity: on secure order (the continuing monarch – cf. 'whom we invite to see us crown'd at Scone'), on the value of felt experience, and on generation.

> The weight of this sad time we must obey;
> Speak what we feel, not what we ought to say,
> The oldest hath borne most: we that are young
> Shall never see so much, nor live so long.
>
> *King Lear* (end)

Certainly the expression of atonement takes on a particularly disturbing force and penetration in poetry – yielding in some writers their richest texture, as in T. S. Eliot:

> '. . . the rending pain of re-enactment
> Of all that you have done, and been; the shame
> Of motives late revealed, and the awareness
> Of things ill done and done to others' harm
> Which once you took for exercise of virtue.
> Then fools' approval stings, and honour stains.
> From wrong to wrong the exasperated spirit
>
> Proceeds, unless restored by that refining fire
> Where you must move in measure, like a dancer.'
>
> T. S. Eliot, *Little Gidding, Four Quartets*, p. 39

Beneath this account of spiritual self-awareness one may detect a deep current of feelings which have their origin in infant experiences of guilt and reparation. The dance-like pattern of continuity, the refiner's fire in which the spirit proceeds – these refer to spiritual chastening and letting 'the fire of God' blow through one.[1] But yet, in the theme of acceptance, 'proceeding' in continuity, and dance-like merging with the flickering flame of the Pentecostal message – these have their psychic origins in the infant's apprehension of the mother's continuity. Mary, the mother, and Pentecostal fire as an assurance of touch with heaven and continuity into a spiritual world are recurrent themes in Eliot's poetry:

> And all shall be well and
> All manner of things shall be well
> When the tongues of flame are in-folded
> Into the crowned knot of fire
> And the fire and the rose are one.
>   *Little Gidding* (end)

Since Eliot's is a quest for the acceptance of spiritual love and humility ('A condition of complete simplicity/Costing not less than everything'), it is also a quest for coming-to-terms with reality of oneself and the world. And this progress has its poetic origins in the universal need to find goodness and hope ('All shall be well') in a sense of the mother's continuing existence – and her survival. We may read the fire and the rose, even, as hate and love – both are obviously deeply sexual images, of the aggressive and phallic flame, and the quiet infolded vaginal and uterine rose (Cf. Blake's *Sick Rose*). Until these are reconciled, and come-to-terms with as having been harmlessly 'infolded' and made into the 'crowned knot' ('crowned' with its deep sense of the triumphant birth, and head-first emergence and progress of the growing personality) – wholeness cannot be attained. Though Eliot is seeking, in one sense, in his *Four Quartets* a spiritual rebirth, he inevitably re-enacts some of the processes of infancy in terms of the birth and growth of consciousness. That he does so gives us an intensity of deep experience which is a guarantee of the genuine-

[1] Mr Eliot possibly had in mind the confident but disturbing harmonic progress in Handel's *Messiah,* in the aria 'He is like a refiner's fire' where the music enacts the transformations in the metal under refinement.

ness of his poetry, which draws on the remembered early experience of guilt, reparation, pain, progress, triumph and the quest for love, goodness and 'wholeness' ('All shall be well and/ All manner of things shall be well').

A similar deep sense of the need for reparation to make good, and find love, pervades *The Winter's Tale*:

> Therefore betake thee
> To nothing but despair. A thousand knees,
> Ten thousand years together, naked, fasting,
> Upon a barren mountain, and still winter
> In storm perpetual, could not move the Gods
> To look that way thou wert . . .

Leontes resolves

> So long as Nature
> Will bear up with this exercise, so long
> I daily vow to use it . . .
>
> (III, ii, end)

The effect is that Hermione, the 'lost mother', is restored. There can be no substitute: all reparative effort has its origins in the original concern to make good again the 'lost' mother:

> There is none worthy
> (Respecting her that's gone) . . .

In the restoration Shakespeare even hints at those areas of infant experience in which magic is exercised to no avail, and cannibalistic impulses which threaten the mother's continued existence:

> If this be magic, let it be an Art
> Lawful as eating . . .

But Hermione *is* restored, as if by reparation, in triumph over Time, by repeated episodes of creative desire ('have (in vain) said many/A prayer upon her grave'):

> Perform'd in this wide gap of Time, since first
> We were dissever'd . . .
>
> (V, iii, end)

The marvellously original form of *The Winter's Tale* was devised by Shakespeare to express poetically deep aspects of our means of triumphing over aspects of experience which we first encounter in infancy, and must continue to grapple with. In this he had penetrated into that territory of unconscious life only now becoming explicitly explored.

The concept of the 'stage of concern' has an educational relevance, too. In teaching and the culture of the child we find the reparative impulse a great mainspring. The child needs someone who is not only loved, but who will accept potency, as expressed in constructive play. They must have the loved person near, apparently involved – being if possible ready to receive, rather than to give. Many teachers arrive at this situation by intuition: Winnicott's paragraph on it (op. cit. p. 271) helps us to see why sympathy and 'love' are so important in teaching, as I suggested in *English for the Rejected*, before I found confirmation in his work.

> For a long while the small child needs someone who is not only loved but who will accept potency . . . in terms of reparative and restitutive giving. . . . This giving is expressed in play, but constructive play at first must have the loved person near, apparently involved if not actually appreciative of the true constructive attainment in the play. It is a sure sign of a lack of understanding of small children . . . when an adult thinks to help by giving, failing to see the primary importance of being there to receive . . .
>
> *Collected Papers*, p. 271

This is not only true of infants and juniors, but especially of older less able children, who 'need the mother' longer, a presence to whom they may make reparation for guilt and so build an 'inner core'.

If the child cannot sort out the inner problems presented at this time, he will 'wet blanket' the inner world and function at a low level of vitality. This mood is depression but it is one which specifically belongs to the 'stage of concern'. Its counterpart is a state called 'manic defence' – a refuge from the problems of the depressive position, in which the necessary development is held off by the negation of everything serious. Winnicott used to call it 'common anxious restlessness' before he encountered Kleinian terms:

> Death becomes exaggerated liveliness; silence becomes noise, there is neither grief nor concern, neither constructive work nor restful pleasure.
>
> op. cit., p. 272

There are many elements of something akin to 'manic defence' in present-day culture and it would be interesting to compare existential accounts of patients' feelings and attitudes at this stage with manic passages in modern novels and poetry. A perhaps related point that Winnicott makes is that in order for a patient in psychoanalysis to work through the stage of concern, he must go through new profound experiences: that is, simply knowing about the stages of this development, or knowing that the problem is in him, and also expressed in culture and mythology, is not enough. There have to be changes which are deeply felt at the intuitive level – and we return to Lawrence's preoccupation with the experience of the 'whole man', and the need for 'the function of art' to be 'moral'. An important element of all growth towards more adequate dealings with internal and external reality is first of all to keep the feelings open, flowing and deep so that the creative and constructive processes can progress, as they need to in all of us. Art and imaginative culture both foster this flow, and provide material for reparative activities, to help us 'work through' the difficulties with which life presents us. Because of 'true guilt' these reparative activities are always an attempt to find 'the good' and to overcome the bad, faults and imperfections.

But, of course, there is a limit to which the individual can help himself, and to what education or culture can do for him. This limit is marked by the existence of mental ill-health, and by the practice of psychotherapy that strives to deal with it.

All the processes I have been describing go on, or are developing, all through life, through imagination and feeling, and their cultural manifestations, as a means to establish contact with reality. To many people, many educators, and even most surprisingly too, many literary people, the 'practical' things of the world come first, and science and externals are pre-eminent. They fail to realize that our inward life is the gateway to perception, even the basis of the growth of effective consciousness, and that it is continually throughout life the area of being in which our 'practical' and ratiocinative functions have their origins. If the affective, intuitive processes of dealing with reality fail to grow and develop, or break down, or collapse, *then we are nothing*, and our 'practical' powers cease to function. Certainly it takes only a little by way of affective dissociation for the more conscious, ratiocinative and executive functions to lose their efficiency. In preserving our practical effectiveness phantasy, and the organized disciplines of imagination, are pre-eminent.

I will close this section with a long quotation from an earlier essay by Winnicott that seems to me to put this matter, from the point of view of his discipline, marvellously:

> It may be asked, what do ordinary people do about this matter of contact with reality? Of course as development proceeds a great deal happens that seems to get round the difficulty, for enrichment by incorporation of objects is a psychical as well as a physical phenomenon, and the same can be said of being incorporated, including the eventual contribution to the world's fertility which is the privilege of even the least of us. And especially the sexual life offers a way round, with the conception of infants, a true physical mingling of two individuals. Nevertheless, while we have life, each one of us feels the matter of crude reality-contact to be a vital one, and we deal with it according to the way in which we have had reality introduced to us at the beginning. In some of us the ability to use the objectively verifiable, to objectify the subjective, is so easy that the fundamental problem of illusion tends to get lost. Unless they are ill or tired people do not know that there is a problem of relationship with reality, or a universal liability to hallucination, and they feel that mad people must be made of different stuff from themselves. Some of us on the other hand, are aware of a tendency in ourselves towards the subjective, which we feel to be more significant than the world's affairs, and for such the sane may seem rather dull folk, and the common round seems mundane.

One of the ways out is the dreaming of dreams, and the remembering of them. In sleep we dream all the time and when we wake we need to carry something forward from the dream world into real life, just as we recognize everyday affairs turning up and weaving themselves into the dreams.

Apart from this, is it not largely through artistic creation and artistic experience that we maintain the necessary bridges between subjective and the objective? It is for this reason, I suggest, that we value tremendously the long struggle of the creator in any art form. For us all, as for himself, the artist is repeatedly winning brilliant battles in a war to which, however, there is no final outcome. A final outcome would be finding what is not true, namely, that what the world offers is identical with what the individual creates.

'Paediatrics and Psychiatry' (1948), *Collected Papers*, pp. 171–2

My incomplete notes on the vast body of psychoanalytical philosophy (of which I have really only taken fragments) are but gestures in the direction of a new kind of art criticism, to suggest a way of looking at works of the creative imagination in terms of that 'bridge-building'. When we approach a piece of writing we need to ask questions like the following. Does this work help us extend our understanding of the outer world, and our inner reality? Does it deepen our insight? These are no simple questions – lying as they do between the world of quotidian morality, and the inner creative forces. Obviously Tolstoy deepens our insight in *War and Peace* and *Anna Karenina* in both worlds: but what are we to say of *Resurrection*, or of his own later belief that continence should be practised even at the expense of the extinction of the human race – which can surely only be seen as psychopathic? But even to say this is of course to postulate a 'good' and a 'norm' – and a future for the human race in which we can believe.

Certainly we may recognize a plain distinction between bridge-building, and demolition or undermining – and here our reference to psychoanalytical philosophy of the growth of consciousness does help, I am sure. As I try to say below in discussing Lawrence, we cannot live without continuously making effort to come to terms with reality, to accept the pain and loss involved, in relinquishing our yearnings for impossible perfection. The baby has to do this, to develop consciousness and live: and to gain our greatest satisfactions we need to go on making this quest, which is intimately bound up with the quest for love. This 'spiritual quest' is abrogated by much of our culture nowadays – and this seems to me to be a form of suicide. Self-destructive people are seeking to involve us in their fear or inanition – and seeking to persuade us that bridge-building is worthless, or impossible. They do this for hate, out of fear, and for the money and success that vindicates the hate and holds away the fear, in an acquisitive and irresponsible ethos, which tends to degrade human nature. As Guntrip suggests, our culture is becoming dangerously schizoid in consequence.

In answer to such destructiveness I hope some connections between imagination, thought, culture and the psyche will be suggested by my stumbling account of the above theories as to how our first consciousness is formed, and my discussions of the works follow, to suggest how they make a positive contribution to our quest for love and an effective reality sense.

TWO

Chaucer's Debate on Marriage

Chaucer was a poet whose responsibility to his art and his language – to England and its civilization – is a great historical fact. One must surely believe that in terms of quality of living such a lifetime's work has been a great influence for good – making possible actual happier lives, of more effective and creative living in many, of greater human accomplishment at large in terms of gentler and more courteous relationships, and in raising aspirations and hopes – as well, of course, as generating a great deal of sheer delight in comedy and the richness of all the varied manifestations of life and human behaviour.

The direct and present value of the metaphorical vitality in Chaucer and its bearing on our lives may perhaps be best demonstrated by examining the quality and meaning of what must surely be the greatest section of the *Canterbury Tales* – those tales dealing with marriage, which make up a debate on human love and its potentialities in the social order. These are *The Clerk's Tale*, *The Franklin's Tale*, *The Merchant's Tale*, *The Wyf of Bath's Prologue* and *Tale*. Here I shall, in fact, only examine in detail *The Merchant's Tale* and *The Franklin's Tale*, with some reference to the others.

In these two tales we have the best of Chaucer's art, and something so civilized and fine that we have yet to prove ourselves capable of possessing the values and attitudes expressed in them. Chaucer will never be 'superannuated': and what he strives for in *The Franklin's Tale* is what many a psychoanalyst is striving to communicate, also in words, if in a different way, to his patient – apprehensions of sexual reality and of love, the nature of the search for a sense of 'good' in ourselves and others, for reality, and for values by which we may try to live more adequately, as of mutual regard between the sexes. How, as a central social issue, can man and woman live their lives together so that stability and enrichment may be bestowed upon future generations? Here Chaucer shares his preoccupations with D. H. Lawrence – and his concern is not, as in so much literature until modern times, with courtship or premarital love, or with the (largely adulterous) love of Courtly Romance, but with love in marriage. This Debate is well on the far side of 'happily ever after' – and so comes very much into its value for our society in which it has become much more possible for all to enjoy fulfilment in marriage.

In *The Merchant's Tale* we have a most subtle comedy, the comedy being bound up with the metaphorical modes – the complex theme is enacted in the figures of the language. By which I mean that the *Tale* 'does what it says', stirs us by a rich awareness felt deep within. In that *Tale* texture of language, with all the force of imagery, alliteration, sound, movement, tone of voice, are brought to play to give us possession of the enacted drama. As we possess this we take in the moral attitude, the poem's criticism of life. These qualities of its language have their roots in compassion for the young bride May, and for her revolting, old, ugly – but also pitiful – husband, January.

So, too, compassion pervades *The Franklin's Tale*: but here the imagery is simpler, and the texture so simple and formal as to be often misread by the modern reader – misunderstood, or even seen to be 'not very striking'. If we feel this it is surely because our powers to respond to language are at fault, for the delicacy and benignity of *The Franklin's Tale* is perhaps only paralleled in English literature by *The Winter's Tale*. And, in the same way as in that play, a different mode is used to convey fresh meaning.

The debate on marriage in Chaucer begins with the consideration of the reality of human sex. What are people really like? To ask such a question about individual make-up is part of Chaucer's modernity, of course, and the pursuit of this theme leads Shakespeare later to make his most profound exploration of the nature of man, culminating in *King Lear*. But to ask about the nature of Man brings Chaucer already to a consideration of prime concern in Renaissance thought, that of appetite. Appetite is a matter of satisfying this flesh in time – and here Chaucer's work enters on a profound poetic exploration of what meaning mortal life, mutable and imperfect as it is, may have in Time, such as Shakespeare was later to make. The preoccupations with appetite and the nature of human nature have their roots in mediaeval theology on the one hand, and on the other in the dominating Tudor and Elizabethan interests in self-fulfilment, as expressed in the hungry wide-ranging exploration of experience and the world made at that period. Although Hamlet's consideration of 'what a piece of work is Man' belongs to the Renaissance and its newer humanist perspectives, yet his pessimistic awareness and his habits of contemplating it – his moral background – are essentially mediaeval.[1] The pressure to study these aspects of human life was coming too, from social changes, and economic developments, which were disturbing traditional patterns and turning minds away from the contemplation of God in submission, towards an assertive humanistic preoccupation with man's potentialities in the world. The seeds of this increased awareness of man's glory, and his tragic state, are to be found in Chaucer's England. Judged against eternity, the ethos of mediaeval religion outwardly proclaimed

> all nys but a fayre,
> This world that passeth soone as floures fayre

and in the attitude to life of mediaeval theological teaching this was the dominating concept: the world is a 'thoroughfare of wo'. But at the same time, of course, as Chaucer's characters in his *Prologue* reveal, there was in mediaeval life an energetically vital hold on this world, and on its temporal worldlinesses and satisfactions. This vitality dwelt on love (both the prioress and the friar wear love-symbols, one a brooch saying *amor vincit omnia* and the other a love-knot pin), on good clothes and household stuff, on food and drink, and on the pleasures of communal life. As Chaucer feels bound to explore human powers to enjoy the richness of the body's life – as he comes closer to the realities of

[1] See L. A. Cormican, 'The Mediaeval Idiom in Shakespeare'. *Scrutiny*, Vol. XVII, Nos. 3 and 4.

human sexual vitality in the *Wyf of Bath*, for example – he is forced to share the preoccupations of the Renaissance with what of man's glory can outlast and transcend the 'crudded puff-paste'. Inevitably, since appetite belongs to the body in time, so an enriched vitality brings us closer to an awareness of man's tragic predicament: despite man's glory and joy, in this world, he is absolutely subject to Time and Death, whatever comes after. Chaucer is already deeply aware of the contrast between the beauty and energy of man's life, and his mortal insignificance in the immediately apparent scheme of things, among the 'congregation of pestilential vapours'. To apprehend such a contrast was a penalty of the easier and richer life for the cultured well-to-do, living mingled with poverty, disease and death. Later the freer love-experience in Renaissance Europe was to bring venereal disease: the rich life of urban and courtly living in mediaeval times already brought other ills, from gout to apoplexy. Civilized living went on in the presence of much squalor and incurable disease and fearful epidemics. Such contrasts emphasized the frailty and mortality of human life. Together with the gravity of mediaeval morality and the all-pervading religious reality, this pessimistic, tragic apprehension is at the centre of Chaucer's poetic contemplation of the nature of man and life, and it stands in a continuous English tradition leading to Shakespeare. At the centre of this contemplation is the problem of human reality. Take this for instance from the *Pardoner's Tale*, the typical mediaeval sermon 'example' on the text, *Radix malorum est Cupiditas. Ad Thimotheum*, 6, given in his Prologue and restated in the Tale:

> O wombe! O bely! O stynkyng cod,
> Fulfilled of dong and of corrupcioun!
> At either ende of thee foul is the soun.
> How greet labour and cost is thee to fynde!
> Thise cookes, how they stampe, and streyne, and grynde,
> And turnen substaunce into accident,
> To fulfille all thy likerous talent!
> Out of the hard bones knokke they
> The mary; for they caste noght away
> That may go thurgh the golet softe and swoote.

Of spicerie of leef, and bark, and roote
Shal been his sauce ymaked by delit,
To make hym yet a newer appetit. l. 534ff

Here the verse conveys in its sound and movement a conflict between the theological condemnation of Gluttony – one of the seven deadly sins – and the natural, and *necessary* vitality of the body. The vitality is there in the cooks, the long line describing whom, 'they stampe, and streyne, and grynde', enacts a vigour which, like pictures of cooks in a Bruegel painting, gives an image of a full vitality in living. Yet they are thrifty ('they caste nought away') and civilized – the sounds of 'spicerie of leef' and other such phrases enact a kind of elegant epicurism in the words, almost like the Prioresse's French, 'entuned in the nose full semely' so refined is it. Yet at the same time all this civilized vital effort goes merely to pack a tube which emits foul noise at both ends, and is filled with ordure and filthy stuff: this is, essentially, the bodily reality. The 'talent' of the belly – 'talent' because it has the value of prolonging and sustaining life – is lecherous, and, like lechery, it needs continual effort to satisfy it. The 'spiceries' civilize this gross thing (for a moment we almost hear Lear asking for water to purify his hand which 'smells of mortality'). The cooks even convert – the wit is in that these are philosophical terms – 'sub-stance' (meat and vegetables) into 'accident' – abstract properties gracious qualities. These belong to good taste, 'the culinary art', civilized living, good, religious living (enjoying the provision God has made for man). Yet later in the same lines, we experience the food actually going down and this is all it is:

... That may go thurgh the golet softe and swoote.

Here the sounds enact the swallowing: we gulp. And in gulping we swallow the reality of feeding which has been laid before us. We have swallowed (almost literally) in these lines a complex attitude – a complex metaphorical exploration of the nature of human appetite. What contributes to the poetic process is the sound and texture of the grosser activities, of the energy of the life-sustaining cooks:

Out of the harde bones knokke they
The mary . . .

The contrast of the sound of this with the 'polite' sounds of civilized eating, underlies the philosophical examination of the process, the contrast between the kitchen work and the potentialities for refined living, where the gross is so refined that it becomes 'accident', a palate-established *appearance* which differs utterly from the reality of the 'stinking cod', just as food 'becomes' civilized, thinking beings. Such acceptance of physical reality, which is yet transcended by human values, and modes of civilization, could never it seems be attained by one such as Swift. He, because he could not accept this fulness of life, a mixture of the gross and the fine, the mutable and the durable, comes in the end to deny – and really, attack – all living reality. (See F. R. Leavis on 'The Irony of Swift' in *The Common Pursuit*.)

In his Debate on Marriage Chaucer takes us through a process of exploring human sexual reality, to find the reality of love. The motivation of the process is to arrive at a better understanding of human beings – pitying them for the reality of the conditions of their lives – and then to offer, positively, transcending values for living which are found in themselves more real than the reality of the bodily beastliness and grossness of man. *King Lear* and Shakespeare's tragedies, of course, take us through a similar, deeper and more complex process, towards the delineation of man's capacities for grace, towards the celebration of ideals and values, as at the end of *Lear*, triumphing over man's physical imperfection and animality. We may here recall the violence of Hamlet's 'Paddling in your neck with his damned fingers' and other violent recoilings from sexual reality in *Hamlet*. In *Timon* it is worse – Shakespeare cannot control his own disturbances, as Timon cries, 'Pash the nose flat . . . she whom the spitalhouse and ulcerous sores . . .' In the later plays a new belief in human good, in love, and continuity – as with young lovers – overcomes the earlier ambiguity of attitude, as expressed in the wonderful phrase in the *Sonnet* 'lilies that fester'. This struggle to embrace sexual reality, and with this the ambivalence and conflict in all reality, was a continual agonized quest for Shakespeare. This struggle is a universal one, whose origins are in our original inner conflict over 'good' and 'bad', closely related, as we have seen, to intense feelings of appetite, with deep sexual connotations and problems of love.

Chaucer's exploration of the reality of love reaches one crux with the *Wyf of Bath*. Her Prologue may be said to be one kind of sex 'education'. She works from 'experience' – from the reality of sex as it is lived. She challenges Holy Writ, often misquoting of course, but asks the crucial question:

> For hadde God comanded maydenhede,
> Thanne hadde he dampned weddying with the dede.
> And certes, if ther were no seed ysowe,
> Virginitee, thanne wherof sholde it growe?
> *Wyf's Prologe*, l. 69

If celibate living were superior to the married state, and this were universally accepted, where would the next generation come from? Whence, then, would there come the beatitudinous condition of virginity itself? The moral reality, in fact, cannot be in 'virginitee' and 'parfit chastitee'; the 'maidenhead' ideal is, really, deathly. Even a virtue such as virginity is born from seed sown by the loss of virginity. What did God give us sexual organs for, if not for use?

> Trusteth right wel, they were nat maad for noght.
> Glose whoso wole, and seye bothe up and doun,
> That they were maked for purgacioun
> Of uryne, and oure bothe thynges smale
> Were eek to know a femele from a male,
> And for noon oother cause, – sey ye no?
> The experience woot wel it is noght so . . .
> In wyfhod I wol use myn instrument
> As freely as my Makere hath it sent . . .
> *Wyf's Prologe*, l. 118ff, 149ff

To accept so much – the actuality of human sex – freely, is a goal for many a psychoanalytical patient seeking touch with 'reality': Chaucer, through the Wyf of Bath, gives us this acceptance, in comedy, but with the humane purpose of accepting one reality before going on to explore a greater which transcends it, and proves yet more real. Her gross reality brings with it a touch of that poignancy of the human situation, which attains its most morbid expression later in seventeenth-century melancholy. This vitality that seems so marvellous a reality, in the enjoyment of our proper sexual and other powers, is but totally subject to Time, decline, and Death. What endures? Thus, the first necessary recognition of reality brings also a painful awareness of mortality, its frailty and its end. The Wyf of Bath confesses herself not one of 'the best', of those that 'wolde live parfitly'. She is not bread of 'pured whete-seed':

> Let us wyves hoten barly-breed.

The coarse homeliness of the image leads to her later statement, that there is nothing left for her but 'the bran'. Acceptance of living at her level, the level of the reality of appetite, transcended by nothing 'beyond', may be good and vital, but it is inevitably tragic, doomed to what Mr Eliot attributes to the 'humanist' end – 'the cold friction of expiring sense'. Here, with great compassion, the verse enacts the physical feelings of remembered joy, and at the same time the bitterness of declining age, tasting the 'venom' of being 'birafte' of very 'pith' and sap:

> But, Lord Crist! whan that it remembreth me
> Upon my yowthe, and on my jolitee,
> It tikleth me aboute myn herte roote.
> Unto this day it dooth myn herte boote
> That I have had my world as in my tyme.
> But age, allas! that al wole envenyme,
> Hath me biraft my beautee and my pith.
> Lat go, farewel! the devel go therwith!
> The flour is goon, ther is namoore to telle;
> The bren, as I best kan, now most I selle;
> But yet to be right myrie will I fonde.
> Now wol I tellen of my fourthe housbonde . . .
>   l. 469ff

'myn herte roote . . . myn herte boote' the movement of the verse enacts the old woman's vigour as do the old shepherd's lines about his wife in *The Winter's Tale*. (IV.iii.60. See below, p. 181.)

> This day she was both pantler, butler, cook . . .

We hear the Wyf's actual living voice: and we take in with its movement her sadness, which is the sadness of resignation to the time-subject sexual reality of the mortal body, and to joy which has a term. We gain many insights from her realism – for instance, from her account of how woman's appetite is enhanced by being tantalized: such a recognition belongs to a wisdom of civilized sexual moeurs such as the classics from Aristophanes to Horace offered the English poets from Chaucer to Marvell and Ben Johnson. In Chaucer this ironic wisdom is given an English local habitation, and is of the native quality to which the folk-songs belong – offering to the next generation a body of un-deceived sexual wisdom – round, full, metaphorical and rich in expression, complex – but in no way negative, cynical, or deni-gratory.

We may possess these wisdoms and weave them still into our attitudes and concepts, our appetances: they enable us to accept our own imperfections, and to escape from isolation, by coming to accept how common our experience is with others. It is not easy for us, because the kind of sexual 'wisdom' offered by present-day popular writers is a form of mental defence against the accept-ance of the wholeness of psychesoma, of love's reality, and is so schizoid. In its concern to enlist others in a distorted view, it has nothing creative or compassionate to offer the next generation. Indeed, it is, rather, immature, cynical, infantile, and dangerous, and tends to reinforce attitudes which can only damage or limit living powers because they are unreal, and partial. Compare the kind of negative ironic 'reality' we are too often offered today with the valuable insights offered in her warm comedy by theWyf of Bath:

> We wommen han, if that I shal nat lye,
> In this matere a queynte fantasye;
> Wayte what thyng we may nat lightly have,
> Therafter wol we crie al day and crave.
> Forbede us thyng, and that desiren we;
> Preesse on us faste, and thanne wol we fle.
> With daunger oute we al oure chaffare;
> Greet prees at market maketh deere ware,

And to greet cheep is holde at litel prys:
Thus knoweth every womman that is wys.
   My fifthe housbonde, God his soule blesse . . .
         l. 515ff

Note the underlying sexual wit and irony: 'queynte' is also the word .for the woman's sexual organ, related to our four-letter word (see *The Miller's Tale*, l. 3276, 'And prively he caught her by the queynte.' Cf. also Marvell's play on the word in 'And your quaint honour turn to dust').

This voice speaks a poetry which, like Herbert's two centuries later, has affinities with folk-sayings, saws, and other embodiments of popular 'experience', in a body of 'auctoritee'. At the end of the tale, representing her constant return to experience in order to challenge authority – for the forces of life *must* challenge it – the Wyf resorts to violence against her fifth husband Jankyn, the clerk. Jankyn is prepared to spend all night haranguing her on women's wicked ways, quoting 'old examples' from his book:

'Bet is', quod he, 'thyn habitacioun
Be with a leon or a foul dragoun,
Than with a womman usynge for to chyde.'
'Bet is,' quod he, 'hye in the roof abyde,
Than with an angry wyf doun in the hous;
They have been so wikked and contrarious,
They haten that hir housbondes loven ay.'
He seyde, a 'womman cast hir shame away,
When she cast of hir smok'; and furthermo,
'A fair womman, but she be chaast also,
Is lyk a gold ryng in a sowes nose.'
Who wolde wene, or who wolde suppose,
The wo that in myn herte was, and pyne?
   And when I saugh he wolde nevere fyne
To reden on this cursed book al nyght,
All sodeynly thre leves have I plyght
Out of his book, right as he radde, and eke,
I with my fest so took hym on the cheke
That in our fyr he fil bakward adoun.
       Wyf's Prologe, l. 775ff

This is not simply a knockabout domestic scene caricaturing 'low

life'. There is a subtle irony in the very fact of Jankyn, half her
age, reading to the Wyf of Bath (of all people!) of the nature of
women! Repeating the age-old prejudices and disparagements –
to her! We need also to have in mind her extraordinary appearance – scarlet hose and gat-toothed – set against Jankyn's images
of the lion and the sow! There is more irony in his puritanical
jibes ('womman cast hir shame away . . .'), addressed to that
exacter of tolls for marital favours, and the feigner of appetite in
bed. And these ranges of irony add up to the comedy of Jankyn
offering her 'auctoritee' – much in the same way as she brings up
'auctoritee' only to dismiss it, and then, really, as John Speirs
points out, acting according to his intuitive reactions after all:

> And he up stirte as doth a wood leoun,
> And with his fest he smoot me on the head . . . l .794ff

But, says the Wyf,

> But atte laste, with muchel care and wo,
> We fille acorded by us selven two.   l. 811ff

This is the 'measure of equanimity' to which D. H. Lawrence
and Frieda came at the end of *Look! We Have Come Through!* (see
below, p. 336). Chaucer's comedy is rich, complex, human, and in
control of his benign belief in human nature: this, he says, is how
human beings behave, despite the tales in 'auctoritee': and, in a
sense, the Wyf of Bath's blow is a blow for feminine freedom,
though there is plenty of irony, in that this is rather a way of dominance, as she has described at length how she holds her 'housbondes'
in thrall, by their own appetites – by the tail, so to speak –

> And when that I hadde geten unto me,
> By maistrie, al the soveraynetee . . .   l. 817ff

In *The Franklin's Tale* Chaucer says:

> Love wol nat been constreyned by maistrye.
> Whan maistrie comth, the God of Love anon
> Beteth his wynges, and farewel, he is gon!   l. 764

The Wyf of Bath's level of sexual relationship, though vigorous
and life-promoting, is yet at the level of 'barley bread' and 'the

bren'. Perhaps indicatively, she never mentions whether she has children or not: there is much lacking in her sensual dominating self-possessiveness, even given the poignant portrayal of that heart, its roots tickled by memory, yet 'envenomed' with time. It is significant that she mentions Time in the context of her resignation – she belongs to the world, and to the modern world.

In all these ways the Wyf of Bath is 'placed' morally, in terms of the 'criticism of life'. She herself, in what is almost a dramatic comedy, is a piece of literary realism on the way to Falstaff, that combination of the moral awareness derived from mediaeval sources, with the realism of a rounded person representing How Human Beings Actually Behave. She is herself an expanded metaphor, as is Falstaff: she takes us, poetically, into the enigmas of how, given these appetites and weaknesses, is it possible for man to be capable of grace, of social order, and inward quality? In answer she has little more than vitality and a robust challenging irony to offer: but this is a beginning. At least we are now less able to deceive ourselves.

The Merchant's Tale though in sequence it follows *The Clerk's Tale* of Patient Griselda – a caricature of an impossible degree of goodness in bearing suffering – follows naturally from the sexual reality delineated in the Wyf of Bath. The Merchant, in his Prologue, reacts sharply against the account of 'Grisildis grete pacience', and relates his own experience:

> 'Wepyng and waylyng, care and oother sorwe
> I knowe ynogh, on even and a-morwe.'
> Quod the Marchant, 'and so doon other mo
> That wedded been . . .
> I have a wyf, the worste that may be;
> She wolde him overmacche, I dar wel swere.'
> *The Prologe of the Marchantes Tale*, l. 1213ff

Yet at the beginning of his Tale the Merchant gives a theologically sound account of the purpose and richness of the married state:

> To take a wyf it is a glorious thyng . . .
> Mariage is a ful greet sacrement . . .
> . . . wyf is mannes helpe and his comfort,
> His paradys terrestre . . .

That this is ironic appears by the time we reach the conclusion of this blissful account – here is the point at which the audience can no longer contain itself and bursts into laughter.

> She kepeth his good, and wasteth never a deel;
> All that hire housbonde lust, hire liketh weel;
> She saith nat onces 'nay', when he seith 'ye'.
> 'Do this', seith he; 'Al redy, sire', seith she.   l. 1343ff

The irony breaks forth because, in these scraps of dialogue the Merchant brings into focus an actual husband and wife, and thus the blissful account of marriage as given by 'auctoritee' is exposed as impossible. Chaucer is on the way to asking what possibilities are there of the 'paradys terrestre' coming about in actual men and women: *The Merchant's Tale* is an exposition of how, with all the best reasons for entering the married state according to the letter, man may come to grief. The old man January does the right thing according to the reasons of 'auctoritee', but, in personal terms, for the wrong reasons. This makes the poem a very modern work, for it emphasizes personal responsibility for good in sexual relationships: January follows 'the code' not the heart – disastrously. There is no love and spontaneity, no selflessness, in his sexual impulses. To him marriage is for *his* pleasure, *his* ease, and *his* redemption – to put right a life spent in sin, before it is too late, at 'the pittes brink'.

This is the moral complexity explored in the Tale. It is a very fine and subtle one, and done with a vigorous irony. In discussing it with adult students one has to protect them from accepting it as they might accept, say, a modern 'sex' novel. Chaucer has a robust and alive tenderness: popular modern novels are immersed in our cult of untenderness – an untenderness which is a symptom of immaturity, and a fear of the flux of sex – that flux in which the self needs to be dissolved in order to find its 'paradys terreste'. A 'sex comedy' writer flatters and reinforces our fears of the loss of personality in the 'death' that passion is: thereby he reinforces our dangerous infantilism, which is involved in fears of 'loss' in love, and even (as we have seen) in fear of satisfaction. Much modern poetry and prose has a flavour of offence to sex, because, as we have seen, the writer fears annihilation, and his preoccupation with sex is a frenetic personal search (albeit false) for 'reality'. So there can be no mutual acceptance of the partner in love, no courtesy or graciousness – no love-reality. If we take such writings as more than 'dirty books' that sell well, as near-pornography written for cash and réclame, we can only find them indicative of a kind of sickness. The writer wants to enlist other in his neurotic distortions, to seek to make them acceptable. If he is successful, the vindication is obviously more satisfying. To many modern poets too, sex seems merely the means to more egoistic satisfaction, where they are not expressing recoil. We have poems delineating the body of the female object, dissertation upon the poet's own physical potentialities and needs, and then the sudden exhibition of infantile (oral) desperation for physical release. The poets want to be loved – as a child does – not *to love*. They have not learnt to *give*. This sex-anxiety in modern 'love' poetry is poles apart from the expression of love as we have it in Chaucer – the link between the 'paradys' of bodily communion, and the gracious–transcending – potentialities of civilized mutual regard. Significantly the poet's woman in much modern poetry is hardly ever described for us so that she becomes known for herself – as Alisoun in *The Miller's Tale*, Criseyde, May, Dorigen eminently *do*. In much modern poetry and fiction there is little respect for women – they are merely a vehicle for the endless accounts of the man-poet's way to his gratifying evacuation, his anxiety-allaying 'detensioning', and his 'contact' with a 'reality' that is often no more than a narcissistic projection. Real women would be too real.

To resort to comparison to Chaucer is to make contact with a mature civilization in which such immaturities could never have been publicly applauded, and probably would never have been exhibited, because they would have been too evidently seen in all their pitiful inadequacy. Our public, alas, because of our prevalent psychic weaknesses, and the suspension of conscience and values in our culture, feels that hard-bitten, untender expressions of sexual experience must be enlightened, emancipated, clever, wise, sophisticated and real. Hence, when we come to *The Merchant's Tale*, and even more so when we come to *The Franklin's Tale*, some readers say that the latter is 'unreal' and 'makes no touch with life'.

Can one imagine such exquisitely human lines as Chaucer's to the Daisy being produced in our Age of Untenderness (the daisy is, of course, a symbol here, of femininity):

> And doun on knes anon-ryght I me sette,
> And, as I coude, this fresshe flour I grette;
> Knelyng alwey, til it unclosed was,
> Upon the smale, softe, swote gras,
> That was with floures swote enbrouded al,
> Of swich swetnesse and swich odour overal,
> That, for to speke of gomme, or herbe, or tree,
> Comparisoun may noon ymaked bee;
> For yt surmounteth pleynly alle odoures,
> And of riche beaute alle floures.
>   *The Legend of Good Women*, l. 155ff text f

Chaucer's generous tender lines convey a deep awe at created life (Cf. the plangent rhythm and soft texture of 'smale, softe, swote gras'). Only because of such regard does Love come to him, 'walking in the mede'. It is a profound psychological observation, that only by such humility, such tender respect and reverence for Nature and human nature can we arrive at love.

It is difficult, for instance, for us today, to see from the opening of *The Merchant's Tale* that the attitude of January from the beginning is placed as wrong, egoistical, and doomed to failure. We tend to say 'this is reality – this is ironic – this is how people do behave'. But in fact, while this tale starts from the 'way people actually behave', it is, too, an expanded metaphor carefully placing the weaknesses in sexual behaviour from the very beginning. The 'worthy knyght' January is 'wyflees',

> And folwed ay his bodily delyt
> On wommen, ther-as was his appetyt . . . l. 1249

He sees wedlock, at the age of sixty, as 'esy' and 'so clene'. The irony is deep; promiscuity, after sixty, becomes less attractive to the pursued women – one has to make do with less good material: better to have sex at home 'esy' to come by and morally 'clene'.

January wishes to 'engendren hym an heir', and to seek both his earthly heaven and his place in the terrestial one at the same time, from the edge of his grave. His desperate sensuality and his tardy yearnings for decent ease are pitiful – they are done compassionately because they are done by a poet who has created the Wyf of Bath who is both 'tickled' and 'envenomed' by her memories:

> And almoost, God woot, on my pittes brynke;
> Upon my soule somwhat moste I thynke.
> I have my body folily despended;
> Blessed be God that it shal been amended!
>   l. 1401ff

This wretched (and damningly tardy) desire to redeem himself by a last gesture towards marriage is linked by Chaucer with the subsequent imagery of appetite and physical hunger and distaste. The 'cold friction of expiring sense' in January is conveyed to us by active images which make us feel, deeply and compassionately, the poignancy of age, and, at the same time, the repulsiveness of his late-in-life frenetic lechery. Psychologically, it is a penetrating portrayal of a man who has virtually blighted his own life by the promiscuous pursuit of 'bodily delit' and is now incapable of *ever* finding the satisfaction he seeks. He is, if you like, a comment on the fallacious belief that early promiscuity is a good preparation for marriage, or a means towards creative and harmonious relationships: it simply may not be, because it may be a symptom of a failure to accept reality. January is an observation that promiscuity is a lesser mode of sexual life because it is essentially *unreal*, a denial of human nature, and its deeper needs, of the exigencies of relationship. There is much in it of infantile egocentricity: January is in his second childhood. He will never find his 'paradys terrestre', because that is only found in love: the true phallic richness is with Damian the lover. January can offer no more than 'the bran' of mere physical conjunction:

> 'Oold fissh and yong flesshe wolde I have ful fayn.
> Bet is,' quod he, 'a pyk than a pykerel,
> And bet than old boef is the tender veel.

I wol no woman thritty year of age;
It is but bene-straw and greet forage.'

l. 1418ff

Before we even meet May, we can foresee that January's wife is to be forfeit to conceptions of marital love in terms of a barren ego-centric gustation – a physical fulfilment such as might be associated with masticating veal: it is *she* who will receive 'bene-straw' in return. And by this imagery, its awakening of our sense of taste and tactile feelings, we begin to enter an awareness of sexual reality that, when January is in bed with May, is to fill us with a deep repulsion at the real consequences, in terms of human suffering, which such depersonalized lust inevitably creates. Perhaps we find it today difficult to enter wholeheartedly and sensitively into May's experience; we are cut off by the cult of denigration from Chaucer's metaphorical search for human potentiality in love. But the gruesome comedy of it has a vital morality.

January's new wife is to be as 'wax' 'moulded in his hands': it is in terms of the domination over a young malleable life that January conceives his marriage. Chaucer's psychological understanding is here profound:

But certeynly, a yong thyng may men gye,
Right as men may warm wex with handes plye

l. 1429

– a 'yonge thyng may men gye' ('gye'=control, govern). Our repugnance at this is given by Chaucer's deep imaginative realization of the reality of an old man's psychological needs – childish, petulant, and requiring absolute acquiescence, as a baby boy demands absolute acquiescence from its mother, to be wax in his hands. He must control the woman he fears. January is a marvellous portrait of the psychic immaturity one may find in such an old man and lecher. Chaucer also deeply understands the origins of 'elde' and 'maistrie', the bullying which becomes a substitute for vitality, once the 'pith' begins to decline. January's 'mental sex' is evidence of his loss of sexual potency in the body. Later in the tale we find the phrase recurring 'he kept his hand on her alway' – the pawing of her body is both a jealous physical

restraint and a reassurance that he is still alive, in the presence of
feminine comfort, with the 'esy' wife in the role of the all-pro-
viding 'mother'. But the wax imagery persists, too, and the
moulded wax becomes the matrix (in its original sense) for the
imprint of the key, symbolic of entry into the garden of hot
creative love and phallic vitality. The symbolism is of the desire
of May's creative body for the awakening phallus of her lover:
Damian's vitality contrasts sharply with the drug-exacerbated,
frenetic, long-drawn out, and studied love-making of the old
man, for his own sense-pleasure. She pretends to be pregnant, to
get to the pear tree. When May climbs on January's back into the
tree the young man mates with her in a trice:

> And sodeynly anon this Damyan
> Gan pullen up the smok and in he throng. l. 2351-2

And we have another glimpse, through January's eyes, of how

> 'Now that this Damyan hadde by the leyn [had with thee lain]
> And that thy smok hadde leyn upon they breast',

and May tells how she 'struggled' with the man upon the tree. The
picture is of a youthful vigour which contrasts with January's
desperate skin-rubbing sensuality. With him, imagery of unpleasant skin sensations abounds – 'the skin of houndsfisshe',
'thikke brustles of his berd', 'he rubbeth her about her tender face'.
Damian, like the lover in *The Miller's Tale*, 'pricketh hard and
deep'! May will be pregnant indeed. January wants to be a fruitful
tree, but he fatally denies the realities of his age: he is winter and
death. The only way in which he could have triumphed over the
reduction of his pith was in love, rather than in following 'his
bodily delit/On wommen'. Inevitably, his nemesis comes – life
will out, and January's garden is entered by the vigorous fertile
Damian, and by love, albeit surreptitious and adulterous love, up
in a tree. The power of sexual vitality as a manifestation of life is
here poetically expressed as it is in *Lady Chatterley's Lover*, as in the
episode of the chicks and the first seduction.

January, unfortunately, describes himself as a tree:

> 'Though I be hoor, I fare as dooth a tree
> That blosmeth er that fruyt ywoxen bee;

And blosmy tree nys neither drye ne deed.
I feel me nowwhere hoor but on myn heed;
Myn herte and alle my lymes been as grene
As laurer thurgh the yeer is for to sene . . .' l. 1461ff

He pronounces himself a laurel, evergreen: this blindness to reality is to become an actual physical blindness. Poignantly he, like Hardy, feels his 'fragile frame at eve' shaken 'with passions of noontide': we sense that he is seeking to exaggerate his sexual vigour (partly by the tree symbol). His shortcoming is in the fruitless uncreativity of one who has not learnt to yield outwards from the egocentric sensual self: there is something unnatural in the image of a January still in blossom, who has not 'woxen' fruit. The growth of wax in the hive concealed in the word 'woxen' reminds us of the young life he is to mould as wax in his hands, and which, like wax, is to take Damyan's phallic impression in the garden, in happy wanton love. It takes Damyan to give May what she needs.

In the telling of the Tale the verse enacts with great vitality Chaucer's exploration of this marriage that may be sanctioned by 'auctoritee', but comes short when examined as human experience by the poet's compassionate understanding. The Tale is a supreme example of poetry *doing what it says*. Here is metaphor at its compassionate task, for we are not merely *told* about the hideousness of such a sexual union as that of January and May – lacking tender feeling, mutual regard, and love – *we live through it* as we read. In doing so it becomes part of each our own experience, and enters into our attitudes to life. We are the more able to contemplate 'what it is like for other people' when they, like January, sacrifice their bodily life to wrong motives, to domination, and cold gratification of appetite. It is a comment, too, of course, on the unsatisfactory relationship which failure of social conventions and modes may bring about – sex must be as loveless as this often when marriages are 'arranged', or have become 'inevitable' because of necessary social or commercial links between families. But having experienced this imaginative episode we shall not in future regard these actual human conditions without compassion – we know better now 'what it must be like'. Our pity extends to the ridiculous old January as much as it does to May because his sexual 'cold friction' and his selfishness are things that are true of all old men, not only those as selfish throughout life as January: but we have experienced a deep 'criticism of life', and change in our moral awareness. We may feel that this poem delineates a failure at the centre of life, at the place where the 'paradys terrestre' should be; but it is a failure which we must not pharasaically condemn, because we shall all experience it at some time or other – our human nature being as frail and imperfect as it is.

'Paraunter she may be youre purgatorie!' says one of January's advisers, l. 1669: there is in this a descant to the ironic description of his marriage night, in that he is not aware of the purgatory which the bridal bed itself has become, certainly for May.

January becomes restless as his marriage feast goes on. For him it does not, like Herbert's feast with God, 'mend in length': he begins in his heart to menace May

> That he that nyghte in armes would hire streyne
> Harder than evere Parys die Eleyne . . .
> > l. 1753-4
>
> Now wolde God that it were woxen nyght . . .
> > l. 1762

Night comes, not without a touch of the ominous:

> Night with his mantel, that is derk and rude,
> Gan oversprede the hemysperie aboute . . .
> > l. 1798-9

January, who boasts of his ability to 'streyne' his bride, takes no chances with his natural potency:

> He drynketh ypocras, clarree, and vernage
> Of spices hoote, t'encreessen his corage . . .
> > l. 1807

. . . we cannot help feeling (though the texture of the language, which grunts strainingly with its 'k' and 'g' sounds) this feverish self-stimulation as a 'menace' to the 'tendre creature'. As January says,

> But God forbede that I dide al my myght!

. . . there is an ominous hint of delight in wounding brutality.
What is to be inflicted on May is a power-lust trained by a lifetime of 'bodily delit' on other women. The night comes. There is
no need to dwell on the texture of the verse ('thikke brustles . . .
skyn of houndsfysshe') and what it enacts here:

> And Januarie hath faste in armes take
> His fresshe May, hys paradys, his make.
> He lulleth hire, he kisseth hire ful ofte;
> With thikke brustles of his berd unsofte,
> Lyk to the skyn of houndfysshe, sharp as brere –
> For he was shave al newe in his manere –
> He rubbeth hire aboute hir tendre face,
> And seyde thus, 'Allas! I moot trespace
> To yow, my spouse, and yow greetly offende . . .'
>
> l. 1819

His conception of sexual union as 'offence' touches in the sadistic
tinge of January's impulse to 'mould her as wax', and to exert his
spice-inflamed skin-stimulating lust on her, as a 'menace'. Like
Leopold Bloom, his mental consciousness of 'the danger' and
'offence' in sex makes up for his lack of sexual 'pith' – his essential
impotence. To the woman, he is, in our slang term, indeed a
'menace'! 'A man may do synne with his wyf' has a superb irony
– that we feel his 'streyning' of her to be as much an offence against
another human being as anything could be – against 'hys paradys'
– apart from the fact, of course, that it is morally, legally, and
theologically unsound to make such a reference to 'auctoritee', to
justify the obscenities January is to practise on the poor girl without the transforming benediction of love's mutual tenderness. The
irony, of course, at the larger level, relates Chaucer's apprehension
of the nature of human life in the body with which we must live:
the division between mere usage of the body and the fulfilment
of true love is not always clear even to lovers, and the physical
robustness of a love union such as that of Damian and May in the
tree contains the same gross physical energy to be found in such
prostituted intercourse as that between January and May – *The
Merchant's Tale* stands, in apprehending this, behind *King Lear*:
'none does offend, none' – because all offend.

Chaucer's own ruth breaks through, in the pitiful image of
January chirruping like a copulating sparrow, as bridegroom:

> And upright in his bed thanne sitteth he,
> And after that he sang ful loude and cleere,
> And kiste his wyf, and made wantown cheere.
> He was al coltissh, ful of ragerye,
> And ful of jargon as a flekked pye.
> The slakke skyne aboute his nekke shaketh,
> Whil that he sang, so chaunteth he and craketh
> But God woot what that May thoughte in her herte,
> Whan she hym saugh up sitynge in his sherte,
> In his nyght-cappe, and with his nekke lene;
> She preyseth nat his pleyying worth a bene.
>
>   l. 1843

Chaucer's irony directed at the old man pretending to be a young
lover speaks through the comedy – 'he chaunteth and he craketh'.
But the irony is charged with pity, for we perceive that his love-
making, though frenetic, is, like his singing, cracked. Women
'over thritty' he had considered 'bene-straw'; May, after her experience of his 'wantoun cheer', considers his (sexual) 'play' not
worth a 'bene'. The phrase 'be hire lief or looth' gives us his indifference to her feelings. The verse takes us into the experience –
it is as if we have been both January and May. The chattering-
sounding words 'flekked', 'slakke', 'cracketh', 'nekke' suggest a
dry and empty quality about the practised approach of the hand
which wishes to mould May as wax, and the body with its slack
skin and lean neck which offers her 'werk' and 'labour' in bed,
'whether hire thoughte it paradys or helle'.

> He laboureth until the day gan dawe

– but the labour is for his own egocentric lust, not, in mutual
consideration, for or *with* her. It is May who has the bean-straw,
and we taste the emptiness, without once losing the touch of
comedy, and robust vitality in the language, of her bridal sexual
experience.[1]

[1] Significantly, because he shares so much with his audience, Chaucer does not
need to describe the sexual union of January and May: he can assume the standards
of tenderness by which it will be judged. Lawrence's predicament was that he felt
it necessary to describe all to vindicate each particular. See below.

The scene is grotesque and hideous: but it is a marvellous comment on the terrible fact in human life of meaningless sex – and much human sex, when so depersonalized and loveless, must be thus meaningless. It is a great triumph of Chaucer's art that he is able to convince us of the lack, here in this bridal chamber, of love, of that ability to give in love which alone makes the sexual life real and significant.

When love comes to May it can only be adulterous love: but it is an awakening to life: the natural heart begins to grow as it could not under the merciless hands of January:

> For pitee of this sike Damyan,
> That from hire herte she ne dryve kan
> The remembrance for to doon him ese.
> 'Certeyn', thoghte she, 'whom that this thyng
>   displese,
> I rekke noght, for heere I hym assure
> To love him best of any creature,
> Though he namoore hadde than his sherte.'
> Lo, pitee renneth soone in gentil herte!
>   l. 1979ff

Damian in his 'sherte' is all to her, as he desires no more than May naked in a sack (in her false vow to January she cries, for Damian to hear, 'Do strepe me and put me in a sak . . .').

These two creatures have no care, even unto death, for 'heritage, toun and tour' – those worldly goods with which January endows his wife, in exchange for a kiss. Life will out, and recks nothing for property. The old man's 'greet prosperitee' is no endowment without love. All January's care in keeping 'a hand on his wife alway', his jealousy, and his doing things 'with speed' in the garden 'of the kind he could not do in bed' – all this 'ragerye' and lust proves, in the end, impotent and nothing against the 'gentil herte' of young love's vitality. May swears she will not be false, but her vow is empty: she is already signalling her lover into the tree where she may give herself to him. Her plea to be stripped and put in a sack is virtually an indirect erotic hint to spur on her lover. Her blind husband she makes cling to the tree-symbol of phallic creativity, by pretending to be pregnant, while she climbs, to be 'dressed' by Damian . . .

> In switch manere it may not be expressed . . .

When Pluto sees this 'grete wrong,' he restores January's sight, and the old husband sees his wife in her lover's arms. She protests that a physician told her that the only way to restore his sight was to struggle with a man up a tree. But January relates the lustful reality as he glimpsed it:

> 'Struggle!' quod he, 'ye, algate in it wente!'

Yet, even though January has seen the actual physical conjunction of the lover with his wife in such graphic detail, she manages to persuade him that he is but 'glymsynge' and he should not believe the evidence of his own senses:

> 'He that mysconceyveth, he mysdemeth.'   l. 2410
> Now, goode men, I pray you to be glad . . .   l. 2416

– we are invited to be glad, presumably that January forgave his wife. But the comic and yet poignant end leaves us with no feeling of gladness: what then? Is there then, no possibility for human love in marriage to be full of rich and lasting potential? Must the reality always be a distasteful union in passionless marriage, while the best potential is represented, as mostly in Courtly Love, by the adulterous alliance, with its culmination in the momentary and furtive passionate act in the pear tree?

From his dissatisfaction with this ironic attitude Chaucer writes *The Franklin's Tale*. Here irony is dropped, and, as in Shakespeare's *The Winter's Tale*, the verse takes on something of a dance-like formality. We leave the 'false solution' of adulterous passion for a new love-reality of marriage. The intense imagery of physical appetite and sexual activity is not here, and we are told nothing of the physical union between Arveragus and his wife Dorigen. But we feel a movement as of achieved harmony in love, of which the sexual details are unspoken:

> O blisful artow now, thou Dorigen,
> That hast thy lusty housbonde in thyne armes,
> The fresshe knyght, the worthy man of armes,
> That loveth thee as his owene hertes lyf.
>
> *The Franklin's Tale*, l. 1090ff

This is significant, because the poem deals with the flux of feeling and attitude at the civilised level, with their roots in a physical delight, obviously there, but absorbed and transcended. We may take the implications of the mutual regard and confidence between Averagus and Dorigen to imply sexual harmony in the bridal chamber, but it is not necessary for Chaucer to be graphic here – obviously their love-making will be something very different from that between January and May. It is significant of the maturity of Chaucer's time that he does not feel the need to describe 'good' sex as Lawrence does, and may leave the indescribable undescribed. Chaucer could assume that his audience could contemplate such a thing as courteous and mutual physical love without a lewd guffaw, or a flight into protesting cynicism.

The Frankleyn is the poetic embodiment of a rich, civilized, vitality. In the Prologue he is described as

> A householdere, and that a greet, was he . . .   l. 339

His complexion is 'sangwyn' but, 'Whit was his berd as is the dayesye,' and his 'anlass' and 'gipser' that 'heeng at his girdle' are 'Whit as morne milk'.

He is 'worthy vavasour', and, 'It snewed in his hous of mete and drinke.'

He is no vulgar gourmandiser however: the whiteness of his beard and girdle suggest discretion and veracity, combined with generosity and good living. He is perhaps of all pilgrims the nearest to Chaucer's own maturity and fecundity:

> For he was Epicurus owene sone,
> That heeld opinioun that pleyn delit
> Was verraily felicitee parfit.

The Frankleyn describes himself as 'burel' – i.e. unlearned, and of 'rude speech': in fact his tale is the summit of the civilized wisdom in the *Canterbury Tales*. It opens with a brief expression of Chaucer's mature perceptions of the nature of love and marriage:

> Thus been they bothe in quiete and in reste.
> For o thyng, sires, saufly dar I seye,
> That freendes everych oother moot obeye,

> If they wol longe holden compaignye.
> Love wol nat been constreyned by maistrye.
> Whan maistrie comth, the God of Love anon
> Beteth his wynges, and farewel, he is gon!
> Love is a thyng as any spirit free.
> Women, of kynde, desiren libertee
> And nat to been constreyned as a thral;
> And so doon men, if I sooth seyen shall.
>
> l. 760ff

– one can imagine the Frankleyn delivering an admonitory glance at the Wyf of Bath in speaking that last line! But how wise is the emphasis on the reality of woman and man! The assurance is that of Chaucer who has behind him *The Wyf of Bath's Prologue*, and *The Merchant's Tale*. So, the expression of freedom and equality in the love-relationship comes as assured in its movement as that of the marvellous line 'Than longen folk to goon on pilgrimages' –

> Love wol nat been constreyned by maistrye...

In all our struggles now towards feminine emancipation, and to liberate our psychic lives by the application of the sciences of mind – our conclusion must be the same as Chaucer's. Yet we fall as far short of living by such a concept of mutual freedom as all the characters do in Chaucer's Tales, including the extremes of the Wyf of Bath, Patient Griselda, and wretched May.

Chaucer being a poet, the concept of freedom is given form and body in terms of imaginative experience, and this is done from the opening:

> But atte laste she, for his worthynesse,
> And namely for his meke obeysaunce,
> Hath swich a pitee caught of his penaunce
> That pryvely she fil of his accord
> To take him for hir housbonde and hir lord,
> Of swich lordshipe as men han over hir wives.
> And for to lede the moore in bliss hir lyves,
> Of his free wyl he swoor hire as a knyght
> That nevere in al his lyf he, day ne nyght,
> Ne sholde upon hym take no maistrie
> Agayn her wyl, ne kithe hire jalousie,

But hire obeye, and folwe hir wyl in al,
As any lovere to his lady shal,
Save that the name of soveraynetee,
That wolde he have for shame of his degree.

l. 738ff

Only in certain circumstances in dealing with the outside world as
a knight must he have 'the *name* of soveraynetee': in all else he
would 'folowe hir wyl'. The verse is formal, as is appropriate to
the account of a knightly romance and marriage. But its formality
is not that of the courtly romantic tale, belonging to a world of
adulterous episodes: the fall of the verse has a quality of real
argument, without extravagance, and progresses convincingly to
postulate balanced symmetry of mutual regard, felt to be possible
in the actual world. The poetic fable is of no ideal world, but is
really gentle (the French sense of *gentil* would be relevant). It is
entirely without irony, and seizes the attention by its quiet, wise,
unflustered and civilized, courteous movement:

Heere may men seen an humble, wys accord;
Thus hath she take hir servant and hir lord,
Servant in love and lord in mariage.
Thanne was he bothe in lordshipe and servage.
Servage? nay, but in lordshipe above,
Sith he hath bothe his lady and his love;
His lady, certes, and his wyf also,
The which that lawe of love acordeth to.

l. 791ff

This verse has that mature quality of simple but profound exposition of universal truths such as we find in Shakespeare's latest
plays, as in Florizel's great lines to Perdita.

The formality of movement in Chaucer's lines belongs to the
same kind of preoccupation, in *The Franklin's Tale*, with what
is durable in human love, in human life. The answer is 'curtesy' –
to the 'fre' – in the sense of yielding generously to other creatures,
and thus escaping from the destructive forces of egotism, isolation
in the self, cut off from relationship with the 'other'. The greatest
human reality, that which triumphs most over human reality and

Time – (If they wol longe holden compaignye) – is the tender, evanescent, abstract value such as the 'curtesy' embodied here in the love-relationship which is also marriage:

> Servant in love and lord in marriage . . .
> Sith he hath both his lady and his love . . .
> His lady, certes, and his wife also . . .

The symmetrical movement of the verse enacts the balance of the mutual regard, the harmony, and the pattern of the marriage which is to endure the assaults of circumstance. The values, the ideals are the most real thing: this is the region in which love may be triumphant over human weakness, mutability and mortality. Of course, in terms of conscious self-determination, in that civilization which is both Chaucer's and ours, this concept of the possibilities of love in marriage was, in his time, perhaps something comparatively new. It is still new for us, in that we have not yet absorbed such civilized concepts as those Chaucer expresses here, enough to show them viable in our own living. And, of course, the problem is universal and eternal. We all have to develop a sense of our own identity, and to develop a sense of the reality of others, so that we may love and respect them: this is part of everyone's 'reality problem'. We all have to learn to love, and all of us are in the throes of a tussle with inherited and assumed prejudices and obstacles deep in the psyche, to such harmonious accord as there is between Dorigen and Averagus. Many marriages come to disaster almost before they start on imperfect and primitive notions of being 'free'. Our need for possessed concepts, ideals and values here is great, not least because we unconsciously tend to repeat the errors of our parents, of our class, or our society.

Thus the subtle balanced movement of Chaucer's verse here, enacting the summit of gentle civilized mutual regard, is a contribution to our powers of living, now. Here the metaphorical activity of Chaucer's language is not in a close-packed texture or in complexity of image and sound, but in the emanation from the gentle rhythm of the lines the felt experience of a character who is deeply realized, in terms of both thought and feeling. We have here the kind of poetic quality which we have in Wordsworth's

sonnet 'Surpris'd by Joy' – a metaphorical force conveyed by the
movement of an inward experience (for an analysis of this poem
see *English for Maturity*, p. 47). In this *Tale* of Chaucer's similar
simple movements of voice, felt deeply in their measured rhythm,
express the profoundly realized emotion of the young wife when
her husband has to go away from her:

> For his absence wepeth she and siketh,
> As doon thise noble wyves whan hem liketh.
> She moorneth, waketh, wayleth, fasteth, pleyneth;
> Desir of his presence hire so destreyneth
> That al this wyde world she sette at noght . . .
>
> l. 817ff

> Which made alwey hir compleint and hir moone,
> For she ne saugh *hym* on the daunce go
> That was hir housbonde and hir love also . . .
>
> l. 920ff

The committed love devotion, as expressed in the simple last line,
is deeply moving. Again, there is the marvellous absence of all
irony, in the impressive presence of the Frankleyn and his civilized
open humane wisdom. The voice needs to be subtly read aloud
('and her love also') to get the delicate feeling of it, and the expression of restless longing in that 'moorneth, waketh, wayleth . . .'

Dorigen's only fault is that which she shares with the
Shakespeare of the *Sonnets*: she sees reality as a threat to her love:
the external circumstances of our life are brutal and indifferent to
that love which seems to us more real than any other thing. We
must come to terms with this reality. Here it is symbolized by the
rocks, over which Averagus's ship must sail:

> Another tyme ther wolde she sitte and thynke,
> And caste hir eyen dounward fron the brynke.
> And whan she saugh the grisly rokkes blake,
> For verray feere so wolde hir herte quake
> That on hire feet she myghte hire noght sustene.
> Thanne wolde she sitte adoun upon the grene,
> And pitously into the see biholde,
> And seyn right thus, with sorweful sikes colde:
> 'Eterne God . . .'

'But, Lord, these grisly feendly rokkes blake,
That semen rather a foul confusion
Of werk than any fair creacion . . .

Why han ye wroght this werk unresonable?'

'An hundred thousand bodyes of mankynde
Han rokkes slayn . . .'

'But wolde God that alle thise rokkes blake
Were sonken into helle for his sake!'

                                        l. 857, et seq.

There is, of course, no answer, from God or from 'auctoritee': there is no disguising nor explaining away of the indifferent universe, the tragic conditions of human existence in space and time. But the rocks are a symbol of the test in relation to the reality which the love of this married pair is to undergo. Thus, dramatically, Chaucer sets out to enact the large metaphor of his poem: to escape from the limitations of the conclusion in *The Wyf of Bath's Prologue* and *The Merchant's Tale*. He is dissatisfied with the limitations of 'seeing reality' in terms of sexual appetite, 'maistrye' and gross expediency in living. He develops here his poetic powers to something beyond the local richness of metaphor, so appropriate for the contrasts of ironic comedy, to the larger expanded, somewhat formal metaphor, dancelike, and enacting a possible whole positive mode of living. This, in Chaucer, parallels Shakespeare's development from *Hamlet* and *Lear* to the dancelike, balletic, masque-like formality of *The Winter's Tale* and *The Tempest*. In these latter plays, in much the same way, Shakespeare, with his ironic exploration of 'reality' behind him, enacts the gracious, creative and delicate promise of the innocent Miranda and Ferdinand, and of Florizel and Perdita as masque-like symbols of mutual regard in the love-marriage relationship, in symbolic terms. To arrive at such ends is in each of these two poets a supreme, rare achievement. It represents great faith in human nature, an assertion that Man is Good and capable of creative altruism – that Man *can be civilized*. It is this which brings tears to one's eyes in the *Franklin's Tale*, at the end of the story. This is surely something word-art, if it is to be significant in human affairs, must always try to move towards, as children in their word-art naturally move towards such celebration of positives and ideals. We shall fall lamentably short of coming anywhere near such hope and confidence as that of Chaucer, in his grasp on life, today. But the threat of failure must be no excuse for not even trying, if we are to take on the honourable name of poet, 'maker'. For the writer 'makes' our ideals by giving substance to values, attitudes and concepts, so giving us hope.

Dorigen's only error is to wish that reality were not real, so that her husband should not be threatened. For this reason, when she is approached by would-be adulterous lover, Aurelius, she playfully promises to be his love if he clears away the rocks. He, of course, represents a more tangible threat to their love than the rocks, and Dorigen's 'fault' is to connive in the least at this, even in play. Aurelius then seeks for a means to clear the rocks. He prays Phebus and the gods to cause a tide to cover them, lasting two weeks – but there is, of course, no response: the nature of reality cannot be changed. But though external reality cannot be changed, inward reality, and thus appearances, can, and thus Chaucer takes us on towards the kind of preoccupations with the nature of things which haunted Shakespeare and which has preoccupied men ever since the dawn of science – until we began to understand the nature of projection, and other psychic hallucinations. For Chaucer the reality of the world could not be anything other than a divine reality, and it is this which will not permit illusion:

> For hooly chirches feith in oure bileve
> He suffreth noon illusioun us to greve.
>
> l. 1133-4

But magic can make things *seem* different:

> By whiche men make diverse *apparences* . . .
> Thus *seemed* it to every mannes sighte . . .

I have heard students in discussion (in this age of mass self-deception!) that the *Franklin's Tale* is 'artificial' because of the 'magic' in the story. (In the age of Hollywood, advertising, and the exposure by psychoanalysis of our irrationality!) Aurelius' magician makes it *seem* that the reality of the rocks can be denied, so that the reality of the love between the married pair can be disrupted by the interposition of the adulterous fairy-tale-lover of courtly love romance. But the reality – a stronger kind of inward reality – of the married love triumphs – and it emerges from this take as a reality more durable and lasting even than the 'feendly grisly rokkes'. Damian, like the day-dreamers in our cinemas, is taken for a ride, out of reality:

> And after this he did him swich plesaunce
> That he hym shewed his lady on a daunce
> On which hymself he daunced, as hym thoughte . . .
>
> l. 1199-20

Aurelius is here like those living in the dream world of unreal feelings as we would say, of Hollywood – the unreality which, at the clap of the magicians' hands, disappears. But to mask reality so from ourselves is deathly, in the end.

So in this tale the climax is approached with a touch of ominousness in the seasonal atmosphere:

> The bittre frostes, with the sleet and reyn,
> Destroyed hath the grene in every yerd . . .
>
> l. 1250

By 'joggelrye' and allusion the rocks are made to *seem* to disappear, and the destructive threat comes close to the married 'paradys terrestre'. Aurelius asks for Dorigen to keep her promise, to love him if he could make the rocks away:

> He taketh his leeve, and she astoned stood;
> In al her face nas a drope of blood . . .
>
> l. 1339-40

> ' . . . wende I nevere by possibilitee
> That swich a monstre or merveille myghte be!
> It is agayns the process of nature.'
>
> l. 1343-5

She clings now to reality, 'the process of nature', when before she had asked for it to be denied. Then, with a wonderful evocation of the gravity of Greek tragedy, Chaucer makes her refer to many women who have died rather than suffer their bodies to be abused.

The lines emphasize the gravity of the moral test which is being applied to this couple's love, and the deadly seriousness, too, of the ethical codes which govern human love relationships. It is a poetic earnest of the validity of 'internal reality', of possessed values:

> Whan thritty tirauntz, ful of cursednesse,
> Hadde slayn Phidon in Atthenes atte feste,
> They comanded his doghtres for t'areste,
> And bryngen hem biforn hem in despit,
> Al naked, to fulfille hir foul delit,
> And in hir fadres blood they made hem daunce
> Upon the pavement, God yeve em mischaunce!
> For which thise woful maydens, ful of drede,
> Rather than they wolde lese hir maydenhede,
> They prively been stirt into a welle,
> And dreynte hemselven . . .
>
> l. 1368ff

Perhaps it is difficult, after so much comic derision of the themes of 'a fate worse than death', for us to take it seriously that there could ever be a situation in which a woman would take her life rather than give her body in dishonour. Perhaps we could benefit from the stern presence of the Frankeleyn, who while he is grave and stern yet seeks delight in civilized fecundity. There is no mistaking the strength of moral gravity in the fierce strength of Chaucer's consonants in the lines above: unbridled aggressive sensuality is the death of civilization, and it is better to die than accept life at the price of submission to the human beast. We should take the reference in a gravity of mind which may recall Maidenek and Belsen, or the rape of German women by Russian troops.

But Dorigen's predicament is to meet an even more prevailing reality than death itself: self-inflicted death here is too romantic, too primitive, a gesture. We are living at the level of the Frankeleyn's (and Chaucer's) maturity. She meets the reality of her husband's courteous regard for her, and his confidence:

> 'Is there oght elles, Dorigen, but this?'
> 'Nay, nay', quod she, 'God helpe me so as wys!
> This is to muche, and it were Goddes wille.'
>
> l. 1469–71

'Is there oght else' – how the line catches the flood of sorrow, fear, and compassion in the man! Her husband urges that she should keep her vow to Aurelius – her truth:

> . . . But if ye sholde youre trouthe kepe and save.
> Trouthe is the hyeste thyng that man may kepe' –
> And with that worde he brast anon to wepe . . . ll 1438–40

As a man, albeit he is a courtly knight, Averagus breaks down: yet against the 'reality' of the situation he urges the greater, transcending, reality of truth and honour. Chaucer warns us

> Paraventure an heep of yow, ywis,
> Wol holden hym a lewed man in this
> That he wol putte his wyf in jupartie.
> Herkneth the tale er ye upon hire crie.
> She may have better fortune than yow semeth . . .
>
> l. 1493ff

Averagus hopes the same – as he contests with his love and truth against the courtly code itself and has confidence in the outcome. Dorigen goes to offer her truth: 'And she answerede, half as she were mad . . .'. Such touches as this, and Averagus' breaking down 'to wepe', brings these characters to us as in a 'close-up'. The action has a psychological realism that makes this tale very modern. We feel the emotional progress of the characters. Yet the verse remains formal, and distancing.

At this point comes perhaps the most moving point in all Chaucer's work – a great dramatic moment, a great poetic moment, and a great moment in English consciousness: Aurelius feels ruth, accepting the reality of the love by which he is confronted, and moves towards the more adult, modern and 'free' conception of personal relationships:

> And in his herte he caughte of this greet routhe,
> Consideryng the beste on every syde,
> And fro his lust yet were hym levere abyde
> Than doon so heigh a cherlyssh wrecchednesse
> Agayns franchise and alle gentilnesse . . .
>
> l. 1520ff

Deeply penetrating is the psychological perception of the lust 'abiding' as Aurelius' compassion flows: he suddenly attains maturity, in becoming aware of the adult reality of the married love which his adulterous courtship and delusions threaten. It parallels the advance a man may make in being released from lustful 'maistrye' in marriage by his developed capacity for respect for his wife, by coming to accept her real identity, and his own. Each character here becomes more 'real' and 'fre' at the end. This growth of 'gentilnesse' in maturity is today one of our greatest needs, towards seeking personal balance and 'reality'. The triumphant reality-sense of the married lovers restores the capacity to be reasonable (the line enacts the balance of wise deliberation in its determined rhythm: 'considering the best on every side') even to an intending lover who has spent much effort and time, even jeopardizing his estate, in the endeavour to disguise the nature of things to the object of his desire. Above all, at the end of this enacted debate, that reality which transcends desire, the realities of 'gentilnesse' and 'franchise' in the mutual regard, trust and confidence of husband and wife – triumphs over the grosser realities of appetite, sex, and weakness, as taken into account, ironically, earlier. The adolescent world of courtly romance gives way to the world of Chaucer's civilized maturity. 'Everich of you dide gentilly til oother' – this is the ultimate human reality – the good – the potentiality of man for grace, the beauty of truths and values that may be found in relationship:

> Lordyinges, this question, thanne, wolde I aske now,
> Which was the mooste fre, as thynketh yow?
>
> l. 1621–22

This 'fre' is something far above the freedom claimed by the Wyf of Bath – the word contains the senses of noble, generous, liberal, gracious. It is a freedom derived from an acceptance of the reality of our feelings and the reality of courteous values and love. The Tale as a whole implies that it is only when we accept reality, from the 'rokkes', to the inescapable social bounds of our life (the bounds which Anthony and Cleopatra can never adequately square with their love in Shakespeare's play), and the reality of love, do we become truly adult and free.

In such poetry do we progress towards important social truths, embodied in a form by which we may take them in as experience which changes us, even by the delight the verse gives us. We take Chaucer's perceptions and include what we can of them in our attitudes and awarenesses, alive in our nerves and blood. This is great art in poetry, a great social force, and a great inward spiritual force for civilization. His is art which is the culmination of a lifetime's contemplation of the nature of human nature, by a spirit which can find it in the end still good and viable, and, in the love relationship, coming to its most triumphant expression – triumphing over the assaults of lust in sexual reality, over separation, and the 'grisly rokkes blak'. As in *Wuthering Heights* and folksong, love is found to be stronger and more durable than the 'external rocks beneath' which are forever undeniable and unappeasable.

Of course, we have to turn to Chaucer's poem again and again to accompany him through the disciplines of his quest for love: but we know we may find in his art a deeper and more positive awareness of human reality and potentialities than we could arrive at unaided. In this, certainly, is Chaucer a 'great analyst', and his art provides a discipline of emotive understanding for us by which we can develop our capacities to deal with life. His poetry can be for those who respond to it a great source of succour, in our inevitable quest for greater inward order, and for greater understanding of the reality of human life.

THREE

Love and Continuity in *The Winter's Tale*

The Winter's Tale seems to me the play of Shakespeare's which is least of all commonly understood. Take for instance this typical notice from *The Times Educational Supplement*:

Shakespearian Panto

The Winter's Tale is jerry built: at every point come such sad shorings-up as the Time chorus that opens Act Four, or Antigonus's notorious bear; even the structural foundation, Leontes's jealousy, is laid down with the comically slapdash haste of an early movie. And besides being jerry-built, it is as much of a stylistic hodge-podge as a Stanmore 'superior residence': some Sicilian melodrama, some knockabout, some pastoral. In production the only thing to do with this play is to accept it for what it is, not try and square it off neatly (as scholars have found to their sorrow, that is pretty impossible anyway).

Times Educational Supplement, 6th January 1961

Our failure to understand the meaning of this play is perhaps due to our inability to see that it is a special form of poetic drama. The kind of comment on experience which Shakespeare sets out to make in *The Winter's Tale* requires a formal balletic structure, and a close collaboration with music. It differs in form from what has gone before, from the great tragedies, as Beethoven's string quartets differ from the late piano sonatas. A new dimension had to be entered to find a different perspective, and a new medium for a particular kind of experience. The form itself is an expression of Shakespeare's assertion of continuity, and this requires a ritual form to convey the greater-than-personal significance of 'the going on of life'. The musical dance-like form itself virtually embodies recreativity as a principle of the universe in which humanity itself lives and creates.

If we can understand what Shakespeare is saying in this last play we may add a great deal to our confidence in feeling that inward personal order and love are the bases of stability in human society and evolution. But, furthermore, we may be brought to accept that improvement in these is obtainable, by the very disciplines of imagination such as Shakespeare embodies in this poetic drama. That is, our attitudes are not changed intellectually – they are re-organized, at the intuitive level, by the constructive art experience which the play is. Of course, for this, we need to be able to respond to it, as the writer in the *Times Educational Supplement* was not.

In order that I may discuss the poetic and balletic themes without being preoccupied with the plot in detail later, perhaps it may be as well to tell the story of the play first.

THE STORY OF THE PLAY

The Winter's Tale is about families and generations, concerning Leontes, the King of Sicilia, his Queen, his son and his daughter; and Polixenes, the King of Bohemia, and his son. The kings have been friends since childhood, and have a 'rooted' affection between them. At the beginning of the play Leontes and Queen Hermione have a young prince, Mamillius, who is of 'great promise' to Sicilia, while the Queen herself is pregnant.

When the play opens, Polixenes is the guest of Leontes and Hermione. Suddenly, as Hermione is pressing Polixenes to stay a while longer in Sicilia, Leontes is seized with an inexplicable passion of jealousy: astonishingly enough it is a discussion of youthful innocence in love which seems to provoke it. Leontes suspects Mamillius of being the child of Polixenes and Hermione. He discusses his suspicions with Camillo, a Lord of Sicilia, a wise and considerate man. In their discussion it becomes plain that the king's reason is quite unbalanced by the way he has abandoned himself to what we would nowadays call hostile unconscious promptings. He falls into the grip of a predatory and destructive envy. Camillo – a statesman – calls it '*diseased* opinion'; Leontes in reply merely abuses him as a 'gross lout' – and while Leontes raves in increasingly emotional language, and employs the invective of the street, his counsellors appear by contrast increasingly reasonable, self-effacing, in deference to traditionally established curbs on human extravagance.

Camillo is commanded by Leontes to kill Polixenes: the courtier is baffled. He goes to Polixenes and reveals that he has been sent to kill him: and tells him why. Polixenes replies by the most extreme denial, swearing he should be linked with Judas, if it were true that he had betrayed his friend:

> Oh then, my best blood turn
> To an infected jelly, and my name
> Be yok'd with his, that did betray the Best . . .
>
> (*Act I, Sc. ii, l.* 417)

Polixenes and Camillo flee in Polixenes' ships. This but confirms Leontes in his suspicions, and he publicly indites Hermione with her 'crime': 'She's an adulteress,' he cries. 'Away with her to prison.' The lords, including Antigonus, a particularly astute courtier, protest, but are told to hold their peace. Leontes despatches to the oracle of Apollo at Delphos for spiritual sanctions for his prosecution of Hermione.

Antigonus' wife, Paulina, who has the traditional loyalty and wisdom of the ancient court family, energetically opposes Leontes' intentions, which, she says, spring from 'fancies as weak as boys'. Hermione has by now been delivered of a daughter in prison, and Paulina takes the new-born child from the gaol and places it before Leontes. Leontes orders it to be consumed with fire, but when the court protests vehemently against this, he commands Antigonus to take the babe to some distant shore and leave it. Antigonus leaves with the child, crying, 'Poor thing, condemned to loss'.

Hermione is tried before the Court, and protests her innocence. The envoys return from the oracle and proclaim:

> *Hermione is chaste; Polixenes blameless,*
> *Camillo a true subject; Leontes a jealous*
> *tyrant, his innocent babe truly begotten;*
> *and the King shall live without an Heir,*
> *if that which is lost be not found.*
>
> (*Act III, Sc. ii, l.* 133)

But Leontes persists in his misrepresentation of reality and cries 'this is mere falsehood'; he orders the trial to proceed. At that moment a servant enters to tell him that Mamillius, who has pined since Leontes accused his mother, is dead. Hermione swoons, and is removed by Paulina.

Leontes suddenly repents, proclaims Camillo's innocence and admits his own guilty intention to poison Polixenes. Paulina enters, however, to tell him that the queen,

> The sweet'st dear'st creature's dead: and vengeance for't
> Not dropp'd down yet.
>
> (*Act III, Sc. ii*)

Leontes in sorrow withdraws to mourn and to a discipline of repentance.

In a brief scene Antigonus lays down the child in the deserts of Bohemia and is killed by a bear. (With total disregard for geographical fact Shakespeare makes Bohemia a country with a sea coast.) The baby Perdita is then taken up by a Shepherd and a Clown, representatives of that raw natural human life and reality of which Lear cried, 'Oh, I have ta'en too little care of this'. The Shepherd, with Chaucer-like realism, takes the child to be a consequence of seduction, a 'natural' abandoned by its mother. His son then brings the terrible news of Antigonus' death, which he relates in a clowning way.

'Time' then marks with a speech the passage of sixteen years, and the second part of the play opens in Polixenes' palace in Bohemia. Polixenes and Camillo are discussing the unhappy past. Camillo wishes to return to his master, now cleared by penitence, but Polixenes restrains him. They discuss the behaviour of his son, Florizel, and relate how he is frequenting a shepherd's house. We are brought at once into another problem of the King's concern with his children as his successors:

> Kings are no less unhappy, their issue not being
> gracious, than they are in losing them, when they
> have approved their virtues.
>
> (*Act IV, Sc. ii, l. 29*)

Polixenes and Camillo disguise themselves and go off to the shepherd's house.

The 'cony-catching rogue' Autolycus now enters, singing of spring, of stealing linen, and of loose women. He cheats the Clown of his purse by pretending to be wounded and robbed (by Autolycus!). There follows the Shepherd's festival, at which the love of Perdita and Florizel is seen to be of an innocent strength which makes all the deformed passion, and the bitter irony, of the first section of the play appear aberrant by contrast.

Perdita is dressed as Flora and distributes flowers: although the actual season is 'on the birth of trembling winter', the spring and May festivals are strongly evoked by the imagery – the spring for which Perdita yearns: 'I would I had some flowers o' th' spring...' There is a dance, and then Polixenes and Camillo begin to question the Shepherd about Florizel (who is disguised as 'Doricles') and about Perdita. Autolycus comes in and sings ballads and sells trash from his pedlar's pack, and 'picks and cuts most of their festival purses'.

Polixenes and Camillo question Florizel about his affection for Perdita, and about his regard for his father – has he told his father of the attachment? Florizel, who has abandoned himself to his feelings as much as did Leontes in the early part of the play, says his father shall not know of the business. Polixenes discloses himself and denounces Florizel, the Shepherd, and Perdita, promising them punishment for 'drawing our throne into a sheep-cote'.

Camillo advises Florizel to wait until his father's temper has subsided, but Florizel continues to follow his love's 'fancy' rather than his 'reason'. The young prince declares he will fly to sea. Camillo advises him to make for Sicilia and marry Perdita at Leontes' court. They meet Autolycus, and Florizel exchanges garments with the 'pedlar'. Camillo reveals his intention to tell the King, Polixenes, to bring him to Sicilia too. There follows an ironic-comic scene between Autolycus, in the Prince's clothing, the Clown and the Shepherd. The Shepherd and Clown are on their way to the court to tell of Perdita's extraordinary discovery as a baby, carrying with them the gold and papers. Autolycus tells them of the fearful fate in store for them at the court, and by various such tricks secures these pieces of evidence. He promises to take the Shepherd and Clown to the King but privately intends to seek advancement by handing the Shepherd and Clown over to Florizel, and to keep the gold.

We return to Sicilia to find Leontes still sorrowing over the terrible past. His courtiers are trying to persuade him to marry because of their fear of a failure of issue. Paulina draws the court's attention to the oracle. Florizel arrives suddenly, and introduces Perdita to Leontes. Polixenes is announced, having arrived as suddenly in pursuit. Leontes promises that he will intercede with Florizel's father, since, the prince's honour not having been o'er-thrown by his desires, 'I am friend to them, and you'.

We then hear (Act V, Sc. ii) indirectly from a conversation between Autolycus and a gentleman of the revelations of the Shepherd and Clown, the astonishment of Camillo and Leontes, and the general recognition and joy while the shepherd stands there like the 'weather bitten conduit of many kings' reigns'. Next we hear of a statue of Hermione which Paulina keeps, 'many years in making', and which Perdita wishes to see.

In the final scene all are present at the unveiling of the statue, which proves to be Hermione herself, not dead, but come forth from hiding. She has lived with Paulina in secret until the oracle should be fulfilled. She is brought to life by music, symbolic of renewed life and harmony. Paulina marries Camillo, and all are united and reunited.

This is the complex and rather fragmentary story of the play: it is only given an artistic wholeness of meaning by the deeper themes, which to discover we must examine in relation to the poetry and its local texture.

A close comparison of this play with Greene's *Pandosto: the Triumph of Time*, the story from which it was taken, reveals something of the nature of Shakespeare's purpose. Some of the larger departures from Greene's story show significant alterations. The most striking change is that Shakespeare brings Hermione back to life after sixteen years. Pandosto in Greene's story (Leontes in Shakespeare's) kills himself from remorse at the end – in Shakespeare's play Leontes is restored to his queen. And we have the addition in Shakespeare's play of the characters Paulina, Antigonus her husband and Autolycus the cony-catching rogue. And we have the bear.

It will not do to merely regard these additional characters and episodes as necessary simply to suit the altered plot: Paulina, say, to engineer Hermione's re-appearance, Antinonus to provide mere sensational stage business, 'exit pursued by a bear'. Why, for instance, does Shakespeare not allow the baby to be reported as put afloat in a cock-boat as it is in Greene? – a question which draws our attention to the significance of the Clown's and the Shepherd's dialogue in Act III, Scene iii. Autolycus is not here merely to give 'comic relief'. As we know from, say, the grave-digger in *Hamlet* or the Porter in *Macbeth*, the 'comics' in Shakespeare's plays usually have a serious relevance to the main poetic theme. A related point – which will become more signifi-cant as we examine the relation between *A Winter's Tale* and folk drama – is that clowning and buffoonery were always associated in ritual with death, and that there are ritual elements in this play. This draws our attention to the reference to 'Whitsun festivals' that enact the renewing of the seasons. In the *Second Shepherd's Play* from the Towneley cycle, which also has ritual elements, Mak, the sheepstealer, who is caught with the stolen sheep, is *not* hung, but tossed in a blanket in lieu. Folk mummers' dances enact beheading by sword-locks and comic mimes. In Shakespeare's later plays the clowning is not sheer fun, but (as with the fool in *King Lear*) an integral part of the contemplation of the nature of human existence. Shakespeare's play takes a more positive direc-tion than Greene's tale, and a more comic direction, towards an irony which is not bitter, but generously humane, and leads to-wards acceptance and the celebration of continuity. The theme of seasonal renewal associates with that of human renewal. The restoration of Hermione and the redemption of Leontes are ex-pressions of great confidence in continuity, reparation and the good in human nature. What is symbolized by Perdita, is, as I have suggested (pp. 67–8 above), of deep psychic significance – the infant 'malicious object' hated, denied as 'lost', and then found again. Hermione is 'the good object' – the mother – restored. Now we begin to see that the play only makes sense at the level of deep inward truth.

In the first scene we learn we are in Sicilia, that the King of

Bohemia has been 'rarely' and 'magnificently' entertained (in Sicilia), and that he intends to visit Bohemia later. But there is (says Archidamus) a great difference between Bohemia and Sicilia, and behind his apology for their inability to be as 'rare' and lavish as Sicilia there lurks (because of his inarticulateness and his 'understanding' and 'honesty') an indication of a real difference – 'sleepy drinks' ... 'your senses (unintelligent) ...' To some extent Bohemia represents the simple, more natural, intuitive bodily life: Sicilia the life of the civilized – or cultivated – mind. We also learn that Sicilia derives great comfort from the King's heir, Prince Mamillius 'a gentleman of the greatest promise' – an 'unspeakable comfort', and of the affection between the Kings of the two countries.

This is the explicit information conveyed to the audience. Implicitly, by the nature of the imagery and the language used, the main poetic themes are struck. We may consider, for instance the preponderance of the imagery of nature to express the quality of the affection between Leontes and Polixenes. And we note, too, the way *time* is first introduced in *The Winter's Tale* by the phrase 'this coming summer'. The affection between the kings is expressed thus by Camillo:

> there rooted betwixt them then such an affection,
> which cannot choose but branch now.
>
> (*Act I, Sc. i, l. 25*)

'Cannot choose' suggests a natural force outside themselves, which is enhanced by the making the relationship more universal by the suggested cosmic perspective:

> shook hands, as over a vast; and embrac'd as
> it were from the ends of opposed winds.
> The Heavens continue their loves.   (*Act I, Sc. i, l. 32*)

Archidamus' reply, 'I think there is not in the world either malice or matter to alter it', with its bringing 'world' against 'Heavens' at once suggests to the audience a tension of expectation of wanting to know 'what happens next?' 'The Heavens continue their loves' has an ambiguity – it may be an exhortation ('may the Heavens!') or it may be a statement of an inevitable development 'embraced as it were from the ends of opposed winds (*thus*) the Heavens continue their loves'.

The affectionate relationship on which our attention is focused is shown to be widely reverberant throughout the nature from which it has sprung: it 'cannot choose but branch now', as if forced by the power of a coming spring. Such a relationship has the power to conquer space and time. The large perspective establishes the large significance of the personal loyalties, and their relation to 'continuity' in natural life. (In the end it will be time and continuity which heal – as they heal the infant psyche of us all, and enable us to achieve sanity.)

The natural imagery of growth and continuance establishes the themes of time and generation. Young Prince Mamillius is 'promise', and has power to make 'old hearts fresh'.

CAMILLO: it is a gallant child, one that . . .
           makes old hearts fresh: they that went on crutches
           ere he was born, desire yet their life to see him
           a man . . .

                                    (*Act I, Sc. i, l.* 42)

There is promise in the continuance of the natural affection between Leontes and Polixenes, which conquers space (division in distance) and in the child Mamillius, who represents the hope that continuity will overcome time (division in generation). The play is to pursue relationships and the growth and maturing of human beings in the wide setting of space and time, and of the rhythmic patterns of nature – winter, spring, summer; birth, maturity, death, birth. As a dramatic poem it is an attempt to answer the question, how can man, in the larger perspectives of his mortal existence, come to be reconciled and resigned to his mortality, and yet maintain hope, a sense of significance, and a sense of continuity?

The next scene is a sudden belying of that 'I think there is not in the world, either malice or matter, to alter it'. There is indeed: all real existence is flawed and imperfect. Polixenes says he must depart: it is nine months since he left his Kingdom. Leontes fails to persuade him to stay longer, and asks Hermione to add her encouragements. She succeeds in persuading the visiting king to stay, and Leontes at once takes this to indicate that Polixenes has cuck-olded him. He is much distracted by this fit of jealousy, questions whether his son is his own, and orders Camillo to poison Polixenes. The energy of his unconscious envy destroys all normal patterns of relationship. Camillo, however, reveals the danger to Polixenes, urges him to flee Sicilia and to take him with him.

On the ground of the rendering of 'individual psychology', or on grounds of 'plot', this sudden development has been found to have little to commend it. Yet it merely enacts what we know (though we may seek to avoid recognizing it) – that the stability of any human being's make-up, or of any relationship, can be wrecked by an inward psychic earthquake, with surprising sud-denness, and *at any time*. But the development is so much faster and so much more unmotivated than in Greene's novel, that ob-viously in *The Winter's Tale* we have nothing of the nature of what any novel or mere tale offers us – the interest is not simply in 'portraying Leonte's degeneration', but in raising a central theme in the poetic organization. The whole play is a patterned dance, and Shakespeare is not interested in *why* Leontes becomes jealous, or in showing us the stages leading up to it. 'Why' he becomes jealous is simply that the human psyche-soma has such weaknesses and is liable to become dissociated, with little justifi-cation, from inevitable inner weaknesses. The poetic drama is compressed beyond the bounds of realistic narrative, as opera, masque, ballet and narrative music may be – to enact the contest with derangement rather than its cause. Rather than naturalism, we have something stylized, masque-like, here, as in *The Tempest* and *Cymbeline*. The whole form and mode of the play implies that we shall not overcome such instability as Leontes's by 'knowing the causes' – but by experiencing an apprehension of the larger rhythms of life, and resigning to its larger continuity, through a harmony brought by the poetic functions themselves. Through Leontes' jealousy and envy the poetic drama explores such themes as the innocence of childhood, the natural development of love, the accompanying complexities of controlling the sexual impulses within the moral pattern of life, and the acceptance of 'the lusts of the flesh' and their decay with age as part of the irrevocable make-up of the human being. The full force of conflicting emotions in the adult man is shown to be liable to swing out of control, for inner reasons. And as this happens he becomes unable to deal with reality – or even to see it as it is. He projects his hate over reality, and feeds his own illusion self-destructively, becoming, we might say, childish in the sense in which his capacities revert to early states before the capacity to deal with reality is developed.

Leontes is contrasted with himself as young, and with Mamillius: the child living and the child remembered in time are present in the scene as Innocence. The marrying of Leontes and Polixenes and their Queens is discussed as an aspect of mature experience. It is, strangely enough, Hermione's recalling of the youth of the two kings which makes effective her attempt to persuade Polixenes to stay, and it is from these themes and the presence of Mamillius that Leontes' fit of jealousy develops. The progress of his jealousy may be studied as a development of verse texture – the poetry itself, by an increase of pace, makes real to us the experience of a nervous illusion feeding on itself. Leontes loses control – his passion overbears reason, not because of truthfulness of vision, but because he is unable to accept reality, because of inner psychic dissociation. The complexities of sexual experience and the ravages of time he finds suddenly unacceptable.

The dramatic poem itself may be seen as part of Shakespeare's own searching after a mature acceptance of sexual reality – and to come to terms with the larger reality – in human life. Shakespeare recognizes that when we contemplate mortality in Time, as focused in fleshly reality, 'human kind can bear very little reality . . .' The poet himself obviously found such acceptance difficult to come by (as indeed we all do). We know this from *Timon*, *Hamlet* and the *Sonnets*, where Shakespeare wrestles with his fears of sex and mortal reality. Polixenes says, speaking of his own Florizel:

> He makes a July's day short as December,
> And with his varying childness, cures in me
> Thoughts that would thick my blood.
>
> (*Act I, Sc. ii, l.* 169)

In this there is an overbearing sense of time: the shortening of a

'July's day' is associated with the 'curing' thoughts – July and December suggest the passage of years, in contrast with both the long July's day and the short Midwinter one. It is the *thoughts* of time as well as the passage of time which would thicken Polixenes' blood. But Leontes' blood is already thickening in jealousy, and he is excluded from such a 'cure' as Polixenes has in Florizel: his contemplation of innocent youth only exacerbates his jealousy because of the possible adulterous origin of Mamillius and the consideration of *how long* he may have been a cuckold. His failure of his sense of reality, and his incapacity to 'bear' Time, are associated with paranoia and depressive attitudes – which will move on to destructiveness to seek relief. The jealousy (which seeks justification though there are no grounds in external evidence) is a means to externalize the terrible feelings of unconscious destructive envy which is both self-destructive and would deny all creativity. So, in the end, it attacks Perdita. To escape the inward torment Leontes stimulates his own jealousy by feeding illusion to illusion, and the normal interplay of reason, appearance and reality – in his thought processes – is dissociated. In presenting this process Shakespeare makes a deep psychological observation. The poet's 'placing' of Leontes is done by maintaining Polixenes, Camillo and the child as norms in the scene, while the developing pace of Leontes' jealousy may be seen by this focus as aberrant. Leontes' jealousy even goes so far in its sickness as to come to an utter rejection of human love and procreation in recoil, because they too are part of reality.

Hermione and Polixenes discuss the nature of normal sexual development within the pattern of moral values. The formal nature of these exchanges (their intricate formal exchanges on the word 'grace' for example) represents a contemplation of sexual truth, in an established moral order, going with a mature acceptance of mortal reality. Values – the good and the best in the moral order – are invoked by the balanced repetition of words such as 'innocence', and 'grace'. 'The heavens continue their loves', the 'promise' of Mamillius – on the continuation of these depend the stability of the kingdom, and whether or not they continue depends on such maturity and acceptance.

POLIXENES: We were, fair Queen,
                    Two lads, that thought there was no more behind,
                    But such a day tomorrow, as today,
                    And to be boy eternal . . .
                    We were as twinn'd lambs, that did frisk i' th' sun,
                    And bleat the one at th'other: what we chang'd,
                    Was innocence, for innocence: we knew not
                    The doctrine of ill-doing, nor dream'd
                    That any did: had we pursu'd that life
                    And our weak spirits ne'er been higher rear'd
                    With stronger blood, we should have answer'd Heaven
                    Boldly, not guilty; the imposition clear'd,
                    Hereditary ours.

                                        (*Act I, Sc. ii, l.* 62)

'Hereditary' means here heavenly hereditary – admission to Paradise. But the word also implies acceptance – by the overcoming of
guilt. The 'weak spirits' have been 'higher rear'd' with 'stronger
blood' – innocence of the child-like kind is impossible to maintain
in the grown man, and the 'imposition', original sin, is more difficult to 'clear'. 'Hereditary' may here be read in the sense of 'coming into one's own', into the birthright of gladly accepted adult
reality.

Hermione returns:

                                        By this we gather
                    You have tripped since . . .

and Polixenes speaks of 'temptations' in the shape of Hermione and
his own Queen. But such 'temptations' and 'offences' are sanctified
and sanctioned by marriage: that is, by coming to terms with the
realities of adult relationship, generation and social life:

HERMIONE: Of this make no conclusion, lest you say
                    Your Queen and I are Devils: yet go on,
                    The offences we have made you do, we'll answer,
                    If you first sinn'd with us: and that with us
                    You did continue fault; and that you slipp'd not
                    With any, but with us . . .

                                        (*Act I, Sc. ii, l.* 81)

Hermione's speeches here explore the sexual norm in marriage ('slipp'd' just gives a sufficient touch of the sensual reality of the flesh) but sanctified by grace, and given significance by mutual contract. The sexual importunity needs to be reconciled (as it could not be for Antony and Cleopatra) with bonds, and the claims of the world:

LEONTES: Three crabbed months had sour'd themselves to death
            Ere I could make thee open thy white hand:
            And clap thyself my love; then didst thou utter,
            I am your for ever.

HERMIONE: 'Tis grace indeed.

                          (*Act I, Sc. ii, l.* 102)

Within the sanctified state of marriage the sexual indulgence Hermione implies ('offences') yet has the energy of the gratification of lust, but the exigencies of civilized living must be as strong to effect a balance: this is made present enough to the senses in the verse by 'crabbed' and 'open white hand'. Within the social recognition of marriage, in love-relationship, the sexual reality can be as vigorous in its vitality as Hermione implies by her 'Your Queen and I *are Devils*' . . . 'the offences *we have made you do*'. The poetry is active under the surface with the imagery of physical love, even with the overtones of the sadism inherent in the normal relationship ('ride us'). Shakespeare is himself seeking to tolerate the sexual reality, to take into account its disturbing elements, and to discover its place in human life as a whole. D. H. Lawrence wrote *Lady Chatterley's Lover* in the same spirit, to seek to take in this 'whole' reality of bodily sexuality:

HERMIONE: cram's with praise, and make's
               As fat as tame things: one good deed, dying tongueless
               Slaughters a thousand, waiting upon that.
               Our praises are our wages. You may ride's
               With one soft kiss a thousand furlongs, ere
               With spur we heat an acre.

                          (*Act I, Sc. ii, l.* 91)

'Cram', 'fat', 'tongueless', 'ride us', 'soft kiss', 'spur', 'heat' – all these establish an apprehension of sexual life and appetite far from

'innocent'. Yet this robust 'temptation' is a joyful aspect of sanctioned relationship. The marriage service itself still contains the
attitude of the mediaeval church that celibacy is superior to marriage, in a quotation from St Paul which it includes. This implies
that marriage is a *faute de mieux*, because of human frailty: fornica-
tion must be provided against by the single union between man
and woman. This consideration lies behind the discussion here,
but also something even more real and vital which Shakespeare
has won out of his own fears and preoccupation with frailty – a
glad acceptance of the reality of bodily sex, such as we have seen
in the Wyf of Bath – bold and brave, more joyful, wholesome
and real than the Pauline attitude.

It is this very glad recognition of sexual wholeness which pro-
vokes Leontes' jealousy:

LEONTES: Too hot, too hot:
    To mingle friendship far, is mingling bloods.
    I have *tremor cordis* on me, my heart dances,
    But not for joy; not joy . . .
                    (*Act I, Sc. ii, l.* 109)

It is difficult for all of us at times and at stages to accept and
recognize sexual reality – the treacherous sensuality of the body –
because of fear, guilt and envy, and our reluctance to accept the
painful truth of mortal reality. In the verse of Leontes' speeches,
the language breaks away from the formal and gracious patterns
of those of Hermione and Polixenes, towards depressive and negative modes. Hermione's love-imagery is refined by delicate ambiguity – her speeches may be taken as formal conceits. The
physical vigour is there, but accepted into civilized terms, as desire
is redeemed by grace and the mutuality of relationship. When
Leontes speaks, however, the civilized mind and coarse feeling
are dissociated, and the grossly physical takes on the more
active life. Leontes' feelings about physical love remind us of those
strange obsessions of Shakespeare's own, to be noted at their worst
in *Timon* and *Hamlet* – as in the strange undercurrent of revulsion
in such phrases as 'paddling in your neck with his damned fingers'.

But Shakespeare's restless pursuit of these areas of disturbance represents something akin to courageous self-analysis. Around his horror of sexual frailty gathered his preoccupation with the question, What, then, is real? Such an awareness as Shakespeare's obviously deepens with the development of his own maturity and its insights. His deeply personal sense of what Time, the approach of death, the treachery of bodily life, and his own frailty as a man could do to destroy love as a source of significance in life, and as an ernest of hope and reality, is seen in the *Sonnets*. The later plays which come after the tragedies – *Timon of Athens* and *Troilus and Cressida* – though they are not altogether without control, seem to shew a dread, and an almost uncontrollable awareness of the forces of treachery, destruction and corruption in human life. *Timon* in particular seems unrelieved by the triumphant positive belief in goodness and continuity which informs the tragedies. Greed and lust are appallingly brought to the sense in that play: the play is heavy with images of disease and corruption, and these seem to express a revolt from sexual potentialities. The elements of destructive envy seem at times in those plays to be in Shakespeare himself, as much as they are later 'placed' in Leontes: his energy almost turns against life itself (as did Swift's). The verse conveys the poet's despair and depressive attitudes as if they were 'his' as much as Timon's:

> TIMON: Destruction fang mankind . . .
> This yellow slave
> Will knit and break religions: bless the accursed;
> Make the hoar leprosy ador'd . . .
>   this is it
> That makes the wappen'd widow wed again;
> She whom the spital-house and ulcerous sores
> Would cast the gorge at, this embalms and spices
> To the April day again . . .

Timon perhaps represents a point at which the frail and mortal nature of man, and perhaps the whole of worldly reality, seemed almost unacceptable to Shakespeare – too dreadful and treacherous ever to bring to hopeful order. The disgust is too strong to control: he cannot accept the bad in himself and others. *Lear* would seem to have been the crucial turning point, towards acceptance, peace, inward order, and a belief in love and continuity. 'Who is it that can tell me who I am?' is answered by what Lear perceives of the good in himself and humanity, and the play ends triumphantly with the resigned and bare recognition, 'as I am a man . . .'.

The later plays *The Tempest* and *The Winter's Tale* achieve and express a calmer and even more hopeful balance by their new, masque-like, formal modes which themselves *enact* the larger pattern and perspectives of life's continuity, as with the seasonal modes of the play under discussion. These plays dance and en-masque resignation and hopefulness. Behind the confidence of their formation is the depth of Shakespeare's self-knowledge, insight, and resignation as attained in *King Lear*. The simple innocence at the end of *Lear* is one attained by leaving nothing unstripped by King Lear's self-awareness attained by the violence of his purgatory: 'I am a very foolish fond old man . . .'. This self-knowledge also marks the poet's acceptance of human reality and the tragic conditions of human life – and his discovery of love as a reality which triumphs over these. The quest Shakespeare made in *Lear*, and its successful outcome, enables him to render the innocence of Miranda and Ferdinand, and Florizel and Perdita, without irony. For we are beyond irony with Miranda's innocent cry, 'O brave new world . . .' – even though we ourselves may take this as profoundly ironical, it is a deeply positive innocence, too. Each of the last plays consolidates this 'brave' affirmation of the continuity of life, as in the young lovers.

This achievement of this affirmation is thus beyond 'realism' – the mere acceptance of the real, of sex or human nature. Shakespeare's task is no longer to explore the reality but to celebrate the affirmation that transcends. He celebrates the values of human bonds, and love, as more real than the imperfect and treacherous reality of the fleshy existence. He chose to consolidate this celebration by the later masque-like plays which enact positive patterns, as of those values and perceptions of significance he has discovered and possessed. It is significant that the later plays are more formal, more symbolic, taking the masque-like forms, of rhythm and pattern as of a dance: for perhaps Shakespeare's profoundest observation is that in order to achieve order we must be changed, by the growth of our personalities, at the intuitive, bodily level. As in infancy, we have to painfully accept the real, but the way to do so, and gain positive hold on life, is by learning to love, and by the experience of a continuity of triumphant and complete experiences. It is this that these masque-like plays *give* us, in a deeply felt way, by poetry and music that enhance our viability. Our effective living is based, as with Leontes, on harmony in the psyche-soma. We experience the torment of hate and despair: then the reparative processes. This is why Shakespeare uses music more and more and makes his poetic art more formal, because music directly affects the nervous system, the depths of the unknown self, and brings order there. The *art* can actually change us, establish in us the joyful reparative feeling, and reinforce our life-seeking impulses. The unveiling of Hermione's statue is a symbol of this power of art to bring renewed life. So in their close relation to the rhythms of nature these later plays embody a deep apprehension of the nature of the natural world and of human nature, and creative processes in these. There is a good deal in the later plays which draws on the 'unconscious' intuitive culture of the rural community – mummings and ceremonies which express its awareness of the seasons, its stoicism and tolerance of suffering and mishap, and its energy of reparative celebration. This provision for the psychesoma was embodied in ritual and folksong, in which were enacted the natural processes of re-creation. But in Shakespeare's work the *acceptance* and resignation are essentially those of an individual soul which has passed through its own purgatory, to find its own personal reality, which is in turn offered for our possession through the works of art. At the centre of his development is Shakespeare's need to accept the reality of human life, not least the reality of its treacherous sexuality, and to explore and define that triumphant reality of love which can offer stability generation to generation. These are our primary needs, too, and by possessing his art we may possess a great imaginative inheritance that can help save us from the disorder such as in himself he courageously approached and confronted with his immense apprehension and vitality. Shakespeare loved life and human life too deeply and capaciously to be willing to accept that it could ever go under or cease: we seem at times today by contrast almost obsessed with self-destruction, because we are unable to find his kind of 'belief in the continuity of life'. In this he has a great contribution to our search for an understanding of reality, and our quest for love, in the modern world.

The distancing into more formal art in the later plays is symbolized in *The Tempest* by the figure of Prospero, in whom there is an obvious relation to Shakespeare himself – the creator of worlds and one who exerts the magical powers of imagination, insight, and moral purpose, to promote belief in continuity. In *The Winter's Tale* there is a personal clue in the story told by Mamillius from which the title is taken:

MAMILLIUS: A sad Tale's best for winter:
            I have one of sprites and goblins . . .
            There was a man,
            Dwelt by a church yard . . .
            (*Enter Leontes*)
                      (*Act II, Sc. i, l.* 24)

'Winter' has an ambiguity – it is Shakespeare's own life's approaching winter, the winter of the 'bare ruin'd choirs' and of 'rosemary and rue, these keep seeming and savour all the winter long'. The poet in later maturity finds he can accept the patterns of human experience which have gathered in his memory, keeping their 'seeming' and 'savour'. In memory are the patterns of resignation, love, reparation, and the sense of continuity established, as they are in the experience of the infant. In this we may see the truth in another way of '*dans ma fin est ma commencement*' – there is a real connection between that belief in the continuity of life that triumphs over death, and the experience of continuity in the infant that enables him to mature. It is no accident that the play contains old men and babies. The title *The Winter's Tale* is offered in the same spirit as the sonnet:

    That time of year thou mayst in me behold
    When yellow leaves or none or few do hang
    Upon those boughs which shake against the cold
    Bare ruin'd choirs, where late the sweet birds sang . . .

– the play is in one sense bare and autumnal (stark and cruel), but yet calm and full of spring, too ('promise'). The play is a piece of work written in reflective maturity – and it has behind it the apprehension of the profoundest horrors of lust, decay and sexual treachery of the later sonnets, the tragedies, and the plays between these and the final masque-like dramas. But it comes from the peaceful state, well advanced in the quest for truth, and knowing, in hopefulness, that life will go on, and glad of it.

To return to Hermione's speech. 'As fat as tame things' evokes a feeling of physical disturbance, even at a deep level, touching on our fear of the vulnerability of the naked body in sexual love. But the wit of the phrase digests and assuages the fear and bravely comes to terms with it. We experience in the conflict a force of bitter irony, and the poet's mature attempt to control and place that bitterness. Shakespeare himself, we know, had experienced the treachery of betrayed affection (if we are to believe *The Sonnets* have their origin in actual events), and this never ceased to be a major preoccupation with him: he knows personal treachery to the bone. So Leontes' irony has powerful authenticity behind it:

> This entertainment
> *May* a free face put on: derive a liberty
> From heartiness, from bounty, fertile bosom,
> And well become the agent: 't *may*; I grant . . .
> (*Act I, Sc. ii, l.* 111)

This is to answer with bitter cynicism a protest such as the audience – or Camillo, with his balanced understanding – might make, that human nature should be given the benefit of the doubt. And beside it – 'placed' – can be seen Leontes' self-irritation, which mounts by dwelling on trivialities in a wilfully self-destructive way under the destructive force of envy, as the verse 'breaks down' in rhythm and texture. The texture enacts his loss of control, by the spitting alliteration and the nervous movement:

> But to be paddling palms, and pinching fingers
> As they now are, and making practis'd smiles
> As in a looking-glass; and then to sigh as 'twere
> The mort o' th' deer:
> (*Act I, Sc. ii, l.* 116)

'That way madness lies' – this the audience or the reader can see, from the nervous consonantal thickening of the verse's texture and rhythm. This reality must be taken into account by the reader too: the word 'paddling' here (as in *Hamlet*) has a flavour of revulsion from manual sexual play. Leontes is driven by destructive envy, by a jealousy which is infantile in the sense both that it marks the inability to accept adult sexuality, and takes total possession of the man's energy and being. Yet he rationalizes this childishness by dwelling on his obsessive preoccupation with the treacherous element in human nature, thus give an external 'justification' for his inward breakdown. The sound and texture of the verse gives us possession of this experience – we feel how in such states the ability to reason and be balanced (to 'derive a liberty from heartiness') desert Leontes altogether – the language becomes thickened, coarse and inchoate, consonantal, and its rhythm angry, subject to the flux of angry sense-feelings. Sensual imagery of coition is mingled with disgust powerfully under the surface:

> Inch-thick, knee-deep; o'er head and ears a fork'd one . . .
> (*Act I, Sc. ii, l.* 187)

– the imagery and oral energy of disgust spreads over Leontes' reasoning ability with such force that we feel it to be the contemplation of one given to *thinking* in his own *dream-images*. He has said (of 'affection'):

> Affection! thy intention stabs the centre:
> Thou dost make possible things not so held,
> Communicat'st with dreams, (how can this be?)
> With what's unreal: thou co-active art
> And fellow'st nothing. Then 'tis very credent,
> Thou may'st co-join with something and thou dost,
> (And that beyond commission) and I find it,
> (And that to the infection of my brains,
> And hardening of my brows).
> (*Act I, Sc. ii, l.* 139)

This statement of disembodied dreams which touch no reality ('fellow'st nothing') is an exact comment on Leontes' mind. The speech is inarticulate, and the reasoning power (by 'the infection

of my brains') is broken down as if envy eats into the mind itself.
Yet the verse also states such truths as we have explored about the
relationship between 'affection' and the reality-sense.

But Leontes is depressive, and wilfully lingers on each item of
physical disgust that chafes and unbalances.

Sully

The purity and whiteness of my sheets
(Which to preserve, is sleep; which being spotted
Is goads, thorns, nettles, tails of wasps).

(*Act I, Sc. ii, l.* 329)

That penetrating irony which underlies the poet's contemplation
of sex, marriage and human bonds, stripping man to 'a bare fork'd
animal' as in *Lear*, takes on its own caricature in Leontes. Leontes
takes his visions for reality, because they affect him physically (as
'*tremor cordans*'):

And many a man there is (even at this present,
Now, while I speak this) holds his wife by th' arm
That little thinks she has been sluic'd in's absence,
And his pond fish'd by his next neighbour (by
Sir Smile, his neighbour).

(*Act I, Sc. ii, l.* 190)

Here the figure of Leontes directs his sickening attitude to sexual
reality at the audience before the stage: the intense dramatic irony
in the theatre embodies Shakespeare's deep troubled awareness at
man's imperfection every time the play is performed. But even as
we enter into this ironic contemplation of life, which is the poet's,
we see Leontes' state as very much a self-stimulated rage – and so
this is presented to us ironically, too, and placed, or 'held away'.
Irony about 'reality' – if it is obsessive – can become a hallucination, too. And we (like Camillo) become aware of the dangers of
this lack of control, consequent upon the refusal – weak and psychopathological as it is – to come to terms with reality. Even
Leontes' contemplation of his own innocent child results not (as
does Polixenes') in 'cure' but in a dangerous tendency to identify:

How sometimes Nature will betray its folly?
Its tenderness? and make itself a pastime
To harder bosoms? Looking on the lines

Of my boy's face, methoughts I did recoil
Twenty-three years, and saw myself unbreech'd,
In my green velvet coat; my dagger muzzl'd
Lest it should bite its master, and so prove
(As ornaments oft do) too dangerous: :
How like (methought) I then was to this kernel
This squash, this gentleman.

(Act I, Sc. ii, l. 152)

– 'makes itself a pastime to harder bosoms' – nature's 'folly' – to
dwell as he does on these is not to seek to 'cure' thoughts that
would 'thick my blood', but rather the opposite. Leontes wilfully
seeks to provoke his own derangement by pursuing depressive
attitudes to the loss of innocence (Cf. 'bite', 'too dangerous'). His
blood is 'thickening' not by the contemplation of the reality of
time, but by morbid obsession, in the absence of sufficient power
to tolerate that reality. His is a 'flight to reality' from inner torment that is unbearable. 'Lest it should bite its master', 'too dangerous' reveal a *fear* that the innocent state is passed: the phallus to
which he obliquely refers is, in the man, a threat that needs be
'muzzl'd'. Hermione and Polixenes have discussed this passing of
innocence as inevitable and acceptable, governable, even as 'tame
fat things' – even as the strange sexual organs themselves can be
governed by civilized use in the sanctioned mutual love-
relationship.

Shakespeare's ironic presentation of Leontes continues with the
King's conversation with Camillo. Camillo has said in the first
scene, 'there rooted between them such an affection which cannot
choose but branch now. . . .' 'The Heavens continue their loves',
Camillo prays, and we are to take this courtier by contrast with
his king as the normal, just, civilized man. ('You pay a great deal
too dear for what's given freely', he says, of mutual friendship.)
In dialogue with him Leontes reveals his own self-deceit, his envious unreason, and its reality-denying dangers. He searches for
evidence: 'Didst note it?', 'Didst perceive it?', 'How came't
Camillo, that he did stay?', 'Lower messes perchance are to this
business purblind? Say?' But he will take a mere word out of
context as 'evidence':

CAMILLO: . . . Bohemia stays here longer.
LEONTES: Ay, but why?
CAMILLO: To satisfy your Highness, and the entreaties
         Of our most gracious Mistress.
LEONTES: Satisfy?
         Th' entreaties of your Mistress? Satisfy?
                              (*Act I, Sc. ii, l.* 232)

In 'satisfy' he imagines he has a hint of calumny – the word is
used by others in its sexual sense – and Leontes runs away with its
physical sense, not its courtesy value, meaning 'clear by proof'. In
a similar way he produces an argument that Camillo is dishonest
which (in its emotional nature) contrasts strongly with the humility and good sense of the courtier. Camillo's verse enacts his
qualities by the movement itself – steady, calm, polite, assured;
they are those of a balanced man's considered declaration:

CAMILLO: My gracious lord,
         I may be negligent, foolish, and fearful;
         In every one of these, no man is free,
         But that his negligence, his folly, fear,
         Among the infinite doings of the World,
         Sometime puts forth in your affairs, my Lord.
         If ever I were wilful-negligent,
         It was my folly: if industriously
         I play'd the fool, it was my negligence,
         Not weighing well the end: if ever fearful
         To do a thing, where I the issue doubted,
         Whereof the execution did cry out
         Against the non-performance, 'twas a fear
         Which oft infects the wisest . . .
                              (*Act I, Sc. ii, l.* 249)

This verse, by its balanced antithetical movement, enacts as well
as states the capacity for insight and self-knowledge of the self-
possessed man who accepts his (and human) limitations as Leontes
no longer can. In its character the verse may be compared with the
exchange in Macbeth between Macduff and Malcolm (*Macbeth*,
Act IV, Sc. iii). What follows (Camillo's 'offence') is sufficiently
'placed' by these lines. From Camillo's standpoint we may watch

how fear bred from envy may 'infect the wisest'. Leontes' processes of argument indeed cannot be called 'reasoning' at all – hallucination fed by sensational feeling gains the upper hand, and Leontes deceives himself further and further as to the nature of reality. The rhythm and movement, again by contrast, are that of a man unbalanced. And his statement is so unconsidered it had better never been made (later we shall see Leontes' remorse and penance for the consequences of such outbursts).[1]

LEONTES: Ha' not you seen, Camillo?
   (But that's past doubt: you have, or your eye-glass
   Is thicker than a cuckold's horn) or heard?
   (For to a vision so apparent, rumour
   Cannot be mute) or thought? (for cogitation
   Resides not in that man, that does not think)
   My wife is slippery? If thou wilt confess,
   Or else be impudently negative,
   To have nor eyes, nor ears, nor thought, then say
   My wife's a hobby-horse, deserves a name
   As rank as any flax-wench, that puts to
   Before her troth-plight: say't, and justify't.
        (Act I, Sc. ii, l. 267)

Leontes' speech, while the imagery has a life of its own, reverts from the formal 'court' language of Camillo ('whereof the execution did cry out against the non-performance') to the crudely emotive language of the London street (or Nashe's journalism) –

---

[1] During this scene there is a progress of distrust, in imagery which would seem to lead to a bitter rejection of life. But this is in fact controlled by the distanced realization of Leontes as being in a state of soul which we understand, but see as a *dangerous* tendency towards rejection, which Shakespeare is seeking, because of his own psychic needs, to 'place' as 'sick'. The flavour of the poetry moves rapidly from the innocence of 'twin'd lambs' and Hermione's soft tactile imagery, to Leontes' verse which progresses rapidly from distasteful imagery of lust ('Virginalling on his palm') to imagery of disgust and disease, and recoil as from dead things. Shakespeare is portraying this progress as in one moving towards a diseased state of mind. As F. C. Tinkler noted in his essay in *Scrutiny*, the play is full of disease imagery:
'Many thousands on's have the disease . . . purblind . . . diseased opinion . . . hoxes honesty behind . . . blind with the pin and web . . . a savour that may strike the dullest nostril . . . the greatest infection that was heard or read . . . my best blood turn to an infected jelly . . . distemper', etc.

'slippery', 'hobby-horse', 'any flax-wench that puts to'. And though he adds a colouring of apparent reasoning ('for cogitation resides not in that man that does not think' – surely as ironically intended as some of Holofernes' euphuistic language?) – it demonstrates, for all Leontes' protests, a complete absence of anything that can be called 'reason'. What he virtually says is that '*If you haven't seen heard or thought my wife is slippery (for you must have) then you have no eyes, ears, or thought: if you say no, then it's impudence. Unless you're prepared to say you have no eyes, ears or thought, then say she's an adulteress.*' This is of course unanswerable, since it leaves room for no answer. And the evidence?

> wishing clocks more swift?
> Hours, minutes? noon, midnight? and all eyes
> Blind with the pin and web, but theirs; theirs only,
> That would unseen be wicked? Is this nothing?
> (*Act I, Sc. ii, l.* 289)

Leontes has come to confuse subjective and objective reality, by feeding his hallucination with the feelings of jealousy. 'Wishing clocks more swift/Hours, minutes? noon, midnight?' is hardly anything that could be *known of someone else*: as evidence it is 'nothing' – mere projections of his paranoia. He is really taking his own projected phantasies as evidence of his senses, attributing to others the hostile disturbances and impulses in himself. The character of Leontes is a poetic embodiment of destructive envy, as Shakespeare perceived it to exist in human nature, with its concomitant disrupted states of feeling and behaviour.

Camillo styles the King's attitude to his face as dangerous. Leontes in reply pronounces him (ironically enough) a '*mindless slave*' and a '*hovering temporizer*'. Leontes retains his illusion now by abusing others and their good counsel, 'You're liars all!' But when pressed Camillo finds he is bound by the bond of allegiance to agree to 'fetch off' Polixenes, on these grounds:

> Provided, that when he's remov'd, your Highness
> Will take again your Queen, as yours at first,
> Even for your son's sake, and thereby for sealing

> The injury of tongues, in Courts and Kingdoms
> Known, and allied to yours.
>
> *(Act I, Sc. ii, l. 335)*

Alone, Camillo describes Leontes as 'one in rebellion with himself', and is in despair, that the stalemate of being ordered to strike 'anointed Kings', when he could never do such a thing, is a 'breakneck'. He chooses to accept the order because he cannot *not* obey – cannot but serve the kingdom, because he is a loyal subject. Herein he counts his own life not worth a straw: the verse is full of contradictory impulse, as is much of Macbeth's in the battle scenes – but here the evil is struggling against the dominant 'good' conscience. The only way out is voluntary exile:

> if I could find example
> Of thousands that had struck anointed Kings,
> And flourish'd after, I'd not do 't: but since
> Nor brass, nor stone, nor parchment bears not one,
> Let villainy itself forswear 't. I must
> Forsake the Court: to do 't, or no, is certain
> To me a break-neck.
>
> *(Act I, Sc. iii, l. 357)*

Leontes, however much 'in rebellion with himself', *is* an 'anointed King' – and so is Polixenes. Leontes 'rebellion' with himself has universal reverberances and Camillo is but the first to find the consequences a break-neck: there is no way out but to withdraw. The personal psychopathology has now led to conscious action – preparation for murder – of a king and brother. As in *King Lear*, dissociation in the psyche inevitably brings moral destruction at large in its wake.

With Polixenes' entrance the language regains its formal court manner from which only Leontes has as yet departed into incoherence and disorder:

> I conjure thee, by all the parts of man,
> Which Honour does acknowledge, whereof the least
> Is not this suit of mine . . .
>
> *(Act I, Sc. ii, l. 400)*

The formality itself conveys that code of relationships, that 'honour', those values in human affairs by which alone can Camillo and Polixenes save themselves.

Of the duplicity Leontes attributes to him Polixenes swears innocence in the name of Christ:

> Oh then, my best blood turn
> To an infected jelly, and my name
> Be yok'd with his, that did betray the Best:
> (*Act I, Sc. ii, l.* 417)

Leontes' psychic disbalance is a real enough obstacle to order, throughout the universe as well as in the Kingdom:

> You may as well
> Forbid the sea for to obey the Moon,
> As (or by oath) remove, or (counsel) shake
> The fabric of his folly, whose foundation
> Is pil'd upon his faith, and will continue
> The standing of his body.
> (*Act I, Sc. ii, l.* 426)

These lines establish powerfully the weight of the consequences throughout, and even beyond, the Kingdom – consequences which are provided by the condition of the one individual psychesoma. Coming to terms with human reality can give stability, and this possible balance between order and bodily life has been expressed in terms of the sanctified grace of marriage, in relationship that resolves fear. A weakness, as of sexual jealousy 'rooted' in the body, is a threat to order, and a failure of our dealings with reality. Now, having erected 'the fabric of his folly', which both obliterates (is 'pil'd on') his (true) beliefs, and is rooted in his (false) beliefs, the kingdom will suffer to its very foundations. Leontes' faulted psychesoma, while it lives, now embodies a universal threat: the effect will be as great as that of the moon on the tides, and seems as unalterable.

Polixenes and Camillo leave the scene. They are at this stage established as normative. Yet later in the play Polixenes is to exert 'reason' and 'custom' *at the expense of* what we feel to be a proper spontaneous impulse of emotions and the impulses of the body, in the love between Florizel and Perdita: there are no clear moral answers, there is no clear distinction between good men and bad men (as *Measure for Measure* makes clear enough).

Significantly, Polixenes and Camillo fly back to Bohemia, the 'country of the body' as I have called it. The solution of the situation is to lead to the restoration of order in Leontes and Sicilia itself, but this requires reference to the processes of natural growth and creativity. The mind has shown itself subject to the disturbances in the body. Now we are to see the problem of the impulses towards life in the body, and of their regulation by the civilized mind, over a long period of natural life.

But first we have to witness the reduction of Sicilia to waste by Leontes' 'fabric of folly'. Leontes' individual degeneracy reverberates throughout the kingdom, because he is king. In the action of the play, with its masque-like symbolism, this involves the death of Mamillius 'the promise', and the apparent death of Perdita (the lost infant) and Hermione (the mother). Perdita and Hermione are reborn later in the play. Mamillius is not, and yet he was stated to be in the first scene 'an unspeakable comfort . . . of the greatest promise . . . one that physics the subject, makes old hearts fresh'. The young princes are in a sense representatives of a symbolic god-head, like the bull or king which is sacrificed in primitive ritual; Mamillius is dead: long live Florizel. But the actual prince Mamillius is destroyed by Leontes' breakdown – because Mamillius is a real part of the reality with which Leontes cannot deal, and so denies, by hate and destructiveness. In the last scene the problem of issue is reconsidered:

DION: You pity not the state . . .
                     consider little
           What dangers, by his Highness' fail of issue,
           May drop upon the Kingdom, and devour
           Incertain lookers on.
                     (*Act V, Sc. i, l. 25*)

LEONTES: . . . the wrong I did . . .
           Heirless it hath made my kingdom and
           Destroy'd the sweets't companion that e'er man
           Bred his hopes out of.
                     (*Act V, Sc. i, l. 10*)

Mamillius was the symbol of the spiritual health of his father and
hence the state: out of him hopes were bred. But over him was
Leontes' hate, and so he, and his hopes, are destroyed. There is a
further identification between Mamillius and Florizel in the first
scene: while Mamillius is not reborn, it is Florizel who replaces
him, as the promise of the inheritance restored.

The oracle is to pronounce:

> And the King shall live without an heir
> if that which is lost be not found.

Florizel is both the means of the finding, and the heir himself.
What is found is not only the actual new generation (refound
Perdita, and Florizel, the flower) but the renewing *belief* in fresh
generation, in the poet, and as expressed in his masque-like poem.

The second act opens with the queen pregnant, with her ladies
and her son: the theme struck is fecundity and continuity, and
again the innocence of childhood is contrasted with the experience
of maturity. Time is the 'good time' of procreation: and the experience of maturity.

MAMILLIUS: You'll kiss me hard, and speak to me, as if
             I were a baby still...
LADY: ... The Queen, your Mother, rounds apace: we
                                             shall
        Present our services to a fine new Prince
        One of these days, and then you'd wanton with us
        If we would have you.
2ND LADY   She is spread of late
        Into a goodly bulk (good time encounter her)...
                       (*Act II, Sc. i, l. 5*)

This emphasis on fecundity stresses that main theme of the play
whose significance we have touched upon: the seasonal rhythm,
related to the rhythm of human generation.

The play is called *The Winter's Tale*. The second half of the play
opens, as we saw, just before winter:

> The year growing ancient
> Not yet on summer's death, nor on the birth
> Of trembling Winter...

It passes later through the spring festivities of the shepherds, at which Perdita is a vegetation deity (a Whitsun goddess or May Queen). In the festival scene she attributes particular flowers to particular ages of man, and the ages of man therefore are related to the seasons of the year. But there is a profound tragic irony even underlying the fertility theme. Mamillius is to die at the beginning of winter. The individual death we must learn to accept: but there is always the promise of new life, to which the succession passes. Antigonus is 'put in the ground': the babe is 'taken up' from the earth. Florizel and the banished Perdita who are to succeed him are now the 'heirs' 'of great promise' and are described as 'welcome as the Spring to the earth'. This spring, as a poetic symbol, represents Shakespeare's own gained confidence in the transcendent values of human love, and their guarantee of continuity in future 'springs' and generations.

Leontes, as a central figure, ages and matures. He advances through his own seasons, from the age which merits 'primroses' that shall 'die before they behold bright Phoebus in his strength' to that which deserves 'rosemary and rue, these keep seeming, and savour all the winter long'. He passes through middle age ('the marigold, that goes to bed with the sun and with him rises weeping'). This progress from innocence to experience is reflected in Leontes between the beginning of the play and the earlier reminiscence of himself as a boy, and the end, sixteen years later, when he is reunited with his time-wrinkled wife. Shakespeare is asking, over such long periods of time, *what counts*, what survives? In offering his poetic answer Shakespeare takes us through stages of developing adequate attitudes to the rhythms of time and to mortality, to find hope in continuity. Leontes' capacity to mature and his capacity to make reparation, are the central progress in the play.

This poetic quest comes as the culmination of Shakespeare's work, and its continual preoccupation with appearance and reality. Man at best is but,

> Man proud man
> Dressed in a little brief authority,

> Most ignorant of what he's most assured,
> His glassy essence . . .
>   (*Measure for Measure*, Act II, Sc. ii, l. 120–21)

Is human good based on appearances only? What and where is the
reality, not least the reality of good? How do we gain insight into
these things?

Leontes' own comment on appearance and reality comes just
after Mamillius has begun his story:

> There may be in the cup
> A spider steep'd, and one may drink; depart,
> And yet partake no venom, (for his knowledge
> Is not infected): but if one present
> Th' abhorr'd ingredient to his eye, make known
> How he hath drunk, he cracks his gorge, his sides
> With violent hefts: I have drunk and seen the
>   spider . . .
>   (Act II, Sc. i, l. 38)

This verse is thick with the imagery, and the sound and movement, of physical force ('cracks his gorge, his sides/With violent
hefts') – and this brings to our apprehension Leontes' sensation-
dominated approach to what he considers to be reality. The lines
enact the overbearing of reason by intense sense 'feelings' which
seem real, but whose basis is hallucination. 'The fabric of his folly
will endure the standing of his body': hallucinations derived from
bodily sensation now dominate Leontes' dealings with the outside
world. There is no real danger in the spider. Leontes says significantly of one who has *not* seen the spider, 'his knowledge is not
infected'. But Leontes' own knowledge *is* 'infected', by images as
unconnected with any actual harm, but yet as real in their effect on
the one who 'sees' as the image of the 'spider'.[1] Without the self-
spun images the physical reaction would not have occurred: there
is no real poison: the reactions of the one drinking are psycho-
somatic. Leontes' own reactions have been psychically self-induced

[1] The spider is an appropriate symbol, as it is a common infantile symbol of
fear of poisonous revenge for having directed hate and destructive impulses at
parents and siblings. As a threat of retribution for bad impulses in phantasy attacks
on others, it menaces relationship and identity.

in the same way: unrelated to any external cause, they are projections, manifestations of inward disorder thrown over reality, in order to blame external things for inward agony. The consequences – death and wrongful imprisonment – are as of a nightmare image which infects knowledge, such as those destructive acts committed by a psychotic who 'lives in' his phantasy. Leontes now lives and acts wholly in his phantasy, and must bring everything into line to justify it: 'How blest am I/In my just censure, in my true opinion.'

Yet from this point forward 'good' and love – the transcendant realities – are established step by step, by their embodiment in the 'good' characters and their actions. Hermione, by her acceptance of the reality of human nature, maintains her view of events in true perspective. Later she says to Leontes: 'My life stands in the level of your dreams . . .'. She upholds loyalty as more real than the death which threatens her from Leontes' psychotic illusions, that threaten to shoot her down (level=aim, as of a gun):

> Sir, spare your threats:
> The bug which you would fright me with, I seek:
> To me can life be no commodity.
> (*Act III, Sc. ii, l.* 92)

And Paulina calls his 'dreams',

> Fancies too weak for boys, too green and idle
> For girls of nine
> (*Act III, Sc. ii, l.* 182)
> (Cf. 'I remain a pinched thing')

'There is the same lack of reasonableness as in the fears of a child in Leontes' convulsive sensationalism,' says F. C. Tinkler. (*The Winter's Tale, Scrutiny*, March 1937, Vol. V, No. 4.) And this physical exposure to sensation of Leontes produces a coarsening of the moral fibre generally, as reason is abandoned to an infantile extent, disastrous in an adult, and destructive of all relationship.

Leontes is to prove redeemable, however – and so he is given an uneasy sense of uncertainty about his predatory assumptions. He seeks to justify his impossible position by progressively more dissociated ploys. For instance, when he comes to formally indict Hermione in the court, he assumes a false and stagey histrionic posture:

> You, my lords,
> Look on her, mark her well
> (*Act II, Sc. i, l.* 64)

Yet at the same time he is inarticulate in his indictment, which becomes mere abuse: 'these shrug's, these hum's, and ha's'. (l. 73.) He is at his easiest with the coarse appellation, in abuse, even though he is aware of the impropriety of such language in the court and proclaims:

> Lest barbarism (making me the precedent)
> Should a like language use to all degrees . . .
> (*Act II, Sc. i, l.* 83)

Yet he goes on to call his Queen a 'bed-swerver'. He is uneasy about 'the fabric of his folly' . . . 'piled on his faith', phrases which he echoes with ironic implications:

LEONTES: if I mistake
In those foundations which I build upon,
The Centre is not big enough to bear
A schoolboy's top.
> (*Act II, Sc. i, l.* 100)

We see the situation as farcical – the building of a 'fabric' of disaster in the state upon deceptive illusions such as that symbolized by Leontes' own 'spider' which only produces a reaction if *seen* – even though it offers no real danger (and, now, even if what is 'seen' is imaginary!). The image of the top suggests the way a kingdom can be poised on a man's infantile whim, a symptom itself of the failure to complete some process of growth of the reality-sense in infancy. We know Leontes' foundations to be false: his image balances them on the whole earth's centre. This suggests powerfully the cosmic scale of the effects of the one man's inward disbalance: this apprehension seems very relevant to the modern world, in which a universal disaster could be precipitated by one man's psychic disbalance.

Antigonus discusses guilt with Leontes even in his own unpleasant terms and imagery of physical coarseness, as if to discomfort him by a caricature of depressive 'realism'. Shakespeare thus indicates how unreal it would be to regard human life in terms of its unruliest 'instincts' only. If the queen is not spotless, Antigonus says,

> I'll keep my stables where
> I lodge my wife, I'll go in couples with her . . .
> *(Act II, Sc. i, l.* 133)

Of his daughters, he says,

> I'll geld 'em all: Fourteen they shall not see . . .
> . . . honesty,
> There's not a grain of it, the face to sweeten
> Of the whole dungy earth
> *(Act II, Sc. i, l.* 146)

– honesty, credit, honour are invoked and their reality called into assertion against Leontes' imputations. The reality is not in (fleshly) imperfection so much as in (abstract) *good*. But Leontes rejects such reason, by 'intuition', as modern dictators do ('what! lack I credit?'):

> Our prerogative
> Calls not your counsels, but our natural *goodness*
> Imparts this.
> *(Act II, Sc. i, l.* 162)

Since we have seen how Leontes' nature is corrupted his assumption of 'natural goodness' seems disastrous. And the nightmare, farcical nature of the action now is suggested by Antigonus' answer to Leontes' proclamation:

> We are to speak in public: for this business
> Will raise us all.
> ANTIGONUS: To laughter, as I take it
> If the good truth were known.
> *(Act II, Sc. i, l.* 196)

But it will be the bitter laughter of a nightmare, of universal human ridicule, for 'fatal Sicilia', for the king's 'natural goodness' is most unnaturally 'infected'. We hear an echo again of those phrases from *Measure for Measure*: 'most ignorant of what he's most assured' and the 'tricks' of an 'angry ape'.

Paulina in the next scene exerts herself as the embodiment of commonsense maturity and honesty in the court. The several loyalties throughout the play are a subtle presentation of differing human sensibilities and their modes of behaviour in a situation where loyalty is called to act on its own responsibility, even at risk to life itself, so that the frail values of human relationship are given the ultimate test. Paulina, for example, never ceases to oppose Leontes, and she it is who later will restore Hermione to life. 'He must be told on't and he shall,' she says, and consistently invokes values by her terms 'honour', 'goodness', 'innocence', 'freed', 'enfranchised'.

By the next scene (Act II, Sc. iii) Leontes' sleep is gone, just as Macbeth's sleep deserts him, and the king can no longer escape the evidence of his own derangement: he seeks desperate ways out, even that of destroying his wife – and with her the sexual reality that he cannot tolerate:

> . . . say that she were gone,
> Given to the fire, a moiety of my rest
> Might come to me again . . .
> (*Act II, Sc. iii, l.* 8)

Mamillius has taken the matter as Leontes (had he not been 'fixed' in his 'condition') should have done: the boy 'declines'. Leontes is torn between love and hate for the child whose innocent re-action (which should be his own) puts him for Leontes among his enemies: yet he shrinks from murdering his son. Mamillius is the 'hated object' as much as Perdita:

> The very thought of my revenges that way
> Recoil upon me . . .
> (*Act II, Sc. iii, l.* 19)

Leontes himself has an inkling (in this lies his deepest suffering – and Shakespeare's profoundest perception) that he is but projecting on his wife and son 'bad' elements from within himself. Paulina enters with the babe. She appeals to the lords.

To connive at psychic derangement is to deepen the distemper:
to uphold the truth of reality is to cure:

> Fear you his tyrannous passion more (alas)
> Than the Queen's life?
> I come to bring him sleep. 'Tis such as you
> That creep like shadows by him, and do sigh
> At each his needless heavings: such as you
> Nourish the cause of his awaking. I
> Do come with words, as medicinal, as true . . .
> (*Act II, Sc. iii, l.* 33)

Paulina's 'test' is an attempt to 'purge' by words – 'truth', 'honour'
– the utmost appeal to moral decency – and this represents a
loyalty to the kingdom, and a desire to cure the community (Cf.
Macbeth's request to the doctor to 'cast the water of my Kingdom'). Leontes fails the test, and reverts even further to the language of social anarchy. The babe, because of its being closer to the
hidden origins of Leontes' dissociation, as a symbol of the sexual
reality he cannot tolerate, now becomes the central object of
hatred:

> Force her hence . . . a most intelligencing bawd . . . crone . . .
> A nest of traitors . . . A callat . . . a gross hag, and lozel . . .

Paulina persists, and the poetry stresses here again, the point that
the rottenness at Leontes' heart is a rottenness in the foundations of
the kingdom. But it is also a remarkable observation of the in-
accessibility of some forms of mental sickness to the reality of
bonds and values – and to pity, since Perdita now becomes the
'malicious object', against whom the hate and destructiveness of
Leontes' sexual jealousy can now be exerted without conscience.
(The analogies between this situation in this play, and the situation
in occupied countries, when Nazism destroyed values of human
relationship, even to the murder of millions of innocent children,
may be studied. In this lies the contemporary relevance of *The
Winter's Tale* to the relation between the conflicts in our inward
nature and politics. Leontes' progress towards his claim of natural-
self-goodness and Hitler's of 'infallible intuition' may be compared. Leontes' urge to destroy his wife and children may be com-

pared with the terrible work of the psychotic Nazi organizations
in killing and burning those over whom they projected their
hatred, even newly-born children, as in the concentration camps.)

Paulina, with magnificent courage, insists on the firm and
normal reality, of sound relationships and governing values,
though she knows in this insistence that she faces death from the
psychotic dictator. Yet she knows, too, that to insist on the norms
is the only way to expose the aberration. So she encourages the
court in its resistance. 'A nest of traitors,' cries the paranoiac
Leontes: 'I am none,' retorts Antigonus. 'Nor I,' cries Paulina,

> But one that's here; and that's himself: for he,
> The sacred Honour of himself, his Queen's
> His hopeful son's, his babe's, betrays to slander,
> Whose sting is sharper than the sword's; and will not
> (For as the case now stands, it is a curse
> He cannot be compell'd to 't) once remove
> The root of his opinion, which is rotten,
> As ever oak, or stone was sound.
>
> (*Act II, Sc. iii, l.* 82)

The court takes the view that Leontes is not able to produce more
accusation 'Than your own weak-hing'd fancy'. But Leontes
defends his dissociation by paranoiac abuse: his whole relationship
with his Court is a relationship with a projected phantasy from
his own disordered inward life, 'You're liars all!' The court warns
of the wider consequences of unbalanced and destructive acts, as
Leontes demands that Perdita be consumed by fire:

> we beg . . .
> That you do change this purpose,
> Which being so horrible, so bloody, must
> Lead on to some foul issue.
>
> (*Act II, Sc. iii, l.* 150)

The sequence reveals Shakespeare's acute perception of how the
unconscious destructive and envious impulses in Leontes – impulses of whose true origin he is ignorant, and about which he
'rationalizes' so irrationally – make it impossible for him to deal
with reality, except by increasing destructiveness and paranoiac

distortions of reality. Even Leontes now shows some uneasiness in his own position.

> I am a feather for each wind that blows . . .
> (Cf. Where were her life if I were a tyrant?
> – but he is!)

His condition is now like that of Macbeth during the Scottish regicide's neurotic state of unbalance in the last battle, a victim of psychic disorder, ineffectual in his disordered reason, impotent in the face of reality, ordering the putting on and then at once the removal of his armour, in bursts of uncontrolled fury. And yet, being king, Leontes can still command by a social system which depends for its functioning on the very values he is wrecking. So, 'liegeman' he calls Antigonus, to command his obedience:

> We enjoin thee
> *As thou art liegeman to us,* that thou carry
> This female bastard hence . . .
> (*Act II, Sc. iii, l.* 172)

Antigonus is made the instrument of Perdita's exposure, on his *'honour'*: the denial of pity is worse than bestial:

> ANTIGONUS: Wolves and bears, they say,
> (Casting their savageness aside) have done
> Like offices of pity. Sir, be prosperous
> In more than this deed does require; and blessing
> Against this cruelty, fight on thy side.
> (Poor Thing, condemned to loss.)
> (*Act II, Sc. iii, l.* 186)

'Casting their savageness aside' is an ironic comment on Leontes' inability to do so, so that he might have pity. Despite all the protestations of a civilized court, he cannot cast his own savageness aside: this, says the poet, is man's most damaging weakness – the ruthlessness of unconscïous envy. It is like that of the bear to whose claws Antigonus is doomed.

Act III, Sc. i opens with a statement of the nature of the Isle of the Oracle. We have seen the dissociation of hate as 'a feather for each wind that blows'. Now goodness and creativity are given solidity as of peaceful place:

> The climate's delicate, the air most sweet,
> Fertile the Isle, The Temple much surpassing
> The common praise it bears.
>
> *(Act III, Sc. i, l.* 1)

This obviously recalls the passage from Macbeth:

> This castle hath a pleasant seat: the air
> Nimbly and sweetly recommends itself
> Unto our gentle senses.
>
>   this guest of summer
> The temple-haunting martlet, does approve . . .
> His pendent bed and procreant cradle . . .

Fertility, air, climate, sanctity are here associated as the positives
to be set against Leontes' (and the kingdom's) dissociation and the
nervous, physically coarse, farce which he has made of human
relationships. The last line of the scene is, 'And gracious be the
issue' – 'grace', as F. C. Tinkler points out, is a key-word in this
play, and it is associated with innocence, goodness and the triumph
of values.

Grace is the apprehension of 'good' that brings resignation and
acceptance, and the urge to make reparation, and thus a release
from guilt and destructive envy.

In the next scene Hermione is in the dock. Her plea,

>   it shall scarce boot me
>   To say, Not guilty . . .
>
> *(Act III, Sc. ii, l.* 27)

recalls Polixenes' earlier recollection of innocence in childhood:

> not guilty; the imposition cleared,
> Hereditary ours . . .

The 'trial' which follows brings against Leontes' disorder formal
protestations of the intangible but none the less real values of
civilized social and personal order. Hermione is for honour, even
at the expense of her life.

HERMIONE: My life stands in the level of your dreams.
                 Which I'll lay down.

LEONTES: Your actions are my dreams.
             You had a bastard by Polixenes
             And I but dream'd it:
                    (Act III, Sc. ii, l. 82)

HERMIONE: . . . no life
             (I prize it not a straw) but for mine honour
             which I would free . . .
                 . . . all proofs sleeping else
             But what your jealousies awake.
                    (Act III, Sc. ii, l. 110)

Hermione's contemptuous rejection of life in favour of honour, and the relegation of Leontes' 'proofs' to 'fancies', 'dreams', that is to the level of hallucinations which are projected by jealous envy, make the abstractions by which men live – honour and virtue – more substantial than Leontes' 'reality' of intuition and the 'evidence' of his senses. Honour, innocence, grace are given body and form: it is physical evidence, and actual appearances which now seem to be dreams and 'blown feathers'. The values which transcend human reality are more real than the coarse reality of the body itself and its impulses, certainly more real and lasting than the unconscious drives that disrupt these. Love and 'good' are more real than that 'reality' of the flesh such as irony dwells on. The deep offence to creativity in the denial is movingly brought out (and suggests Shakespeare's intuitive awareness of the origin of such destructive envy and paranoid tyranny in a fear of woman and her creativity):

HERMIONE: My third comfort,
             (Starr'd most unluckily) is from my breast,
             The innocent milk in it most innocent mouth,
             Hal'd out to murder . . .
                    (Act III, Sc. ii, l. 99)

The Oracle proclaims, and Leontes makes one last fatal attempt to maintain his position, his 'faith', even against the gods – 'This is mere falsehood'.

> *Enter Servant.*
> The Prince your son . . . is gone.

PAULINA: Look down
        And see what Death is doing.

                              (*Act III, Sc. ii, l.* 142)

It is deathly to deny the reality of the truth of human goodness. Leontes' perception must take in this reality at last, and his verse at last resumes the balanced movement of sanity, of wise consideration, recognizing painfully the good values and norms:

                              which had been done,
        But that the good mind of Camillo tardied
        My swift command; though I with death, and with
        Reward, did threaten and encourage him,
        Not doing it, and being done – he (most *humane*)
        And filled with *honour* . . .

                              (*Act III, Sc. ii, l.* 162)

With this one may compare Camillo's speech on 'negligence'. The abstract concepts 'humane', 'good', 'honour' now have form and substance in the enacted drama: we, like Leontes, know better what they mean. But the next passage – Paulina's entrance – reveals how the consequences of 'sick fancies' may not, in a real world, be escaped simply by good intentions and sudden conversion. Leontes, with a lack of realism complementary to the madness, from which, by sudden shock, he recovers, cries,

        I'll reconcile me to Polixenes,
        New woo my Queen . . .

– but Paulina reappears with the news that the object of this reparation is already dead. Paulina's taunts ('Racks? Fires?') are expressed in intense imagery which reminds us of Leontes' derangement and its intensity. The universal consequences of such a diseased state of soul are not as lightly overcome. The acceptance of reality brings inevitable pain, and the need for great reparation. The verse parodies Leontes' nervous rhythms ('hours, minutes, days, weeks?') and Paulina now brings reality home to him in verse whose texture has equal physical force to his. Only by accepting the reality of the damage he has done, and the reality of his need to atone can he begin to restore and reconstruct:

> But O thou Tyrant,
> Do not repent these things, for they are heavier
> Than all thy woes can stir; therefore betake thee
> To nothing but despair. A thousand knees
> Ten thousand years together, naked, fasting
> Upon a barren mountain, and still winter,
> In storm perpetual, could not move the Gods
> To look that way thou wert.
>
> (*Act III, Sc. ii, l.* 208)

The 'fabric of his folly' having collapsed, the 'trespasses' come crowding in: restitution is a matter of common and laborious concern ('a thousand knees') – the consequences and the guilt spread through 'fatal Sicilia'. Leontes' noble heart is touched ('shame') and he devotes himself to penance: mere involving of 'honour' will not do – it must be actively given pressure and form, and acted out in living terms. Reparation is required in terms of a series of constructive acts. As Bunyan was to know, there is no short cut to the apprehension of truth and reality: *il faut souffrir*, unless we are to go the way of Ignorance:

> And tears shed there
> Shall be my recreation . . .

So we end the first part of the play on the coast of Bohemia.

We may compare the two halves of the play with the first and second part of *The Pilgrim's Progress*. Now, the 'ordeal' of Leontes is over, and his 'cure' is to be expressed in a much more benign dramatic phase whose effect is to give us, involve us in, an experience which seeks to convey to us the poetic truth by which Shakespeare found himself able to redeem Leontes, and maintain his own confidence in life and human good.

This point in the play marks the wintry depths of *The Winter's Tale*: it is now, as it were, the shortest day, and the 'darkest night of the soul', in the season-like pattern of the total dramatic poem. Leontes represents Man whose reason may be unbalanced by yielding to the evidence of sensation and to a diseased imagination deceived by its own hallucinations, and to drives of the passions biased by unconscious energy. He has severely damaged his commonwealth. He has (apparently) driven his Queen to her death, has killed his son (on whom the succession depends), and has flouted successively both reasoned wisdom (in the person of Antigonus) and the vitality of traditions of honour (in the person of Paulina). He has apparently destroyed the babe as a hated object, an outward symbol of the bad in himself. Then, at last, he flouts justice, and divine judgment. The consequences to him and the state are of that kind which inevitably follow the human disintegration of reason.

The play now comes to draw on the old rituals and fertility ceremonies such as flower festivals, Twelfth Night ceremonies and mumming-plays in which was enacted the death of the old year, and the rebirth of the new. As a metaphor the play now explores in related modes the seasonal passages of decline and renewal. These are related to human life in time, and the renewal brought by love and the fresh generations it brings. Thus the play enacts acceptance of 'the continuity of life', as 'an expanded metaphor'.

The Leontes, into whose experience Shakespeare so deeply enters, the 'man (who) dwelt by a church yard', is a deathly, wintry thing, until he is reborn and regenerated in the second half of the play. The virtues by which he is 'reborn' are almost symbolized by the herbs Perdita gives Polixenes – rosemary and rue, remembrance – reflection in maturity in Time. It is by this activity that he makes access to Grace, and is redeemed.

There is a significant compression or fusion of the seasons now, as in memory. The play within the play, of Act IV, Scene iv, is in late autumn:

> ... the year growing ancient
> Not yet on summer's death, nor on the birth
> Of trembling winter...

– but yet the Festival is like a 'Whitsun Festival' at which Perdita is a May Queen or vegetation goddess. (These renewal rites would have been celebrated in every village in England at the time.) In the second part of the play Autolycus enters singing of daffodils and is a mythical figure in disguise – a version of the traditional thief-god, disguised as a pedlar who goes down to the underworld to fetch the spring. All the concern with disguises in the second half of the play relates to the theme of natural change, because it is in spring that the bare land assumes its variegated cover and in autumn that it loses it. Florizel and Perdita when they arrive at Leontes' court are welcomed as being, 'As the spring to th'earth'.

To bring about the maturation of man's nature, and balance in men's affairs, the play implies, time and the passage of seasons are needed. Time, seasons of suffering experience, and triumph over these by constructive experiences and acts, make for healing, balance, continuity, order and stability in subsequent generations.

When we are in the middle of the play in the darkest winter, the one hope (as the oracle indicates) is in 'what was lost' – Perdita. The abandoned babe is the new seed, as it were, in the earth, the seed of new life and a reviving goodness in each new life, which ever escape man's most aggressive and destructive intentions, and his envy directed at creativity. The destructive 'Caliban' in nature and in human nature is represented by the bear, a symbol of the kind of destructive worse-than-beast which Leontes has become because of his disordered psychesoma.

By the time we arrive at Antigonus' death there seems – as in winter – nothing left: the blind deathly impulses of Leontes have brought universal ruin and destruction, even of pity. The combination of the abandonment of the child in the wilderness and the destruction of Antigonus by a wild beast bring the nadir of human potentialities forcibly to us. This is the reason for that most bizarre of stage directions – 'Exit pursued by a bear'. To us it seems ludicrous, and we explain it by supposing the availability of some convenient animal at the Globe. But the bear is no comedy item, nor is the use of it mere expediency – to the Elizabethans bears would be familiar as dangerous and savage beasts, for they would have seen them baited by dogs, and their claws and teeth at work on flesh, torn and bloody. They represented the most conspicuously present natural life in London, savage and predatory, and would be unconsciously associated with brutal sadistic feelings, even among the exposed bodies of dismembered and beheaded criminals. Shakespeare sought not only to accept the reality of human life, and the inevitable individual decline and decay in Time, but to become serenely reconciled to the savage truths. The greatest obstacle in the soul to such serenity is envy, and envy is destructive of creative attitudes. Melanie Klein points out that:

> The capacity to give and preserve life is felt as
> the greatest gift and therefore creativeness becomes
> the deepest cause for envy . . .

Leontes' destructive envy seeks to destroy Perdita, the growing point of future generations in the false attempt to destroy the hated bad object within himself: this aberrant impulse does, of course, destroy Mamillius. Melanie Klein notes in the same passage the way in which envy is portrayed as a biting animal (which she links with infantile feelings towards the mother's breast, and unconscious urges to consume or destroy it). Spenser, she points out, describes envy as a ravenous wolf:

> He hated all good workes and vertuous deeds . . .
> He does backbite, and spightfull poison spues
> From leprous mouth on all that ever writt . . .

In *The Winter's Tale* the delineation of envy concludes with the bear, representing the consequences of envy, grievance and persecution, in death. The second half of the play explores the means whereby this savage envy – an aspect of an infantile failure to accept mature reality – may be escaped and overcome, and ruth found.

We begin anew with the baby – Perdita, that which was lost – the new creature who is to become the next generation, to grow to sexual creative power, to fall in love (even in defiance of the older generation), and become accepted as 'great promise' herself. Sanity, reconciliation, peace, could not be found 'until that which was lost is found'. 'What could have been lost' was belief in creative life. The marvellous quality of Shakespeare's last play is his acceptance of the young lovers as being earnests of continuity, of the continuation of life. Such an attitude to life, if it can be achieved, writes Melanie Klein,

> includes gratitude for pleasures of the past and enjoyment of what the present can give, expresses itself in serenity. In old people, it makes possible the adaptation to the knowledge that youth cannot be re-

gained and enables them to take pleasure and interest in the lives of young people . . . Those who feel they have had a share in the experience and pleasures of life are much more able to believe in the continuity of life . . . Goethe said, 'he is the happiest of men who can make the end of his life agree closely with the beginning'.

Envy and Gratitude

Goethe's remark quoted here seems to me very relevant to *The Winter's Tale*, in which play the seasons are intermingled and merged, until there grows a sense of large perspectives of time and generation, until the sense of continuity becomes a timeless apprehension that transcends time. We begin with the pressure of destructive envy in Leontes, as of the older man who feels debarred from the ecstasies of others, 'which perhaps he feels he never had': yet, by suffering the consequences of his own envy, and by assuagement brought by Time, he is able in the end not only to bless the 'continuity of life' in the young lovers, but also to be reconciled to his own long-lost wife. 'The end agrees closely with the beginning'; we should read into this not only a glimpse of Shakespeare's own personal quest for a deeper sense of meaning in his personal life, but a working from his own inward conflicts towards an expression in his art of the contest with envy and the quest for love as universal redeeming and reparative elements in all human life. That Perdita who was the 'internal object', which Leontes cannot embrace, but denies and attacks as malicious, because to it adhere his fears of sexual reality and his envy of creativity, is, in the second half, refound, and becomes the focus of hope and regeneration. In this, poetically speaking, Shakespeare himself is finding inward 'goodness', and love.

Antigonus' last speech was formal, distanced, masque-like, and the play now withdraws from its more realistic modes into the more formal pattern of its second, pastoral, ritualistic, restorative part.

The scene in which Perdita is found is the pivot of the play, and contains the pivotal motto of the dramatic poem:

> Now bless thyself: thou met'st with things dying,
> I with things newborn.

(Act III, Sc. iii, l. 116)

We are at a moment of significant contemplation of time and re-generation – of unchanging patterns of recurrence, but yet of the continual emergence of new life – which is beyond tragedy, and is a clue to the growth of a capacity for resignation, gratitude, and hope. This growth must, however, keep reality in mind, as with the ironic pronouncements of the old shepherd's 'I would there was an age between ten and twenty-three. . . .' He takes Perdita for an abandoned bastard. Like Hermione's and Polixenes' earlier speeches about human nature, his lines are a recognition of human truth. His resigned compassion is close to the spirit of stoical resignation found in folk-art, and its acceptance of the nature and conditions of human life.

But here, as in the court, humane values are as triumphant, even in the resigned, ironic depths: 'I'll take it up *for pity*,' says the shepherd. The clown's description, the shepherd's recognition of tenderness, are given as in direct physical imagery again, as in Leontes' speeches. But significantly, while Leontes' speeches played on our nerves, these, though concrete in their imagery, have a stoic zest of mature acceptance of troubled reality, rather than the depressive bitterness of Timon:

> Betwixt the firmament and it, you cannot thrust a
> bodkin's point . . .
> Swallowed with yeast and froth as you'd thrust a cork into
> a hog's head . . . to see how the bear tore out his
> shoulder-bone . . . how the poor souls roar'd and the
> sea mocked them; and how the poor gentleman roar'd
> and the bear mocked him.
>
> (*Act III, Sc. iii, l. 86*)

It is painful but it is comic: it is clowning such as accompanies death in the folk-ritual: it is one way for us to accept death, by a resigned wry grimace. This language – 'Mercy on's, a barne', 'thrust a cork into a hog's head' – is full of life-promoting energy, and springs directly from the lusty idiom of a fine and vigorous folk life, which knows savagery and privation, but which maintains a hold on life, positive, resigned attitudes to it – and knows pity and mercy, too.

By this release into another mood, by ironic buffoonery drawn from the folk-tradition in the presence of death, we are prepared for the transition over the sixteen years interlude, and to the spring-coming, of Perdita's return:

'Tis a lucky day, boy, and we'll do good deeds on't.

We are still deeply disturbed from being involved in the episode of Leontes' jealousy, and its destructive march to ruin. But now the Clown's stoical attitude to death, the Shepherd's to birth, make the exposure of the nerves bearable – life must go on, does go on, despite the agonies and tragedies of individuals. Here is hope. The seasonal pattern, the pattern of generation, the rough vigour and the new life, transcend the individual obsession. The men find gold, the child, bury Antigonus: we return to the normal every-day world with the promise of 'This is fairy gold, boy', and in the 'wise' country of Bohemia. The mood of almost intolerable ferocity, culminating in the bear, lightens, towards hope.

'Time' at the beginning of Act IV makes a formal speech, again distancing the play and establishing the freshness which perspective may perceive as life renews itself. The character Time might be the composite figure Prospero-Shakespeare himself speaking. In the light of the larger realities the reality of the present is mere 'glistering':

> I witness to
> The times that brought them in; so shall I do
> To the freshest things now reigning, and make stale
> The glistering of this present.
> (*Act IV, Sc. i, l.* 11)

In Act IV, Scene i, attention is drawn to Polixenes' 'reasonableness' (as embodied in the prose he speaks) and at once the parallel is drawn between Mamillius and Florizel.

> Of that fatal country Sicilia, prithee speak
> no more, whose very naming, punishes me with
> the remembrance of that penitent (as thou call'st
> him) and reconciled King my brother, whose loss
> of his most precious Queen and children, are even now

> to be afresh lamented. Say to me, when sawest thou
> the Prince Florizel my son? *Kings are no less*
> *unhappy, their issue not being gracious, than they*
> *are in losing them, when they have approved their*
> *virtues.*
>
> (*Act IV, Sc. ii, l.* 21)

The problem here is that of the degree of grace in Florizel. Polixenes is almost *over-wise* in the event: though he is only prevented from being so by Perdita's being Perdita, a Princess. The considerations of princedom are similar to those explored in *Hamlet* ('He may not, as a Prince, carve for himself') and *Henry IV*, *i and ii* (as when Harry rejects Falstaff, 'I know thee not, old man').

Autolycus enters in Act II, Sc. iii, and he brings references to spring and daffodils at once, in his song. But this renewal has no naïvety – there is enough irony in his song (in 'doxy' and 'my aunts') to preserve the presence of the recognition of the truth of human nature and its sexual reality, to which the play seeks resignation. Even in the freshest, most fertile, season we hear the notes of irony: belief in the continuity of life, to be real, requires acceptance of the gross realities, before moving beyond them. Autolycus was 'littered under Mercury', the patron saint of thieves. And he bears a relationship to the tricksy spirit of myth who brings the seasonal change, wayward and uncertain, as John Speirs shows in his book on mediaeval drama, where he relates him to Loki, the Norse god, and other antecedents in folk-lore – the shiftless, face changing, double-dealing thief who moves between this world and the underworld to bring back the spring, and to change the face of the earth.

This double character of Autolycus and his use of disguises associates with the poetic theme in the play of deceit by disguise, and the deception of appearances. The play asks, where is the reality of life, or character, of values, behind all outward semblances, and given our inward darkness, about which we rationalize? Later the Clown and Autolycus will change social class by changing clothes. But yet in all the deceptive appearances, what matters is the underlying relationship between the 'bare fork'd animals'

Perdita and Florizel are truly lovers, whether they are disguised or undisguised, foundlings, princess, rejected son, or shepherdess – the reality of love lies beneath 'robes and furr'd gowns' and 'glassy images'. This we find in *King Lear* – love as a truth persisting in the face of the collapse of all bonds, of Lear's inward disintegration, and universal chaos. Here this truth is embodied in the young lovers, as a promise for the future, for the continuance of human life and order, despite all the switches in appearances which change the outward aspects of human life, as the seasons change the aspects of the world, under the influence of Time.

This first section of the play ends in death. The second section opens with a reference to death ('a death to grant this') but it begins a movement of resurrection – Camillo returning to his home country, Perdita refound, Hermione brought back from the dead, lovers united, friends reconciled. Time, growth, season, maturity themselves are essential to the bringing about of these things. As well as bringing about change and decline, Time and the natural rhythms also heal and regenerate. Even such an ironic creature as the impish Autolycus may be an agent of renewal.

In Act IV, Scene ii, the heirdom, passed from Mamillius to Florizel, is established as continuous. The struggle now is to maintain the *quality* of that continuity:

> Kings are no less unhappy, their issue not
> being gracious, than they are in losing them,
> when they have approved their virtues.

So we now have further, formal considerations of honour, loyalty and service, and their exigencies on the individual.

In Autolycus' first song the note of the passage of the seasons from spring to summer is sounded, a passage associated with changes in the blood, and hence with the development of a human being in his life, as through the seasons of the year, through the states of maturity (with sexual connotations) represented by Perdita's primroses, marigolds and rue. The theme is of human blood rising like sap – as in 'the red blood reigns in the winter's pale', 'pale' meaning both the 'enclosure' of winter, its limited

confined life, and the 'pallor' of the winter complexion, starved of
health and sun. (Cf. 'a sudden pale . . . Usurps her cheeks', *Venus
and Adonis*.)

There is now a significant change in imagery from what has
gone before – 'sweet o' the year', red blood, quart of ale, sugar,
currants, rice, nosegays, saffron, warden pies, mace, dates, nut-
megs, 'prewins', raisins. The flavour of the second half of the play
is less bitter, and less nervous, and not pre-occupied with physical
disgust. The conquest of envy goes with an increased relish for joy.
Life seems less gross, more sweet, with the sweetness of mature
resignation. There is a delight in appearances, even accepting that
they are deceptive, as with Autolycus' tricks and his appearing as a
pedlar whose wares are trash. Autolycus is 'a snapper-up of unconsidered trifles' – 'when the kite builds look to lesser linen'. The
exploration of appearance and reality takes a different form – is
Autolycus' 'white sheet bleaching on the hedge' snow? – or
blossom? The depressive reality which Leontes supposed he saw
('paddling palms') gives way to joy in even transitory appearances, such as the brave daffodils of 'the sweet o' the year'.

The whole scene is concerned with disguise and even with that
joy in surface delights which cheats destructive envy and fear. Jane
Harrison points out that in folk ritual such disguises are common in
spring rituals – e.g. 'one of the girls is dressed in the Death's dis-
carded clothes' (see *Art and Ritual*, p. 70). Disguise is seen as something innocuous, even capable of bringing a healing delight as may
the temporary dress of leaf and blossom in seasons – the spring
festival with its assumed costume is an acceptance of the natural
order. The renewed appearance of things (as in the cheats practised
by Florizel and Perdita) is a natural way of finding in appearances
– like blossom – means to be creative, and to express a life's continuity – as against that morbid irony that seems to see into 'reality',
and destructive forces built on hallucinations. In the place of the
depressive distrust of appearances (as in Leontes, when he comes to
distrust everything except his own 'weak fancies' – inward hallucinations like those focused on the 'spider') we now can *afford* to
be deceived by pleasurable seemings. To live in constant distrust
of appearances would be intolerable. So Florizel says:

> These your unusual weeds, to each part of you
> Does give a life: no shepherdess, but Flora
> Peering in April's front.
>
> (*Act IV, Sc. iv, l.* 1)

'Does give a life' – the bedecking, as with flowers and plumage – is creative, an April thing. Florizel is *disguised* as a swain, Perdita as Flora: she is already *disguised* as a Shepherd-girl, Polixenes and Camillo are to come in *disguise*. Yet there is another danger here, as of self-deceit by appearances:

> PERDITA: But that our feasts
> In every mess, have folly, and the feeders
> Digest it with a custom, I should blush
> To see you so attired.
>
> (*Act IV, Sc. iv, l.* 10)

The custom – the celebration of the greater-than-human thing, in the ritual – justifies the disguises: the festival garments are not mere disguises but have the quality of poetic symbol and metaphor, as means to insight and understanding. Spring is changing the appearance of the earth: the emphasis (in the spring and summer of the mood of the poem) is on 'the sweet of the year'. The seed left by Antigonus is growing. 'I'll put him in the ground . . . thou met'st with things dying, I with things newborn.' So the human motives and actions in the second half are much stronger and surer – they represent the behaviour of those who have learnt from the experience of Leontes' tragedy (or, if you like, what Shakespeare himself has learnt) and who can now grow into fresh life.

Although we are with Shakespeare at this advanced stage of experience, and have experienced much bitterness, we return with him now to unironical acceptance of the simplicity and innocence of the natural love of Florizel and Perdita. This innocence, like Lear's, at the end of *King Lear* has been refined from a profound assay of the reality of the whole range of the conditions of human life, including its most terrible aspects. Because it is won from awareness of such suffering, this love is given us as profoundly valid and transcendent, being a concept created by a poet resigned to the reality of human nature, and yet able to believe firmly in human goodness, and life's renewal.

Perdita is aware of the contrast between true self and pretence intuitively:

PERDITA: Or how
          Should I (in these my borrowed flaunts) behold
          The sternness of his presence?
                              (*Act IV, Sc. IV, l.* 23)

But they are sure in their love. It is virtuous, and lives in the transcendent truths of love and loyalty in the personal relationship:

FLORIZEL: My desires
          Run nòt before mine honour: nor my lusts
          Burn hotter than my faith.
                              (*Act IV, Sc. iv, l.* 33)

But the future of their love depends upon the need for seeming impossibilities to come to fulfilment:

PERDITA: One of these two must be necessities,
          Which then will speak, that you must change this
              purpose
          Or I my life.
                              (*Act IV, Sc. iv, l.* 38)

Yet they recognize, as folk myths often imply, that the means to triumph is to be true to oneself and one's lights:

FLORIZEL: For I cannot be
          Mine own, nor any thing to any, if
          I be not thine.
                              (*Act IV, Sc. iv, l.* 43)

The very formality of Florizel's verse conveys the civilized relationship in which their love exists, the reality of mutual courtesy, and of their 'separateness in togetherness'. Each lover must recognize his or her own identity and reality.

Florizel and Perdita belong to the court; the shepherd stands for the vitality of common life which has made their survival possible. ('I'll take it up for pity'.) When he speaks of his wife –

> Fie, daughter! when my old wife liv'd, upon
> This day she was both pantler, butler, cook;
> Both dame and servant; welcom'd all, serv'd all,
> Would sing her song, and dance her turn; now here,
> At upper end o' th' table: now i' th' middle:
> On his shoulder, and his; her face o' fire
> With labour, and the thing she took to quench it
> She would to each one sip . . .
>
> (*Act IV, Sc. iv, l. 55*)

– the movement of the verse enacts the vigorous generosity of the peasant community, with its capacities, too, for social graces. The festival is a folk-ritual, and Perdita's distribution of flowers becomes part of it, suggesting a common capacity in human beings of all degrees to explore experience poetically. Her attribution of flowers to the several ages of man links the play with the poetic wisdom expressed in folklore and folk-song. Like the 'group unconscious' expressed in folk-culture, Perdita has the intuitive natural perception of the innocent soul (such as we find in each new generation of young children). To Polixenes and Camillo she says,

> For you there's rosemary and rue, these keep
> Seeming, and savour all the winter long:
> Grace and remembrance be to you both . . .

(Rosemary stood in popular flower symbolism for remembrance, and rue for grace.) Polixenes replies,

> . . . well you fit our ages,
> With flowers of winter.
> (*Act IV, Sc. iv, l. 74*)

The festival seems so obviously a spring or Whitsun festival that it comes as something of a shock to hear that in the time-scale of the play it is autumn, 'the year growing ancient . . .' the seasons and ages seem so fused by the juxtaposition of images. This fusing marks in the poetic drama the resignation achieved by a Shakespeare reconciled to the continual press of 'hungry generations', and able to see life as a blend of cycles and recurrences or

living power. He commingles the generations, and thus escapes
from the sense of being imprisoned in one – and so 'makes old
hearts fresh', finds 'promise', and escapes destructive envy.

The realities of the situation of Perdita and Florizel in relation
to the real world are now touched on in the significant exchange
between Perdita and Polixenes, in a symbolism similar to that of
folksong, sexual and metaphysical:

> POLIXENES: We marry
> A gentler scion to the wildest stock
> And make conceive a bark of baser kind
> By bud of nobler race...
> (*Act IV, Sc. iv, l.* 92)

There is an irony in the dramatically present fact that Perdita is
(apparently) a 'base' 'bark' to whom Florizel hopes to graft himself: this Polixenes will soon reject as impossible, because a prince
must recognize the claims of his own social reality and its exigencies. Polixenes now seems in his turn to reveal something of the
old man's envy of the young. But the natural imagery focuses our
attention on the creature beneath the outward rank of appearance
– on true love rather than arranged liaison, on natural renewal and
generation rather than considerations of mere forms. Perdita
makes her plea for proper worth, for distrust of appearances, and
the rejection of the forced manipulation of nature, by grafting, to
create 'dissemblings'. And we have seen how, despite her being
brought up by peasants, Perdita, as in a folk tale, preserves her
courtly qualities, for they come naturally in her verse and the
attitudes it expresses.

> PERDITA: No more than were, I *painted* I would wish
> This youth should say 'twere well: *and only therefore*
> Desire to breed by me.
> (*Act IV, Sc. iv, l.* 102)

The underlying force of the imagery is that of sexual attraction as
one of our 'unreal' snares – the lovers face, in another form, the
same problem of image and reality such as there has been for
Leontes. Sexual, too, are some meaning of the flowers she distributes, representing flowering, the decline of potency, and aspects of

memory and sorrow in relation to the growth and decline of human passion. This imagery, so similar to that of folksong, springs from Shakespeare's mature attitude of resignation to time and season: its pregnancy gives extra force to Florizel's plea for an arrest of time and season in the famous lines:

> when you do dance, I wish you
> A wave o' the sea, that you might ever do
> Nothing but that: move still, still so,
> And own no other function . . .
> (*Act IV, Sc. iv, l.* 136)

Florizel pleads here for an impossible arrest of the waves of growth and decay, of movement in time, an arrest which is enacted in the symmetrical movement of the poetry, so that we feel both the movement and the desired arrest of it. The movement is that of the wave held at its crest – 'move still: still so' – 'still' having the sense both of the adverb, meaning 'always' and the verb, *to still*, meaning 'arrest'. As with the desire in *The Sonnets* 'that you shall shine as bright in these contents', or Keats' *Ode to A Grecian Urn* and his 'Bright star were I as steadfast as thou art', we feel the universal longing for permanence, and yet at the same time feel the poignancy that this can only be expressed in terms which prompt a yet deeper sense of transience, because the words inevitably evoke Time and Process (in the context of flowers) by contrast. This is why they move us so deeply. Yet Florizel's lines 'still' for a moment the flux of human mutability, arrest the concept of love from the flux, in a larger perspective, as the play itself stills, and fixes in a pattern 'love' and the creative continuity of human life. There is both an incessant procession of waves, yet the molecules in each wave stay still, simply move up and down. So in the waves of time, moments and elements of great beauty and significance, such as love, may be held, and subsist. The lines come from the same impulse in Shakespeare as the *Sonnets*, to 'make war upon this bloody tyrant, Time'. But here the tone is quieter and more simple.

Yet the rhythm in the simplicity of these lines is not the rhythmical simplicity of inexperience (it is the verse of an early play such as *Romeo and Juliet* which is by comparison 'garish', callow

and 'taffeta phrased'). It is a simplicity achieved by deep experience: it has behind it the deep insight achieved by writing *King
Lear* as expressed in the simplicity of Lear's later statements about
himself – 'as I am a man'. Lear's is mature insight: Florizel's intuitive and innocent. Both are created by a poet who has stripped
human nature to its bare truth, and found it still beautiful. So this
simplicity itself, in its urgent poignant expression of brave constancy in love, and of continuity, expresses the powerful force
of human desire and hope against the disintegrative effects of
Time, that plucks 'the keen teeth from the fierce tiger's jaws' and
leads all to death. It is a triumphant moment. The poetry actually
stills the wave: and thus it is an expression of Shakespeare's art, of
his 'powerful rime', whose embodiment of human experience and
human values endures, out of the turmoil and flux, and the loss of
the individual in death, as 'a living record' (see *Sonnet* 55).

Perdita cannot 'own no other function'. Time, and the conditions of life inevitably assail her since she is living. Yet her ritual
movements which Florizel commends distil from the universal
flux a transcending image ('how can we know the dancer from the
dance?'). This image is the expression of the true love that
triumphs over change and decay. Human passion here becomes a
permanence, in the lover's expression of his wishes. It is Florizel
and Perdita who are 'welcome as spring to the earth' – it is they,
young lovers, who shall maintain continuity and hope. The recurrence of young true love in 'honour', constancy, and marriage,
with the creative 'promise' for the future, is the most triumphant
'value' of all – the most enduring reality.

This expression of the value of true love maintains its strength
of innocence even more substantially in the presence of the ironic
contemplation of sexual reality. Autolycus' ballads, the servant
proclaims, are not bawdy. Perdita demands they be not scurrilous.
But, of course, they all turn out to be filthy, in the end, by *double
entendu*. The coarse reality persists even during the transcendent
ritual – but the greatest reality is still felt to be not in the coarseness or cynicism, but in the love and goodness that endure testing,
even by Autolycus' scurrilous irony.

The last problem remains, however – how to reconcile the in-

tuitive confident love between Florizel and Perdita to adult reality
and the patterns of social life. To endure as lovers they must
accept the conditions of service to the community which their
place in generation obliges them to accept. Polixenes and Florizel
discuss the latter's marriage (as a shepherd), and his father's part in
it, Polixenes meantime having become aware that Florizel is his
son:

Have you a father?

Intuition – the life of the body – is strong, but reason must bear a
part: so must the bonds of relationship. The claim of the world and
inheritance must be recognized: Polixenes speaks from age and
maturity:

POLIXENES: Is not your father grown incapable
          Of reasonable affairs? is he not stupid
          With age and alt'ring rheums? Can he speak? hear?
          Know man, from man? Dispute his own estate?
          Lies he not bed-rid? And again, does nothing
          But what he did, being childish?... reason my son
          Should choose himself a wife, but as good reason
          The father (all whose joy is nothing else
          But fair posterity) should hold some counsel
          In such a business ...

(Act IV, Sc. iv, l. 410)

Shakespeare recognizes that, as T. S. Eliot says, there is

only a limited value
In the knowledge derived from experience ...
Do not let me hear
Of the wisdom of old men, but rather of their folly ...

– the mounting condemnation of Florizel begins to savour, in its
rhythm, imagery and movement, of Leontes' envy, and the iras-
cibility of the old man in authority, 'most ignorant of what he's
most assured' – the Lear destructive (Cf. 'Hours, minutes? noon,
midnight?' – this verse has the same nervous movement).

But the traditions Polixenes invokes have, we have seen in the
first part validity, too, so there is, again, a stalemate, – which only
time can solve and heal.

The shepherd (who said when he discovered Perdita, we remember, 'this is a lucky day') senses the shame:

> You have undone a man of fourscore three,
> That thought to fill his grave in quiet: yea,
> To die upon the bed my father died,
> To lie close by his honest bones . . .
> (*Act IV, Sc. iv, l.* 466)

The *honour* of the common tradition (Cf. Joseph in *Wuthering Heights* 'I had aim'd to dee where I've sarved for sixteen years') is impugned.

Camillo once more, in his ability to give flexibility and thus reality to the traditions, once more provides a balance. Time will amend: 'Then till the fury of his Highness settle . . .'. But Florizel speaks now possessed by an impulse towards the abandonment of reason in favour of intuition such as proved so disastrous in Leontes:

FLORIZEL: It cannot fail, but by
                    The violation of my faith; and then
                    Let nature crush the sides, the earth together, 1er
                    And mar the seeds within . . .
                                        I
                    Am heir to my affection . . .
CAMILLO: Be advis'd.
FLORIZEL: I am: and by my fancy, if my reason
                    Will thereto be obedient: I have reason;
                    If not, my senses better pleas'd with madness,
                    Do bid it welcome
                        (*Act IV, Sc. iv, l.* 489)

Here we recall 'fancies as weak as boys'. This *is* a boy's weak fancy – more appropriate in a young lover than in a middle-aged jealous husband. Yet it is the vigour of natural renewal, too, the attitude in love that 'nothing else matters'. But the problem Leontes presented recurs here once more, and again there must be a recourse to values to circumvent disaster. The disaster, once more, could be of universal reverberation – a loss of 'promise' – a sequel of ruin and disorder, crushing the sides of the earth to-gether – as is suggested by Florizel's cosmic image.

Camillo's ability to deal with this situation, which he does for honour's sake, is more effective *because of his experience (which is our experience) of the mistakes of Leontes.* The ironic knave Autolycus now becomes an instrument of disguise, and of the revelation to Polixenes of the lovers' flight:

> every lane's end, every shop, church, session,
> hanging, yields a careful man's work.

In Autolycus' behaviour and his attitudes, which are the reverse of conventional, and in the success of his disguises ('this cannot be but a greater courtier'), we have ironic comment on Polixenes' anger which springs from 'reason'. Autolycus' remarks on the shepherd's guilt – 'draw our throne to a sheep-cote', and on the tortures ('scratched with briars'), – parody the sound, rhythm and fury not only of Polixenes, but of Leontes in his jealousy. The destructive impulses of unconscious envy are held in suspension in the background to give gravity to the resolution of Florizel's predicament. But Leontes has by now been brought to the capacity to be creative in his attitudes, by suffering, and the painful achievement of insight. So he welcomes the lovers thus, as in April's front:

> Welcome hither
> As is the spring to th'earth.
> *(Act V, Sc. i, l. 151)*

Leontes, in age, and with the tragedy of 'fatal Sicilia' behind him, is no longer predisposed to suspicion. He is capable of a profound compassion. The revelation of the lovers' deception makes him 'sorry... sorry... sorry'. In the end the reconciliation is recounted as being of wide reverberation:

> They look'd as they had heard of a world ransom'd ied
> or one destroyed.
> *(Act V, Sc. ii, l. 16)*

The old shepherd stands by as 'the weather-beaten conduit of many kings' reigns'. Time has again brought both wisdom, tolerance, and reparative achievement.

The account of the reconciliation and discovery of Perdita's real self is given more force by being related by messenger. The word 'world' repeated, the general sense of history and time by which this must be seen, emphasize the importance of continuity in the succession, of the parallel between the stability of the state and the stability of the king's mind and soul, and of the stability of the values of love and relationship in community. Personal order is again related to 'world order'.

> If all the World could have seen't, the woe
> had been universal.
> (Act V, Sc. ii, l. 103)

That the stability must be no deception, that it depends on the real inward health of the men in the community is underlined by the scene in which the 'comics' dress as courtiers:

AUTOLYCUS: I know you . . . a gentleman born
CLOWN: Ay, and have been so any time these four hours
(Act V, Sc. ii, l. 154)

Real worth does not come simply by 'lucky' circumstances, but only by genuine acceptance, by the discovery of positive attitudes to reality.

In the final scene Hermione, albeit wrinkled by time, is restored. Leontes contemplates a final madness, as Florizel contemplated a madness in rejecting real life and real situation for his love:

> Make me to think so twenty years together:
> No settled senses of the World can match
> The pleasure of that madness.
> (Act V, Sc. iii, l. 71)

But no rejection of 'the settled senses of the world' is implied. The formal masque-like close has need for few explanations. Camillo and Paulina are married, and thus rewarded for their embodiment of values and human goodness. The close of the work of art has a confidence purified of anxiety, and enacts in a masque-like way the triumphant rewards to be found in a persistent discipline in the quest for acceptance, resignation and hope. There is a joy and calm not wrested from bitterness, but rather found in positive confidence in human nature.

The second half of the play glows with a confidence in the positive movements and rhythms in human life which make for healing, continuity, propagation, tradition, stability. The poet asks what is the nature of those values which may uphold reason and order. He finds not only values which transcend human frailty in the bestowings of divine grace – but finds a capacity in living creatures themselves to generate wisdom – poetic wisdom – and positive life-growth themselves, renewed in each generation. The young of each generation, like the daffodils,

> Come before the swallow dares, and take
> The winds of March with beauty . . .

– these simple lines, two of the loveliest in Shakespeare, gain their power from the underlying deep compassionate respect Shakespeare has achieved for the beauty of that courage in young people as a manifestation of flowering and creative natural life, a courage which greets the adversity that comes too soon 'with beauty'. (For adversity comes from the beginning of 'promise'.) They convey his hard-won belief in the continuity of life and love, and his gratitude for the joy to be seized from life's evanescence in Time. Shakespeare's values are Christian but do not depend upon adherence to Christianity, or even to supernatural sanctions. Patterns of behaviour in society and as between individuals governed by values – these have transcendent validity, as given in the constant loyalty of Camillo and Paulina. But Shakespeare also perceives that human life could not go on, and be the marvellous manifestation it is, were it not that an altruistic capacity for goodness is continually being re-created and re-exerted by each fresh generation – and that this can even overcome the derangement of reason in the individual by a warped 'intuition'. So there is much forgiveness, pity and repentance in this play. We may continue to maintain an honesty to our intuition (as in Florizel), by continually seeking to distinguish between false and true apprehension of reality, and to know our best selves. The great number of disguises suggest perhaps that an intuitive trust and loyalty ('there is none worthy/Respecting her that's gone') and a continual re-examination of values, a continual testing of the embodiments of human wisdom, must go with a distrust of immediate appearances, in the quest for insight. And this must happen continually in each of us at a deep level, poetically, as creative living. Just as the death of winter is only apparent, the essential continuity of life, of generations, of traditions and values, depends on a long-term belief in enduring values in relationship which are our greatest reality. Shakespeare offers us an earnest of love continually returning to human life, to ensure rebirth and continuity – as 'welcome as the spring to the earth'.

The extreme ugly points of reality, such as the madness of hallucination, and destructive projection, are extremes which can be overcome, balanced and brought to order in Time. The ordered sensibility – as symbolized by the harmony in music and poetry – can sustain meaning and significance in human life against Time and Death. Music in this play, as in *The Tempest*, enacts the ordering power in human nature and creativity itself. The use of music, formal verse, and masque form are themselves a recognition of our need to 'change ourselves' – to heal and forgive – to meet the exigencies of reality, as we may be healed and helped towards inward order by the play itself. The balletic form of the play is a pattern which we possess by experiencing it: Shakespeare does not 'tell' us of the truths he perceived, but seeks to bring us to possess them, by possessing this celebration of them, so we may share his triumphant regaining of hope. The play is an expression of the value in human affairs of reason, love, integrity and social bonds – the play has a sound intellectual 'message'. But, at a much deeper level, it goes beyond telling us about these personal qualities and values – it *enacts* the contemplation of the continuity of life and seeks to change us by our possession of the total experience, by its great creative power. The music and verse may bring order to the unconscious regions where the struggles between creativity and destructiveness, between sanity and dissociation, between love and hate, take place, while we are engaged with understanding the explicit meaning. Such a work is a great force for balance and order in human life. If we can possess the poetic drama, then we can possess something of Shakespeare's achievement of confidence and hope. This may help us towards a greater sense of 'belonging' in the universe, and towards a gladness in life's creative continuity. Such benefits from a great work of art can help us towards personal maturity and order, may help us in striving with the disbalanced and destructive impulses such as are delineated in Leontes, or in the uncertainties of a young Florizel – and found in all of us, with the same bearing on human life at large.

FOUR

The Fiery Hill – *Lady Chatterley's Lover*

A Note

My feelings about *Lady Chatterley's Lover* were so intense at the time of the trial that I wrote at once a long series of notes on what seemed to me the falsity of the book. The process marked a major turning point both in my writing and in my attitudes to life. So absorbed was I in unravelling my attitudes to love, and to Lawrence's treatment of it, that I preferred not to read the comment of anyone else on the subject, beyond F. R. Leavis in his book *D. H. Lawrence, Novelist*, where he has a paragraph or two on *Lady Chatterley*. This was no doubt unscholarly, but it was the way I chose to work. I did not read Leavis in *The Spectator* at the time of the trial and have not read him since. I have not read Professor Wilson Knight on the anal elements in the book in *Essays in Criticism*: my essay was virtually complete by the time this appeared. I had also completed my analysis before the penny dropped at Oxford about 'the secret places of shame'.

I
LAWRENCE'S FALSE SOLUTION

Then I saw that there was a way to hell, even from the gates of heaven, as well as from the City of Destruction!
John Bunyan, *The Pilgrim's Progress*

As everybody in England now knows, *Lady Chatterley's Lover* is the story in novel form of a young titled married woman who falls in love with her husband's gamekeeper, Oliver Mellors, and has a clandestine, passionate affair with him in the grounds of her home, Wragby Hall, in the Industrial Midlands, in the nineteen twenties, or thereabouts. The story recounts the pains and joys of their sexual life together, and their progress towards 'a measure of equanimity'. In the end Mellors is working away on a farm, and

writes to Lady Chatterley that 'what I live for now is for you and
me to live together'. She is pregnant, and there is desire on the
part of both, apparently, to marry, after having divorced their
respective spouses. The story has been called by some a' definition
of marriage'. It is the first story to be published at a popular price
in English which gives full accounts of sexual intercourse in all its
details, using the Anglo-Saxon words which many privately use,
but which are publicly taboo, for the act of coition and for the
private parts of the body, without substitution or inhibition. The
book has sold several million copies.

Its release has been acclaimed as a triumph of enlightenment and
no doubt in a sense it was. It was also a *succés de scandale* which arose
from a publisher's business acumen in the first instance. The
question of what contribution this work makes to our culture has
been too little examined. The question is not whether Anglo-
Saxon words of direct sexual meaning should be printed in books,
or whether descriptions of sexual intercourse should be available
to all who want to read them, but, fundamentally, an artistic one.[1]
Is this a good novel? We know it to be by a sensitive artist. But
are the possessed values it may give, in the end, good ones, leading
us forth – as Lawrence would have consciously wished to lead us
forth – towards more adequate, more truly civilized, fuller living?
Will it, as a work of art, enrich and develop the concepts of those
who read it?

The question of the popular influence of such a great imaginative artist and his effect on attitudes to life is crucial today. As
Lawrence himself declared, the 'intuitive' aspects of the whole
being in us, linked as they are with phantasy and imagination, are
suffering from starvation. In consequence our reality sense and our
power to find meaning in life are weak. Rich imaginative nourishment is scarce and so our concepts – as of values in human relationship – are impoverished. What a Lawrence can offer to the popular
mind and to the mind of the intellectual minority counts a great

[1] One unfortunate effect of the book's release was of course an increased tolerance of pornography such as that of Henry Miller and other writers without even
his pretensions. Publishers have been quick to take commercial advantage of this.
No one can pretend the impulse to market *Fanny Hill* or Frank Harris is a 'literary' one.

deal, because we have so little of the truly creative and positive today in popular and minority culture.

Our concepts and attitudes to life, and our capacities to employ them more or less effectively in living, as in sustaining the free flow of feeling in love and family life, depend to a degree on cultural influences, including books. As culture has become so generally trivial, our life nowadays seems to suffer from the absence of what may be called spiritual challenge, the pursuit of constructive aims and values in contest with our inward nature and the nature of external reality. Lawrence was the last great English writer to offer us such a contest in which to engage ourselves. Our culture since the war seems to have abrogated this positive concern, and many of our works of literature and entertainment picture human beings as helpless victims of a hostile environment, depressively. Meanwhile entertainment culture offers phantasy which has no relation to reality at all, except to disguise it or defend us against it, like a drug. Yet our phantasy life, as we have seen, is crucial to the growth of our capacities to deal with reality: without phantasy there is no effective consciousness. The conscious exercise of the imagination, metaphorically, to come to terms with the painful aspects of reality – with our mortality and our aspiration to transcend it – may be called 'spiritual discipline'.

England had before this century a popular tradition of spiritual discipline. In Bunyan, who was from about 1650 to 1850 England's greatest popular writer (after 1850 he shares the honour with Dickens), we can see the process of this search for something 'beyond' us, greater than, 'outside' the individual. Bunyan's Christian cries that the City of Destruction is doomed: he must fly! Life! Eternal Life! The implication of his work may be taken in non-religious as well as religious terms: as a recognition that our mere existence merely dies – to live well we need to achieve a perception of something which does not die with us. Even if not believers, we may, like Bunyan, still accept that there are values and truths greater than the individual such as may be found in love and personal relationship, or in a sense of life's continuity that transcends mere personal existence, as Shakespeare portrayed these in his work. Christian in *Pilgrim's Progress* progresses through all manner of spiritual challenge. He seeks the wicket-gate of Christ's grace – nowadays in modern terms we might consider this experience as one of undergoing a progress of personal integration – coming to terms with inner and outer reality. Such a process moves, as we have seen, from infant to man, towards toleration of the reality of human existence and towards acceptance of the mortal condition of human life, in search for values, a perception of 'good', and a belief in life's continuity, that transcend the mere reality. Acceptance of such truths must be a real acceptance – the false acceptance is indicated by Bunyan by the fate of Ignorance, who seems to have run the course, but who is seized and thrust into a fiery hill, even from the Gates of Heaven – because his self-discovery is not complete, and so his access to Grace is not complete either. He attains only a 'false solution'. He comes, at the end of his quest, only to destruction. This is a perception in Bunyan's art of the need to continually discipline ourselves to come closer to accepting the reality of our predicament: we never come through. This is the true quest, and it can bring self-fulfilment. We may perhaps accept that equally in creativity, in study, in devotional disciplines, or in psychoanalysis, the quest for insight and understanding must be unflinching if we are to find peace in a profound sense of 'felt order' in life, and of meaning in the individual life. In the long contest we must continually seek to combat distortions and falsifications – as of By-Ends and Mr Worldly Wiseman – as Bunyan did.

Christian, the protagonist of this poetic projection of Bunyan's own spiritual quest, enters the heavenly gates at last. Because of the successful outcome of his ordeal, in the second part of *The Pilgrim's Progress*, the artist is able to offer the world a benign compassionate humanity, a power of succour in living, a tender, triumphant awareness of life's perplexity, even unto death – in the end an earnest of how the human spirit may triumph over death. There is a release from the stern egocentricity in Part One, to a warm sense of community life in Part Two. The people – *all* the people – pass over the River singing, and even the Daughter of Mr Despondency goes through the river singing, though 'none could understand what she said'. It is a deeply moving passage, rendering a compassionate vision of the shared spiritual experience of humanity that can triumph over death itself. All are portrayed, at the end, in the sympathetic light of an apprehension of the universality of human experience. This escape from isolation into compassionate at-one-ness Bunyan discovered through the solitary spiritual torment which he describes in *Grace Abounding*. He attains a compassion springing from the achieved assurance of 'something beyond the self', found in the common vitality of humanity, as a great manifestation of life. It is a truly democratic vision, because Bunyan portrays *all* as able to make access to grace.

In the second part of *The Pilgrim's Progress* Puritan life in the community is depicted warm and humane – it is even in the bath scene virtually erotic:

> When they were returned out of the garden from the bath, the Interpreter took them, and looked upon them, and said unto them, Fair as the moon . . .

Mercy, humanly weak, womanly weak, is granted even the indulgences fit for a young pregnant girl:

> But Mercy being a young and breeding woman, longed for something that she saw there, but was afraid to ask . . . so they called her and said to her, Mercy, what is that thing thou wouldst have? Then she blushed, and said, The great glass that hangs up in the dining room. So Sincere ran and fetched it, and, with a joyful consent, it was given her . . .

This is the essence of English Puritanism, that first the solitary individual must set out alone, sternly to fight the personal battle of self-discovery, driven by conscience, listening to the voice of God, speaking to him alone. *Pilgrim's Progress* is the poetic rendering of the quest described in *Grace Abounding* for peace in the soul. No one can complete the quest for self-awareness for another by proxy, so each one goes alone. And, then, when 'Grace Abounding' is found, the self is released to a fulfilled recognition of the beauty of creation, and not least of the beauty of physical life and human love: the solitary Puritan, after his grim ordeal, becomes benign and tolerant. Bunyan's own affection for his wife and children tenderly and beautifully colours the Second Part of *The Pilgrim's Progress*. But the essence of the devotion, the humanity, the happiness, the great spiritual elation and satisfaction conveyed in *The Pilgrim's Progress* as a whole depends upon Christian's earlier lonely struggle against Appolyon, Doubt, Despair and the Valley of the Shadow, in the First Part, to find his personal reality, the true voice of God in his soul, his inward reality and the tragic truth of man's state on earth. In *Pilgrim's Progress* we see how the Puritan tradition has affinities with the deep stoical attitudes, born of suffering, in English folksong: these express with gravity a commitment to life as a whole, especially to the experience of the heart. Whether Christian or stoical, spiritual discipline obliges each first to seek to understand himself, and gain his sense of significance in finding how much he 'belongs' to the human family: then he may understand and succour others. Only then can he *afford* to do so, wholly (Cf. Wordsworth of the leech-gatherer, 'He could afford to suffer, with those whom he saw suffer . . .').

The Puritan tradition has decayed, and among the disciplines lost has been this kind of contest with experience in the quest for truth – the struggle to find something 'beyond' ourselves, the wicket-gate, of triumphant values, of Christ's mercy, if we are believers; or of the truth of ourselves and the world whether we are or not. *Pilgrim's Progress* corresponds closely with the process of self-discovery, escape from obsessions and delusions, the overcoming of the falsifications of manic defence, and effective release to the world, in the psychoanalytical patient. Bunyan made his quest first in *Grace Abounding* by expressing, ordering and analysing his own spiritual conflicts, and then gave a metaphorical account of this process in *Pilgrim's Progress*. Interestingly enough, he was able to effect this development of his soul because to him words had a forcible, actual, felt existence in the reality of human life: 'That sentence lay like a mill-post at my back.' For him the creative quest in words affected the depths of his being and wrought changes there. So Bunyan exemplifies the value in English life of the vital, metaphorical richness of the English language, its poetic power to enable us to come at our inner truth, and that of the world. Bunyan's language is the rich language of the old English rural community, with all its cadences of gravity. As in folksong, issues of the deeper psyche are enacted out in metaphor, by a 'carrying across' from inner to outer reality. This traditional verbal power and its effectiveness has been weakened in our own time by an uncreative education, by the loss of vernacular idiom, by superficial forms of communication and entertainment, by the prostitution of words, images and emotion in advertising, and other media. The word 'love', for instance, is polluted now by meretricious use in the language of advertising ('People love Players'): so it is less possible to use it well in our relationship with God or in significant relationships between man and woman. Because we can only use the word 'love' in its lessened way, we are that much less able to come to explore reality through love. We are consequently the less able to reach, as Bunyan did, our personal truth, because we have not the good words. Because we cannot find this ourselves, we are less able to attain the release to community, to give out succour and compassion. But a Lawrence can help to refine language again, and so help refine our thought and feeling.

And so in this situation it is crucial to consider the work of such a distinguished and influential artist as Lawrence – a clear, vivid writer, whose background gave him affinities with the same Puritan conscience that produced Bunyan. Lawrence was such a creative and deeply religious man, albeit he was an agnostic, that he was driven to seek into the heart of things.

Lawrence's last book *Lady Chatterley's Lover* is now one of the most widely read novels in the English language. In terms of sales it is second only to the Authorized Version of the Bible. It is having as much influence as any imaginative work can have in an illiterate world, of trivial culture. What effect will this have, if any?

In a way the book is very much like *Pilgrim's Progress*: it is an imaginative search of a kind for insight into personal reality and understanding of the author's own behaviour, by analogy. Lawrence himself was in the Puritan tradition and touched the world of Bunyan from the world of the working-class chapel which was his inheritance. He wished to explore his own personal reality, to discover something 'beyond the self' which could give life significance and meaning, even in our industrial and mechanical age, even though he was agnostic: he sought this in love. He experienced – albeit at a distance – the destructive cataclysm of the Great War. He could see the final disintegration and loss of an England which had existed for several hundreds of years, and saw the population being made by commerce into money-conscious 'money-boys and money-girls', devoted to a meaningless pursuit of material possessions, to making things 'go' simply for the sake of the 'go', in an acquisitive society. What was lacking? To Lawrence. it was wholeness of being, of spontaneous-creative being, of the flowing of the intuitive faculties. He took as the central index of this lack the relationship in love between man and woman. To every man his parents' relationship is crucial in forming his own capacities to love, and his attitudes to love. In his own life Lawrence had experienced as a child, as he records in *Sons and Lovers*, a deeply disturbing awareness that this relationship, over his own stripling head, had broken down. His own mother and father had not had a rich relationship in marriage. That he perceived this we know from several places in his work. In *Sons and Lovers* Paul Morel's mother says to him, 'I've never had a husband, Paul, not really'. In *Odour of Chrysanthemums* the woman protagonist realizes the same thing. In life Mrs Lawrence, it would seem, came to relate to her son almost as a lover, turning to him the polarity due to her husband. In trying to cherish his mother, to whom he became the son-as-lover, Lawrence comes to attribute the failing in her sexual life (which affected him in consequence deeply) to the effects of the industrial society which had degraded men to toilers in the pit – the pit to which his father wanted to send *him*. Obviously this connection established itself powerfully in his mind. His father would have committed him in subjection to industry: his mother prevented this and strove to see that he was educated. So his mother represented 'civilization': she becomes in his work a symbol of the best in English social life, and in her is the inspiration of Lawrence's zeal. He wanted to restore 'England' and the countryside as reparation to the mother. Of the woman of the English Midlands he says:

> Looking out, as she must, from the front of the house towards the activity of man in the world at large, whilst her husband looked out to the back at sky and harvest and beast and land, she strained her eyes to see what man had done in fighting outwards to knowledge . . . She also wanted to know, and be of the fighting host. . . . It was this, this education, this higher form of being, that the mother wished to give her children, so that they too could live the supreme life on earth . . .
>
> *The Rainbow*

The women, in industrial England, as Lawrence pointed out in *The Rainbow*, kept up the civilized values in the working class life, degraded as it was by bad living conditions, hideous conditions of work, and the meanness of industrial wage rates. They struggled amid *laissez faire* justifications of the inhumanity of utilitarian attitudes. They saw the English countryside being made hideous. They felt the indifference to social welfare, and indifference to social order of the industrial magnates. The women were oppressed by the meaningless trashiness of commercial provision-mongering – as nowadays they still are, in a different and more affluent way.

> The car ploughed uphill through the long squalid straggle of Tevershall, the blackened brick dwellings, the black slate roofs, glistening their sharp edges, the mud black with coal-dust, the pavements wet and black. It was as if dismalness had soaked through and through everything. The utter negation of natural beauty, the utter negation of the gladness of life, the utter absence of the instinct for shapely beauty which every bird and beast had, the utter death of the human intuitive faculty was appalling. The stacks of soap in the grocers' shops, the rhubarb and lemons in the greengrocers! the awful hats in the milliners' all went by ugly, ugly, ugly, followed by the plaster and gilt horror of the cinema with its wet picture announcements, 'A Woman's Love!', and the new big primitive chapel, primitive enough in its stark brick and big panes of greenish and raspberry glass in the windows . . .
>
> *Lady Chatterley's Lover*

There is, of course, an unfair exaggeration in the passage – industrialization can hardly be blamed for lemons and rhubarb, stacks of which can surely sometimes restore a little beauty to the urban scene? But the scene is evocative of Connie Chatterley's feeling – which was Lawrence's – that the deadness of her own life is reflected in the ugly industrial world. The personal life had been made squalid by circumstances, especially for women, who wanted beauty. Lawrence feels this because he wanted to make the world beautiful for his mother. The ugliness and oppression extended, Lawrence suggests, to the sexual lives of the women in industrial society – indeed to the intuitive life of the body in all of us.

We must accept the deep and relevant truth in Lawrence's analysis of this aspect of modern life. And, of course, this analysis is the basis of many writers and educationists in their approach to present-day problems of culture and environment. There *is* an intuitive failure in us, and it has something to do with the industrial revolution, the dissociations it brought about in family life, and the make-up of English people.[1] But the problem with Lawrence comes when the life-seeking impulse turns, as it does in *Lady Chatterley*, to an utter rejection of the modern world, and to something approaching malevolence: the industrial workers in this book are, in the end, described as 'carrion bodied'. How did Lawrence's impulse come to be reversed?

There is as we know the Luddite side of Lawrence:

> And so it will be again, men will smash the machines . . .
> (*Work*)

There is a Lawrence who is hysterically offensive about procreation: 'How can they commit the indecency of begetting children . . .' He is quoted in the same vein in Catherine Carswell's *The Savage Pilgrimage* (p. 60):

> There are plenty of children, and no hope . . . even the mice increase, they cannot help it. What is this highest, this procreation? It is a lapsing back to the primal origins, the brink of oblivion. . . . There are many enceinte widows with a cup of death in their wombs.

[1] See E. P. Thompson, op. cit.

This Lawrence is one with no belief in the continuity of life and who rejects education: 'Never teach the mass of the population to read and write. Never!' Allowing for occasional extravagances, we must still admit that Lawrence often wrote savagely not only bombast or nonsense, but with a disturbingly destructive misanthropy. These elements culminate in *Lady Chatterley's Lover*.

This negative and destructive side of Lawrence we need to reject. To do so we must try to discover why he became so negative. The reasons are deep – so deep and complex that we can no longer fully unravel them, since Lawrence himself is dead, and we cannot examine his mind. But from his writings we may piece together a number of symptoms of a fundamentally disturbed attitude to experience – against which he strove himself courageously. Yet he could not overcome these distortions, and so his attitude to life contains dangerous elements, which lead to falsifications, and to disastrous social and political attitudes. The root of these is in the fear of woman, which has something to do with Lawrence's too-close attachment to his mother. He himself records the possessiveness of his mother, and her will to dominate him in *Sons and Lovers*: this he must have experienced in reality, and more deeply, as infant and child. The effect of this over-mothering seems to have been that he came, as an adult, to find it impossible ever to tolerate, much less to cherish, the mother-child relationship.

How the fear of woman and woman's domination became a deeply implanted fear in Lawrence we cannot tell because such a deep fear must surely have very early origins. It would obviously be wrong to judge only from his own autobiographical account of his relationship with his mother, since that is a biased account of later stages in his life. But we need to note that nowhere in Lawrence's work does a normative love-relationship culminate in family life – except perhaps for episodes in *The Rainbow*. The typical situation is one in which the man flees family life, as in *Aaron's Rod*, or the children seem apart from the love-relationship, or the protagonists devote themselves to chastity (as in *St Mawr*).[1]

The relationship between mother and child, and its importance in human life and society, are truths so evident that we tend to

---

[1] See Lawrence's attitude at its worst in Appendix A from *Aaron's Rod*.

take them for granted, and so fail to give them sufficient emphasis. In Tolstoy, of course, we may see this truth of human experience made central in a way it certainly is not in Lawrence. In European art it is symbolized in the innumerable depictions of the Virgin and Child. But nowadays it is sadly possible for large numbers of people to protest that they can only 'fulfil' themselves, and their love-relationships *without* children – giving for this such reasons as the fact that one cannot 'choose' one's own children – 'they might not be attractive or intelligent' – or they would 'limit their careers' or even 'their enjoyment of one another'. No doubt there always were such people who were prepared to rationalize so their own incapacities in living: what disturbs one about the manifestation (as when one sees it exposed for sensational purposes, uncharitably, in a newspaper: see *The Observer*, Sunday, 14th July 1963) is the degree of fear of life it manifests. Children are, for these people, feared as representing the unknown quantities, the unbiddable and uncontrollable elements which may at any moment emerge from the flux of their living. They must be in control, and so they cannot give themselves up to life: at some time or other, inevitably, one feels, these people's capacities to deal with life must break down, because the unknown and unavoidable cannot be so controlled, and to try so to live is unreal. That is, the degree of procreative failure in our society marks a failure to accept certain primary aspects of reality. This fear of reality perhaps centres on that 'primary maternal preoccupation' which is a psychic 'illness', necessary for the infant's growth, but too disturbing for those whose intuitive life is inhibited or suppressed.

Acceptance of sexual creativity is necessary to our relationship with the life in us, and the natural world in which we have our being, even if we have no children. This is no condemnation of the 'selfishness' of those who don't have children. What we must be concerned with is concepts and *attitudes* to love and procreation in human life. In these must be included, for the whole truth, an adequate appreciation of the creativity of love and the importance of the mother-child relationship, in human society. To deny this may involve both an inability to accept reality, and this may have its roots in a fear of or denial of woman.

Some of the relevant connections between the fear of woman, her creativity, and politics, are made by Dr D. W. Winnicott in *The Mother's Contribution to Society*, an essay in his *The Child and the Family*. Here he links fear of woman's dominance and the refusal to recognize the mother's role, to the impulse to dominate. He urges us to recognize 'the immense contribution to the individual and to society which the ordinary good mother with her husband in support makes at the beginning, and which she does simply through being devoted to her infant'. He speaks of the 'infinite debt' any sane person owes to a woman. 'At a time when this person knew nothing about dependence, there was absolute dependence.' To accept this, he says, should not give rise to 'gratitude or even praise' but '*a lessening of fear in us*'. (My italics.)

Lawrence could not accept the immense importance of the mother-child relationship, at times and in part of him. Of course, elsewhere, Lawrence is marvellous, both about children, birth, pregnancy and the baby (see the poem, 'As a drenched, drowned bee . . .'). But the impression one has of his work is never associated with the kind of happy and rich relationship between mother and child, such as we gain from Tolstoy, in his portrayal of Kitty and her baby, for instance. On the contrary, much of his work manifests a deep fear of woman and her creativity.

Winnicott goes on, significantly when we think of the Lawrence of *Lady Chatterley's Lover*, *The Plumed Serpent* and *Aaron's Rod:*

If there is no true recognition of the mother's part, then there must remain a vague fear of dependence. This fear will sometimes take the form of a fear of woman, or fear of a woman, and at other times will take less easily recognized forms, always including the fear of domination. Unfortunately the fear of domination does not lead groups of people to avoid being dominated; on the contrary it draws them towards a specific or chosen domination. Indeed, were the psychology of a dictator studied one would expect to find that, amongst other things, he in his own personal struggle is trying to *control* the woman whose domination he unconsciously fears, *trying to control her by encompassing her, acting for her, and in turn demanding total subjection and 'love'.*

(my italics)

Lawrence fears the woman's domination, as we know from many places in his work. In return he demands that she accept the man's domination. Much of his bad work is given to enlist us in this attempt – to act out the encompassing, controlling and 'acting for' the woman – and in *Lady Chatterley* he does this with intensity. These astute observations by Winnicott suggest a link between the woman-fearing and the Lawrence who wanted a man-controlled dictatorship, with all his dangerous urges towards such dictatorship, as in *The Plumed Serpent*, *The Woman Who Rode Away* and *Kangaroo*.

Yet the origins of Lawrence's fears of woman are inseparable from the springs of his more creative impulses. They have roots in the powerful unconscious feelings Lawrence has about the relationship between his father and mother, and their function in the community of industrial society. These unconscious feelings are symbolized by this artist in various forms. Industry is to be rejected, for instance, because of Lawrence's hatred of his father and the father's ill-treatment of the mother. Yet because he loved his father, industry is also to be hated for what it did to his father, too, reducing him to a slave of the machine, and lessening his capacity to be a good husband to the mother. Yet, while Lawrence wants to give his mother a 'good' husband he is at the same time so much still in love with his mother that he enters into the person of the phantasy-father (such as Mellors who has escaped from the pit and, indeed, from all connection with industrial life, reality and time – and is 'temporizing'). In consequence of this incestuous impulse he fears retribution. The retribution seems to gather from the same industrial 'Thing' that also symbolizes the father and has 'blotted out' the countryside, which, again, Lawrence associates with the mother (and so he makes Connie Chatterley – who is in a sense an image of his ideal mother – a *landed* aristocrat).

The extended analysis of the book in these terms would run something like this:

Lawrence's mother was 'in love with him', to an extent which left no room for the father – and which was too much the intense expression of a personal need. She could not, that is, give her sensitive and acutely perceptive son a 'good-enough' environment. In the early stage, as Fairbairn emphasizes, the mother's role is to convince the infant that she is 'loving him in his own right as a person'. Because of some failure here in his early environment Lawrence found, as a man, huge impediments in himself to the formation of adequate object-relationships – as we know from *Sons and Lovers*, and autobiographical material. Of course, because he is a great artist and a courageous soul, he wrests his *oeuvre* from the struggle to overcome the weaknesses of his psyche. But the truth is that in his own make-up there remained strong elements of infantile attitudes to relationship and love, because his 'too-close' relationship with his mother had inhibited his maturation.

My theory here is that Lawrence failed in *Lady Chatterley* to approach adult relationship at all, and loses his way altogether. He depicts a picture of neurotic genitality, conditioned by infantile oral aggressiveness: thus, both the book and its direction are virtually an act of infantile oral sadism. A quotation from Dr Harry Guntrip is relevant here:

> Neurotic genitality, which is compulsive, expresses oral sadistic rather than truly genital attitudes . . . [Guntrip says of truly genital relationships that they 'represent the co-operative mutuality and giving of two equal partners'].
>
> *Personality Structure and Human Interaction*, p. 291

I shall try to demonstrate how Lawrence cannot attain a picture of 'truly genital' 'co-operative' relationships, involving equal partners, and how his conception of genitality remains infantile. Infantile too, I consider, is the oral-verbal assault, which the book, with its explicitness and its 'direct' language, is.

Another failure in the artistic elements of the book, and the direction it takes, with origins in the failure to leave behind infantile concepts, is in its concentration, as we shall see, on sensuality. Lawrence cannot discover here that 'the ultimate goal of the libido is the object' (Fairbairn). He tries to solve the problem of love in terms of erotic pleasure merely. To quote Guntrip again, this false quest is inevitably doomed, since man's chief need is in mutual and equal relationship, and not in libidinal expression in sensual pleasure:

If one switches attention away from the object to the pleasure of the object-relationship experience, the object is lost sight of, the experience of a satisfying object-relationship is lost, and the pleasure soon evaporates. Those who seek pleasure only find the unpleasurable kind of excitement of the continuing tension of a never satisfied quest.

op. cit., p. 288

This is both a description of Lawrence's doom in this novel, and our response in reading it: 'the pleasure soon evaporates', as it never does from a book which gives us the essence of problems of object-relationships, such as *Sense and Sensibility*, *King Lear*, or *Odour of Chrysanthemums*.

The infantile modes pervade the whole of the story. In presenting the coition between Connie and Mellors the art seems to be satisfying an unconscious need in Lawrence to phantasy his own unconsciously desired coition between himself in the place of his father with his mother. (I call the composite hero-author figure Morelorence.) Because of the degree of identification and projection in the phantasy this is of course virtually a narcissistic coition with himself, and reality is thus totally evaded by short-circuit. In this relationship there must be no child – it would be rival to the son's demand on the mother or her projection: so there can be no real acceptance of a child in the love-story. Again, since the book is an act of 'control' over the feared woman, there can be no child, for it is the woman's creativity that is essentially subject to destructive attack.

At the outset Connie's urge is related to the chicks in Mellor's care, as a symbol of the natural desire to procreate. But after this episode the procreative theme is suppressed in favour of mere sexual docility on her part, and moves towards a denial of her separate existence, and of her creativity as woman. Lawrence unconsciously seemed not to be able to tolerate the creation of a child: he cloaks his reasons as we shall see under comments on the state of the world ('and not have many children . . .'). But the hostility to creativeness lies deeper than that. So his portrayal of love inevitably becomes distorted, limited, and the reverse of life-promoting, while reality is increasingly denied.

The sex between the protagonists in *Lady Chatterley's Lover*
becomes a mere 'rather awful sensuality', anxious and even perverted, leading not towards a sense of significance, to the security
of 'the rainbow' which triumphs over death and time, or a hope in
continuity, achieved by love and generation, but instead towards
a haunting sense of doom and strangulation. The book ends in a
splenetic denial of the best in human nature, a pharisaical attitude
to industrial society and the people in it. It conveys a deathly
attitude to the unborn child, a vacillating attitude to marriage, and a failure to accept that mutual regard in equal
right, in 'disquality', between man and woman – though such
concepts of identity and 'separateness' are so crucial to our future.
A 'measure of equanimity' is achieved (as in the poems, from
which the phrase comes): but the novel implicitly denies the
values in his best work. The sensual love culminates not in the
creative vulva, but, symbolically, in the anus, a parallel to Birkin's
urge to have a relationship with a man, at the end of *Women in
Love*.

Lawrence's very agonies of trying to escape from his own toils,
because he is a brave, sincere, sensitive artist are in themselves of
major interest and value, because he was a genius. Such portrayal
of tenderness as he does achieve, such escape from the self, in the
discovery of love and reality is marvellous. But in this work it is
blocked, and *Lady Chatterley's Lover* is an embracement of the self:
it is narcissistic, self-enclosed, and denies reality. Lawrence falsifies
the world and sex – as the Hindu text has it: 'he who embraces the
self knows neither within nor without'. The book becomes a
barrier to understanding and insight, rather than an illumination:
falsification rather than truth.

There is a sense in which any work of writing is a narcissistic
work, and even an exhibitionist act in narcissistic ways – any
writer experiences uncertain pleasures and agonies in seeing his
name or work in print, and in exposing his private suffering to
public view. He obtains relief and satisfaction from the very act of
narcissistic exhibitionism and oral aggressiveness that writing is,
because he is sharing it with others, and 'taking the world into his
mouth' as it were, as a baby wants to do. All the creatures in any

man's work, including Shakespeare's, are spun out of himself, part
of himself. How much he succeeds, of course, depends, as Mr
Eliot has said, on how far he 'separates the man who suffers from
the man who creates': how much he translates his private agony
into terms by which it can be apprehended as universal experience,
seen afresh, and seen in its place as an aspect of our shared compassionate humanity, so that we may gain insight and understanding,
feeling, 'Ah, yes, I recognize this experience, that I too have had.'
But in this book the narcissism is a prison – a *huis clos* – from which
Lawrence does not escape.

We may begin looking for proof of the over-personal nature of
the novel even in the names of the characters. Here the imaginative processes are perhaps similar to the ways dreams are 'used' by
patients in psychoanalysis, to discuss emanations from the psyche
which can only emerge in metaphorical and cryptographic disguise: in this word-play often plays a major part. So it does in
imaginative creation.

Lawrence perhaps began to compose his names thus. From the
'cry' for 'life' maybe comes the name OLIVER (O-live-er) for the
hero. But certainly MELLORS is an anagram of MOREL, the
name Lawrence used for his father in *Sons and Lovers*. MELLORS
also contains the syllable LOR having the same sound as the 'Law'
in Lawrence.[1] Where is the rest of Lawrence's own name concealed? It is in ConstANCE. I suppose it might be possible that in
the sensitive verbalizing activity of Lawrence's mind 'Constance'
also echoes alliteratively 'Jocasta', and there is some significance in
Mellors' christian name beginning with an 'O' – Lawrence could
not disguise from his subconscious mind or even his aware intelligence that he was writing an Oedipus 'tragedy'. Clifford is Laius:
but his name also contains the L O R syllable, albeit divided up.
There is also the distant echo of Lawrence's aristocratic confidante
Lady O. Morrell, to whom he wrote to tell her that she 'needed'
his kind of verbal aggression.

The most important aspect of these verbal-anagram clues seems

[1] This clue suggests also an identification by the letter-code AWR with St
MAWR of *St Mawr*, with the Stallion for whom *Lou* (with whom Lawrence
identifies) has such affection.

to me that which suggests that when Mellors is making love to Constance there is an aspect of Lawrence making love to himself, and this draws our attention to the narcissism of the book. Lawrence is, as it were, ravishing himself with words: and though Constance is perhaps called Constance because the one *constant* love in Lawrence's life was his mother ('The bonds of love are ill to loose', he says in *Lady Chatterley*, and in a poem to his mother, written on honeymoon, 'I shall always be true to you'),[1] she is also *him*. Lawrence in this was embracing himself, and ends by making an anal possession of himself, in final oral-anal aggressive verbal sensuality. This process of intense identification with his heroine would explain why throughout Lawrence's work he is so pre-occupied by the female experience; concerned, too, to demolish the female self since he wants to take the woman's place; and why in this book there is a continual concern with Connie's feelings in sexual union and orgasm, and much less with Mellors'. Lawrence wants the woman to have 'good' sex (because his mother 'never had a husband really'). Yet it is to himself he wants to make sex good – the self which has suffered from the mother's sexual inadequacy (she was not properly polarized towards the father). This egocentric preoccupation is so monistic and unwilling to en-compass reality that any actual woman he wants to destroy, be-cause he fears her reality. Mellors the 'actual' lover is thus pre-occupied, on the other hand, largely with his feelings of doom, fear, mistrust, with his sloganizing, and the preservation of his 'integrity'.

This self-ravishment – more and more prevalent in modern

[1] Perhaps Lawrence reverts to the idiom and metre of cheap greetings cards in this poem because he associates these with the boyhood for which he is nostalgic, when thinking of his dead mother. *Lady Chatterley* is dogged by similar intense but sloppy feelings, as he attempts in the book to resurrect the dead mother as an act of 'constancy'. Note the title and that his soul 'lies helpless' beside her death bed.

> And so, my love, my mother,
> I shall always be true to you.
> Twice I am born, my dearest:
> To life, and to death, in you;
> And this is the life hereafter
> Wherein I am true.
>
> *The Virgin Mother*

literature among Lawrence's imitators, particularly in American
novels concerned with 'sexual reality' – is done in words. The
verbal aggression is itself a defence against reality – an attempt to
throw the closed-circuit hallucination over it. It is done 'chatterly'
– talkatively, wordily. This explains the name in the title – for
Lady Chatterley's Lover is virtually a symbolic dream-statement of
self-ravishment by words – the very thing Lawrence makes a
scapegoat in the castrated Laius-self of Clifford, as we shall see,
the thing that he himself fears to become, the ball-'less' verbalizer
who cannot escape into creation from his own will-driven mill-
wheel of words, and who cannot engage with experience potently.
Lady's Chatterley Lover, Lady's Lover Chatterley – the talkative
(or word-) lover of Her Ladyship: but yet Lady Jane and John
Thomas are both aspects of the one creature, in the writing, for a
man can only describe his own experience. Law*rence*, who has
much in him of wanting to be a woman, perhaps so that he could
'warm-heartedly fuck' himself, merges into Cons*tance*, and the
book *Lady Chatterley's Lover* is a verbal act of self-embracement,
Lover Verbally Loving Himself. The whole is a projection of narcissistic phantasies which touch reality at no point. In this lies the
contradiction that Lawrence should so much condemn the word-
mill, and the mind-mill in sex – yet offer us, even to the point of
a national scandal, the 'four-letter words' scandal, a great quantity
of tedious verbalizing of what should never have been described
in words and of what *cannot* be described in words. Ironically, we
have at the end of this story of ideal, idyllic sex, his hero *verbalizing
about his own satisfactions* at the moment when his seed springs
forth in the 'creative act that is more than procreative'! At the
point when, in the arms of his beloved, he should have been in
forgetfulness of the world within and without he *thinks in words*,
'I stand for the touch of bodily awareness. . . .' And we are left with
a mental-verbal conscious anxiety (as to whether we have 'good
sex') instead of enriched intuitive awareness.

This negative translation of a personal psychic agon into a
cultural act of narcissistic exhibitionism ('as beautiful as the naked
self') explains the insistent, over-insistent tedium of much of the
story. It explains the sense we are left with afterwards that the

indescribable should not have been described. It explains the strange sterility of the book. It leaves us in no way with our life flowing in new discriminative sympathy, with no renewed sense of the act of sex being more 'valid and precious'. It leaves us disconcerted, less able to bear our own reality. The qualitative failure of the book goes with its quantative success now: the millions of popular readers do not read, mark and learn in a compassionate mood: they read for that tittilation that satisfies anxiety – many only read, in fact, the 'good bits', and the 'rude words'. The result is an increased inhibiting mentality about sex, if anything. As with Freud, the world has exaggerated Lawrence's bad rather than his best side.

Lawrence could not conquer his psychic Appolyon. Perhaps the point where he meets his Arch Enemy is the explicit discussion through Mellors of his own unfortunate experiences with women. Mellors could not find access to grace at the wicket-gate of Connie's body, because Lawrence was not able, in his whole psyche, to accept the conception in the woman's womb, nor was he able to accept the essential equality – or 'disquality' – of woman. Lawrence can record, in Mellors, his striving towards accepting his own yielding to woman – something which Mellors fears as deeply as Lawrence did. Lawrence explores Connie's yielding as a woman to a man. But, right at the end, Mellors retains his mental separation, his willed domination over the woman, his denial of female reality, by preserving his egocentric 'integrity' ('Thank God *I've got a woman*') – *and Lawrence applauds*. The hero ends in loving 'the chastity that flows between us'. And, as in other books by Lawrence (at the end of *St Mawr* for instance) there is a strange preoccupation with chastity rather than the glad acceptance of the established rhythms of a love-relationship. From this we may deduce that it was Lawrence himself who found physical sex and the reality of love intolerable, and found in them no gateway to a belief in continuity, through procreation. At a less deep level we will find some faults in the book arising from the fact that for Lawrence the sexual act may well have been something of an offence to the female because he resented his father's relationship with his mother. He loved his mother, and

wanted to make love to her himself, Oedipus-wise, unconsciously
– remaining in the infantile attitude. This would have been shameful and taboo, because it was incestuous, and the mother must
not, of course, enjoy such a shameful thing. Also, the 'infant' mind
finds it intolerable to allow the mother to be in any way imperfect
and for her to enjoy such a guilt-laden thing as sex cannot be
allowed. Again, the son would fear the father's vengeance for
incest, and this vengeance may come from 'within the woman'.
Certainly for such reasons – common manifestations but exacerbated in him by his deeper fears – for Lawrence the sexual act with
any woman seems to have been filled with trouble, as it always is
to some degree for all of us.

He may have been impelled to write most of his books unconsciously to seek to overcome this trouble, and did so with
great courage. His characters seem at times to be seeking to prove
their normal potency as Lawrence must have needed to do himself. But the sense of doom and shame inherent in sex never leaves
him, even though he seeks to exorcize it by words which are often
almost incantatory.

Lawrence sets out to 'resurrect' for his 'ladyship' mother a
creative sex his own mother did not have. For the reasons I have
suggested he sets out to prove himself, in Morelorence, sexually,
a 'proper' man, a 'better' man than the usurped father.

Here Lawrence falls into the humiliating situation we all experience in our love and marriage situations – he repeats, for
unconscious reasons the mistakes of his own parents, and, being
unable to gain insight into them or recognize their bad aspects,
endorses them. Here, obviously, for one thing, his Oedipal feelings for his father link with his class feelings. Lawrence, in the
person of Mellors, feels humiliated to think he has working-class
origins: he will not be 'kept' by a lady: he will not be a mere 'my
lady's fucker'. But, Mellors reflects, you don't ('*after all*') lose
your integrity as a man by going into a woman. And moreover –
so implies the sexual experience as delineated in the book – you
can *humiliate* her into the bargain even, really, destroy her.
Lawrence, as I have argued, is unconsciously having sexual intercourse with his mother, the aristocrat of his family, the cultured

one, the 'her ladyship' of the Bottoms. But of course, he has related feelings about his own wife who was an aristocrat too. He
enters 'her ladyship' by entering the person of his father, and the
consequent guilt, in which he seems to fear the retributions of
impotence, castration, humiliation, links with his feelings of
possible retribution for this from the Industrial scene on which he
has projected his feelings about his father. Or he fears that the
'aristocratic' woman (i.e. – the one 'above', as is the mother) will
laugh at him, humiliate him, possibly hurt or attack him from
within. Thus he invents a woman who will not laugh (the book
is unbearably solemn), and who will *submit* and be controlled.
She must be humiliated to see how much 'mummy' will endure –
if she will endure all, then the infant son is truly loved and his
fears of retribution or separation – and death – can be at last
allayed. Her body must be exorcized of its inner threats, including
the anus.[1] In Mellors Lawrence invents a super-potent working
class man who will 'burn out all' the 'shames', in the deepest
places, by force of sensuality (though the sensuality is really
verbal), by sheer aggression.

But this dominant exorcizing male becomes in fact, in the process, worse than the brutal and unrefined Morel! He becomes,
with Lawrence's full endorsement, a creature whose impulsive
domineering is not far from that of the drunken miner come home
to his comforts – 'a real man!' –

> He jerked his head swiftly . . . she took it obediently . . . it was a night
> of sensual passion. And how in fear, she had hated it. But how she
> had really wanted it! At the bottom of her soul. . . . To find a man
> who dared to do it . . .
>
> What liars poets, and everybody were! They made one think one
> wanted sentiment. What one supremely wanted was this piercing,
> consuming rather awful sensuality. . . . How rare a thing a man is . . .

How far we are here from the recognition of 'disquality in
equality', such as Lawrence explores between Birkin and Ursula!
The old working-class brutality is strangely vindicated in Mellors –

---

[1] Some patients under psychoanalysis are said to be found to actually believe
that the vulva may contain teeth or other destructive and dangerous forces.

the brutality of the man driven into untenderness by the circumstances of the wretched life of industrial poverty - children coming, the wife worn-out, tired, unable to live the 'life of the mind'.
Hopeless, the husband tries to be tender for a time, then exerts his
will on her: sexual relationship becomes a matter of humiliating
rape.[1] But it is this very failure to achieve mutual genitality
that Lawrence virtually *vindicates* in Connie and Mellors: and
Connie does not even complain – she 'really wanted it'. He is *man*!

The whole book, therefore, is a disastrous projection of
Lawrence's own psychic difficulties. These are projected over the
face of reality, so that *the nature of things* may be blamed for his
own troubles. Outer reality is 'blamed' for troubles of his inner
reality. The distortions enable him to find an *external cause* in
industrial society for the unacceptable inward truths which he
finds too painful for acceptance.

These aspects of the book will be further explored here, together with further themes. There is his profoundly uncompas-
sionate and punitive attitude to Clifford, the usurped and castrated
Laius, and the fear of impotence associated with him that leads to
the impulse to assert potency by verbalizing. There is Lawrence's
identification with Constance, to experience and exhibit her
sexual experience, which has consequences in further over-
straining of the function of prose in the book so that it is forced
beyond tolerable limits. The narcissistic 'embracing of the self'
here becomes both a loss of knowledge and a failure of communication. There is the treatment of the Oedipal usurper Mellors or
Morelorence and his ambivalent relationship to the industrial
world, causing a collapse of the function of intelligence in the
argument of the book which becomes splenetic, misanthropic,
hysterical, and at times ludicrous, implying an utter rejection of
reality and of the hope for continuity in life. This culminates in a
malevolent denial of the potentialities of human nature and so of
possibilities in education and culture – even to do what Lawrence
supposes himself to have set out to foster.

---

[1] A correspondent quotes a working-class man's comment: "Tain't much con-
jure being married. They all want it at first, but it soon wears off. I have to take it
pract'lly by force – not nice when it's me right, is it?'

Finally, we may consider the lack of love's reality in this book altogether – while we may go on to find more of love's truth in *Look! We Have Come Through!*

2

THE REALITY OF LOVE

So energetic and persuasive is Lawrence in defence of his distortions that only by working very hard to unravel his tangles can we protect ourselves, and expose his untruths, in order to come better at his truths. It is important to do so, because Lawrence is often recommended as healthy and creative in his attitudes to love and sex. I think this belief is a very dangerous one. Lawrence often seeks to involve us in neurotic and distorted attitudes. One central aspect of this process is the cunning distortion of sexual truth he weaves in *Lady Chatterley's Lover*. What we may first accept, perhaps, from evidence in his work, is that, in confirmation of my analysis of his symbolism above, whenever he gave himself to a woman, Lawrence, like Mellors, was seized with a sense of impending retribution and doom, sometimes in terms of strangulation, sometimes in terms of a threat of mutilation from within the woman ('the beak-like clitoris'). Sometimes this threat associates with 'money-getting' (as are Mellor's 'white hands') that threaten strangulation to anyone who tries to 'live beyond money' – so possibly this manifests the memory of a childish fear that the father wanted to send the son out to work in the industrial machine, and thereby 'squeeze the life' out of him. Another underlying reason for this fear is perhaps in the unconscious intense incestuousness of Lawrence's feelings for his mother: even on his honeymoon, as we shall see, Lawrence wrote love poems to his mother wishing she could be having his experiences 'through his eyes'. These are couched in intense phallic imagery ('I am a naked candle *burning off* on your grave'). Such incestuous urges, as they accompanied Lawrence's sexual activity (as we can tell from his poems), would naturally be followed by guilt and fears of retribution.

What is not true is Lawrence's explanation of this fear in terms of it being a consequence of that 'will' in man to 'make things go' that produced industrial society, and that industry threatens man. This is a projection over outer reality, and a paranoiac projection of his fears of retribution from the 'industrial' father.

These unrealities both perhaps associate with a reality problem over love. The clue here is in Lawrence's post-coital woe. The melancholy frequently expressed by Lawrence as following sexual satisfaction, and his desire to have the mother present in his honeymoon experience, suggest that for him sexual desire, the image of the loved one, and the rhythms of sexual relationship were deeply informed with feelings which were nostalgic – in the sense that they were commingled (as they tend to be in all of us) with a desire to return to an impossible state of bliss such as the infant hallucination 'invents': 'eternal happiness':

> So I hope I shall spend eternity
> With my face down buried between her breasts
> (*Song of a Man Who is Loved*)

This may be linked with failures of the reality sense and the sense of continuity. In a man who has limitations on his capacity to accept the reality of adult love – who finds it hard to accept mutual genitality and to recognize his own and his partner's separate identities in togetherness – his confusion of infant states of relationship with adult states may prove disastrous. It may confuse his dealings with the 'other' – because the realities of both the self and the other are confused by projected images, and by identification and introjection. Even desire and satisfaction then become tormented – because adult modes are imbued with the aggressions and fears of the infant.

We have seen earlier how the baby 'makes' the mother's breast when he is hungry. Winnicott speaks of the other faculty in the baby of 'making the breast disappear when not wanted':

This last is most terrifying and is the only true annihilation. To not want, as a result of satisfaction, is to annihilate the object. This is one reason why infants are not always happy and contented after a satisfactory feed. One patient of mine carried this fear right on to adult life and only grew up from it in analysis, a man who had an extremely good early experience with his mother and his home. *His chief fear was satisfaction.*

(My italics)

In a footnote Winnicott adds:

I will just mention another reason why an infant is not satisfied with satisfaction. He feels fobbed off. He intended, one might say, to make a cannibalistic attack and he has been put off by an opiate, the feed. At best he can postpone the attack.

These two aspects of satisfaction, in their relation to adult sexuality, will be found to be most significant when we turn back to Lawrence, and his preoccupation with the gloom and anxiety which, in him and his protagonists, follows even the most 'successful' coition. The anxious comparisons ('That 'twere the best yet' etc.) are a symptom of this fear of satisfaction, and anxiety as to whether states of 'flop' will prove bearable. The satisfaction brought by coition may even bring a threat of 'ceasing to exist'.

In *Look! We Have Come Through!* we can find expressed some of these moods in coital experience, as of a man re-experiencing in an intense love-relationship problems related to those of infancy. Lawrence, being a 'terrifyingly honest' man records fits of violence, fear, rage, and depression associated with sexual satisfaction. No doubt one of our most disturbing experiences is to find that even our happiest sexual experiences can leave us with a sense of anxiety, anger, depression, restlessness, and even hostility, and to find that these associate with a whole reality-problem.

How can these things be overcome? Here lies the crux of the problem which Lawrence tackles in *Lady Chatterley's Lover*. Briefly and crudely it may be said that in this work Lawrence sought to overcome the post-coital anxiety he knew from his own experience, by insisting on sensuality – on 'deepening' the erotic experience. His attention, we must note here, is totally given to *erotic impulses*, and the *desire to put them right*: if they could be put right, then everything else (i.e. the rest of reality) would follow. This is to invert the truth. The roots of the anxiety are not in the erotic impulses at all, since these have been satisfied, by sexual gratification, as by a feed in the baby. The anxiety is a matter of our *whole* reality sense. The anxiety has its roots in the fear that one has 'annihilated the object' – that is, in the difficulty of holding on to a sense of the reality of one's self and the reality of the beloved when all desire is gone. This has to do, obviously, with one's sense of the reality of one's love and being, to things which belong to *other areas than the erotic*. The problem is one of our dealings with reality altogether, and with love, not simply the reality of sex. Again, another source of the anxiety is in the frustration of aggressive and destructive impulses, which were directed, as in the baby, at 'eating' the beloved. (Cf. 'I could eat you' in popular use.) Of course, in normal adult sexual inter- course, these impulses are present as slight sadism – biting, and aggressive movements in coition. But inevitably, since one cannot devour the beloved any more than the baby can devour the breast, some aggression and destructiveness may remain polarized, post- poned, but not resolved. This may well become associated with all our other many fears connected with sex – of incestuous feel- ings, retribution for these, fears of harmful things 'inside' the partner, and so forth. But certainly, we may note, again – these are problems of '*finding the object*' in mutual relationship. They have to do with problems of our inner reality, in terms of unresolved aggressive impulses. The solution of these has to do with our capacities to make reparation, capacities developed at the 'stage of concern'.

Anxiety over sexual relationships, then, has its origins in a complex combination of impulses, erotic, aggressive, destructive, and to do with one's whole hold on reality. Lawrence's error was in supposing he could exorcize the anxiety by *concentrating on the sensual alone*, and by aggressive verbal-oral *accounts* of the erotic. He pre-occupies himself, that is, too exclusively with sex and sex- talk – and forgets all those complexities and realities which belong to love. But because the anxieties are not caused by the sex, rather by the other aspects of the realities of self and of love, he was inevitably doomed to failure and to error.

Nor is aggressiveness, oral or sexual, a way out. The way out of such anxieties is by restoring a whole reality sense:

In early stages [of an infant's life or of a course of psychoanalysis

which is following the pattern of the child's early development],
when the *Me* and the *Not-me* are being established, it is the aggressive component that more surely drives the individual to a need for
a *Not-me* or an object that is felt to be *external*.

Winnicott, op. cit.

In the love-relationship this seems to me to imply that the way to
overcome the torments and unresolved anxieties of loving is by
seeking to become more aware of the reality of the partner – of
her 'separate, separate' being – of her 'MYSTIC NOW' – to use
Lawrence's own terms. As the mother's continuing existence,
love, and care help the child through torment and trial after
torment and trial, so that he can gain experience of triumph over
difficulty, and knowledge of constructive whole experiences,
towards wholeness and balance, so in the adult lover, to develop
a respect for the 'other' existence of the partner is the means to
survive and triumph over the torments and trials of love. (This
sense of the continuity of the partner is exquisitely expressed in
The Winter's Tale, as particularly in Florizel's lines about Perdita
and the waves, see above, pp. 183–4). Winnicott goes on:

> The erotic experience can be completed while the object is subject-
> ively conceived or personally created, or while the individual is near
> to the narcissistic state of primary identification of earlier date.
>
> The erotic experience can be completed by anything that brings
> relief to the erotic instinctual drive, and that allows of fore-pleasure,
> rising tension of general and local excitement, climax and detumesc-
> ence or its equivalent, followed by a period of lack of desire (which
> may itself produce anxiety because of the temporary annihilation
> of the subjective object created through desire). *On the other hand, the
> aggressive impulses do not give any satisfactory experience unless there is
> opposition. The opposition comes from the environment, from the NOT-
> ME which gradually comes to be distinguished from the ME.*
>
> *Aggression in Relation to Emotional Development*,
> op. cit., p. 215 (my italics)

Although Winnicott is here describing a progress in psychoanalysis, which follows a progress in the baby's mind, he might
well also be describing the progress of a love-relationship. The
important point is that which draws attention to the need for

'opposition', so that aggressive impulses can be *satisfied*: for 'opposition', we may read 'touch with reality' – the reality of another person, and their existence in the real world. As we shall see, in *Lady Chatterley*, Lawrence provides himself, in his ideal relationship, with a partner who is neither real nor exists in a real world – and provides no 'opposition'. All is still 'subjectively conceived' and 'narcissistic'. Lawrence's novel is too much enclosed in the monistic *Me* – and so is the attitude to sexual relationships he recommends by implication. Even Connie, the created love-object, has no 'opposition' to offer – as Ursula offers in *Women in Love*,[1] and as Frieda eminently did, as a real woman, who threw pots at his head.

The sense of continuity in a love-relationship that can transcend periods of anxiety and 'deadness' depends upon a complexity of shared elements between the partners that belong to the civilized plane. A love-relationship that was solely erotic, such as Lawrence tries to postulate here, would find periods in which desire was allayed, with the love-object 'annihilated', that might be intolerable – one has to learn, as it were, to let things 'die' for a time, without fearing death or loss because of it. Related to this is the energetically idealizing title of the poem-sequence – *Look! We have come through!* Nobody has ever 'come through', and no-one ever will. We all need to go on contesting, seeking and recreating – coming through, yes, but never come through. To cry, 'Look! We have come through!' is to court disaster, because it is implicitly to make impossible demands on life and insist that it *must* be good now, at will. Of course, a confidence in a relationship can grow, but even so, here, the very insistent note of that 'Look!' suggests a lack of confidence against which Lawrence is exerting a destructively idealizing urge.

What Lawrence is unable to do in *Lady Chatterley* is to find the clue to continuity – by allowing the sexual and erotic fall into place in the larger complex of relationship and love. This larger complex includes the aggressive, the destructive, and the sense of the external *Not-me* – and civilized values by which conflict and set-backs can be resolved and transcended. In these civilized areas

[1] See Appendix C.

are to be found possibilities of continuity and survival: the lover who relies solely on the erotic is doomed to fear from time to time, because he has allayed desire and thus destroyed the object of his love for the time. To quote Guntrip again, 'the object is lost sight of' and 'the pleasure soon evaporates'. We all know this kind of deep anxiety from our honeymoon days – and *Lady Chatterley's Lover* fails because it never develops beyond the honeymoon stages of touch to a mutuality that enables us to transcend moments of separation, anxiety, the subsidence of passion, and the fear of ceasing to exist. Dr Winnicott's final paragraph is illuminating here:

> In adult and mature sexual intercourse, it is perhaps true that it is not the purely erotic satisfactions that need a specific object. It is the aggressive or destructive impulse in the fused impulse that fixes the object and determines the need that is felt for the partner's actual presence, satisfaction, and survival.

Here we have, in the language of modern psychology, an expression of that need for mutual regard, in freedom and 'separate, separate' togetherness such as we have seen Chaucer and Shakespeare exploring, in the quest for love, and such as we know Lawrence to have explored in his best work.

Lawrence's error, in this bad work, was to concentrate too exclusively on the erotic, at the expense of the need to find the actuality of the partner in love, in the world 'out there' – in those areas where aggressive and destructive impulses find 'opposition', and can be fused and brought to civilized association. In one sense the partner given Mellors is annihilated by him (brought to 'the nought of her last solution'); in another sense Lawrence, because both his partners are unreal, and are himself, is enclosed in his narcissism like a foetus – and has annihilated everything except himself. He makes the world as monistic as it is for the new-born baby. In this his work becomes as far from reality as it is possible to get.

Until we devise more effective modes of discussing these deeper aspects of an author's psychology, however, we cannot hope to continue literary analysis at such a level. It will be necessary to discuss the book for the rest of this essay at the level of more accessible themes. We should, however, remember and try to recognize the deeper elements which belong to areas of Lawrence's consciousness formed in his primitive early relationship with his mother – at the time of feeding and weaning – and long before the later time of son-lover-to-the-mother whose experience he records in *Sons and Lovers*. Everything we examine of, say, Lawrence's Oedipal impulses towards his father and mother has earlier concomitants, in which were formed his very capacities to utter images at all, and to explore experience in phantasy as he does in his writings. The very nature of his sexual phantasy, as I have suggested here, is inevitably closely linked with intense feelings for the mother – and so, inevitably, she and every heroine merge. But the sons-and-lovers problem is but an extension of a much deeper dissociation caused by traumatic experience, or failures of the maternal environment, in Lawrence's earliest infancy. Our further discussion of the book will be largely in terms of more 'secondary' problems – but the analysis of these continues to indicate a grave fundamental dissociation from reality.

Certainly we shall have no difficulty in accepting that sex for Lawrence (as E. T. reports in her memoir) was full of trouble: so he makes it so for Mellors, and so, in many of his books he seeks to allay this trouble, and, by coming to the root of it, to exorcize it.[1]

The trouble, however, was so deep (and Lawrence was, we are forced to say, so neurotic) that in fact, despite all his brave, creative,

---

[1] See the poems *Monologue of A Mother*, p. 19, Vol. I. *Complete Poems*, a statement of the mother's intense need for the son; *Lightning*, p. 36, 'love lost in a thaw of fear'; *The Bride*, p. 83 – the dead mother a 'bride'; *The Virgin Mother*, p. 83 (quoted above). Also note the very telling end to the poem *Snap-dragon* about the symbolic strangling and erotic touching of a flower (Cf. 'the white hands in the air' that threatened Mellors):

> And I do not care, though the large hands of revenge
> Shall get my throat at last, shall get it soon,
> If the joy that they are lifted to avenge
> Have risen red on my night as a harvest moon,
> Which even death can only put out for me:
> And death, I know, is better than not to be . . .

– the expectation of 'revenge' for sexual joy is the neurotic ghost which haunted Lawrence as a lover, and haunts many of his characters.

and supreme efforts, he could never overcome his sense of doom, following on the sexual expression of love. In personal love he could but attain the 'measure of equanimity' such as is reached by Mellors and Connie, and the protagonists of *Look! We Have Come Through!*

Possibly, as we would consider now, psychoanalysis might have helped Lawrence personally to overcome this difficulty in his living. But it is because he could not overcome these problems as an artist, despite his genius, that he became in the end malevolent and destructive. He could not redeem his inner reality and its agonized distortions; so he protected himself by projecting the distortions on to external reality – on to the industrial world, and to England, and, in the end, over human nature.

3
THE QUEST FOR LOVE

Let us first take the story as Lawrence meant it to be – a quest for love. This may help us to discover at which points he, like Christian, is turned aside from the true path. In the story which Lawrence meant to write we have a work we might well compare with Bunyan's. Lawrence's *Grace Abounding* is to be found in the record of his life. His marriage with Frieda was stormy, as one may glimpse through biographies, poems and letters. But there was a beauty in it which he expresses in his wonderfully tender poetry, particularly in the sequence *Look! We Have Come Through!* The title of this sequence lies behind *Lady Chatterley's Lover*. Look, says Lawrence, at the spiritual struggle which marriage is – the *Pilgrim's Progress* we have to make in loving. If we are successful there, at this centre where man meets woman in the creative act of love, then all will be well. There we shall discover the spiritual, creative significance of life. The body in the whole being must be resurrected:

> The body's life is the life of sensations and emotions. The body feels real hunger, real thirst, real joy in the sun or the snow, real pleasure in the smell of roses, or the look of a lilac bush, real anger, real sorrow, real love, real tenderness, real warmth, real passion, real

hate, real grief. All the emotions belong to the body, and are only recognized by the mind.

Apropos of Lady Chatterley's Lover

A dichotomy opens in this passage between mind and body, which proves fatal in *Lady Chatterley*. It is true that the roots of mental life are in the whole being, but mind and body are not as separate as here suggested. Lawrence rightly recognizes the body's complex, intangible, unbiddable existence as a whole. In this he certainly touched on an important aspect of our present difficulties and also on the schizoid trends of our civilization: but, again, it is a half-truth which lies behind the final distortion. The soma is no more to be divorced from the psyche than the mind from the body.[1]

The discovery of love, Lawrence insisted, was not to be a mere 'mental' one: it must belong to the life of the body. The modern world had denigrated the body, and modern neglect of the intuitive faculties had neglected the whole being, 'blood imagination and intellect running together'. As an artist, of course, Lawrence was concerned, too, to help people to experience with him, in felt terms, his own movement towards the truth, in the phantasy experience, just as Bunyan was: they share the same concern with the power of the word in life. Lawrence seeks to restore beauty and meaning to life through his books, to restore beauty and life to the creative act of sex itself, to make it 'valid and precious' – *by words*.

Thus he seems to have felt towards the end of his life that he must go beyond the very great work he has done in *The Rainbow* and *Women in Love* to reveal the connections between successful love in the being, and the effectiveness and fulfilment of the individual in the social context. In *Women in Love*, in Gerald and Birkin, he symbolizes two possible attitudes to love and life, to mutual regard and sympathy between man and woman, and the processes of industrial life. He is never finally able to offer us a substantial positive in these, but makes a courageous advance in terms of dramatic symbolism. Gerald, the embodiment of the sacrifice of

---

[1] See D. W. Winnicott on the origin of the fallacy that 'mind' is located in the 'head', *Mind and its Relation to the Psyche-Soma, Collected Papers*, p. 243.

the body, of the whole being, to will, and to making things 'go',
even at the expense of finding oneself by entering into a love-
relationship with a woman, fails and dies. Birkin finds harmony
in mutual regard with Ursula, and lives into the promise of the
future – though, as W. W. Robson has pointed out, there are
uncertainties in this positive, and in the end Birkin seems to yearn
for a relationship with a man to which the man-woman relationship would be 'lesser'. This very dissatisfaction must also have been
a driving force behind the writing of *Lady Chatterley's Lover*.

F. R. Leavis quotes from *Women in Love* this symbolic enactment of mutual regard:

> 'You like this, do you?' she said, in a gentle solicitous voice.
> He laughed shortly.
> 'There is a space between us,' he said, in the same low, unconscious
> voice, as if something were speaking out of him. And she was as if
> magically aware of their being balanced in separation, in the boat.
> She swooned with acute comprehension and pleasure.
> 'But I'm very near,' she said caressingly, gaily.
> 'Yet distant, distant,' he said.

Leavis goes on:

> What is symbolized is that normative relation between the man
> and the woman which Birkin ultimately achieves with Ursula, and
> in which alone Gerald escapes disaster . . .
>
> *D. H. Lawrence, Novelist*, p. 194

But Gerald does not escape disaster, attempting as he does to
retain the will's domination over the intuitive life of the whole
being. The truth of Gerald is magnificently epitomized in the
incident of the Arab mare at the railway crossing gates; the passage
can bear extensive quotation, as it has all the drama and economy
of Lawrence's best writing – so lacking in *Lady Chatterley*. It is the
drama and economy of rightness in the artist's perception:

> In spite of the ironic smile at his picturesqueness, Gudrun liked to
> look at him. He was well-set and easy, his face with its warm tan
> showed up his whitish, coarse moustache, and his blue eyes were full
> of sharp light as he watched the distance.
> The locomotive chuffed slowly between the banks, hidden. The
> mare did not like it. She began to wince away, as if hurt by the un-

known noise. But Gerald pulled her back and held her head to the gate. The sharp blasts of the chuffing engine broke with more and more force on her. The repeated sharp blows of unknown, terrifying noise struck through her till she was rocking with terror. She recoiled like a spring let go. But a glistening, half-smiling look came into Gerald's face. He brought her back again, inevitably.

The noise was released, the little locomotive with her clanking steel connecting-rod emerged on the highroad, clanking sharply. The mare rebounded like a drop of water from hot iron. Ursula and Gudrun pressed back into the hedge, in fear. But Gerald was heavy on the mare, and forced her back. It seemed as if he sank into her magnetically, and could thrust her back against herself.

'The fool!' cried Ursula loudly. 'Why doesn't he ride away till it's gone by.'

Gudrun was looking at him with black-dilated, spellbound eyes. But he sat glistening, and obstinate, forcing the wheeling mare, which spun and swerved like a wind, and yet could not get out of the grasp of his will nor escape from the mad clamour of terror that resounded through her, as the trucks thumped slowly, heavily, horrifying, one after the other, one pursuing the other, over the rails of the crossing.

The locomotive, as if wanting to see what could be done, put on the brakes, and back came the trucks rebounding on the iron buffers, striking like horrible cymbals, clashing nearer and nearer in frightful strident concussions. The mare opened her mouth and rose slowly, as if lifted up on a wind of terror. Then suddenly her fore feet struck out, as she convulsed herself utterly away from the horror. Back she went, and the two girls clung to each other, feeling she must fall backwards on top of him. But he leaned forward, his face shining with fixed amusement, and at last he brought her down, sank her down, and was bearing her back to the mark. But as strong as the pressure of his compulsion was the repulsion of her utter terror, throwing her back away from the railway, so that she spun round and round, on two legs, as if she were in the centre of some whirlwind. It made Gudrun faint with poignant dizziness, which seemed to penetrate to her heart.

'No – ! No – ! Let her go! Let her go, you fool, you fool – !' cried Ursula at the top of her voice, completely outside herself. And Gudrun hated her bitterly for being outside herself. It was unendurable that Ursula's voice was so powerful and naked.

A sharpened look came on Gerald's face. He bit himself down on the mare like a keen edge biting home, and forced her round. She roared as she breathed, her nostrils were two wide, hot holes, her mouth was apart, her eyes frenzied. It was a repulsive sight. But he held on her unrelaxed, with an almost mechanical relentlessness, keen as a sword pressing into her. Both man and horse were sweating with violence yet he seemed calm as a ray of cold sunshine.

Meanwhile the eternal trucks were rumbling on, very slowly, treading one after the other, one after the other, like a disgusting dream that has no end. The connecting chains were grinding and squeaking as the tension varied, the mare pawed and struck away mechanically now, for her terror fulfilled in her, for now the man encompassed her; her paws were blind and pathetic as she beat the air, the man closed round her and brought her down, almost as if she were part of his own physique.

This writing springs in its power as art from Lawrence's perception of the fatal consequences of the imposition of 'will' on the natural being, and all its rich potentialities, towards narrow, 'ideal', intellectual ends, pursued at the expense of the body. And the writing enacts that bodily life – given here, dramatically and symbolically, to foster in us the claims of that bodily existence against dominating will.[1] Yet is it, essentially, *will* that is the enemy of the psychesoma? Isn't it, rather, those impulses in us to deny the reality of our needs for object-relationship?

Why did Lawrence need to go on further, to be more explicit, as he did in *Lady Chatterley's Lover*? For several reasons, I think. He could no doubt recognize the unsatisfactoriness of the end of *Women in Love*. He must also have felt he was not understood. He hated the attitudes to sex that were gaining ground (or seemed to him to be gaining ground) – that, for instance, sex was an unpleasant 'function', that evolutionary processes would eventually rid us of this indignity of having to live with a troublesome body, in which the gates of the alimentary system are combined disgustingly (as some saw it, and some still do) with the gates of sex.

[1] It also has disturbing undercurrents as a symbolic rape, seen in 'a disgusting dream' – 'she's bleeding', etc. In a sense the passage enacts a phantasy of the industrial father raping the mother as seen by a child ('it was almost as if she were part of his own physique'). See Appendix B.

He hated the way people had become satisfied with the mere outward appearance of marriage, people who secretly seemed to detest the reality of sexual union (as he unconsciously feared it). He hated the verbalizing mentality of the modern world in its attitudes to sex, and associated them with the separation of mind from body, in a deathly and dangerous, life-hating way. Men were becoming irreverend and over-proud, valuing their clever minds and an assumed 'pure' soul at the expense of the body which they despised. And in *Lady Chatterley's Lover* such attitudes are caricatured, rightly, in those people who hope that soon babies will be bred in bottles, or consider that having a child 'given you' is 'like a visit to the dentist'. He hated, too, even the 'good','emancipated' talk about healthy sensuality, without any real sensuality behind it – the way in which Tommy Dukes talks in this book, (and the way, we might add, sex is often discussed in our 'quality' press). He deplored the way in which, deprived of sex, and cut away from it, as it were, men devote themselves, their sexual energy, to industry, to pursuits which have the energy in them of infantile toy-play. With these attitudes and modes of living he classed the effort of the bad artist, the bad writer, who sought kudos, material gain, the 'bitch-goddess success', as Henry James had called it. This latter trend seemed to Lawrence an acquiescence in the industrial drive, really, as servant of the whole industrial-commercial degradation of humanity in our time. This world and its attitudes he considered castrated, impotent, fallen into deathliness and meaninglessness. Connie Chatterley is made to feel the world has gone grey and dead. We need only to look round at our intellectual world (from advertising to university academism) to see these diagnoses essentially confirmed in part. The English Sunday papers are typical foci of this world – with their concepts of 'success' in terms of kudos and gain merely. Or one may consider the total deficiency of positive comment on public matters of morality, or the emotional life, in the weeklies. One cannot but endorse Lawrence's diagnosis of the tendency to deny life, and to vilify human nature, abroad in our culture and civilization.

Other less effective reasons for going on to write *Lady Chatterley* are more personal to Lawrence. Despite the success of *The Rain-*

bow and *Women in Love* as creative works of art, things must have seemed to him no better, in fact or promise, either for him or England. His own peace must have seemed no nearer than 'a measure of equanimity', however much he cried, 'Look! We have come through!'

Alas, the ghosts remained in him threatening extinction even as they do at the end of *Lady Chatterley's Lover*, where Mellors still feels 'great grasping white hands in the air, wanting to get hold of the throat of anyone who tries to live, *live beyond money and squeeze the life out*'. Lawrence sought to 'squeeze the life out', with all his verbal powers as artist. He sought, in this book, to expose, for himself and the world, every detail of a progressing sexual experience between two new lovers in a search for creative 'life'. In this he hoped to come at the Gates of Heaven, the wicket-gate of significance and meaning in human life, that creative truth which would release him from fear, and redeem the world. He is making the artist's driven effort to make the world 'good' by his pen, by seizing the truth of it.

So Connie Chatterley is portrayed setting out with the commendable intention, with all Lawrence's fertile and life-seeking impulses in her creation, to become a part of the life-regenerating processes of the natural world. Married to a castrated aristocrat engaged in futile verbalizing for the sake of kudos and display, she feels her life and the world are ended. After an unsatisfactory affair with a popular playwright (by which Lawrence means to give us to understand that what will redeem Connie is no mere sequence of 'affairs', no mere 'good time' in promiscuity), in spring, one year, she sees a man washing himself. He is their gamekeeper, a man who has quit the industrial scene, is 'temporizing', has been 'civilized' by some unusual experiences abroad, is 'almost a gentleman', is good with animals, and keeps himself to himself, in fear of being hurt in his spirit. He is 'a really exceptional being' – according to Lawrence – though we find it hard to accept him as one as things turn out: we know very little about him in fact. But while his whole background is shadowy, Lawrence concentrates with surprising energy on one particular aspect of Mellors – his fear of those women who 'exert their will' on him, to gain satisfaction. Here we have the clue to Lawrence's pre-occupation with 'will': Mellors has suffered feminine rape. He has been hurt inwardly by women who have exerted their will on him – sexually, by bringing on his orgasm too quickly, and then using the penis after ejaculation as a tool to bring about their own relief.

Later I shall discuss this as part of the whole question of how representative are the sexual truths in the book. Here it is enough to note that Lawrence offers this as a symbol, of the female impulse to dominate, which must be broken and subdued.

Lawrence links 'bad' women with 'bad' sex, symbolically – and links them with industrial society. The 'worst' sex is this:

'And when I'd come and really finished, then she'd start off on her own account, and I had to stop inside her till she brought herself off, wriggling and shouting she'd clutch, clutch, clutch with herself down there, and then she'd come off, in fair ecstasy . . .'

For the time being we will accept Lawrence's postulated link between sex and attachment to the industrial 'Thing'. In fear of being humiliated in this way, by the implications he feels in it against his male potency, kept in that 'inferior' state by the women deliberately, as if to insult his potency, Mellors has given up his wife, and kept out of women's way for five or six years. He is 'temporizing with life'. He has a little pension. He has given up the search for sex, believing there was no 'proper' sex left in the world.

Connie Chatterley on her side is aware of a growing restlessness, having lost touch with the vital world. Her marriage is all appearance and no reality. Clifford is paralysed below the waist: yet he goes on 'believing' in the marriage.

One day Connie goes to the keeper's hut in the woods, where he raises chicks. The world is full of renewed life and spring. While he is showing her the chicks, she lets fall a tear, because of the beauty of creative life, and in sorrow at her own infertility, her own uncreativity. Mellors, in a surge of tender passion, comforts her, and then, with very little introduction – it 'just happens' as sexual relationship often does – has sexual intercourse with her in the hut. Her flesh is docile, submissive: he is unwilling, but life, as it were, takes over, and drives them to the creative act of love. This is a very beautiful passage, and is central to the (intended) theme of the book:

Yet it was spring and the bluebells, were coming in the wood, and the leaf-buds on the hazels were opening like the spatter of green rain. How terrible it was that it should be spring, and everything cold-hearted, cold-hearted. Only the hens, fluffed so wonderfully on the eggs, were warm with their hot, brooding female bodies! Connie felt herself living on the brink of fainting all the time.

Then, one day, a lovely sunny day with great tufts of primroses under the hazels, and many violets dotting the paths, she came in the afternoon to the coops and there was one tiny, tiny, perky chicken tinily prancing round in front of a coop, and the mother hen cluck-ing in terror. The slim little chick was greyish brown with dark markings, and it was the most alive little spark of a creature in seven kingdoms at that moment. Connie crouched to watch in a sort of ecstasy. Life, Life! Pure, sparky, fearless new life! New Life! So tiny and so utterly without fear! Even when it scampered a little, scrambl-ing into the coop again, and disappeared under the hen's feathers in answer to the mother hen's wild alarm-cries, it was not really frightened, it took it as a game, the game of living. For in a moment a tiny sharp head was poking through the gold-brown feathers of the hen, and eyeing the Cosmos.

Connie was fascinated. And at the same time, never had she felt so acutely the agony of her own female forlornness. It was becoming unbearable.

She had only one desire now, to go to the clearing in the wood. The rest was a kind of painful dream. But sometimes she was kept all day at Wragby, by her duties as hostess. And then she felt as if she too were going blank, just blank and insane. . . .

. . . She arrived at the clearing flushed and semi-conscious. The keeper was there, in his shirt-sleeves, just closing up the coops for the night, so the little occupants would be safe. But still one little trio was pattering about on tiny feet, alert drab mites, under the straw shelter, refusing to be called in by the anxious mother.

'I had to come and see the chicken!' she said panting, glancing shyly at the keeper, almost unaware of him. 'Are there any more?'

'Thirty-six so far!' he said. 'Not bad.'

He too took a curious pleasure in watching the young things come out.

Connie crouched in front of the last coop. The three chicks had run in. But still their cheeky heads came poking sharply through the yellow feathers, then withdrawing, then only one beady little head eyeing forth from the vast mother-body. 'I'd love to touch them,' she said, putting her fingers gingerly through the bars of the coop. But the mother-hen pecked at her hand fiercely, and Connie drew back startled and frightened.

'How she pecks at me! She hates me!' she said in a wondering voice. 'But I wouldn't hurt them!'

The man standing above her laughed, and crouched down beside her, knees apart, and put his hand with quiet confidence slowly into the coop. The old hen pecked at him, but not so savagely. And slowly, softly, with sure gentle fingers, he felt among the old bird's feathers and drew out a faintly-peeping chick in his closed hand.

'There!' he said, holding out his hand to her. She took the little drab thing between her hands, and there it stood, on its impossible little stalks of legs, its atom of balancing life trembling through its almost weightless feet into Connie's hands. But it lifted its handsome, clean-shaped little head boldly, and looked sharply around, and gave a little 'peep'. 'So adorable! So cheeky!' she said softly.

The keeper, squatting beside her, was also watching with an amused face the bold little bird in her hands. Suddenly he saw a tear fall on to her wrist.

And he stood up, and stood away, moving to the other coop. For suddenly he was aware of the old flame shooting and leaping up in his loins, that he had hoped was quiescent for ever. He fought against it, turning his back to her. But it leapt, and leapt downwards, circling in his knees.

He turned again to look at her. She was kneeling and holding her two hands slowly forward, blindly, so that the chicken should run in to the mother-hen again. And there was something so mute and forlorn in her, compassion flamed in his bowels for her.

Without knowing, he came quickly towards her and crouched beside her again, taking the chick from her hands, because she was afraid of the hen, and putting it back in the coop. At the back of his loins the fire suddenly darted stronger. He glanced apprehensively at her. Her face was averted and she was crying blindly, in all the anguish of her generation's forlornness. His heart melted suddenly, like a drop of fire, and he put out his hand and laid his fingers on her knee.

'You shouldn't cry,' he said softly.

But then she put her hands over her face and felt that really her heart was broken and nothing mattered any more.

He laid his hand on her shoulder, and softly, gently, it began to travel down the curve of her back, blindly, with a blind stroking motion, to the curve of her crouching loins. And there his hand softly, softly, stroked the curve of her flank, in the blind instinctive caress.

She had found her scrap of handkerchief and was blindly trying to dry her face.

'Shall you come to the hut?' he said, in a quiet, neutral voice.

And closing his hand softly on her upper arm, he drew her up and led her slowly to the hut, not letting go of her till she was inside. Then he cleared aside chair and table and took a brown, soldier's blanket from the tool chest, spreading it slowly. She glanced at his face, as she stood motionless.

His face was pale and without expression, like that of a man submitting to fate.

'You lie there,' he said softly, and he shut the door so that it was dark, quite dark.

With a queer obedience, she lay down on the blanket. Then she felt the soft, groping helplessly desirous hand touching her body, feeling for her face. The hand stroked her face, softly softly, with infinite soothing and assurance, and at last there was the soft touch of a kiss on her cheek.

Connie's search is given to us here with tender poignancy and compassion in that fresh direct prose such as we find in his best short stories. She is claimed by life for 'the creative act that is more than procreative'. In this latter phrase, however, he seals his own doom, by separating sex from procreativity, as he has already separated mind from body. But already, even in the language here, he begins to move towards the pastoral idyll which recognizes none of the claims and exigencies of actual living. So far, all seems life-promoting and beautiful – unless it be for a suspicion that this 'broken-hearted' and easily acquiescent woman ('queer obedience' . . . 'semi-conscious') already represents an unreal woman who can be easily *controlled* out of fear. This unreality is already present in this passage, in such wish-fulfilling phrases as 'helplessly desirous', and 'infinite soothing and assurance'. In these emerge Lawrence's infantile concepts of genitality.

When the couple begin their sexual relationship Lawrence turns to explore the nature of 'good sex'. Here again we have to cross beyond the bounds of literary criticism, in order to question the truth of this book as we need to do. The unreality of the book inevitably suggests that in it Lawrence is writing about an ideal sexual experience which he himself had never experienced. If he had he could never have made it so impossibly unreal: indeed, and I shall suggest at the end of my essay, and in discussing *Look! We Have Come Through!*, the best reality of love is something much quieter and calmer, belonging much more to relaxed civilized togetherness, and much more forgetful of sensuality, than *Lady Chatterley's Lover* ever allows us to be. Such peace is never achieved in this book.

The couple, perhaps somewhat idyllically, are fortunate in their 'sexual adjustment', securing mutual orgasm in their second act of coition. Connie gradually learns to relinquish her feminine impulse to dominate the man; Mellors gradually overcomes his inward fear of giving himself to a woman, though never completely. He strives against his resentment at being driven by the forces of life, and his fears of 'giving himself', without 'loss of dignity' or 'pride'.

Hurt as he has been by women, Mellors gives a very unsympathetic account of his experiences of neurotic women and of Lesbian women in particular with whom he has slept. He has, he says, 'suffered' from 'Lesbian women' ('they're nearly all Lesbian'). He wants, 'Nothing more to do with women any more – I wanted to keep to myself: keep my privacy and my decency':

> I thought there was no real sex left: never a woman who'd 'come' naturally with a man: except black women, and, somehow, well, we're white men: and they're a bit like mud.

This, in the mouth of a sympathetic character, seems to me as offensive, in terms of attitudes to human nature, as anything could be. Lawrence – who had had plenty of experience of racial problems abroad – should have placed that 'a bit like mud' with more care.

Because of all these misgivings, Mellors has a sense of doom when he becomes involved with Lady Chatterley:

'There are black days ahead' . . . 'And now he had taken the woman, and brought on himself a new cycle of pain and doom. *For he knew by experience what it meant.*'

Taking a woman, brings him terrible anxiety, emotional torment, and a sense of pain and trouble. But his admission of these difficulties is part of the quest for truth:

'You seem to have had an awful experience with women,' she said.
'You see, I couldn't fool myself. That's where most men manage. They take an attitude, and accept a lie. I could never fool myself. I knew what I wanted with a woman, and I could never say I'd got it when I hadn't.'

'To me it's the core,' says Mellors, of his need to have a good relationship with a woman. So a failure of the partners in sexual relationship to 'come off together' was for him crucial: such people are lesser creatures.

'Don't people often come off together?' she asked with a naïve curiosity.
'A good many of them never. You can see by the raw look of them.' He spoke unwittingly, regretting that he had begun.

Lawrence, in Mellors, however, for a moment, is also capable of recognizing that 'bad sex' may be the man's fault, too:

'And perhaps the women *really* wanted to be there and love you properly, only perhaps they couldn't. Perhaps it wasn't all their fault,' she said.
'I know it. Do you think I don't know what a broken-backed snake that's been trodden on, I was myself!'
'But you're not now,' she said . . .
'I don't know what I am. There's black days ahead.'

The fundamental fault, however, lay in industrial society itself:

It was not woman's fault, or even love's fault, nor the fault of sex. The fault lay out there, in those evil electric lights and diabolical rattling of engines. There, in the world of the mechanical greed, sparking with lights and gushing hot metal and roaring with traffic, there lay the vast evil thing, ready to destroy whatever did not conform. Soon it would destroy the wood, and the bluebells would spring no more. All vulnerable things must perish under the rolling and fuming iron.

Thus the sensual quest made by the lovers now becomes an act of defiance of the industrial world, a purging of their souls of its ghostly hands that threatened to 'squeeze the life out of everything'.

Their joint 'creativity' in sex is, then, the central issue of the book: very little else happens than a long series of enthusiastically described acts of sexual intercourse. Connie learns to 'touch' Mellors, and to submit to him (even to the extent of anal possession) and to 'adore' him. In the end the couple are alienated from industrial society and have no great confidence in their future, or in continuity. Mellors and Connie can only see Industrial England in terms of 'the anima of material disintegration'.

What would come after? Connie could not imagine. She could only see the new brick streets spreading into the fields, the new erections rising at the collieries, the new girls in their silk stockings, the new collier lads lounging into the Pally or the Welfare. . . . There was a gap in the continuity of consciousness, almost American: but industrial really. What next?

Connie felt there was no next. She wanted to hide her head in the sand: or, at least, in the bosom of a living man.

The world was so complicated and weird and gruesome! The common people were so many and really so terrible. . . . She . . . saw the colliers going home. . . . Men! Men! Alas, in some way patient and good men. In other ways, non-existent. Something that men *should* have was bred and killed out of them. Yet they were men. They begot children. *One might bear a child to them. Terrible terrible thought!* They were good and kindly. But they were *only half, only the grey half of a human being. . . . Supposing the dead in them rose up!* But no, it was too terrible to think of . . . a life with utterly no beauty in it, always 'in the pit'.

Children from such men! Oh God, oh God!

(My italics)

In the end we have a suggestion of marriage in a letter from Mellors, but chiefly his assertion that it is a flame made by their 'fucking' that matters – even the child is a 'side issue'.

> You can't insure against the future, except by really believing in the best bit of you, and in the power beyond it. So I believe in the little flame between us. For me now, it's the only thing in the world, I've got no friends, not inward friends. Only you. And now the little flame is all I care about in my life. *There's the baby, but that is a side issue.* It's my Pentecost, the forked flame between me and you. The old Pentecost isn't quite right. Me and God is a bit uppish, somehow. But the little forked flame between me and you: there you are! That's what I abide by, and will abide by, Cliffords and Berthas, colliery companies and governments and the money-mass of people all not-withstanding.

> (My italics)

This is a pathetic message, the hopelessness of which is not disguised by the religiose language, from such a distinguished writer of our century. What went wrong with Lawrence?

4
CREATIVITY A SIDE-ISSUE?

A good point to fix on, in our discussion of the unsatisfactory nature of the comment which *Lady Chatterley's Lover* makes on experience is that phrase in Mellors' last letter, 'Then there's the baby ... but that's a side-issue ...'. Lawrence makes a similar error of realization when he makes Connie say to herself in Venice, '*after all*, he was the father of her child' – only '*after all*'? These parenthetical and hostile references to procreation endorsed by the author are surely so un-Lawrentian! They are certainly unreal in the light of the reality of human sex: no man would actually write like that; no woman think like that. The clue to the origin of the failure to realization here is in the line in a poem to Frieda: 'I have learnt to curse your motherhood.'

Lawrence has an unconscious hostility to any children born of his mother by the father whose place he wished to usurp. At a deeper level yet, in the impulse to dominate woman whose reality he fears, he must seek to deny her creativity, and finally annihilate her. For these reasons the whole course of *Lady Chatterley's Lover*, which sets out as Connie weeps over the chicks because she cannot have a child, turns away from procreation, and takes a sterile path towards barren sensuality, irresponsible to procreation. In doing so it fails to climb towards love at all, but regresses to a dominating and sadistic infantile sexuality that unconsciously seeks to annihilate the woman, and her creative role, and becomes in the end a hostile attack on the reality of all human nature as 'carrion bodied'.

This aberrant progress in the work begins as soon as Lawrence allows the fatal distinction between 'procreative' sex and 'creative' sex. Of course we may follow that Lawrence wanted a sexual creativity that wasn't mere 'breeding mice' nor cohabitation 'for the sake of the children'. But it must be insisted that, in truth, the act of sex in love does not culminate in orgasm, but in the birth of the child, and the next generation. The child enriches the love of the parents, and draws its own happiness from its awareness of their love. To come to terms with this larger reality is as important as it is to have 'good sex' at the basis of a marriage relationship: indeed if love is to grow the acceptance of the procreative reality must be taken into account more at the centre than it is in this book. The creative-procreative element in sexual love is undeniably there, even if no children are possible, or after all children have been born to a couple. To come to fulfilment – to its happiest and most given – love must accept its procreativity that enriches the lovers' creativity.[1] The sexual act in love is at the centre of a whole complex of which the least intelligent human being is aware – a complex of the family and love in reality, in Time and generation. The procreativity of love is its germen, and by it love is linked with the reality of the world and civilization. Because he unconsciously wishes to deny reality in this narcissistic work,

[1] I don't imply here that those who decide not to have children are being uncreative, or are being 'selfish', etc. Nobody can be called selfish who forfeits the greatest of all satisfactions – to have children and bring them up. I am talking about concepts, awarenesses and acceptances. One finds immensely creative attitudes in single people – as in some teachers – who have no children, but who are closer to wholeness of personal reality than some parents. These attitudes enable them to make great creative contributions to the community.

Lawrence plays down and ultimately denies these links. In consequence the love between Mellors and Connie can only turn in upon itself and becomes self-consuming.

If we explore further the treatment of procreation and children in the book we become even more surprised – that the author of *The Rainbow* and *Women in Love* can have so failed to remember the sense he gives us in those great works, of the psychic connection between one generation and another, and the need for the child to walk to its fulfilment under the evanescent arch of the rainbow of parental care. One of the greatest moments in modern literature is the birth of the child to the Brangwens in *The Rainbow*, and especially the account of Tom taking Ann into the cowshed to calm her. In such a passage Lawrence's sympathy is totally engaged in the all-important relationship between parents and children: and there are several places in his work where he penetrates marvellously this crucial complex in human life. At this level – the level of 'felt life' that enlarges our awareness of the reality of the family and of the child in it – his novels have great power to enlarge our sympathy, and our living. His work complements the developments in the philosophy of child care, as manifested in the work of John Bowlby, and the whole new creative approach to psychodynamics so largely associated with work with children.

But in *Lady Chatterley's Lover*, Lawrence virtually rejects this reality of 'the rainbow', the creative function of each generation in love and procreation. A bitterness emerges from his work, a splenetic quality, in relation to children and procreation. An element in the story, for instance, soon forgotten, is the fate of Mellors' first child. Mellors is brutal to his own child:

> 'Ah shut up, tha false little bitch!' came the man's angry voice, and the child sobbed louder . . .

and when Connie asks him what is the matter,

> . . . a faint smile like a sneer came on the man's face . . .
> Connie felt as if he had hit her in the face . . .

The passage is worth studying: Connie's mettle is up – as it seldom is in confronting Mellors ('her blue eyes blazing *rather vaguely*' – the latter phrase seems uneasy, a hint that Lawrence essentially despises her mother-instincts as he himself despised Frieda's).

> 'I asked *you*,' she panted. . . . 'You did, your Ladyship,' he said: then with a return to the vernacular, 'but I canna tell yer.' And he became a soldier, unscrutable, only pale with annoyance.

(We may compare the scene from *Sons and Lovers* where Morel strikes his wife over the baby's head. The difference is that Lawrence here in *Lady Chatterley's Lover approves* of the man's impassive hardness. He approves elsewhere of Aaron's defection, which we can only see as a deplorable flight from reality.)

Connie turns to the child 'with the conventionalized sweetness suitable'. The disparaging latter remark shows Lawrence's own prejudice: the child's need is something tender and humane, and Lawrence despises Connie for giving it: with Morelorence he is 'inscrutable'. Mellors remains 'laconic', 'satirical' – and Lawrence invites our respect for this very quality: 'A man very much alone and on his own.' The passage has something of that marvellous sympathy of Lawrence's with children:

> 'The child looked at her, with bold dark eyes of scrutiny, sizing her up, and her condolence.'

This is penetrating. But the passage is weighted, carefully, in favour of – to excuse and vindicate – Mellors' very inadequacy as parent: 'Connie disliked her: the spoilt false little female'. This has an important psychological significance: Lawrence is able to see that for both Mellors and Connie, who are drifting together, the child represents their awareness of his sexual relations with Bertha Coutts. What Lawrence is *unable* to see is that the child represents his *own* jealousy of procreativity.[1]

Only at one point in the book does Lawrence accept gladly the urge of procreative sex, but even this passage culminates in misrepresentation. This comes after one of the lovers' most successful acts of love, in which Connie is able to achieve 'the loss of herself

[1] See note A on *Aaron's Rod*.

to herself'. Lawrence for once is able to convey a feeling of the body having 'spoken' love sufficiently for him to avoid the over-insistent verbalism such as I shall come to analyse below:

> 'he seemed to have nothing whatever to say. Nothing left.'

Then, once Connie is alone, the record of her mental rumination begins again. At first it is sweetly concerned with creation – Lawrence is really much aware of woman's concern with the child she may have, even if he denies it elsewhere by implication. But this preoccupation does not last long before Lawrence enters into his own female consciousness and exerts his hatred of the very self-respect, of the very *claim to equality*, and creative impulse, of the woman. Her preoccupation is with creativity, true creativity, with her potential child, following the successful sexual act with her lover (though he has contributed nothing except potency to that act's success - certainly no great consideration for 'mutuality'). But this very creativity Lawrence at once comes to resent, and mis-represent, in her. The turn spoils the whole tenderness of the scene, reduces it to pointless sensuality, and immerses us again in 'the bitter tastelessness of shadow fruit' as the product of their union. For a time the recollection is creative:

> . . . she realized the immense difference between having a child to oneself, and having a child to a man whom one's bowels yearned towards. The former seemed in a sense ordinary . . .

Strange to find Lawrence so often floundering as in this book – whatever can 'having a child to oneself' mean? But the passage is good:

> to have a child to a man whom one adored in one's bowels and one's womb, it made her feel she was very different from her old self, and as if she was sinking deep, deep to the centre of all womanhood and the sleep of creation.
>
> It was not the passion that was new to her, it was the yearning adoration. She knew she had always feared it, for it left her helpless . . .

But then, significantly, Lawrence turns from conception to his insistent preoccupation with breaking down the resistance in a woman, bringing her to be devoted to her 'master', 'helpless', 'adoring'. Mellors has mastered her, and in this Lawrence exults. Yet he is not content even with adoration and her 'loss of herself to herself'. The woman for him is still a limit to man's self-realization. So, now, instead of going on to celebrate their mutually regardant togetherness-in-separation, he goes on to relate their struggle – her struggle against male domination, the male domination Lawrence offers as *inevitable* for successful union.

The woman remains, that is, a remainder of that 'threat in the air' which never leaves Mellors, and never left Lawrence, and must be exorcized. Even in the creative passage above, Connie is the enemy-woman:

> She must not become a slave. She feared her adoration. She knew she could fight it. She had a devil of selfwill in her breast that could have fought the full soft heaving adoration of her womb and crushed it. She could even now do it, or she thought so, and she could then take up her passion with her own will . . .

Mellors and Connie having 'come off together' marks them to Lawrence as being on the right side, morally – on the side of life and intuition rather than the selfish will of industrial life, and the Lesbian women who 'grind their own coffee' with the 'beak-like clitoris'. But why? What is in them that *is* different? 'Warm-hearted fucking', yes – a sensual rich wild passion without courtesy or creativity – and some progress towards mutual regard. But in what is this embodied? In what lies the difference between the good thing, 'the full soft heaving adoration', and the bad thing, 'taking up her passion with her own will' – by which Lawrence means the woman finding her own orgasm after the man's climax? In what lies the difference? The difference, according to Lawrence, lies in being *mastered* by the man, who is a 'real man'. In 'adoration'. But how do we know Mellors *is* a real man, worthy of adoration? Any possible answer would not be in the over-written account of the whirlpools of sensation, nor in the subsequent post-mortem on the quality of their act of coition: we demand it where it ought to be in a novelist – in the account *of how Mellors treats her* otherwise than in bed. That is, it cannot be found in the exclusively erotic, but in the areas where are resolved such impulses as aggression, and in which the reality of love is found – in mutual relationship. But here, surely, Mellors deserves neither respect nor 'adoration'?

Lawrence is driven by his need to control the woman he fears. So he means us to find Mellors *admirable* in his taciturn refusal to offer her more than his physical manhood, take it or leave it, rough and smooth, as he is. Mellors treats her in a masterly, half-insolent manner, his aggressiveness unresolved by tenderness – and Lawrence approves of this. To drive home the aggressiveness, the direct details of coition are delineated – and the effect of these is to subject us to something of the same negative power Lawrence seeks to exert over the woman. Connie attempts to imagine a possible rebellion:

> Ah yes, to be passionate like a Bacchante, like a Bacchanal fleeing through the woods, to call on Iacchos, the bright phallus that had no independent personality behind it, but was pure god-servant to the woman? The man, the individual let him not dare intrude. He was but a temple-servant, the bearer and keeper of the bright phallus, her own.

The bright phallus is the lingam – the embodiment of universal creation. Lawrence could not bear Connie to be devoted to such a symbol of universal life, forgetting her 'master': he goes on (did a woman ever think like this of a man with whom she had just had her first mutual orgasm?)

> So, in the flux of her new awakening, the old hard passion flamed in her for a time, and the man dwindled to a contemptible object, the mere phallus bearer to be torn to pieces when his service was performed. . . . She would not give up her hard bright female power; she was weary of it, stiffened with it; she would sink in the new bath of life, in the depths of her womb and bowels that sang the voiceless song of adoration. It was early yet to begin to fear the man . . .

This is a strange passage. Lawrence is exploring the nature of resistance in the 'Lesbian' woman, the wilful side of woman, such as Mellors describes above. This must be broken down. The woman must *adore* the man – Lawrence is neither satisfied with 'love' nor with the significance of the phallus as universal creative force to which they *both* submit in awe and creativity. The man must be *feared*, the hard bright female power must be 'broken'. This springs from the fear which in Lawrence is a mixture of terror of being humiliated by a woman, of being thought contemptible by the woman for impotence, and ultimately, of annihilation by her. It is as though he fears her *because* she is 'with him in the end'. At a deep level it is Lawrence who fears being torn to pieces.

So Connie is progressively beaten out of her female power into submission, from the first:

> 'You lie there,' he said softly. . . .
> With a quiet obedience, she lay down on the blanket. Then she felt the soft groping, helplessly desiring hand touching her body, feeling for her face. The hand stroked her face softly, softly, with infinite soothing and assurance, and at last there was the soft touch of a kiss on her cheek . . . and he had to come into her at once, to enter the peace on earth of her soft quiescent body. It was the moment of pure peace for him, the entry into the body of the woman . . .

Again 'pure' – but the point to notice is the suddenness with which Mellors always seeks *his* peace: in her lack of will is his peace.

> the peculiar haste of his possession.
>
> p. 178
>
> he lay with her and went into her there on the hearthrug
>
> p. 217
>
> Then suddenly he tipped her up and fell with her on the path, in the roaring silence of the rain, and short and sharp, he took her, short and sharp and finished, like an animal
>
> p. 231
>
> 'Quick! Lie down! Let me come!' Now he was in a hurry.
>
> It was a night of sensual passion, in which she was a little startled and *almost unwilling*, yet pierced . . .

Having been suddenly taken, she is 'fulfilled' by the recurrent return of Mellors to the capacity to perform again, and on occasion, yet again, with little interval. But there is a strange sense in which there is no progress – no deepening or growth – in their physical sex – no increasing tenderness, no calmer approach to the act, no subtle maturity of physical togetherness, no harmony, despite the fortuitous early occurrence of their original 'coming together'. Of course, the descriptions of the acts of sexual intercourse become more enthusiastic – but they also became less convincing, because the verbiage spills over and becomes more insistent, even at the expense of those quieter harmonies at the civilized level *in which sexual togetherness would show*. It is in this sense the book is far from a 'definition of marriage'. Having been quickly taken, Connie is as summarily sent off home in the same humiliation: she must be controlled, and kept in that ignominy that disarms her power to annihilate:

> 'There then, there then, I'll undress thee, tha' bob-tailed young throstle.'
> And he took the leaves from her hair, and kissed her damp hair, and the flowers from her breasts, and kissed her breasts, and kissed her navel, and kissed her maiden-hair, where he left the flowers threaded. 'They maun stop while they will,' he said. 'So! Thou'rt bare again nowt but a bare-arse lass an' a bit of a Lady Jane! Now put they shimmy on, for tha mun go, or else Lady Chatterley's goin' to be late for dinner, and where have you been to my pretty maid.'
> She never knew how to answer him when he was in this condition of the vernacular. So she dressed herself and prepared to go a little ignominiously home to Wragby. Or so she felt it: a little ignominiously home . . .

During the strange, banal, flower-adorning scene Mellors has said many cuttingly cruel things which Lawrence does not see as destructive of relationship (as they are) ('Who'll be puttin' blossoms on you next year'). And the 'caressive vernacular' as Lawrence calls it (a voice he knew from his father) becomes here the teasing voice of the father as to a little girl, with sinister sadistic and destructive undertones. Speechless, complying, 'almost unwilling', Connie is progressively humiliated by her master – her hard female spirit broken. She loses dignity, she loses sexual disquality (to use Lawrence's own term) – she is a Lady bloodywell shown where she belongs, and how a *man*, a *Man* – a working man – can treat her sort. Gathering his balls in her hand, and rubbing her face in his belly, she listens submissively to his pompous – and often ludicrous – pronouncements on the world. He, holding her buttocks, gathering up 'her lovely, heavy posteriors one in each hand and pressed them towards him with a frenzy' – touching her secret entrances insolently, exulting in his familiarity with her 'arse', he claims his right to exert a masterly contempt for her femaleness and creativity, and the industrial system which makes women exert their will in sex:

> Industrial system or not! . . .
> Bit by bit let's drop the industrial life an' go back . . .
> You ought ter be alive and beautiful . . . if man had fine red legs, that'd change them in a month. They'd begin to be men again, to be men! . . . an' in time pull down Tevershall and build a few beautiful buildings that would hold us all. An' clean the country up again. *And not have many children because the world is overcrowded* . . .
> But I wouldn't preach the men, only strip 'em and say, Look at yourselves . . .
>
> (My italics)

Connie, mercifully, returns to talking about how many different kind of hair he has, and the pronunciation about the industrial system rouses itself again, only to be broken by the lady dashing invitingly into the thunderstorm where she is taken like an animal by her gamekeeper, ridiculous in her canvas shoes.

Lawrence, we know from his poems, had an aversion to being asked by a woman if he loved her: her assurance, he insisted, should be 'felt' in the bodily life of sex. Yet, as we shall see, the kind of sexual approach which Lawrence approves of in Mellors takes no account of the large physical rhythms of the woman which belong to her creative nature. A woman takes time to arouse: Mellors is always importunate and seldom caresses her body before coition.[1] It is as if Lawrence had an aversion to

---

[1] The exceptions are at the first occasion with the chicks; then later when he touches her breast with a kind of insolent familiarity in the presence of Clifford, and again when he touches the 'gates of her body', also insolently. What I mean is that he does not arouse her by gentle fore-play, but is always aggressive in his 'touching'. He is always on the defensive, on guard against possible attack.

caressing the breasts and body, as indeed he makes Mellors averse to mouth kisses – how aberrant Lawrence is! Yet a woman has a biological need for both the caress and the reassurance: Lawrence fails to register any great anxiety in Connie as to the consequences of conception. Whenever she asks for reassurance, Mellors, with Lawrence's approval, denies her right to it.

> 'You love me, don't you?'
> 'Ay, tha knows!' he said.
> 'But tell me!' she pleaded.
> 'Ay! Ay! asn't ter felt it?'
> 'You do love me!'
> 'Say you'll always love me!'

– there is to be no 'loss of dignity' on Mellors 'part by giving in to her pleading for conscious assurance of love and security: only feeling, touch, she must take it from his body – "asn't ter felt it'. But the touch will be aggressive, never gentle. Meanwhile their minds are singularly amputated from their bodies – and Lawrence sternly refuses to countenance lovers' needs for verbal love-making reassurance, and conscious bonds of tenderness. Perhaps for him the mouth, whether for words or kisses, belonged too much to the mother?

So while Connie's pleas for reassurance are denied, and even made a little babyish (because she can be controlled best so), Mellors' attitude to sexual intercourse is painfully unmanful – indeed, at times it is pathetically infantile. At one point Lawrence confesses this, after the conversation about the 'bits of mud' that 'come off';

> 'And now, are you glad of me?' she asked.
> 'Yes! When I can forget the rest. When I can't forget the rest, I want to get under the table and die.'
> 'Why under the table?'
> 'Why?' he laughed. 'Hide, I suppose. Baby!'

While there is a babyishness about all lovers at times, possibly because intense love revives the primal feelings of infancy, there are also extreme babyishnesses here which Lawrence approves –

because his own concept of a love relationship was as that of an infant to the mother, as we have seen.

Coition, for instance, is a healing for Mellors – gratification for the man's wounded psyche, and an allaying of anxiety:

> 'I love thee that I can go into thee,' he said.
> 'Do you like me?' she said, her heart beating.

– the grateful, possessed child-mother must be maintained in the position of dependency, baby-asking for reassurance: this increases the son-father's sense of power over her, and goes with the 'healing' benefits he draws from her as demanding-infant. There is, of course, here the general truth, too, that coition temporarily allays a man's unconscious anxieties about his potency, and also his fear of retribution from within the woman. But Mellors' gratitude goes with a degree of patronizing condenscension:

> 'It heals *it all up*, that I can go into thee. I love thee that tha opened to me. I love thee that I came into thee like that!'
> He bent down and kissed her soft flank, rubbed his cheek against *it,* then covered *it* up.

When Clifford calls the child 'it', Lawrence – in Connie – bridles: here 'it' stands for the Morelorence woe at sex, the psychic woe, and the other 'its' refer to her body. The use of the impersonal article suggests a strangely depersonalized sex. Sir Clifford's 'it' was a convenient avoidance of sex-gender: Lawrence reviles. But Lawrence does not bridle at Mellors' disastrously depersonal and egocentric attitude ('Thank God *I've got* A *woman*').

There is both a realism in this passage – in the man's gratitude for what a woman can give him for instance. But there is also a strange lack of maturity, of that maturity which grows in terms of mutual respect – in mutual healing and creativeness, and not in sexual gratification conceived as of a healing service provided by the woman for the man. Connie asks, as if to claim her side of the balance in togetherness,

> 'And will you never leave me?'

This is childish, baby-wise – but also the woman's anxious real concern for security *because she may have his child*:

'Dunna ask them things,' he said.

'But do you believe I love you?' she said.

'Tha loved me just now, wider than ever that tha thought tha would. But who knows what'll 'appen, once tha starts thinking about it!'

'Wider' – the search is for the deeper, more open 'cunt' in desperate sensuality: no thinking, for that inhibits. Yet it is not *deep* love, but 'wider' physical plunging. It is the baby's satisfaction he seeks (with Lawrence's approval) rather than that of the adult civilized man: and a loss of anxiety in the utmost sensual experience, sex as an anodyne, mere detensioning. This baby-need is commonly found in men, but it is doomed because it falls so short of adult reality. Certainly it is 'not love'.

Morelorence both resents the claims of the world and the claims of the woman who may become a mother: the conversation goes on:

'. . . you don't really think that I wanted to make use of you, do you?'

'How?'

'To have a child – ?'

'Now anybody can 'ave any childt i' th' world,' he said as he sat down fastening his leggings.

'Ah no!' she cried. 'You don't mean it?'

'Er well!' he said, looking at her under his brows. 'This wor t'best.'

. . . And she lay and wondered at the wonder of life and of being.

The phrase 'the wonder of life and of being' and Connie's contented gratitude as depicted by Lawrence (unreal as it is) conceal the destructiveness and unreality of Mellors' attitudes, which he unconsciously approves. There is a recurrent insolence on Mellors' part as, having had his 'good cunt' he buttons his trousers or does up his leggings, and refuses to be 'ax'd' about love, the world, children, life. He is always demandingly discriminatory in his comments on her, in a way that would be destructive in life, shockingly destructive of the relationship: 'this was the best yet'. Connie must just lie down: no woman must use him 'as a tool' – she must 'take the rough with the smooth'. But for Morelorence it must always be '*good* cunt', 'wide', 'deep'. Mistrust is escaped, but by the humiliation and denial of the woman: she is simply reduced to the 'good cunt' with the 'proper arse'.

The remark 'anybody can 'ave any childt i' th' world' is given us with Lawrence's approval: sexual love counts more than procreation. To hell with procreation – you or anyone else can have what children they like – I have had 'good cunt'. This, to a woman to whom he had just given his seed!

The mistrusting Mellors never gives Connie the assurance of his love in words: he never responsibly accepts the possibility, nor the future of the possible child. Would Mellors' first child – motherless and abandoned – be capable when she grew to adulthood of 'good' sex? This Lawrence – even the Lawrence of *The Rainbow* – does not consider – she is simply abandoned.

I am not merely pressing the 'claims of parental duty'. Obviously a continued loyalty to a sexually dead marriage 'for the sake of the children', for instance, might not be preferable in comparison with a relationship fulfilled in sexual love. But even so, such 'duty' is not always to be despised. What I am attacking is this elevation of sexual love to a high symbolic value while being so savagely negative about procreation: this is to deny a large aspect of love's reality and to ignore deep elements in any such relationship as it would have been.

The failure comes because Lawrence is saying, through Mellors, 'If I could only secure my complete satisfaction in sex as it was as an infant with Mummy I could bear the world – this gloom and horror that I feel would dissolve and evaporate – I would be freed'. Unfortunately as long as the need *is* that of seeking Mummy – satisfaction with the world can never come right, for a man is a man, not a baby, and his woman is a woman, a free adult 'separate' in her own right in all her creative reality. To seek a total bliss in sex detached from adult exigencies – a bliss such as the infant supposes it has at the breast – is to idealize, to demand something which never was and never can be – and this, since reality can never approximate to the expectations, is bound to cause destructive criticism, schism, and unhappiness. Indeed, it is a barrier to the deeper satisfactions of love in 'co-operative mutuality'.

But, alas, at the level of *moeurs*, the effect of this condonation of Mellors' egoistical indifference is to endorse an attitude to family life which is essentially that of the old Morel-working-man, of Lawrence's father, of a whole degraded generation of working men, who drank, took their women in drink, burdened them with children, of which they took no great care nor interest, only to regard them as a burdensome visitation from God. Here Lawrence condones the very root of the psychic woes of working-class life, and the root of many of our prevalent disabilities in dealing with reality. Mellors bears (with Lawrence's approval) all the marks of that inhuman insouciance of the industrial working-class husband, which belongs to the dissociation already referred to, which undermined self-respect and courtesy in family life. The old self-sufficiency, the old decency of the world of the English village, with some capacity for deep feeling, and its basis in family life, despite some peasant savagery, was broken by rapid and disastrous change and deliberate degradation, in the creation of modern industry. In this situation the families suffered hardship and lasting scars not only of material living, but also of the soul love between man and woman and a viable mother-child relationship. A deep bitterness ensued, which has never left English life: it lies under the guilt and frigidity of working-class attitudes to sex (as a correspondent points out, working-class wives traditionally don't let their husbands see them naked). Despite their sexual sorrows, however, these generations often strove to make their marriages whole and sound *for the sake of the children*. And while this is not the best ideal, it is a greater thing in life, a greater contribution to the future, and to the human triumph over time and death, than the inversion Lawrence makes of it, in his rejection. Such loyalty to the family is a means to overcome dissociation. (We may see elements of this aspect in *Sons and Lovers*.)

Mellors wants 'good cunt' first: the child can come if it likes. Security is rejected – 'don't ask me to be responsible'. 'Dunna ax me to think' – there was no point in the working-class father thinking, because all was hopeless. Thus the presence of Lawrence's father in the man is so urgent, and Lawrence so biased against what his mother endured – he so wants her to have sexual fulfilment first, with the child-care left out altogether, and so to be denied as a woman. And in this he brings himself to distort sexual reality altogether.

5

SEXUAL UNREALITY

The unsatisfactory treatment of procreation in *Lady Chatterley's Lover* is, then, the most obvious indication that in the book Lawrence is unconsciously seeking to deny aspects of the whole reality of human love. He denies, implicitly, the great truths of 'the rainbow', the primal need of every human being to have a good environment in the mother's love in infancy, with parents' love fortifying the nurture. On this complex of the growth of love depends all sanity.

From this we may go further in examining the book, to see what other aspects of reality are denied, in the life of sex. In doing so we shall come to see that the book is less an achieved piece of imaginative creativity than a phantasy expression which is a symptom of a profound and intolerable anxiety – in terms of thinking about other people's sex and wondering whether our own sex is 'all right'. Such anxiety about *the exclusive sexual reality* is a manifestation of fear of life – and it is on this that commercial entertainment battens, in the 'X' cinema and a near-pornographic popular culture at large through the popular press and bookstall dirt. Culturally, these things are a mark of the sexual inadequacy such as Lawrence diagnosed in us. At a deeper level they are a mark of a reality-failing. Lawrence was able to diagnose it in us because he knew it in himself, and sought to allay the anxiety in himself. To really allay such anxiety would require the acceptance of certain truths. So Lawrence's choice lay between projecting a pretend-world of sexual unreality, dissociated from the actuality of the world and of human nature, and accepting the painful reality. Where the truths were evident, since they could not be hallucinated away, like Dorigen's rocks, they must be rejected. The rest of the book is a consequence of this false solution. Hence the malevolence: all the industrial world must be swept away, with its 'carrion bodied' inhabitants. This is the basis of much of our social thinking in literary criticism – yet its roots are in Lawrence's sexual fears!

The sexual untruths in this book may be bluntly stated thus:
1. Undoubtedly sexual 'adjustment' in terms of mutual orgasm is the 'best' sex. But it is a mechanical-minded fallacy to suppose that such 'good' sex is a *sine qua non* of a good marriage or love-relationship. (Even such a popular writer as Dr Benjamin Spock characterizes this false belief as 'the American fallacy' and as too mechanical a theory.)

2. Far more important in marriage than sexual adjustment (as figures for marital breakdown show) are such considerations of larger aspects of reality as whether the partners love one another, their mutual respect, courtesy, recognition of each other's separate identity and rights, and such elements of shared civilized living. These are dealt with, as we have seen, in Chaucer – and in Lawrence's *Rainbow* and his poems. Such love and shared civilized living, in good terms with the world, are missing from *Lady Chatterley*.

3. The solution of difficulties in relationship is not by sensuality merely. Or, to put it another way, if the 'fucking' is to become 'warm-hearted' this release of libidinal potential does not come by mere sensual intensity or energetic exploitation of the body. Certainly not by anal possession or by 'daring to do it' – these might well have a reverse effect. The way to release potentialities in the body is by love, tenderness, courtesy, mutual understanding and sympathy. The whole reality sense needs to be restored. In the end medical help or psychotherapy may be necessary, or an adult may not be released until he has overcome some other crisis such as grief when the reality sense is affected, or the need to establish himself in his work in the world, by which he gains confidence in his prowess and identity. These approaches require a recognition of personal and outer reality, and the use of feeling and intelligence to gain a sense of identity, and integration. The domineering bodily aggressiveness of Mellors by which Lawrence here symbolizes the 'phallic power' would be as much use in seeking sexual fulfilment, in overcoming reticence or fear as flogging a mental

patient or making a child with a spinal weakness do strenuous
exercises. It is noticeable, as I have said, that Mellors makes no
concession to the needs of the woman to be reassured and to be
aroused patiently and tenderly until she is ready for sexual intercourse. He takes her 'like an animal': and in this Lawrence symbolizes his unconscious urge to annihilate and deny feminine nature.
By the intensity of his vision he defends himself against even the
possibility that the 'unanimal' intelligence might find him out in
this attack. Our devotion to Lawrence shows how successful he
was.

4. Comparison of our sex with that of others, awareness of the
sex of others, and discriminatory considerations of each sexual act
we perform are, to say the least of it, unhelpful and inhibiting.
They provoke disturbing feelings of envy and pain associated with
our memory of infantile unconscious awareness of parental sex.
Indeed, it is perhaps more true to say that such comparisons and
awarenesses are a *symptom* of grave anxieties, at the root of which
is a fear of impotence, and an anxiety about reality altogether (as
is the preoccupation with 'sexual reality' in such books as Henry
Miller's). The whole of *Lady Chatterley's Lover* is itself an act of
anxious comparison, which is really self-questioning ('to me it
is as beautiful as the naked self'), a mark of a deep fear of impotence, and the inadequacy of reality-sense in Lawrence for which
he compensated by compulsive aggressive verbalizing.

5. The symbolic equation Lawrence makes between those who
have 'good sex' and people who are 'good characters' in the moral
sense is unreal.

Our sexual capacities are determined by a complexity of influences and inherited potentialities. In forming them our experience in infancy of the mother and the father is crucial. Thus inevitably, since mothers, fathers, homes and cultures are imperfect
(like us), we grow up to learn to love imperfectly, in imperfection.
In this state of affairs, as with everything else, the distribution of
happiness and fulfilment in love-relationship is unequal and flawed
so everyone has to contest with difficulties and imperfections of
some kind. But it is true that our world in particular, because of
dissociation brought by severe social change, tends to give us, as

infants and adults, much too often, a 'not good enough' environment for our best fulfilment. This has been so far the price of the development of a higher material standard of life.

But there are servants of the industrial machine, 'carrion bodied' workers, business men and even 'money boys and girls' whose sexual lives are so fulfilled that they have no anxiety about them at all. And at the same time there are gamekeepers, 'natural' men, Lawrentians, artists, and others on Lawrence's 'good' side whose sexual lives are inadequate and troubled.

One cannot become a good lover by becoming an adherent of Lawrence's attitude to life, nor even by reading his books. Nor can one, merely by having the best education of one's sensibility, or the best of intentions. Our best culture, certainly can help us with our quest for love, and suggest possibilities of fulfilment (it may, of course, add fuel to our capacity for destructive anxiety, too). But our main capacities for love are determined in our infancy, and if things are gravely wrong there (as they were for Lawrence) then possibly only psychotherapy can bring us to fulfilment.

It is true that for most normal people a positive attitude to the possibilities of love helps, and that Lawrence gives this in his other writings, among others. And, as I have said, attention to aspects of civilized living are paramount – and Lawrence helps us here, too. The growth of love depends upon our whole reality sense. *But what is not true is that 'good' people have 'good sex' and 'bad' people 'bad sex'*. Nor can you bring yourself to 'good' sex merely by adhering to 'good' attitudes to life.[1] This Lawrence dared not accept. It must have seemed to him terrible that one such as himself, so full of life-promoting energy and beliefs in life should be so doom-laden and guilty about sex. Yet, of course, his work may be seen as a great creative effort to rectify this: in such an effort, some of the output is bound to be idealizing and erroneous, and this is true of *Lady Chatterley*.

[1] Of course, the lack of direct and simple connections does not mean there are none: our conduct is helped or hindered by cultural influences and the influence of others. Those who proclaim their right to denigrate life because such connections don't exist, do actual harm to living. It is also possible to be a destructive influence by promoting a cult of it 'not being worth bothering' and obstructing insight.

It may be disastrous for us to follow the unrealities, however. Lawrence's suggestion that it is 'industrial' women who don't 'come off', as it were, is ludicrous, in so far as he even seems to go so far as to blame 'the machine' for their sexual ineffectiveness. It would have been more correct to blame fathers and husbands who behaved like Mellors: and mothers who were as over-demanding on their sons such as Mrs Morel.

There are, then, untruths which Lawrence seeks energetically, with all his unconscious power, to persuade us to accept. His persuasive phantasy is compelling, and so there has been very little protest at his implications in this book. We are all afraid of exposing our own weaknesses and shortcomings in sexual matters, possibly because of our deep fear of being thought deficient in potency, and our fear of humiliation. Sexual activity helps us to feel 'alive': to be undermined or found weak in it may seem a touch of death or annihilation. So we, too, easily lead ourselves to manic persuasion over sex.

So when such an authority as Lawrence puts forward what he believes to be truth it is difficult for us to say that this does not accord with our experience.

But there are other not easily noted implications about sex in the book which are unreal, some connected with the above untruths, others not.

One gets a sense, first of Mellors' extra-potency - a potency which belongs to a dream idyll. It is true there are (as Kinsey showed) people of extra-potency. But Mellors is offered as normative. It is true that he had not known a woman for a long time: but it is also true that he is thirty-nine, and has recently suffered from pneumonia. When he pushes Clifford's wheelchair up a hill he has to pause and rest because he is out of breath. This is one contact with the physical reality of the outside world the lovers make - the only bit of work they do together, outside sexual activity - 'this bit of work had brought them closer together than anything else'. (Here is a tiny touch with the *Not-me*!) It is about the only recognition between them of the existence of the outside world at all - and of the flow of compassion, or hate, in aggressive and destructive elements that belong to the real. There is a refreshing touch of realism in Mellors' need to recover from exhaustion after lifting the chair, one welcome touch of real life on the stuffy, close, covert, unreal sensuality of the pastoral relationship. But the sexual actuality belongs to a dream – nothing ever goes wrong, all is 'perfect', insistently so, and 'god-like' – never a touch of that note in the poems, 'Last night was a failure – why not?' And Mellors, despite his state of convalescence, can make love three times in immediate succession, without once being out of breath, or even having to pause to regain his potency – yet such love work is surely infinitely more taxing than pushing a wheel-chair! But we do not see the unreality because we are carried away into the dream of super-potency. And the potency never flags – the lovers never settle to a normal quiet established rhythm, despite their good fortune in adjustment. They continue at the breakneck pace of the initial surge of a love relationship. It is as though Lawrence sought to elevate to an ideal an experience that may have happened to him once, or to postulate a richness for which he yearned but never knew.

Having noticed this one unreality, we may come to note others (and it is important that we should, because the anxiety in the book inevitably makes us anxious about our own reality).

The lovers make the kind of explorations any young newly-married couple make of the ranges of bodily sensation: there is nothing to which one can object in this: this is how people behave, and it accords with our experience. There are elements in all human sex of the slight sadism Mellors displays – breaking Connie's clothes, ripping her nightdress, tipping her up on the path.

But one sinister misrepresentation in *Lady Chatterley's Lover* is in the fact that the woman is made always 'half-unwilling', a little ashamed, submissive, 'a little frightened', and is made in this something of a baby-girl, while the man is allowed to retain his enigmatic, contemptuous, self-preserving attitude, refusing to accept his procreative responsibility, and his social responsibility. The picture is of a man-woman relationship which is distorted by gravely immature elements – but yet Lawrence neither sees nor places this. He approves the woman's submissiveness and the man's domineering attitudes, and presents them as normative. The book becomes at times as we have seen a special plea for a kind of masculine untenderness and brutality, and its exertion in domination and control of a partner, whose equality – or 'disquality' as Lawrence would want us to call it – is denied. He does not want an adult woman. Of course, as we have seen, he is 'controlling' the woman he fears.

Lawrence was a perceptive man, however, and there are valuable renderings of features of the sexual life whose portrayal here may enlarge our discriminative sympathy. The lovers learn what they have to do for instance – learn to accept new and strange sexual posture, or the 'slight messiness', to come to terms with the intractable body, beyond access of will, and to overcome their inward psychic resistances to the flux of the body's responses. The book is also valuable in conveying what lovers inevitably have to go through – and their occasional tendernesses in this.

But there are aspects of Lawrence's portrayal of these which are surely false to universal experience – chiefly, for instance, as I have said that it is Connie who always 'learns', while Mellor has little to learn, and instructs her. In reality, surely it is more true of love that – while the man may be said to lead, to take the initiative in making love and to work in bodily love for the woman – it is the woman's pace, cycle, rhythm to which *both* have to submit, because she is the creative creature, and has the larger and slower complex of rhythm and development? Because she has the greater need for security she can't surely really 'give' herself until she is happy about her creative and family future – a large point, touching civilization? Again, she completes her love in her creative role as mother. Significantly, because Lawrence's Mellors refuses to submit to the feminine creative rhythm, to the woman's need, to the truth of female reality, for fear of a 'loss of dignity' – and for his fear of loss of the self to the woman's 'dominance', he simply doesn't make love well, even considered in mere terms of physical sexual behaviour.

Again, as I have said there is a falsification of sexual growth: resistances are not overcome – sexual difficulties are not overcome – by Mellors' kind of masterliness, by such romantic wildflower wildness, by sensuality, by reckless phallic and anal exploration: that is the way to a kind of doom, to the Fiery Hill. These overcome nothing, where there are barriers to overcome. Difficulties have to be overcome in terms of the whole civilized complexity and personal reality of love. Mere 'warm-hearted fucking' may be a mere false solution.

Then, again, Lawrence's use of sexual maladjustment representative of a common weakness seems questionable (no survey of sexual behaviour in our time seems to consider it a central aberration) in terms of 'lesbian' women making the man 'stay inside them' while they 'bring themselves off'. It is certainly questionable in its symbolic implication, as of the selfish will in women of an industrial society. Mellors' wife has left him after a marital breakdown brought about by this very practice – which Lawrence renders as a one-sided, will-impelled mere cold 'use' of the male, painful and repulsive.

> But when I had her, she'd never come off when I did, Never! She'd just wait. If I kept back for half an hour she'd keep back longer . . . she'd tear at me down there, as if it was a beak tearing at me . . .

The angry blame and fear in this tells us more about Mellors – and Lawrence – than Bertha Coutts, for the language shows Lawrence's attitude to be punitive and hate-filled, attacking the woman because he fears her. The woman's sad inadequacy gains no pity or tender co-operation from Mellors – or Lawrence.

> tear, tear, tear, as if she had no sensation in her except in the top of her beak, the very outside tip top that rubbed and tore . . . it was a *low kind of self-will* in her . . .

(My italics)

The obsessed intensity of this passage reveals Lawrence's deep guilt and hostility towards woman's normal and proper right to her own sexual satisfaction. The woman's sexual organ and needs are regarded with contempt ('low . . . self-will'), and feared as having a predatory 'beak'. Such an introduction, in this tone, to the difference between clitoral and cervical orgasm would seem unhelpful to say the least – and yet Lawrence meant to help us.

Lawrence, in Mellors, takes this to be the representative sexual failure of our time – is it really so? The clinical investigations of our time by Chesser and Kinsey, for what they are worth, seem to suggest a wide variety of sexual 'failures', but the surveys seem to yield no certain correlations of sexual success with marital 'success', and certainly no correlations of 'good' sex with 'good' people! The picture seems to be one of failure on both sides, at the level of civilized living, rather than anything due to feminine attempts to dominate. 'Good' or 'bad' sex cannot be taken as indices in such a direct way, in the social and moral human pattern. People cannot be *blamed* for their unhappy sexual difficulties. They are not 'bad' and they may be able to do nothing about them. Interestingly enough, for instance, in many broken marriages the partners have had 'good sex' right up to the end – what has broken the marriage has been some straight-forward issue of daily living such as problems of money, bad behaviour one to the other, forms of aggression or power-seeking, and such common civilized aspects of daily life. Love relationships are neither consolidated nor do they break down on merely erotic, sensual matters *alone*. These are but indices – the other areas, where we resolve aggression and such impulses, and the whole reality sense, count more largely. The whole problem of co-operative mutuality counts more than sex, though it is, of course, integral with the discovery of 'giving' in adult genitality.

But Lawrence in this book has separated mind from 'heart, belly and cock': and seeks to prove to us the need for us to learn to live in the body, to learn 'the touch of bodily awareness'. Feeling, he implies, must be made to flow by feeling: sensuality frees the touch, and the touch brings awe and adoration. But cut away from the intelligence, it does not bring love. Here is Connie on feeling, in the sexual sense:

'I want to touch you like you touch me,' she said. 'I've never really touched your body.'
. . . 'How do I touch you?' he asked.
'When you feel me.'
He looked at her, and met her heavy anxious eyes.
'And do you like it when I feel you?' he asked, *laughing at her still.*

'Yes, do you?' she said.

'Oh me!' then he changed his tone. 'Yes,' he said. 'You know without asking.' Which was true.

Mellors is supercilious and sardonic at her anxiety about touching her body: such derision, which is to 'heal' her, is the thing the *man* most fears. When they meet she is not able to respond to his touching.

> ... she was afraid, afraid of his thin, smooth naked body, that seemed so powerful, afraid of the violent muscles ... something in her spirit stiffened in resistance ... stiffened ... from the terrible *haste of his possession* ... the butting of his haunches seemed ridiculous ... [the] little evacuating crisis seemed farcical ... surely a complete evolution would eliminate this performance, this function ...

Her resistance to 'feeling' associates her with the misuse of mind (about 'evolution' 'saving' us from sex) which Lawrence characterizes rightly as anti-life. But by potent return Mellors, by his very standing there buttoning down those absurd breeches ('so assured in himself'), by his very physical insolence, overcomes her resistance:

> She let herself go. She felt his penis rise against her with silent amazing force.

The ravishment is an attempt to verbalize the intelligence away: note the novelette language – as in the 'silent' 'force' of the penis (was Lawrence afraid the penis might one day speak?) 'Amazing' force – such hyperbole reveals the desire to establish a super-potency – by words[1]:

> ... it came with a strange slow thrust of peace, the dark thrust of peace and a ponderous, primordial tenderness, such as made the world in the beginning ... On, and far down inside her the deeps parted and rolled asunder ... as the plunger went deeper and deeper ... till suddenly, in a soft, shuddering convulsion, the quick of her all was touched, she knew herself touched, the consummation was upon her, and she was gone. She was gone, she was not, and she was born: a woman. Ah, too lovely, too lovely...

[1] The god-like, plunging, 'silent', 'amazing' penis is notably more nobly described than the 'beak' that 'rubbed and tore'.

Earlier she had said, like a submissive baby-girl, 'I want to love you but I can't . . . it seems horrid . . .' Connie's resistance had to be broken down by 'rather awful sensuality': by *feeling*. And the waves of feeling, the whirlpools of sensation bear the woman away to her rebirth, the resurrection of her body. She is lost, only to be reborn. But in fact it is not happening in bodily life – rather in the surge of such over-insistent verbiage.

But here we may observe of the sexual reality portrayed that Connie learns, after 182 pages, to touch her man:

> And now she touched him and it was the sons of god with the daughters of men. And the strange weight of the balls between his legs! What a mystery!

Note that it is the mere *daughters* of men, but the *sons of god*. The woman must be so *awed* by her godlike partner that only after so much sexual experiment dare she 'touch' him – feeling takes that long to overcome feeling. This may be true of some women who find it difficult to accept sexual reality. But this touch is made after two acts of coition immediately preceding, at the moment when, surely, most men find such touch unwelcome? Lawrence reacted strongly against Frieda's touch *at all* – she 'wouldn't dare to touch a snake so'. But Mellors' potent phallus rises again, and this time it was 'all soft and irridescent, purely soft and irridescent, *such as no consciousness could seize*'. Lawrence, however, persists in trying to bring to our consciousness something which no consciousness could seize. All Connie knows is that 'she could not know what it was. She could not remember what it had been. Only that it had been more lovely than anything could be' – the language becomes that of *Peg's Paper*, as the woman is reduced to 'awed submission'.

But we note, as we go, that the religious overtones of the description are rather to instil awe for the 'son of god' who is the dominant male, and to deny the woman and the creativity of sex. *Connie is made to have more reverence for Mellors' 'balls' than they have between them for the great mystery of her conception.*

In the end Mellors triumphs over her completely by forcing her 'almost unwillingly' to commit anal intercourse with him (p. 258).

This latter is hinted at most coyly and pruriently by Lawrence. Only later do we learn that Mellors has had his wife 'all ends' and 'in the Italian manner': where the incident occurs it is 'reckless, shameless sensuality. . . . Burning out the shames, the deepest oldest shames, in the most secret places. . . . She had to be a passive consenting thing, like a slave, a physical slave. . . . She really thought she was dying.' In the end Mellors is shown virtually crowing mentally over her submission as he performs the act:

> And she realized as he went into her that this was the thing he had to do, to come into tender touch, *without losing his pride or his dignity* or his integrity as a man. After all, if she had money and means, and he had none, he should be too proud and honourable to hold back his tenderness from her on that account . . .

(My italics)

Why should Mellors be so concerned at not losing his 'dignity and integrity' in the very act that gives a man creative dignity and fortifies his pride and integrity? Why should anal intercourse be necessary to 'burn out' 'shame'? The answer, as we have seen, is that Lawrence unconsciously fears that the woman hides in the anus the threat that will annihilate. The verbal act which the book is associates with this act: both emerge from infantile modes of 'attack', oral-anal sadism in the place of shared adult genitality.

The greatest irony of Lawrence's fate comes towards the end, at the passage we have just looked at, when Mellors is in the throes of his last sexual act with Connie. Here is the culmination of a book whose point is to oppose the tyranny of conscious 'will' over the 'body'. But in the end it shows the hero verbalizing strongly at the moment of supreme passion – as he approaches his crisis:

> 'I stand for the touch of bodily awareness between human beings,' he said to himself, 'and the touch of tenderness. And she is my mate. And it is a battle against the money, and the machine, and the in-sentient ideal monkeyishness of the world! Thank God I've got a woman who is with me and tender and aware of me. Thank God she's not a bully, nor a fool. Thank God she's a tender, aware woman.' And as his seed sprang in her, his soul sprang towards her too, in the creative act that is more than procreative.

p. 292

Here is his hero, at the moment of consummation. The woman has just confirmed her pregnancy. The lovers move towards consideration of marriage, after a whole series of episodes in which they seek to give their whole beings to one another in sexual union. And yet the man is *thinking out a kind of self-saving manifesto, in abstract verbal terms*, at the very utmost moment of being 'gone to body'! Yet he neither considers 'us', *nor their child*! And thinks of her as 'a' woman. By any experience, of course, this is absurd, and a denial of the very 'warm-hearted' coition which Lawrence recommends. It is also unreal. Mellors is making love, but he is more interested in his thoughts. This is both un-Lawrentian – and a comment on Lawrence and his need to write this book. The oral-anal attack is more important to Lawrence than love. 'But have you got it now?' Connie asks, knowing that he *has* got 'it' – 'good' sex – now, if 'coming off together' is all he wants. The book says *this* – warm-hearted coition – is all we need for perfection, for happiness, for a reformed society – what more do we need? But there *is* something more, because Morelorence never loses his sense of doom, but Connie and Mellors don't find 'it' – however much they try in frantic sensuality. In the merely erotic 'it' can't be 'got'.

Lawrence cannot explain Mellors' continuing dissatisfaction: he can only say that what he wants is 'warm-hearted fucking':

'Then why are you so pale and gloomy?'
'Bellyful of remembering: and perhaps afraid of myself.'

(This is courage from 'the broken-backed snake' as he describes himself. He goes on, revealing that to Lawrence 'right relation' belongs too exclusively to 'body', and is spoiled by fear of bodily giving.)

She sat in silence. It was growing late.
'And do you think it's important, a man and a woman?' she asked him.
'For me it is. For me it's the core of my life; if I have a right relation with a woman.'
'And if you don't get it?'
'Then I'd have to do without.'

Again she pondered, before she asked:

'And do you think you've always been right with women?'

'God no! I let my wife get to what she was: my fault a good deal. I spoilt her. And I'm very mistrustful. You'll have to expect it. It takes a lot to make me trust anybody, inwardly. So perhaps I'm a fraud too. I mistrust. And tenderness is not to be mistaken.'

She looked at him.

'You don't mistrust with your body, when your blood comes up,' she said. 'You don't mistrust then, do you?'

'No alas! That's how I got into all the trouble. And that's why my mind distrusts so thoroughly.'

'Let your mind mistrust. What does it matter!'

This comes just before Connie says her piece about the women who wanted to be 'there' with him, and who were not to be blamed. The perception put into Connie's mouth in this passage is acute, and it is great courage on Lawrence's part to admit as much as he does about himself, and about any man. Mellors admits he had not always been 'all right' with women: much of the trouble is his fault, he admits, 'a good deal'. But the exact nature of the fault he does not admit, nor does Lawrence – it is not in 'spoiling' or 'letting get to what she was'. But there are revealing phrases here. 'Tenderness is not to be mistaken' means 'taken wrongly, and used to humiliate me': and Mellors' (and Lawrence's) predicament is to wish not to 'mistrust' with his body, but is forced to mistrust in the exertion of something like will over his body. There is much in that 'mistrust' (the speech is strangely unconvincing until this point, as though Lawrence was on uncertain ground). But 'I'm a fraud' is a brave clue to the whole book. Mellors' speech here reveals the profound mistrust Lawrence himself had in yielding, giving himself to a woman. It is not Connie who had so much to learn: Morelorence had more to learn about his own complementary sexual and psychic weaknesses. One truth Lawrence certainly could not accept was that 'marriage is a relationship in which psychopathology plays a part on both sides'.[1] He wants to project his own difficulties over 'woman', and then

[1] H. C. Scott, Senior Psychotherapist, Addenbroke's Hospital, in a private communication to the author.

attack her, as he attacks 'the industrial world' – to prove his inner troubles were in them, not in him.

At the conclusion of this consideration of the unreality of the sexual love portrayed in *Lady Chatterley's Lover* we may appropriately wish Lawrence had told us about love rather than sex. Love, when we find peace in it, releases us to the world, to devote ourselves to effort for humanity. We go from the satisfactions we find in our own love, children and home to give out in our work and for the community. The end of our quest for love is an escape from envy, in creative attitudes abroad, joy in the joy of others, and 'belief in the continuity of life'.

And any change for the better in our complex attitudes to sex can only come by slow and deep changes pervading the whole being, *the whole moral perception*, and the whole civilized context of love, in one generation, as it grows to bring up the next. While this involves a study of the love experience of others, in fact an anxious contemplation of the coition of others is not only impertinent – is a valueless help to our quest, but a symptom manifestation of our fear of sexual reality. Other people's coition can only be disturbing, even disgusting, and the contemplation of it destructive.[1]

In his books, however, Lawrence was impelled by his inner anxieties to describe sexual activity. The compulsive reasons for this are suggested by one quotation given above:

> 'Don't people often come off together?' she asked with a naïve curiosity.
> 'A good many of them never. You can see by the raw look of them.' He spoke unwillingly, regretting that he had begun . . .

The last sentence betrays an uncertainty. One wonders whether Lawrence ever regretted having begun *Lady Chatterley's Lover*, having once felt it necessary? He would, I think, be sorry now. The word here, 'regretting', suggests that Lawrence found a compulsive interest in people's 'raw faces' which showed that they did

[1] This explains the negative and dissociating effect of 'sex education' separated from imaginative culture in education, of books on sex, and manuals of contraception, etc. Of course, there are times when we need to look at sex thus, but it is always at a cost – 'the poetry' is lost or damaged, temporarily.

not 'come off' together – and so a compelled inquisitiveness about their sexual lives. To those to whom it is given to have rich and 'successful' sex there can be no such anxious concern to explore the nature of 'good' and 'bad', 'ideal' and 'wrong' sex – or to look at the faces of others to see if they were those who 'came off' – certainly never to condemn those who 'fail' in order to defend themselves against being classed as one of them. Indeed, an adequate sexual relationship surely exorcizes the destructive impulse to compare? Such impulses belong to trouble in our attitudes to sexual experience which may in fact lead us to suppose there is a degree of sexual experience we are not having, or cannot have – *when we are probably actually 'having it' if only we could see we were* and if we could only *accept* it as 'good'! That is, our whole reality sense is at fault if we yearn for a hallucinatory 'perfect' sex, because we cannot accept our real sexual life, with all its inevitable imperfections. Lawrence's impulse to compare, as conveyed by this book, can only exacerbate the discomforts and difficulties of those who have limitations, through no fault of their own. Thus he contributes to our prevalent psychic symptom of sex-anxiety.

In many places in the book we meet this self-exploratory courage of the 'broken-backed snake', who seeks to explore experience without mercy to himself. By contrast with the self-deception, the 'touch of a man' and all it means, for instance, is much better given us in the remarkable passage in sympathy between Mrs Bolton and Connie. Here 'heart and belly and cock' – sufficient for Mellors – become linked with the social context and the intelligent contemplation of the place of love in it, and the family, as an aspect of civilized living. Here is the real, intelligent 'vibration of the working people', alive. Here is Lawrence able to convey the deep reality of love and 'touch'. It is a superb passage – would the rest of the book were as good! Extraordinary that Lawrence should have been diverted from this human warmth of common life, into the pastoral, classless, unreality of his humiliated aristocratic girl and the woodlander, temporizing gamekeeper!

It was a sunny day, and Connie was working in the garden, and Mrs Bolton was helping her. For some reason, the two women had drawn together, in one of the unaccountable flows and ebbs of sympathy that exist between people. They were pegging down carnations and putting in small plants for the summer. It was work they both liked. Connie especially felt a delight in putting the soft roots of young plants into a soft black puddle, and cradling them down. On this spring morning she felt a quiver in her womb too, as if the sunshine had touched it and made it happy.

'It is many years since you lost your husband?' she said to Mrs Bolton, as she took up another little plant and laid it in its hole.

'Twenty-three!' said Mrs Bolton, as she carefully separated the young columbines into single plants. 'Twenty three years since they brought him home.'

Connie's heart gave a lurch, at the terrible finality of it. 'Brought him home!'

'Why did he get killed, do you think?' she asked. 'He was happy with you?'

It was a woman's question to a woman. Mrs Bolton put aside a strand of hair from her face, with the back of her hand.

'I don't know, my Lady! He sort of wouldn't give in to things: he wouldn't really go with the rest. And then he hated ducking his head for anything on earth. A sort of obstinacy, that gets itself killed. You see, he didn't really care. I lay it down to the pit. He ought never to have been down pit. But his dad made him go down, as a lad; and then, when you're over twenty, it's not very easy to come out.'

'Did he say he hated it?'

'Oh no! Never! He never said he hated anything. He just made a funny face. He was one of those who wouldn't take care: like some of the first lads as went off so blithe to the war and got killed right away. He wasn't really wezzle-brained. But he wouldn't care. I used to say to him: "You are for nought nor nobody!" But he did! The way he sat when my first baby was born, motionless, and the sort of fatal eyes he looked at me with, when it was over! I had a bad time, but I had to comfort him. "It's all right, lad, it's all right!" I said to him. And he gave me a look, and that funny sort of smile. He never said anything. But I don't believe he had any right pleasure with me at nights after: he'd never really let himself go. I used to say to him: "Oh let thysen go, Lad!" – I'd talk broad to him sometimes. And he said nothing. He didn't want me to have any more children. I always blame his mother, for letting him in th' room. He'd no right t'ave been there. Men makes so much more of things than they should, once they start brooding.'

'Did he mind so much?' said Connie in wonder.

'Yes, he sort of couldn't take it for natural, all that pain. And it spoilt his pleasure in his bit of married love. I said to him: "If I don't care, why should you? It's my lookout." – but all he'd ever say was: "It's not right." '

'Perhaps he was too sensitive,' said Connie.

'That's it! When you come to know men, that's how they are: too sensitive in the wrong place. And I believe, unbeknown to himself, he hated the pit, just hated it. He looked so quiet when he was dead, as if he'd got free. He was such a nice-looking lad. It just broke my heart to see him, so still and pure looking, as if he'd wanted to die. Oh, it broke my heart, that did. But it was the pit.'

She wept a few bitter tears, and Connie wept more. It was a warm spring day, with a perfume of earth and of yellow flowers, many things rising to bud, and the garden still with the very sap of sunshine.

'It must have been terrible for you!' said Connie.

'Oh my Lady! I never realized it first. I could only say: "Oh my lad, what did you want to leave me for!" – That was all my cry. But somehow I felt he'd come back.'

'But he didn't want to leave you,' said Connie.

'Oh no, my Lady! That was only my silly cry. And I kept expecting him back. Especially at nights. I kept waking up thinking: "Why he's not in bed with me!" – It was as if my feeling wouldn't come back, it took me years.'

'The touch of him,' said Connie.

'That's it, my Lady, the touch of him! I've never got over it to this day, and never shall. And if there's a heaven above, he'll be there, and will lie up against me so I can sleep.'

Connie glanced at the handsome, brooding face in fear. Another passionate one out of Tevershall! The touch of him! For the bonds of love are ill to loose!

'It's terrible, once you've got a man into your blood!' she said.

'Oh, my Lady! And that's what makes you feel so bitter. You feel folks wanted him killed. You feel the pit fair wanted to kill him. Oh, I felt, if it hadn't been for the pit, an' them as runs the pit, there'd have been no leaving me. But they all want to separate a woman and a man, if they're together.'

'If they're physically together,' said Connie.

'That's right, my lady! There's a lot of hard-hearted folks in the world. And every morning when he got up and went to th' pit, I felt it was wrong, wrong. But what else could he do? What can a man do?'

A queer hate flared in the woman.

'But can a touch last so long?' Connie asked suddenly. 'That you could feel him so long?'

'Oh my Lady, what else is there to last? Children grows away from you. But the man, well! But even that they'd like to kill in you, the very thought of the touch of him. Even your own children! Ah well! We might have drifted apart, who knows. But the feeling's something different. It's 'appen better never to care. But there, when I look at women who's never really been warmed through by a man, well, they seem to me poor doolowls after all, no matter how they may dress up and gad. No, I'll abide by my own. I've not much respect for people.'

This is the great Lawrence of the short stories (cf. *Odour of Chrysanthemums*) mingling compassion with critical understanding, a sense of sympathy between the women going with an understanding, too, of how far they are apart. But how the blood flows here in enacted poetic drama of reality and people as they are – as it hardly does elsewhere in this book, with any real life! The reason is not the over-preoccupation with bodily awareness elsewhere, so much as the stifling of the mind, and the civilized heart, and a loss of discriminative power in Lawrence who enters too compulsively into the Philistine Mellors, for deep and destructive unconscious reasons, and so compromises his capacity to render a true picture of sexual reality.

6
SONS OF GOD, DAUGHTERS OF MEN

One of Lawrence's own characteristic ploys is to assert his normality so forcibly, even when denying such things as the nature of the sun, that we accept him as less fallible than other men. F. R. Leavis says, 'What is misfortune for a genius?' and implies defiantly that Lawrence triumphed over his inward difficulties. In many ways he did, but there are ways significant to his work in which he could not, and because he refuses to accept this Leavis, as W. W. Robson implies, gives more credit to Lawrence for positive comments at the end of his great novels *The Rainbow* and *Women in Love* than we may, in fact, find in them. Whereas to indicate Lawrence's shortcomings does in the end make his courage and contest in spite of them seem more marvellous and helpful to us.

Lawrence, we must accept, was as neurotic and imperfect as anyone. That he had a horror of neurosis perhaps confirms this, as Catherine Carswell notes:

> Although the fullness of his admissions, and the sensitiveness of his abandon to the impulses of life might give to the superficial observer the impression that he was a sufferer from a neurosis, Lawrence was emphatically no neurotic. Of this I am convinced. If I add that he hated neurotics, even while he had the misfortune to find in them more immediately than in others a kind of response which sprang from superficial understanding, I suppose I shall call forth the gibe of the analyst – 'Thou sayest it!' 'The real neurotic is half a devil,' said Lawrence, 'the cured one' with his 'perfect automatic control,' is 'a perfect devil'. And again, '*Spit on every neurotic and wipe your feet on his face if he tries to drag you down.*' Yet I know what I say is true. Lawrence hated, he feared, he fought and he was obliged to consort with neurotics. But he was himself untainted.
>
> *The Savage Pilgrimage,* Catherine Carswell, p. 224 (My italics)

On this passage perhaps we may comment to allay strong reactions in protest against Lawrence being called neurotic. As I have tried to suggest above, it is now recognized that everyone has neurotic elements in their make-up: we are all sufferers from the inevitable consequences of the natural faults in the circumstances of our mysterious and complex growth to human consciousness. Every psyche suffers from the consequences of early deprivation and failures in the development of a reality sense. Such disabilities in us are the curse of Adam: they are the price of consciousness. Conversely, there is no 'cured' neurotic, as is suggested here. There may be a person who supposes that he had conquered his psychic difficulties by the exercise of the will and intellect, but this is likely to be rather a manifestation of a defence against the acceptance of truth than a 'cure'. Lawrence was, by the evidence of his work, in some areas of experience, a very neurotic man, and his great value as creative artist was in the courage of his struggle against the neurotic distortions by which his own unconscious mind strove to delude his better vision. At times, however, as in *Lady Chatterley*, and many of his poems, and in *The Plumed Serpent* – and, of course, in much of his Old Moore's Almanacking as in *Fantasia* and *Psychoanalysis and the Unconscious*, Lawrence writes drivel – anti-scientific, anti-reason, and against even his better poetic judgment as artist. This activity in part, despite its flashes of occasional 'terrifying honesty', marks the attempt to project neurotic distortions over reality, to disguise it. There were some insights, and some apprehensions of the reality of the world, which Lawrence could not accept – such as the equality in dis-quality of women – because he feared women unconsciously. He therefore strove bravely, but erroneously, to belabour the world into accordance with his own neurotic view of it. In this, and be-cause the activity has its origin in his deep attachment to his mother, whose goodness he seeks to restore in the world, he assumed a Messianic role. Naturally, he comes into conflict with a similar impulse in such a person as John Middleton Murry, who also identifies strongly with Christ himself. The deep envy that seems to have motivated Murry was obviously bound up with the com-petition between himself and Lawrence to 'be' Jesus Christ: Catherine Carswell's account of the celebration at the Café Royal at which Murry kissed Lawrence, like Judas at the Last Supper, makes this plain. Murry wanted Lawrence-Christ crucified, so that he could take his place as Murry-Christ. The Messianic appeal in Lawrence is still among us, and it causes those who support his work as artist to be guilty at times of regarding 'treachery' to Lawrence as a kind of blasphemy, or Judas touch. But this is only part of Lawrence's 'defence' – to involve us as disciples in the domination he seeks to exert, to 'control' us, as he wants to control the woman.

This urge to be a 'son of god' in the special relationship with the holy mother must be inherent in every man, but in the creative artist it takes perhaps a particular intensity, related to the positive inspiration which the mother has given in infancy.

The urge to bring the mother (who is at times also 'England') a renewed life links here with Lawrence's desire to 'resurrect the body' – to bring back to our living now the wholeness of life we have lost – as the mother had lost her life, and had previously become subject to the half-life of being a miner's wife.

But, of course, such an identification of oneself with the Christ-child, with large elements of feeling to do with being an omnipotent son who is to make the world good for the mother, contains inevitably strong Oedipal feelings.

We can confirm this Oedipal content of *Lady Chatterley's Lover* from the autobiographical material in *Sons and Lovers*, and we can find in this some of the origins of Lawrence's denial of the realities of love, and woman's creativity.

His anxieties as we have seen impel Morelorence to seek 'healing' in the woman – and to demand of a woman the attention and healing, anxiety-allaying comfort such as a mother gives a child. Such demands, of course, are very destructive of adult relationships (though in real life we all make them at times): and so disaster inevitably comes – and further sense of doom. Who shall be blamed for this doom? Truly, of course, the man who has the anxiety should blame himself, some fault in his inner reality. But the pain of recognition would be great, and so with Morelorence, *it is the women who are blamed*. It is the women who will not yield: the women who tear at the men with their 'beak-like clitoris'. But in fact, as 'E. T.' points out in her memoir, in life it was possibly Lawrence who found sex 'difficult', not his women at all. But to him, they have been made like that by the industrial 'Thing'. (This industrial thing is also, as we have seen, the father.)

In Lawrence's life he had to put up with real women. But in this idealizing phantasy, a real woman such as Frieda Lawrence,[1] who would demand respect as a mature adult equal, would not do. So, in this work, Lawrence invents in ('true') Constance the completely compliant woman who is willing to sink all her personal integrity and self-respect into a union which in life could only be humiliating to her, because it demands total attention and submission such as a child desires from the mother (but never gets) though it hallucinates it in its phantasy. Yet Constance is called 'a lady': her essential humiliation, her inferiority in the sexual role,

[1] See Appendix C on Ursula and Birkin.

is disguised by the idyllic, boyish, romance of the story, and by her 'aristocracy'. She is, if we look at her dispassionately, something of a whore – the whore who will gratify like the mother, but who can also be attacked and despised, and will do anything we make her. But we have already noted the force of identification at work – by which Lawrence identified himself with both Connie and Mellors. Lawrence needs to make the woman in his own image thus because he cannot accept feminine 'otherness' and reality: he can only really accept 'fucking' when he is 'fucking' himself.

In *Lady Chatterley's Lover*, Lawrence takes his father's place – Mellors being, as I have said, a not very complicated disguise for the fact. His vernacular speech, with its 'thou-ing' going with a certain kind of tenderness, is perhaps the tenderness he perceived and loved in the father. The mysterious creature maleness (notably Connie first sees Mellors washing himself *like a miner*) is the aspect of his father he loved. The theme recurs – and in *Odour of Chrys-anthemums* it is this loved washed miner's body which the wife had so distressingly not 'known', the woman who then also perceives she 'hasn't really had a husband'.

We may remember that it is his father Morel in *Sons and Lovers* who says 'Shonna', and talks in the Northern vernacular. It is his mother who addresses Morel ironically as 'milord' – which is transferred in *Lady Chatterley's Lover* to Mellors' ironic, insolent, 'your ladyship'. And Mellors' tenderness in addressing Connie as 'my little lass' comes, too, from Morel's mode:

'What has it done to thee, lass?' he asked, in a very wretched, humble tone.

This is from the striking passage where a drip of blood falls from Mrs Morel's wound, given her by her husband's drunken blow, on to Paul's baby head:

. . . his manhood broke. 'What of this child?' was all his wife said to him . . .

The scene is recalled in the moment when Connie's tear falls on to her wrist as she holds up the baby pheasant chick, when Mellors' manhood breaks towards her, in her desire for creative life. But a child for Constance-Mummy would be rival to baby-Morelor-ence, and thus in resistance to his mother's poignant cry, 'What of this child?', with all Lawrence's love for his mother rendered in it, his compassion for her predicament, and his hatred of his father – in *Lady Chatterley* sex is made childless. One memory that may have been upmost in Lawrence's mind as he wrote *Lady Chatterley* is the scene where Morel seeks to be tender to Mrs Morel at his own birth:

> 'Bless him!' he murmured. Which made her laugh, because he was blessing by rote – pretending paternal emotion which he did not feel just then. 'Go now,' she said.
>
> 'I will, my lass,' he answered turning away. Dismissed, he wanted to kiss her, and he dared not. She half wanted him to kiss her, but could not bring herself to give any sign. She only breathed freely when he was gone out of the room . . .

Lawrence possibly set out to seek in phantasy to redeem this moment of his own birth and infancy, unconsciously seeking to give his mother the tenderness he indicates here as lacking between Morel and his wife, and to seek true feelings of 'paternal emotion'. The child's wish that 'all should be well' between the parents becomes the adult author's need to give in phantasy the dead mother a husband (through the son) she did not have in life. The whole movement of the book up to the first seduction is in the direction of the creation of new child-life: after that it turns away, because of the complications in Morelorence's attitudes to birth, and woman's creativity.

Certainly Mellors is Morel, made into a 'good' father – re-deemed as an 'unusual man', as Lawrence intended. In the end he becomes as inhuman as Lawrence's own father. In the father's role Mellors assumes, enters, and does to his mother in the person of Connie what Lawrence wanted to do with his mother. Thus Lawrence hopes, by the imaginative phantasy, to overcome his sense of doom in sex, and make it 'all right'. But yet, as I have suggested, he becomes aware in the most explicit scene – p. 212 – that something stands in the way. Here the other side of Mellors is meant to come into the picture, as an 'exceptional being'. He is a 'reader' (though his books are a pretty poor selection!). He has been civilized by his first girl (as Lawrence was, by E. T. – 'Miriam' – in their shared literary interests). He is 'almost a gentleman', embodying Lawrence's feelings of wanting to be considered as good as an aristocrat, retaining an undercurrent of class inferiority shame. But Mellors speaks at other times – in English which is not vernacular – with Lawrence's voice, prophetically, and with that tediousness of his creator's 'Old Moore's Almanacking'. Lawrence fails to make a good father, and Mellors is a strange and unconvincing amalgam. This is the source of Lawrence's failure. Who can this Morelorence blame for his sexual difficulties? For the discomforting sense of dissociation from reality that haunts the idyllic sexual relationship with Lady Chatterley? For his strangle-threatened joy with the phantasy-aristocrat, the goddess of his daemon, behind which the mother's figure lurks with a hint of incestuous voluptuousness? Who can be blamed for all this impingement of reality, and the recognition that sex can never really be as phallic, Panlike, utterly magical, primaeval, and religious as it is between Mellors and Connie? For the failure of life's reality to come up to the idealized pastoral?

The answer takes the malevolent extreme – first, the reality of human nature – *all real people* other than Morelorence and Her Ladyship, the monistic self having coition with the self: hence the general malevolence of the book, its misanthropy and destructive hopelessness. And secondly, *industrial society*, because industrial society had made Morel – Lawrence's father, that is – what he was, a troglodyte, and had therefore robbed his mother of the joy which, had she had it, would have released him, Lawrence, for adequate, untrammelled adult sexual relationships. Also, Morel would have had Lawrence in the pit, which he must have feared in retribution for his intense love of his mother. The tale itself is thus from the beginning doomed to take the opposite direction from acceptance of reality: Lawrence could not accept these inner realities and must falsify outer reality and the reality of sex to accord. We must go on from these to examine further why these things undermined the art, and damaged Lawrence's social attitudes.

7

IMPOTENCE AND WORDS

Lawrence's extreme rejection of industrial society is based on his projection of his inward difficulties, many of them to do with his feelings about father and his father's relationship with his mother. So he falsely accounts for many of our sexual shortcomings by implying that these are the fate of those who embrace the spirit of industrialism. Chief of these is Clifford, who is the usurped Laius in Lawrence's Oedipal myth. Clifford is a victim of the 1914–18 war: it is not his fault he is ball-less, literally – but he receives no sympathy for his disability, certainly not from Connie – *as if it were his fault*.

There are veracities in Lawrence's delineation of possible reasons for Connie's hostility to her husband. There is Connie's mounting restlessness, her realization that she wants an entire man and a child by him, her exacerbation with Clifford, and with the pretend-life they lead, under the slogan of 'there is something eternal in marriage'. But in Clifford the argument against the 'carrion-bodied', against the industrial system, against modern England, is disastrously weighted. The man is castrated not by a consequence of his own acts, but, as it were, with perverse unfairness, by Lawrence, who seeks to give the industrial magnate dog a bad name and then maims him. Clifford is very different from Gerald Crich in that the latter takes the volitional path to willed self-destruction. Clifford doesn't castrate himself. He may represent 'England', chuffing about in his mechanized wheelchair, exerting his will childishly, first on verbalizing experience in cliché ways, then with the industrial toys in the production of coal and iron. But his impotence after all (we protest) comes not from some moral weakness in himself, for which he might be blamed, but from a chance fate of the large impersonal incidents of modern times for which no individual alone is to blame, whatever his weaknesses.

Clifford has been castrated, of course, in the war: but we may say he has been castrated in the phantasy by Lawrence's own Oedipal impulses. The book opens with the statement, 'Ours is a

tragic age.' Ours is not a tragic age: far from it. We have not the
transcendent values for tragedy, for taking into account the conditions of man's existence as 'a poor bare fork'd animal', and to
find a 'belief in the continuity of life' that transcends such an
apprehension of the reality. Lawrence's impulse is akin to Hardy's
desire to 'be' tragic in *Tess* and *Jude* – a somewhat literary pose.
Lady Chatterley has an underlying tragic myth – the Oedipus myth,
but it turns false. Oedipus went blind and destroyed himself, and
this is what happens to Lawrence in this book.

The flower-thunderstorm scene no doubt sprang from
Lawrence's tragic intentions and reveals his unconscious sense of
tragic myth underlying this novel. The storm which expresses a
storm in Lawrence's mind over the explicit revelations of his
predicament, echoes *King Lear*, and so does the flower-winding
and the nakedness in the tempest. In such elements are revealed
the tragic aspirations of the book: alas, they are brought down by
Connie's canvas shoes, by a petty 'realism' that never attains the
courageous insight necessary for tragedy. Clifford, as the tragic
protagonist, is never realized: he is never more than a caricature, a
mere projection-target, with his 'yellow' rage, of everything
Lawrence hates. What Lawrence hates is here too often what we
are forced to protest to be desirable – the man's energetic courage
in the face of his disability, his attempt to keep his marriage in
existence as something valid, his desire that his wife should have a
child. (How poignant is his, 'I mind not having a child when I
come here more than at any other time'.) Clifford is the projection
of some part of himself that Lawrence hated: so here he is sometimes uncomfortably like an embodiment of a reality Lawrence
wants to deny. Clifford is virtually persecuted for desiring aspects
of reality which Lawrence unconsciously fears – to have a child,
to be 'a part of things' with Wragby, marriage, to *belong* to a
locality and to reality.

In a sense Clifford is the father Lawrence loved as well as hated.
In order to punish and destroy these 'good' qualities in Clifford,
Lawrence weights him by piling on his impotence other negative
qualities, related to the social and personal worlds, in which there
is no coherence of moral inevitability: Lawrence is simply unfair

to a paradigm of everything he dislikes – and fears. There is no attempt to come to terms with the fears, merely to punish them and deny them by attack. Yet there is a sense in which poor Clifford is closer to adult reality than the somewhat infantile pastoral lovers.

Clifford stands for the war-wound:

> . . . it was the bruise of the war that had been in abeyance, slowly rising to the surface and creating the great ache of unrest, and stupor of discontent. The bruise was deep, deep, deep . . . the bruise of the false inhuman war. It would take many years for the living blood of the generations to dissolve the vast black clot of bruised blood, deep inside their souls and bodies. And it would need a new hope.

The 'living blood of the generations . . . a new hope' – it is this that Connie seeks to exert against the wound of the war epitomized in Clifford. But what hope remains at the end of the book? Lawrence kills it on the way. Clifford represents a mock.

> Clifford's mental life and hers gradually began to feel like nothingness. Their marriage, their integrated life based on a habit of intimacy, that he talked about, there were days when it all became utterly blank and nothing. Just so many words. The only reality was nothingness, and over it a hypocrisy of words.
>
> There was Clifford's success: the bitch-goddess! . . . display! A display!

Lawrence means us to feel that marriage without sex is nothing, and that words without bodily life beneath are nothing too. Clifford's writes his words to seek to find kudos and worldly success only: he lives only in the medium of the schizoid intellect, that seeks power and kudos rather than closer touch with life. Here Lawrence touches, indeed, on the blight of our intellectual life, in which intellect is so often enlisted against feeling. But there is no analysis here, in a helpful way, yielding insight, of *why* Clifford should be like this. We are simply told that he is so – and prompted to hate him. So in Clifford Lawrence mixes together a number of his dislikes without much organic connection or adequate grounds for their origin. Why should Clifford's wound symbolize post-war society, except in the crude sense of attributing to it a sym-

bolic 'ball-lessness', splenetically? How does Clifford associate
with industrial energy and drive, really – except to proclaim that
there is a kind of purposeless, immature, unmanliness about devotion to machines? Is it so? Were Brunel and the Wright
Brothers or Leonardo da Vinci such men? One can see how the
ball-lessness relates to the hypocrisy of pretending a marriage is
valid when it is no longer a marriage – but is the implication that
every woman whose man loses his potency should desert him?
Isn't even this disability, so terrible to Lawrence, surmountable
by something other than desertion?[1] Lawrence's argument here is
heavily – and unrealistically – weighted against all altruism and
compassion. It would have been so much more effective had our
sympathy with Clifford been alienated by his withdrawal from
married sexual relations by force of will or indifference – which
is what happens between Rico and Lou in *St Mawr* (where
Lawrence approves of Lou's chastity). We might even have taken
an impotence brought about unconsciously by the deathly influence of willed mechanical living – as in Gerald, as a symbol of
life-denial. But Clifford is given no such chance to involve our
compassion and sympathetic discrimination (in which we would
be accepting his predicament as part of ours – 'there but for the
grace of God go I'). His unconscious Oedipus urge dictated to
Lawrence that Clifford should be actually castrated: and because
this physical amputation, however symbolic it was intended to be,
is undeserved, we find Connie's desertion cruel and her self-satisfaction sickeningly wrong. This reaction alienates our sympathy.
This is not only in that it might be *possible* for a woman to think
so, but in that (again) Lawrence *approves*, even relishes her cruelly
crowing thought behind Clifford's back, 'What would he think
if he knew I had sexual intercourse today with his gamekeeper?'
   How could Lawrence do this? The answer we may find, if we
see Clifford as embodying something to which Lawrence is unfair
– which he castrates – because he is afraid of it. Lawrence fears

---

[1] It is possible for many people to lead chaste lives. It is possible for widows to
live a life of renunciation of sex in memory of a love. It would not be impossible
for a wife of a Clifford to live devotedly with him, and not necessarily uncreative
for her to do so.

sexual impotence as a revenge for castrating Clifford and usurping his place in Morelorence. Thus his own verbal exertions are a compensatory striving against the threat, as well as an attempt to allay anxiety about potency by oral aggression. Clifford also stands for impotent verbalizing, and here there is a strange and interesting confusion because Clifford is thus both Laius and Lawrence himself. No one in the present century has verbalized as much as Lawrence in this book: its *succès de scandale* even added the phrase 'four-letter word' to popular speech. Its use of Anglo-Saxon words was an act of oral aggression disguised as an attempt to 'redeem the vocabulary'. Yet in Clifford Lawrence hates this very verbalizing activity:

> She was angry with him, turning everything into words. Violets were Juno's eyelids, and windflowers were unravished brides. How she hated words, always coming between her and life: they did the ravishing, if anything did: ready-made words and phrases, sucking the life-sap out of living things.

But Lawrence's words have ravished sex too, ravished all our violets of sexual sweetness by exposing the very Mystic Now to verbal view, as it were. Indeed, this was the unconscious intention of his anxiety, to allay his ghosts by conquering with words the secret places of his own 'shame', and laying the 'naked self' bare. Somewhere in himself he hates what he is doing, hates the exhibitionist narcissistic act – and so projects the hatred on to poor usurped Clifford, his cast-out Laius 'father', and a scapegoat for the bad side of himself.

Lawrence's book has an insistent quality that goes with something of the compelled looking of a *voyeur*. The compulsion associates with Lawrence's need – as seen in his treatment of Clifford – to assail those things he feared – the woman's sensual reality, impotence, humiliation and revenge. Because of this compelled verbalizing the book is insistent beyond boredom – we feel assaulted. *Lady Chatterley's Lover* is dreadfully literary – not least in the stilted quality of the descriptions of sexual intercourse. If we take such a passage as the following we find how very like Clifford's wordy literariness Lawrence's writing is here, as full of 'quotations' as is Clifford's talk:

The first windflowers were out, and all the wood seemed pale with the pallor of endless little anemones, sprinkling the shaken floor. 'The world has grown pale with thy breath.' But it was the breath of Persephone, this time; she was out of hell on a cold morning. Cold breaths of wind came, and overhead there was an anger of entangled wind caught among the twigs. It, too, was caught and trying to rear itself free, the wind, like Absalom. How cold the anemones looked, bobbing their naked white shoulders over crinoline skirts of green...

Never has Lawrence written so much like Patience Strong, with a studied, child-like eroticism. And this may well be because in a sense he is writing as a child for his mother, as he leads Her Ladyship (Constance) to himself as Morelorence. So his prose is indistinguishable from the verbalizing of Sir Clifford that he attacks so vehemently:

She wanted to be clear of him, and especially of his consciousness, his words, his obsession with himself, his endless treadmill obsession with himself, and his own words.

Surely this is Lawrence speaking of himself as Clifford, of himself in the shame of seeking, anxiously, to verbalize, through his sexual experience, in order to achieve the peace, from the sense of doom, he never, or 'Morelorence' never, found? Instead, the words become the pastoral, studied, Swinburnian falsification which Lawrence detects in himself. 'How ravished one could be without being touched. Ravished by dead words become obscene, and dead ideas become obsessions.' But this is a fair description of *Lady Chatterley*! The phrases come at the very moment when Mellors first appears, to serve the forces of life. But henceforward in the book this is what Lawrence goes on to do, leave us ravished, obsessed, deadened, by words 'become obscene'.

8
THE WORD-MILL AND THE WHIRLPOOL

Lawrence set out to 'render the sexual act valid and precious' – by words. Elsewhere, in writing to his mother he says, 'so many words because I can't touch you', a betraying phrase. In the end, in

sensuality, Connie is said to die 'a poignant marvellous death' –
but we feel only the press of the words, and no deep sensuous stir.

The failure of the word-art may be related to the impossible
task that Lawrence set himself – and the even more impossible
one he is trying to do, for unconscious motives, in his phantasy.
He is trying to 'redeem the vocabulary' and to make the act
'valid and precious'. He is trying to 'resurrect the body' – but in
our word-absorbing minds. By this he seeks to make the world
right by promoting warm-hearted coition ('if only the men and
women would . . .').

But, as we have seen, at the unconscious level Lawrence is
following other paths – and the dissociation mars his language.
Much of his verbal activity is directed at cloaking these deeper
meanings, and diverting us away from reality into the pastoral
dream.

In trying to 'resurrect the body' with words, he comes to
foster the very mental consciousness he is assailing as destructive.
Yet, at the same time, he wants by words to allay and deny the
mind – that questing intelligence that might expose the huge self-
deception he is perpetrating.

'What liars the poets were.' But they are not. Man has a mind,
and civilized capacities which distinguish him from the beasts, and
which give his life – and love – significance. Lawrence will not
have this here: society is 'insane', the life of the mind deadening.
His intellectuals have gone dead. In this book his attack on 'mind'
becomes a caricature of his vindication elsewhere – penetrating
and intelligent – of the life of the body. Here he does not want to
recognize all the aspects of relationship, of mind as well as body,
in which man and woman meet, and must meet, on equal terms
if love is to grow.

Now arises an artistic problem. Lawrence defined sentimentality
as 'taking out on yourself feelings you haven't got' – and this
exactly is what he does in describing sexual intercourse.

We have no feelings to feel in the consciousness the feelings we
are supposed to have when we have submerged our consciousness
in bodily life. In sexual union we are lost: in reading Lawrence we
are *not* lost: we are being mental, having mental sex. There are no

feelings corresponding to our being immersed in 'primordial tenderness' to be received *in our consciousness from words*. This is the fallacy underlying Lawrence's book. He seeks to exorcize our resistance to bodily life by whirlpools of sensation, as Mellors breaks Connie's resistance with his extra-potency. No mind. But to write a novel *is* a thing of the mind and consciousness of feeling, and by his verbal-oral aggressiveness Lawrence impinges only on our minds. So the whole undertaking breaks down.

It breaks down on the fallacy of attempting to bring primordial feelings to the consciousness, to refine our powers of the whole being, in an area which Lawrence conclusively argues elsewhere to be beyond the beck and call of will and mind. And, as Lawrence should have known, we can't be conscious of our unconscious inner reality, except by metaphor, because it can't be made explicit. Certainly we can't speak what only can be spoken by the body gone to body ('There seemed nothing left to say'). We can't feel the primordial feelings because they are only to be experienced, as Lawrence says they are, primordially, primally. You can't experience *anyone else's* 'warm-hearted fucking'. And in any case mere 'fucking' by itself is meaningless, too: its meaning is only to be apprehended in other non-erotic terms. What we need to gain through a work of art is a sense of the significance of love, to give meaning to the love-making: what we really need is to forget about the 'going to body', not to be made conscious of it at great verbal length – though we can certainly be conscious of the love-complex it enriches, in relationship.

But Mellors' and Connie's sexual life in the larger complex, and their love, simply do not develop in the book. It cannot, because other 'components' than the bodily erotic are not there. There is no progress towards anything, except a mere recognition of the social 'complications' (not a coming to terms with them) and more and more verbally conveyed sensuality which we can't really take in, can't really experience, desperate as its energy is. We respond only with boredom and embarrassment. Development would in fact have required consideration of things of the whole being, largely here of the mind, and this Lawrence will not do: it would lead him to considerations of mutual regard and thus equality, then to the child to procreation and 'the rainbow' – and these he simply refuses to accept. So we have only the 'continuing tension of a never satisfied quest'.

> They all believed in the life of the mind. What you did apart was your private affair, and didn't much matter.
> 'The whole point about the sexual problem,' said Hammond, who was a tall thin fellow with a wife and two children, but much more connected with a typewriter, 'is that there is no point to it. . . . We don't want to follow a man into the W.C. so why should we want to follow him into bed with a woman? . . . a matter of misplaced curiosity . . .'

Such caricatures cloak the unconscious reason for Lawrence's extraordinary work.[1] The attitude Lawrence means to characterize here he does not represent fairly. Hammond is splenetically projected from Lawrence's hatred of normal creativity. The criticism of Lawrence's narcissism and his misconceptions in writing *Lady Chatterley* implicit in Hammond's remarks are not fairly put up to be answered, but maliciously caricatured in order that they may be abused and denied. The uneasiness of the author is manifest in the spleen.

At one point in his portrayal of Constance, Lawrence reveals that he was aware of two fallacies in his book: one, that his attribution of fault to the 'carrion-bodied' industrial and intellectual men was wrong, and, second, that he himself – or 'Morelorence', despite the courage of a 'broken-backed snake' – had lost the essential clue to his problem.

> 'And perhaps the women *really* wanted to be there and love you properly, only perhaps they couldn't. Perhaps it wasn't all their fault,' she said.
> 'I know it. Do you think I don't know what a broken-backed snake that's been trodden on I was myself!'
> 'But you're not now,' she said . . .
> 'I don't know what I am. There's black days ahead.'

The verbalizing is virtually a blind energy, seeking beyond that limitation: 'I don't know what I am.' Lawrence was unable to see

---

[1] Lawrence was surely connected with his typewriter in a strangely compulsive way too, and is here a pot calling the kettle black!

that the trouble was in him rather than in the woman, or the world, over which he projects his difficulties. The futile verbal intensity of belabouring vainly this projection, an attempt to talk reality round by 'taking it into the mouth' to squaring with Lawrence's own distorted view of it: so, inevitably, it is doomed as a literary undertaking.

The detailed description of coition, the use of the vocabulary of sex freely, in fact, as F. R. Leavis says, can only be 'an offence against taste'. But not only are they an offence against taste: they simply can never have the salutary moral effect, or the regenerative effect *as art*, which Lawrence set out to use them for. The 'broken-backed snake' could neither cure himself nor us with these words. Lawrence hoped to 'make the sex relation valid and precious instead of shameful. And this novel is the furthest I've gone. To me it is beautiful as the naked self. . . .' 'To me' – Lawrence virtually wrote the book to endeavour to prove *to himself* that the sex relation was valid and precious, narcissistically.

Lawrence describes in a famous passage what he set out to make the novel:

> After all, one may hear the most private affairs of other people, but only in a spirit of respect for the struggling, battered thing which any human soul is, and in a spirit of fine, discriminating sympathy. For even satire is a form of sympathy. It is the way our sympathy flows and recoils that really determines our lives. And here lies the vast importance of the novel, properly handled. It can inform and lead into new places the flow of our sympathetic consciousness, and it can lead our sympathy away in recoil from things gone dead. Therefore the novel, properly handled, can reveal the most secret places of life; for it is in the *passionel* secret places of life, above all, that the tide of sensitive awareness needs to ebb and flow, cleansing and freshening . . .

Lawrence writes 'in a spirit of respect' – but can we maintain a 'fine *discriminative* sympathy' in descriptions of sexual physical acts? Lawrence reached a point of blockage in his exploration of his inward life in this novel. But there is also a point of blockage in our response to the novel. There is a limit to how much can be revealed in words, and a limit to how far our sympathy can

become engaged through descriptions of sexual acts. We cannot
truly accept, in words, an account of other people's sexual behaviour beyond a certain point. Perhaps that point is the actual
entering of the woman by the man, or perhaps the point at which
the sexual organs are displayed. At this point thought, awareness,
moral discriminative sympathy, cease, both in the creatures, our
consciousness of them and our sympathy with them. Art is only
of value while our discriminative sympathy is engaged (as
Lawrence always intended it to be). But the poetic symbolism
breaks down, in a realistic mode such as the novel when characters
are 'gone to body'. This is because sexual acts necessarily manifest
forms of aggression, seem even more aggressive as 'seen' in others,
and yet more so as described in words. (The proponents of pornography fail to take into account this aggressive-destructive element
which by no means promotes love.) Described sexual acts must
by their nature seem to us invasions of the privacy of another
being. This invasion we are glad to enter into as lovers in life
ourselves – but we find it difficult to tolerate it if *we witness the
possession being made by others*, or have it described to us. No doubt
the roots of our inability to tolerate these things lies in our infant
difficulties of accepting our parents' sexual lives. But certainly
sexual acts cannot easily be taken as poetically symbolic, as can the
acts of courtesy and contact between man and woman, at the
civilized plane. A kiss can be a poetic symbol: an act of sexual
intercourse, while it can be acceptable, as in Hindu erotic sculpture, as a formal symbol of cosmic creativity, depicted in a
stylized mode, supra-human and remote, it cannot be easily
accepted as a symbol in a realistic work of art such as a novel,
especially in one in which everything depends upon our apparently 'seeing' events as real. We can only feel discomfort, once
characters are gone to body, if our attention is kept on seeing
them and following their sensations in the act. Certainly, verbal
accounts at this point are fraught with disaster, because they evoke
intense feelings, such as we experienced in infancy, around oral-
sexual feelings of aggression, in our awareness and phantasy of
adult sexuality.

Loving creatures are in the grip of the life-processes of the body, which Lawrence so rightly and insistently urges us to consider valid and precious – as an aspect of our whole life – they are 'to bodies gone' (see Donne's *Ecstasie*). But we cannot enter into this with them because *words* cannot convey to us the experience of being 'lost to body'. We can only 'see' or 'know of' the experience from the outside as 'other' and apart. This arouses feelings of recoil and rejection, and of being subject to aggression. The greatest writers about sexual love such as Chaucer and Shakespeare, seldom felt there was more to say, once the male enters the female, virtually, except for comic purposes as in *The Miller's Tale*. Today, our anxious writers, many of them following Lawrence, stay to describe. This is obsessional, and does not, often, in fact have the effect intended: it repels, bores or angers. This may be linked with what I have said earlier about reality and love. To the dissociated mind the 'reality' seems to be 'in sex' – and in such works as Henry Miller's we have the pursuit of reality in sex. But the reality is not in sex, exclusive of the whole complex of psyche and soma. To hurl oneself at the woman's body may indeed be no more than a symptom of a vestigial infantile craving. In this a man may erroneously suppose that a dissociation consequent upon a lack of love can be restored by phantasies of physical acts or by the oral aggressiveness of accounts of sex. Some writers do this deliberately to involve others in their own disturbances, as when Lawrence Durrell discovers a copulating couple as 'victims of some strange cosmic accident' or Miller describes, with conceited defiance, the antics at an 'orgy' in Greenwich Village.[1]

To deliberately seek to witness sexual acts in life obviously manifests grave psychic sickness, the vestiges of infant curiosity, a deep dissociation of the reality-sense, and a sadistic tendency, containing a desire to see the woman humiliated because one fears

---

[1] 'Now and then one of us had an orgasm . . .' That such 'group' sexual activities are at the level of infant sex-play, and sadly short of adult genitality, does not trouble Miller, who with boring portentousness presents it all as sophisticated and significant. The astonishing thing is that his acclaim suggests that his audience has too few standards of mutual sexuality themselves to find his assumptions laughable and destructively degrading. Far from being a 'protest', his obscene tantrums but complement the depreciation of human value by the ethos of an acquisitive society.

femininity. Melanie Klein traces many disturbances in children
to witnessing 'the primal scene'. Even dogs manifest discomfort in
the presence of other dogs copulating, and Lawrence distantly
recognizes this in one of his scenes in which the keeper's dog is
awed by the coition of Mellors and Connie: we feel like the dog.
We should not be there. There is no room for a third presence in
coition. Kingsley Amis' near-pornography as incipient in the title
Only Two Can Play deliberately plays upon our anxieties and obsessions with overlooking the sexual act for sensational reasons,
and in fear, associated with deeper fears about the nature of reality
itself, and our own identity. (Amis' sex is, like Henry Miller's,
'knee-stuff' or 'fiddling with peckers', never whole or adult.)

The root of the sterility in Lawrence's prose in this work lies in
the sterility of his erotic attitude which denies a reality he has
come to fear. This eroticism is self-enclosed, and, as I have suggested, the book is an embracement of self, narcissistically, to fight
an agon with the inward psychic ghosts. This marks the difference
between Lawrence's eroticism and that, say, of Hindu erotic
sculpture:

> In the embrace of his beloved a man forgets the whole world – every-
> thing both within and without; in the very same way, *he who em-
> braces the self knows neither within nor without.*

The sculptured figures on the Temples of Khajuraho show couples
in ecstatic union: the supporting figures hide their faces and avert
their eyes in awe or are formalized as supporters in heraldry. The
formalized expression of the ecstasy is a rendering in stone of the
human bliss in sexual love which Hindu religion (unlike much of
Christianity) fully accepts and approves. But the point of the
sculptures is that this human bliss and creativity are but a shadow,
a minute reflection only of the Divine Love, its Eternal Bliss,
and Creativity in the cosmos. The couples are united in love-
creativity, not in 'mere sensuality'. The whole is a pattern, stylized
and symbolic. Here we do not expect the real nor do we experience the exclusively personal. The sensuality embodied in such
symbolic works of art is intended to induce the spectator to seek
the universal, the eternal truths of creative life and being, beyond
the personal self, beyond the one sexual union – the universal

significance of the sexual act that is creative, *in procreation* – a
'contribution to the world's fertility and continuity'. The supporting figures avert their eyes, in awesome modesty, or seem to be
assisting at a ritual. We see, of course, and are awed by the spec-
tacle of ecstasy in coition. But the statues are not realistic – they are
extremely formalized, emphasizing both the pitch of ecstasy, the
balanced mutual satisfaction of sex, and expressing the philosophy
of Hindu religious writings. The full love reality here generates
a transcendent value.

We may compare Lawrence at his crudest: compare this with
the formalistic effect of distancing and making universal in the
Hindu sculptures of sexual love:

> '. . . th'art a lot besides an animal, aren't ye? – even ter fuck? Cunt!
> Eh, that's the beauty o' thee, lass!'

Lawrence's eroticism sometimes seems, as here, mere callow
sensuality – the lover's flowers are not fertile symbols of seasons of
life as in *The Winter's Tale*, but mere sterile adornments of pastoral
fun in sex-play. For erotic truth we may consider some of the
statements in ancient mythology and mysticism about eroticism
and creativity (these are quoted from an interesting article by
Aleain Danielou on *Hindu Erotic Sculpture* in *Marg*, Volume 2,
Number 1):

> The yoni and the lingam symbolize the creation of the world. Their
> union represents Action (karma).

> The woman is the fire, her womb the fuel, the invitation of a man
> the smoke. The door is the flame, the entering the ember, pleasure
> the spark. In this fire the gods pour the offering. From this offering
> springs forth the child.

All the richness of the Eastern eroticism seeks its highest expression
in creation of the child. Lawrence's beauty of sex lacks this
essential creativity, so the sensuality becomes frenetic, desperate,
and in self-embracement, 'knowing nothing', because it makes no
touch with the reality of universal creativity.

To examine some of Lawrence's realistic descriptions of sexual intercourse reveals that the sadism we find in Mellors, as manifest in the description of sexual acts, associates with the desperate oral act of aggression, to seek reality so. Looked at thus we may also see poor Lawrence as virtually having oral sadistic coition with himself in a mental mirror, to exorcize inward ghosts. In this the partner of course can therefore be as submissive as he chooses to make her. The woman's reality is aggressed away, and denied totally. For Connie to have thrown a pot, or even to have bridled, would have been a relief, for the reader, and as refreshingly real as the Wyf of Bath's sexual realism, when she shoves her husband in the fire. There is aggression in his idyll, but it is not an aggression which is resolved, as it is in the realism of Chaucer: it is rather destructive in its effect under the surface.

Mellors 'has his way' with Connie, and demands submission, with many touches of dominating sadism.[1]

> He threw one or two dry ones down, put his coat and waistcoat over them, and *she had to lie down there* under the boughs of the tree, *like an animal,* while he waited, standing there in his shirt and breeches, watching her with haunted eyes. But still he was provident – he *made her lie properly, properly. He broke the band of her underclothes, for she did not help him, only lay inert.*
>
> He too had bared the front of his body and she felt his naked flesh against her as he came into her . . .
>
> p. 138

Throughout the book, as I have said, Mellors never submits to the rhythm of the awakening of the woman. There is only a hurried force to overcome her 'resistance'; and make her lie 'properly, properly'. The woman is passive and inert. Allowing for the over-whelming force of passion, and the degree of sadism in every normal sexual act, the brusqueness goes with the masterly over-bearing nature of Mellors *of which Lawrence fully approves.*

That the woman must be passive reveals Lawrence's deep fear of woman's nature, and so of woman's sexual satisfaction. Mellors

---

[1] Melanie Klein points out (*The Psychoanalysis of Children,* p. 275) that children sometimes desire their parents to have sadistic sexual intercourse. If Lawrence is here having a phantasy of parental sexual intercourse then this might well explain in part why he makes Mellors so sadistic.

begins to move 'in sudden helpless orgasm' (Lawrence does not here mean orgasm surely, but movement *towards* climax?). But the slight sadism now turns to verbal ravishment. Connie awakes in her 'new strange thrills rippling inside her. Rippling, rippling, rippling, like a flapping, overlapping of soft flames, soft as feathers, running to points of brilliance, exquisite, exquisite, and melting her all molten inside'. This overwriting, describing the indescribable, is a narcissistic indulgence, bringing us to strange disturbed feelings, or an urgency we would rather not feel – 'melting her all molten inside' – we fell the impotent wish for such experience which, since it is the woman's experience, Lawrence can never have had, but only seeks to have, given by himself to himself. 'It was like bells rippling up and up to a culmination.' – the sentences dissolve into meaningless gesture: how can 'bells' 'ripple'? (If we accept this as referring to waves of sound, then we need more direct and definite poetic meaning given to 'bells'):

> She lay unconscious of the wild little cries she uttered at the last. But it was over too soon, and she could no longer force her own conclusion with her own activity. This was different, different. She could do nothing.

We have seen how Morelorence resented the woman's search for orgasm after the man had had his: here is the 'different' thing. The 'difference' between this coition and any earlier ones is not that Connie has been filled with a different kind of passionate desire, and has been somewhat brusquely taken out-of-doors by a roughish man not of her class, whose body she finds attractive, but that she has not 'forced her own conclusion' and 'she could do nothing'. The woman who is feared because she seeks her own sexual satisfaction, is reduced to inert submission, totally controlled and denied. It is perfectly acceptable, I suppose, that a woman might under such circumstances – the sexual urge being so mysteriously unique in each of us – find this act 'different'. But our problem in reading about sexual acts is that they seem too tediously the same (an impression sexual love never gives in life). The description of each act gives us no feeling of this being 'different' from any other act of coition, in the strained language of describing the indescribable. Again, this is a matter of 'what is real?' The reality of sex is in love. The only thing that could convince us of the special quality of an act of coition – and this could and should be done by implication – would be the love and tenderness preceding it, the creative care for the woman's rhythm of excitement and her rising arch of creative fulfilment by her lover, and the satisfaction afterwards, in love and ease, mutual regard and tenderness, and a deep awe at the momentousness of possible conception. In fact, to convey 'difference', love would have to be described in terms which belong to love, to the civilized areas of relationship, taking in other aspects than the erotic. The only thing that could make the 'difference' is *love*. But love here is absent, because here Lawrence seeks to undervalue it, in favour of sensuality, with the 'aggressive component' unresolved. So, he cannot convey the 'difference' at all, and because of this treads his sterile round of impotent verbalizing.

The other convincing way of conveying the 'difference' in a new relationship would be in the closer civilized, shared, togetherness and mutual regard which follows love-making, guaranteeing a successful dealing with life and security for the created child between the lovers. All we have, immediately here, in fact, is a verbal post-mortem, albeit followed by one brief beautiful sequel, which again dissolves into a diatribe, as we have seen, *against woman's nature*. Lawrence wishes away the female urge for self-satisfaction, by his verbal incantation:

> She could no longer harden and grip for her own satisfaction upon him. She could only wait, wait and moan in spirit as she felt him withdrawing . . . whilst all her womb was open and soft, and softly clamouring like a sea-anemone under the tide, clamouring for him to come in again and make a fulfilment for her. She clung to him unconscious in passion, and he never quite slipped from her, and she felt the soft bud of him within her stirring, and strange rhythmic flushing up into her with a strange rhythmic growing movement, swelling and swelling and swelling until it filled all her cleaving consciousness . . .

Lawrence must have written these passages in a state of febrile, incantatory excitement, the excitement of narcissistic self-intercourse. What seems unbelievable is that he rewrote and rewrote this book! Of course, there are flashes of beauty: here Lawrence renders the relaxed stirring, distant sensations of deep physical passion as no other writer could – the sea-anemone image is a beautiful one, and springs perhaps from the submerged arche-typal symbol of the sea as mother – even the mother to whom he so deeply desired to give satisfaction. It is a lovely perception that the felt stirrings in the womb's mouth in sexual intercourse have the strange life of their own, submerged in the depths of the whole being, such as a sea-anemone has under the tide. But one such image of the reality would have been enough: Lawrence's fault is to tug and tug at the words, as though he were having intercourse with them – which, of course, he really is, Chatterley. From the intense oral aggressiveness comes the bad, repetitive urgent writing – 'strange', 'strange', 'rhythm', 'rhythm', 'swelling', 'swelling' – the effect of which is far from making us feel the uniqueness of bodily experience, but conveying rather something of tedium, as of a depressing similarity between every act of sex. And it is so. Considered quantitatively sex is meaningless. The sexual act tends to be very much the same kind of experience in described terms (compare what would be the effect of a number of descriptions of the mere experience of eating). Yet to a lover, as a psychologist recently pointed out, the sexual act is in fact the one act we can repeat endlessly and yet find a continuously re-created sense of order and meaning in it. But such significant moments as may be found in the sexual act are inevitably richer or lesser according to how much *love* is in them.

To think of sex as this book forces us to, quantitatively, in-volves something of a denial of its 'mystic now'. Where there is love, anxiety about 'performance' flies out of the window. If our loving is rich then we do not want to ravish it all out of ourselves in words, but keep it inward and private – forgotten, really, in its uniqueness, with no before or after, except as part of the larger and more all-embracing complex of the love bond.

But Lawrence must make the verbal cerebral ravishment, until Connie's consciousness is 'cleaving away' – but *not* – be it noted – our consciousness of Connie's consciousness!

> Then began again the unspeakable motion...
> (Would God that it had been unspeakable!)
> ...that was not really motion...
> (what then was it?)
> ...but pure deepening whirlpools of sensation swirling deeper and deeper through all her tissue and consciousness, till she was one perfect concentric fluid of feeling, and she lay there crying in unconscious inarticulate cries. The voice out of the uttermost night, the life! The man heard it beneath him with a kind of awe, as his life sprang out into her. And as it subsided, he subsided, too and lay utterly still...

If only the motion (which was 'not really motion') had been 'unspeakable', we feel: the inconsistency betrays Lawrence's own uncertainty of what he was doing. This is as perfect a description of 'coming off together' as our greatest writer can write: the fact that he fails to give us anything but words shows well enough that the task should never have been undertaken. There are marvellous touches, but there are also banalities which sadly lower the tension of the prose – its uncontrolled rhythm which is the rhythm of desperate gesture, rather than mounting climax, the 'with *a kind of* awe' with its sentimental vagueness the gushing 'utterly', and the internal contradictions of 'not real motion', then 'whirlpools' – which suggest motion surely to most of us? But why 'pure' whirlpools – or even whirlpools of 'pure' sensation? The 'pure' – which recurs again – shows a desire on Lawrence's part to rid his sexual reality of disgust and make it valid, the guiltless, because he fears it. Then we have 'tissue and consciousness', suggesting an unfortunate dichotomy, and the mechanical terms, 'perfect concentric fluid of feeling' – why 'concentric'? And so on: the words to compare Lawrence with, surprisingly enough, are those of Eliot, evocative of spiritual experience in sensual terms, and closer to the experience of loss of the sensual in the mystical:

> Neither from nor towards; at the still point,
> There the dance is
> But neither arrest nor movement...
> Descend lower, descend only
> Into the world of perpetual solitude,

World not world, but that which is not world,
Internal darkness, deprivation . . .

A moment of ecstasy, demands, in fact, not such descriptive
realism as prose is capable of, but the reminiscent poetic celebration of aspects of experience. Poetry, however, would move
towards love: Lawrence wants 'real' sensuality. Had Lawrence
been drawing on actual remembrance of sexual love (as in *Roses
on the Breakfast Table*, see below, p. 341) he would perhaps have
done something of the kind: but his words are in themselves a
ravishment, falsifying, and unsatisfactory narcissistic arts in themselves. Yet the 'whirlpools' of sensation leave one in the end with
a strange sense of sterility, despite the reference to life: 'The voice
out of the innermost night, the life!' The cries of a woman in
sexual union induce a deep response of tenderness in her man:
overheard by others it can be a disconcerting shock. Here Lawrence produces the cry with a kind of male triumph at having
touched 'life' at last. But it is the life of the body's apartness from
mind – the 'night' – of terrible sensuality – not a cry of love in the
being. Lawrence's excitement at producing this orgasm on himself, on the phantasy woman who is so grateful, submissive and
undemanding, strikes one as an over-insistent preoccupation
extracting from the woman the voice of that life, for the *mind* to
know, in defence.

There follows a beautiful description of their loss together of
sensation and 'the world':

> And they lay and knew nothing, not even of each other, both
> lost . . .

But Mellors quickly recovers, becoming aware, significantly, of
fear and mistrust of 'his *defenceless* nakedness'. She feels, however,
that he 'must cover her now for ever', and later 'Another self was
alive in her, burning molten and soft in her womb and bowels,
and with this self she *adored* him'. She is full of creative power: 'It
feels like a child,' she said to herself: 'it feels like a child in me.'
'And so it did, as if her womb, that had always been shut, had
opened and filled with new life, almost a burden, yet lovely.'
But Mellors must make his verbalizing post-mortem: 'We

came off together that time', and his generalizations about other
people not coming off, refusing the while to commit himself:

> 'Glad,' he said, 'Ay, but never mind.'
> 'Have you come off like that with other women?'
> He looked at her amused.
> 'I don't know,' he said, 'I don't know.'
> And she knew he would never tell her anything he didn't want to
> tell her. She watched his face, and the passion for him moved in her
> bowels. She resisted it as far as she could for it was the loss of herself
> to herself.

Here there are good qualities in Lawrence's writing – as where
he portrays the uncertainty, the mistrust, between the two, both
fearing giving in love as a loss of self, both suffering from the
furtiveness of their relationship, he unwilling to reassure her, she
unwilling to yield herself entirely. Lawrence renders beautifully
the touch of the rawness in their relationship. But even so there
seems to be a strange dichotomy between their richness of bodily
experience and their lack of tenderness to one another, their mutuality in relationship. Love is absent. But Lawrence, where he is
content with drama, at the proper level, is here as good as Lawrence as artist can be. 'He seemed to have nothing whatever to say.
Nothing left.' -this feeling of the body having 'spoken' the love
sufficiently had it been used more in the book to escape over-
insistence, would have made it a much greater work – might indeed, have saved it. But we return, as I point out above, to yet
another post-mortem on the last sexual act.

In his verbal ravishment of Constance, Lawrence is looking at
a reflection in his occult mirror: this is no better than merely considering the duplicated topside of 'mentality'. Indeed the verbal
sensuality belongs to the topside, and bodily living is more denied
than it would be if the book were pornographic and stirred actual
physical excitement.

There is much in love we cannot, merely, feel as 'whirlpools of
sensation' and if the 'unspeakable pleasure beyond consciousness'
cannot convince Connie that Mellors loves her, then on what do
we rely for assurance of what love *is*? Here Lawrence is again in
the throes of his dilemma: he has invented a kind of sex which,

described in a verbal flurry, we must take as the highest sexual
potential, unearthly sensation, self-loss and god-like. Yet it leaves
Connie still anxious, and Mellors still taciturn and unable to reassure her, in any intimacy of personal regard and expression of
intelligent, civilized, conscious love – "asn't ter felt it?" But because of the confusion of response we *can't* feel it, and neither can
she, except that the author tells us it was 'lovelier than anything'.
'This wor t'best' says Mellors a little later, and refused to speak of
their child and its future – anybody in the world, he says, *can have
any child they like now*. That was lovely: thank you. But how do
we know any more about *love*? Love requires the capacity to give
as well as receive, and this Mellors – and, one suspects, Lawrence –
never learnt.

9

THE LOWER HALF OF FATHER

How do Lawrence's falsifications affect our social and cultural
attitudes, in so far as we follow him, in his attitude to our world?
We may trace these from his desire to 'make a good father'.
Would that he (Morel) had been an aristocrat – to match his
mother's refinement! Would that he had not been bound to the
pit, but escaped, like Mellors, to be his own master, with a little
pension, and a life in the woods! To the child Lawrence that side
of the collier – the poaching, wood-walking, rabbiting, Sunday,
rural, side – was the glad side, connected with the happier times
between the holiday father and mother, and belonging to the
organic community such as a child can feel secure in, by contrast
with the urban dissociation. That woodsense went with a gentle-
ness in the miner, and thus Lawrence embodies it in his phallic
character, Mellors. But he wants to *be* the father and show that *he*,
as a naturally aristocratic and fine soul (as indeed he was), could
have awakened the mother.

Lawrence's analysis of the difficulties of our way of life today
has thus involved us in falsifications, as well as in discrimination.
Perhaps from his very resentment of his father has come our own
too prevalent spirit of nostalgia for the old rural England, and the

defeatist attitude of many of the intelligent minority who are deeply influenced by Lawrence, to industrial society and its future. In *Lady Chatterley* the attitude to industrial society is totally negative, and this is surely an uncreative and ineffective position? The falsification perhaps emerges, through Lawrence, from the very pattern of working-class life, which centres so much on the mother who, in that life, as Lawrence showed, has some matriarchal power and is at the centre of its traditional values, and its search towards spiritual good. The women upheld the chapel, and the best traditions of Nonconformist, Puritan English popular life – self-respect, a sense of decency, family togetherness, sexual loyalty and child care. The men were betrayed, degraded, to the machine. The suffering of the women was caused by the machine that took father away, by the breakdown of traditional family patterns in a self-subsistence rural economy (as idealized in, say, George Eliot's Mrs Poyser), and increased her burden. The sons therefore – since they loved the mother – came to hate the 'greedy' machine, and all machine civilization – out of unconscious loyalty to her. Yet the respect for the mother seems in working-class culture not to go with a respect for the mother's role with her baby as D. W. Winnicott urges us to respect it – but seems to go with a fear of feminity, rather, and a guilt over feminine eroticism, as we see from many working-class taboos about pregnancy, sexual love, and such matters: conditions seem to have damaged the capacity to let love flow.[1] The women sought other satisfactions, in power.

The woman's power in working-class life is portrayed superbly in *Lady Chatterley's Lover* in Mrs Bolton, and her eulogy of the 'touch' of a man. The breakdown of these matriarchal values is delineated by Lawrence in this woman's development of a ferocious mother-domination over Clifford Chatterley. Sir Clifford is reduced to babydom, and plays with Mrs Bolton's breasts, when Connie leaves him, in a strange, infantile and repulsive way. In this way Lawrence rejects in the image of his usurped father the weaknesses of his own mother-dependence, related as it is to the

---

[1] A correspondent writes of a factory worker, a woman, who said how different it was after marriage – they '*could see it in your face*' that you had sexual intercourse, and this made for shame.

whole mother-dependence pervading traditional working-class life. But in this grotesque relationship Lawrence expresses his fear of woman in yet another form. The working-class matriarch becomes the mother-inspiration of (boy-baby) Sir Clifford in his devotion to machine-industry projects: the more he becomes a baby, the more he is able, boyishly, to make things 'go' at the mine. But for this he sacrifices his living powers, and replaces them by a vacant receptive preoccupation, tinkering with his radio. (His fate is parallel to that of Mrs Bolton's husband who so feared her creativity that it 'spoilt his bit of married love'.)

There is, it is true, something infantile in the preoccupation of the industrial world with 'making things go', but it is too unfairly guyed here since some industrial trends have in fact enabled us to make possible a more advanced maturity and fulfilment for many, through education, the improvement of material living, and increased leisure. Significantly enough the Lawrentian position has become the orthodox attitude to the 'collapse of the organic community' in the hands of Denys Thompson and F. R. Leavis – yet the students most submitted to this argument are the very people from working-class homes who would never have been given their superior education – indeed might never have survived to adulthood at all – *had it not been for the advance of material civilization.*

It is worth considering the psychic origins of the appeal of this nostalgia for the rural-organic past. The present writer remains an exponent of our need to give attention to the best in that past, to continuity, and to aims in civilization beyond material affluence. But the psychic origins of the prevalent nostalgia for the rural past, very much associated with Lawrence's influence, are I think in a profound uncertainty, and self-distrust become a distrust that anything 'good' can ever come of this society. In F. R. Leavis I think – and in the young men he has influenced – this attitude has become dangerously uncreative and a damaging distrust of human nature as it is, necessarily imperfect in a world that will always be imperfect. With its roots possibly in the traumatic experiences of 1914–18, it marks a deep lack of confidence in continuity. It is a kind of refusal to accept any human society except a postulated

ideal that never existed, and could never exist – and so is a denial
of any possible actual reality. Its roots may even be, as in Lawrence,
in a nostalgia for a 'rural past' that in fact stands symbolically for
the 'mother's lap' –

> 'He lay us as we lay at birth
> On the cool flowery lap of earth . . .'

I wonder what F. R. Leavis would say if one suggested that our
nostalgia for the 'old organic past' was an aspect of a refusal in us
to accept adult reality and maturity in some way – in fact,
another form of dissociation? A nostalgia for yet another hallucination? Certainly in some way it marks a refusal to have hope in
human nature, to express belief in the continuity of life and hope
in its recurrent creativity – such as Shakespeare achieves, as I have
shown. The characteristic of this fear is an intolerance of all failings and weaknesses. It marks a fear, in a particular intellectual
minority, of the uncertainty of life, even including creative drives.
A disturbing aspect of the 'Lawrentian' following has been its
increasing lack of interest in creativity while such cohesion as it
has manifests a resistance to fresh ideas, not least to those about
inner reality.

In a sense, socially, Lawrence's picture has, of course, been
prophetic. It has been the fate of working-class traditions themselves – imbued with the character of the bourgeois commercial
mind (a public-school product) – to have been drawn, through
advertising and mass media, into the infantile preoccupation with
'making things go'. Distractions have become substitutes for the
richer pursuits of spontaneous living. Working-class people have
accepted a culture in terms of defence against reality by forms of
hallucination which seem to offer immediate satisfaction.

Maybe it is true, then, to an extent, that the over-dependence
created by the over-dominant working-class mother has been to
blame for the infantile dependency of so many on *unwon*, undemanding, satisfactions, such as Sir Clifford finds at Mrs Bolton's
breasts. Even perhaps for the immature obsession of men in
machine-society with 'things' and with making things 'go' rather
than *being*. In working-class people, their warm-hearted energy

too easily becomes a dupe to exploitations of greed. Lawrence was right to oppose this world of distraction and 'go', and to insist on the quest for love and reality. So we may commend the attempt to *be* on the part of Mellors, who has escaped from a working-class life, and of Connie Chatterley, who has escaped from a dead aristocratic life, based on exploitation of the working people, on 'coal, sulphur, iron', and on human degradation, following the decline of the older traditional rural patterns of life.

But it is also true that millions are healthier, more aware and *alive* at all, even because of industrial 'go'. And in the child at school we come to know a human creativity that is by no means 'carrion-bodied', with immense possibilities in education to bring about a new popular culture and creative possibilities in social living. The relationships now between lovers, married men and women, children and parents have infinitely greater opportunities for fulfilment, if we can overcome our problems of psychic dissociation (even these are of course, in part, consequences of survival, since all survive, and there are more imperfections viable).

The retrograde falsity of *Lady Chatterley's Lover* is in that the escape the characters make from the industrial 'Thing' is too dreamlike: it offers no possibilities of effective escape or protest such as Lawrence's own. It belongs rather to the middle-class Sussex week-end world of the London Twenties, rather than Lawrence's Nottingham or even Vence or Taos. It has something precious and even rather twee – olde worlde – about it. It is implied that the lovers develop their intuitive faculties, their capacities for life in 'whole being' – this they poetically represent. But Mellors' 'exceptional' qualities come from no civilized refinement, and he makes no creative contact with the world – as Lawrence did. Mellors, like so many of Lawrence's 'natural' men, has been in touch with horses, is 'good' with them, and has gained a 'different' kind of civilization and self-respect, by chance, in the Army abroad, and by cutting across geographical and social boundaries, much as Lawrence himself managed to do. But how naïve of Lawrence to take the *Army* as a civilizing nurture! And how conveniently he forgets how much of a higher education was his own process of refinement at the hands of his mother, 'E. T.', and even

school and college – those products of the 'social man' he despises.
Mellors belongs with Phoenix, Lewis (in *St Mawr*), the escaped
Aaron in *Aaron's Rod* and 'the lost girl': 'natural creatures'. But
none of these justify the confidence in 'being' the author places in
them – they are often really uncivilized because they are emptied
of the intelligence of a Lawrence. If they are looked at in a way that
makes no allowances for Lawrence we may even find them rather
what we would nowadays call layabouts. (I find adult students in
evening class work particularly aware of this.) Aaron, especially,
forfeits all our sympathy as he flees from his personal reality, and
tediously justifies himself. (See Appendix A.) Civilization does not
come by nature or blood, but by disciplines, as Lawrence knew –
disciplines of intelligence, of *mind*. By contrast, Birkin in *Women
in Love*, who is closer to the civilized, cultivated Lawrence himself (the name 'Birkin' no doubt being echo of 'Bert', the familiar,
easy, self) *is* civilized, complex, intelligent and uncertain of himself in the right kind of way. Mellors is unconvincing in his arrog-
ant ignorance. Aaron is a selfish, self-deceiving bore. Birkin con-
vinces us he is real, not least in being uncertain and imperfect (not
a 'Son of God' at all). Yet it is very difficult to know even what
kind of man Birkin is if he be not Lawrence: the qualities are not
quite adequately enough embodied and placed as a being separate
from the author.

Moreover, this element represents a serious flaw in Lawrence at
large, and his value to education and criticism – such implications
as we find here are less conducive to new growth, than to a misanthropic, mysogynist, egotistical, personal flight from 'doom'.
Mellors, despite his lack of cultivation, his lack of real existence,
does not stop at abusing the life of mind, and modern art, or being
thoroughly, gratuitously, rude to Hilda (who represents common
sense, even if of a limited kind: she might have been a positive in
a novel by E. M. Forster), or mocking the 'rulers', refusing to
kowtow to them, and pronouncing on the future of the world or
humanity: he has no future, and comes to terms with no society.
He is dismally close to Cassandra of the *Daily Mirror* in his prejudices. Certainly he is not a man of intelligence employed in the
arts of living: he represents 'the life of the body' – merely because

he is a gamekeeper, a servant of the old landed aristocracy, that ruled before industry – and before democracy. But his psychic origins are really in a nostalgia for infant states of being, in which the complex realities of adult life are denied.

Of course the picture becomes confused, because the grounds for Mellors' attitudes and moral choice are not *there*, except as wish-fulfilments. Morelorence is a strange amalgam, only coming to life during the sexual act, compiled of part of Lawrence himself – and part of Lawrence's father. Much of what he is and says is only acceptable had Mellors himself written Lawrence's other books – just as much else of Lawrence is only acceptable because Lawrence wrote it. Mellors' phlegmatic dumbness, his refusal to 'think' about the 'complications' make him much of a moral coward, as do his attitudes to Connie's unborn child. His refusal to give Connie the assurance of his love she craves, his grudging tenderness and concern with his own gratification in sex, combined with his humiliation of the woman, embody the worst sides of the *Plumed Serpent* aspect of Lawrence, and the worst of working-class attitudes. Mellors has their iconoclastic, destructive, sardonic, untender, insolent distrust of delicacies of civilization, of *moeurs*, of subtlety, of mutual respect, and a lack of true courtesy. All these are legacies of the degradation of our industrial-urban era, and it is these bad qualities which are going to make it so difficult to educate the new generations of a leisured working, and middle class in England and bring them to a full release of their potentialities for living.[1] Mellors is a philistine, a prig, and pigheaded. He is often stupid. Sexually he is a clumsy boor and infantile. Yet he is cock-sure of himself, because he can make a woman 'come off': his attitudes to sex are virtually those of a navvy. And in fact, Lawrence has offered us in this book this 'rather awful sensuality' taking itself for the centre of a new human life, and a new civilization in terms of 'the resurrection of the body'. For the multitude to seek this without true civilization is too appalling to consider: it is, in fact, what they are too much encouraged to seek by an

---

[1] In this sense Eliot was right to bemoan the lack of 'raffinements' when Lawrence's characters 'faisent l'amour'—the fault in Eliot's attitude is revealed more in the word '*supportable*', with its Swiftian recoil.

acquisitive society, and by the urge to depersonalized sensuality
– that suits commerce well.

In this book, besides rejecting mind, Lawrence seems to reject
the potentialities offered by education. He rejects the possibility of
the problems of industrial society being solved, and seems to have
no hope in the creative powers of fresh generations. There is no
answer to 'What next?' in *Lady Chatterley's Lover,* except the
hopeless self-enclosed gesture towards 'warm-hearted fucking' –
and the inevitable consequent deeper sense of futility and doom
even in seeking to escape these.

Lawrence's argument in this book – the argument that it is
loyalty to the 'industrial system' which prevents people achieving
orgasm adequately – implicitly denies the life-seeking impulse in
human nature and its creativity. What is needed for our society to
develop towards finer living is the development of more adequate
concepts to foster the growth of love, the cherishing of the 'rainbow' between man and woman in love under which the child
walks in security. The child can enrich the parents' sexual love, and
their sexual love can enrich the child. This 'rainbow' is sought for
unconsciously by the human soul, as we know from children's
imaginative writing and folksong. This quest is evolutionarily and
biologically a necessity for human development. We need a
better environment, as infants and adults. Altruistic love, however much Lawrence distrusted it, is a *fact* in human development,
a biological fact, and all the best values connected with this development are natural growths, too, as Suttie argues and Guntrip
confirms. We do not have to implant sexual values on young
people: they develop them intuitively, and find them out where
they can in our civilization. We only have to foster them.
Children will draw, at the age of eleven or twelve, beautiful
pictures of the arch of marriage, full of beauty and security, expressing this truth as does Lawrence's *Rainbow* or Blake's picture
The Angel of the Divine Presence Clothing Adam and Eve with Skins.
This natural poetic concept of the love-relationship goes in
children with an unconscious readiness to accept love and sexual
enjoyment as 'valid and precious': it is noticeable from children's
writing, unless they are disturbed, that there is no inevitable block-

age of their growing up into rich sex.[1] The trouble comes with the need to form conscious concepts to help guide living and imaginative nourishment for unconscious living. Here the schools often abrogate, and here our culture is deficient. The better influences of home and school come under powerful influences from advertising, Fleet Street, television, cults of precocious sex-awareness, and the prevalent taboos on tenderness, as I tried to suggest in *The Secret Places*. This is the whole wrong pressure of our material, distraction-seeking society, to direct and lure young people's attention away from reality, and to undermine their pursuit of long-term satisfactions in life. To foster the development of adequate sexual potentialities in all is a social need, and a deep and complex problem. Important tasks for us are to cherish and celebrate the mother's function with her baby, and the love-complex in marriage. *But* it was not necessary to write *Lady Chatterley's Lover* to convince the majority of young people that sex and love are fine, beautiful things, or to help them achieve joyful sex and creative procreation in living. Most normal individuals know this as well as Lawrence knew it himself: most lovers do not need the anxious exhortation of his phallic book – they get on very well by themselves. Each generation makes its fresh approach, and challenges traditional concepts. As with good health, physical and mental, 'good' sex is first a matter of chance and luck in life, and then working hard to foster what one has. To fulfil ourselves will tax our whole capacities to come to terms with ourselves and the conditions of human life. Moral issues are bound up with our reality-sense. Interestingly enough, school-children are more interested in the morality of *Lady Chatterley* (will Mellors marry Connie?) than in the sex. But unconsciously the effect of his book must adversely affect us by communicating Lawrence's fear of woman, by isolating the sexual from all the other more important aspects of love, and thus weakening our reality sense.

It is possible that this failure in Lawrence to have confidence in

[1] D. W. Winnicott is also concerned to stress, in *The Child and the Family*, that mothers *naturally* do the good thing with their babies and enjoy them naturally. Destructive attacks on this natural enjoyment come from others, of course, – from mothers-in-law to midwives. 'Creativity', as Melanie Klein points out, 'is the greatest source of envy.' (*Envy and Gratitude*.)

following generations, in their creativity and in education, has to do with his increasing isolation from any actual community, and with his own childlessness. Of course, the flight from the actual English community and even the childlessness may have been determined in him by the unconscious motives discussed here. It is true Lawrence affirmed that he was writing for later generations of England – and in this lay his marvellous creativity. But in *Lady Chatterley* hope at times seems gone – as though he did not seem to know for whom he was writing the book.

Of course, one section of society Lawrence wrote to denounce was the upper middle class and the literary, artistic set of the twenties. Against these 'carrion-bodied', 'men without balls', people whose 'spunk has gone dead' he exerted all his sense of bodily sex being valid and precious, albeit splenetically. In this one feels, from a glance round this milieu, he may have been fully justified: but, again, one feels that he over-estimates the importance of such people in our cultural patterns. One has from him elsewhere such a penetrating analysis of the relationship between love, parent-hood, marriage, the child and social order (as in *The Rainbow*) that the failure of *Lady Chatterley* is all the more surprising. Idyllic and unreal as it is, to call this book a 'definition of marriage' (as did A. Alvarez) seems to me naïve in the extreme.

But certainly the emerging working class intelligence should have strong reservations – stronger than Richard Hoggart allows himself to have – over Lawrence's attitude, and his social recom-mendations – in this work. In this book Lawrence divagates too disastrously close to the world of Bloomsbury and 'protest' at the level of the cults advertised in the *New Statesman*.

Ponderous, without an ounce of humour, and ungainly, there is something painfully rustic about Lawrence's presentation of these narcissistic selves, sitting with their pubic hair adorned with flowers in the ''ut', pronouncing that men must strip and wear red trousers – and that this would change them, and reform humanity. 'And have a few children!' The eurhythmic dancing in the rain, the coition, the whirlpools of sensation are as far from truly changing Connie and her lover – or us in our capacities for loving. It is all so unreal! One might as well suppose Dalcrose

Dancing or vegetarian meals will redeem mankind, or that dried
bananas will restore our lost youth: the episode goes with all the
Plumed Serpent, nudist, despotic, ritual loving, naturist crankiness
of Lawrence at his worst, and associates with the most unreal ot
the precious literary milieux of Bloomsbury and the twenties. The
storm conceals a storm in Lawrence's mind, the impotent storm
against the world, which will not be changed to suit him. It is he
who could not be changed, so that he could come to accept sexual
reality and woman. He would have needed to have been changed,
to have accepted the reality of woman's separate right to respect
and dignity, the right not to be humiliated, to be an equal partner
in sex – and in love. Not to reject the world, not to become
malevolent, Lawrence would have needed to recognize woman's
biological need for *love* – not for mere good sex, but for the
security of civilized love, as the creative bearer of the child. At the
deepest level he would have had to allow woman to exist. But he
could not, and so he cannot find civilized love. Mellors can only
emit a humourless spleen, a spleen directed at castrating and
annihilating the world. Only Mellors and Connie must 'warm-
heartedly fuck': the rest must perish: the lack of compassion is
malevolent: geld and splay all! It is a return to the total narcissism
of the infant, all the reality of the 'not-me' denied. So Mellors
expresses the ultimate misanthropy of the Lawrentian neurotic
position, in the most dreadful prose:

'the English middle classes have to chew every mouthful three times
because their guts are so narrow . . . arse-licking prigs, with half a
ball each. . . . The Tommies are just as priggish and half-balled and
narrow gutted. It's the fate of mankind to go that way.'
'The common people too, the working people?'
'All the lot. The spunk is gone dead . . . rabbity generation . . .
indiarubber tubing for guts . . . tin legs and tin faces . . . making
mincemeat of Adam and Eve . . . what is cunt but machine-fucking
. . . pay 'em money to cut off the world's cock . . . when the last real
man is killed . . . and they're all tame . . . then they'll all be insane. . . .
Because the root of sanity is the balls. . . . To contemplate the ex-
termination of the human species . . . it calms you more than anything else . . .'

There is much in this book in the same vein, tedious, hysterical, humourless, unplaced: then –

> 'But if you have a child?'
> He dropped his head.
> 'Why,' he said at last. 'It seems to me a wrong and bitter thing to do to bring a child into this world.'
> 'No! Don't say it! Don't say it!' she pleaded. 'I think I'm going to have one. Say you'll be pleased.' She laid her hand on his.
> 'I'm pleased for you to be pleased,' he said. 'But for me it seems a ghastly treachery to the unborn creature.'
> 'Ah no,' she said, shocked, 'Then you can't ever really want me! You can't want me, if you feel that!'
> Again he was silent, his face sullen. Outside there was only the threshing of the rain.
> 'It's not true!' she whispered, 'It's not quite true! There's another truth.'

'I'm pleased for you to be pleased' – as impotent a sentence as Lawrence ever wrote! The exchange is appalling, however much it is also true at times to a possible gamekeeper and a possible woman. Appalling, in that Lawrence shows no sense that he disapproves of Mellors' procreative irresponsibility, or even shows his sense of disapproving of or placing the man's sulky shame, petulant, taciturn, and childish. Yet at the next page Mellors takes her again in the 'creative act that is more than procreative'! Lawrence was left – judging from Connie's continual questioning – with an uncomfortable sense that no woman would ever take 'good sex' as the end – as all there is to a love-relationship – and he is right. He wants sex to be sex limited to man-sex: he shrinks from accepting the full reality of the man-woman-child reality. Yet his uncanny insight into woman, and his better daemon, make him strangely aware that there is 'another truth', which he cannot see.

Yet we are invited, quite ironically, by Lawrence, to suppose that this uncultivated Mellors, who spurns art, reading, education, work, would be a fit partner for Connie Chatterley (some of whose perceptions are as sharp as Lawrence's). And to concur in his malicious, even idiotic pronouncements on the end of industrial civilization and man. We are to join in the narcissistic pastoral in the hut and the rain with this de-industrialized Adam and Eve, in the classless, workless, moneyless world of Lady Jane and John Thomas, without the creative responsibility even of our first parents.

10
MORELORENCE'S MALEVOLENCE

A consequence of these psychic distortions as they are projected over 'England' is the malevolence Lawrence exerts at the end, against 'the anima of material disintegration':

> What could possibly become of such a people, a people in whom the living intuitive faculty was as dead as nails? And only queer mechanical yells and uncanny will-power remain? . . . Shakespeare's England! No, but the England of today . . . it was producing a new race of mankind, over-conscious on the money and political side, on the spontaneous, intuitive side, dead, but dead. Half-corpses, all of them: but with a terrible insistent consciousness of the other half. . . . When Connie saw the great lorries full of steel-workers from Sheffield, weird, distorted beings like men, off for an excursion to Matlock, her bowels fainted, and she thought: Ah God, what has man done to man? What have the leaders of men been doing to their fellow men? They have reduced them to less than humanness; and now there can be no fellowship any more! . . . With such creatures for the industrial masses, and the upper classes as she knew them, there was no hope, no hope any more. Yet she was wanting a baby. . . . She shuddered with dread. Yet Mellors had come out of all this! Yes but he was as apart from it all as she was. Even in him there was no fellowship left. . . . There was only apartness and hopelessness . . . and this was England . . .

> p. 158

This follows the famous piece about the children singing in school, 'a strange bawling yell', a passage much used by us who follow the work of F. R. Leavis and Denys Thompson, who offered it in *Culture and Environment* as a statement about the loss of intuitive faculties. It is a shock to find the falsification here that follows, from Lawrence's neurotic sense of 'apartness' – his own sense of compassionate 'fellowship' gone: 'they' are 'such creatures'.

It was no more true then than it is now that 'there is no hope any more': look at a mass of people in the back streets of Leeds or Widnes and you might think so – but get to know a family, working class or middle class, or know their children at school, and it simply is not so. Each is full of creativity and hope. They can be beautiful, and they can spontaneously create new things. Nor is it true that the English people are 'half-corpses', either as lovers, or men and women, or even culturally. We may make such generalizations, if we think of the mass, the mass televiewer audience, the hordes at racing meetings or the seaside – upper class or working class – the banality of our popular press, advertising, and popular dance and song. But leave the mass to think of individuals such as one knows – an eager boy in school here, an adolescent girl blossoming there, parents, students, teachers, individuals – and one's faith in human nature is restored, by the continual fresh lights one receives, impressions of courage and aspiration, of each urge to gain mastery over circumstance, of unique individual qualities. In each is found the child's natural desire for the fine, good and beautiful. The preponderance of human nature is good. If we do not believe this, then all effort is worthless. The artist expresses this faith in the individual, against the generalization and against the mass: Lawrence has done much of this. But here he has lost hope.

There is a great deal in Lawrence's work, alas, of the Pharasaic – at its worst, perhaps, in *Aaron's Rod* – a touch of 'thank God I am not as other men are' – 'Thank God Morelorence is not as other men are'. Lawrence says of Mellors, 'Yes, but he was as *apart* from it all as she was.' They have 'good' sex: all other people's sex is 'two-second spasms'. The clue is there again in that 'yet she was wanting a baby, an heir to Wragby – *she shuddered with dread!*'

So the workmen in the lorries do not invoke compassion, but a Pharasaic disgust:

> 'God knows where the future lies. . . . This is history. One England blots out another. . . . And the continuity is not organic, but mechanical . . .'

– except for one fact: organically, there must be another generation, because the love-urge that draws Connie into the arms of the
gamekeeper draws all of us, for continuity. We must accept that
organic continuity, and do what we can to restore the intuitive
life, and increased possibilities for sanity and enrichment, through
education, through the dissemination of ideas, through responsibility to stay and redeem the world – bleak as it sometimes is –
which we inherit. But this social responsibility must maintain its
sense of reality, and it links with personal responsibility, to the
needs of the whole being, and to creation and its mystery. Connie
Chatterley may lie after coition with Mellors pondering on creation and its mysteries, but such pondering should oblige her to
exert some kind of protest, one would have thought, against his
abrogation of the imminent parenthood. Creation may be a
fresh shoot thrusting even through the stoniest and least promising
of ground. But no: there is no future:

> What would come after? Connie could not imagine. She could only
> see the new brick streets spreading into the fields, the new erections
> rising at the collieries, the new girls in their silk stockings, the
> new collier lads lounging into the Pally or the Welfare. . . . There
> was a gap in the continuity of consciousness, almost American:
> but industrial really. What next?
> Connie felt there was no next. She wanted to hide her head in the
> sand: or, at least, in the bosom of a living man.
> The world was so complicated and weird and gruesome! The
> common people were so many, and really so terrible. . . . She . . . saw
> the colliers going home. . . . Men! Men! Alas, in some way patient
> and good men. In other ways, non-existent. Something that men
> *should* have was bred and killed out of them. Yet they were men.
> They begot children. One might bear a child to them. Terrible,
> terrible thought! They were good and kindly. But they were only
> half, only the grey half of a human being. . . . Supposing the dead in
> them rose up! But no, it was too terrible to think of . . . a life with
> utterly no beauty in it, no intuition, always 'in the pit'.
> Children from such men! Oh God, oh God!

There is here a strange withdrawal in recoil from humanity –
strange for the Lawrence who wrote so sympathetically of the life

of the miner! Had Lawrence seen these 'half-men' walking with
bayonets into a wood fighting as they thought to save the world
from the end of civilization, even if their altruism was confused,
perhaps he would have checked some of his spleen at 'grey halves'.
If he had read their pathetic letters home to their wives and children he would not have despised their capacities to love – their
truly intuitive capacities. Had he contemplated one or two working-class girls with their babies – even those with psychic difficulties![1] In teaching the children of 'such creatures' he experienced
as one may, moments of deeply moving beauty. Had he, indeed,
not shrunk from working men, or had been able to contemplate
them as individuals, without fear, he would not have written
those paragraphs. It seems impossible that the author of *Sons and
Lovers* could write them. But he did: there is a kind of splenetic,
impotent fear behind such passages – and the reason is apparent in
the next passage:

'Yet Mellors had come from such a father. Not quite...'

Morelorence has a miner for a father: the father was 'patient' and
'good' – but to Lawrence the thought of Her Ladyship bearing
a child to one is as intolerable, unconsciously, as it was to him to
think of his father having coition with his mother. This is why he
must spin out to himself the falsified legend of the working masses
being 'half-men' with no beauty, no intuitive life in them. In bad
times it may have been so that working people's lives were so
mean that they had little chance to transcend ugliness and a sub-
human life. But to meet working men as persons anywhere, or to
teach their children, or to know their sons as young men, is enough
to call Lawrence's bluff: human beings are entitled to be considered as individuals, with the same order in every soul as there is in
Bach's music, in greater or lesser degrees, whether they belong to
one class or another. There is not a child of a working man which
does not have in school some 'ray of celestial beauty' in its soul,

[1] The compassionate and creative qualities of the best psychoanalytical writers
such as Melanie Klein and D. W. Winnicott whose lives have been lived in touch
with suffering and who have found in this a deep belief in human nature and its
capacities for transformation contrast sharply with the malevolent *noli me tangere*
tone of rejection of Lawrence at his worst.

somewhere. Lawrence is preaching here, manifestly; and he is preaching a doom, the doom of the neurotic who cannot bear the rest of the world's reality, but projects on to it his own distortions. It is beyond a sense of superiority or snobbery – it is a misanthropy with its origins in fear, a failure to accept the continuity of life, and even life itself. As an attitude, a philosophy, in our time, it is totally disastrous, as disastrous as those impulses to self-destruction in humanity which centre round the hydrogen bomb:

'Perhaps with the passing of the coal they would disappear again, off the face of the earth . . .'
'The anima of material disintegration . . .'

The threat of the animus of material disintegration – of fission – is not in the miners, but in Lawrence's neurosis. From these doom-laden phrases Connie Chatterley is glad to get back to the motherly talk of Mrs Bolton, and to make her way, directly after lunch, to the wood for another 'fuck'. But there is grit in our response to the delicious pastoral: 'Everywhere the bud-knots and the leap of life!' After their coition Mellors says, 'Now anybody can 'ave any childt i' th' world . . . this wor t' best.' It is as if we left the miners in fear of conception among them: 'Children from such men! Oh God, oh God!', only to find, in the wood in spring, the figure of the very man-miner who denied life to Mrs Lawrence – Mrs Morel. There is Morelorence standing over Connie, fastening his breeches, thanking her for 'healing' him, admitting she is 'a lot besides an animal', and the best 'bit o' cunt on earth. When ter likes! When th'art willin'.'

'Is it?' she said. 'And do you care for me?'
He kissed her without answering.
'Tha mun goo, let me dust thee,' he said. . . . the world seemed a dream . . .

The world of Industrial England seemed a few pages before 'like a nightmare'. Between the dream and the nightmare, the story and the neurotic, idealistic-phallic phantasy, Lawrence can still not see that the only real thing in the falsified drama is the humiliating discourtesy and life-denying tyranny of Mellors, and the absence of civilized love and its creative power. Had Connie looked closer at the industrial scene she would perhaps have found more of creative life there, and more hope, too, even than in the ''ut'.

Clifford turns the tables on Connie. She says of the working people:

> 'Their lives are industrialized and hopeless, and so are ours!' she cried.
>
> 'You don't look at all a hopeless figure standing there, Connie, my dear.'

In the light of this truth from his hated alter-ego, we see Connie for once as a true woman – as real as Frieda.

> 'The masses are unalterable . . . we've poisoned our masses with a little education . . .'
>
> Connie was frightened. There was something devastatingly true in what he said. But it was a truth that killed.

Lawrence can comfortably place his own fatal truth in the mouth of his usurped scapegoat, and later he can caricature the man's attitude as that of 'the function determines the individual'.

> 'Then there is no common humanity between us at all!'
>
> 'I believe there is a gulf . . .'
>
> Connie looked at him with dazed eyes.

Yet it is Lawrence's withdrawal of compassion and hope that creates the gulf, not the attitudes he caricatures in Clifford.

The most ludicrous statement of all is Mellors' Lawrentian sermon in the embarrassing storm-flower scene:

> 'I like it! An' if I only lived ten minutes and stroked thy arse an' got to know it, I should reckon I'd lived one life, see ter! Industrial system or not!'
>
> '. . . Here's one of my lifetimes.'
>
> '. . . Kiss me . . .' she whispered.

We may make allowances for the extravagances of lovers: but there is a sense in which Lawrence really meant this – make away with the industrial system, for ten minutes with a woman's 'proper arse', in a wood in spring. All for love! Except that it is not love, but 'rather awful sensuality': and he denies the child who will come from it. Here Lawrence merges with Hollywood and the cheap novelette: and at a deeper level with all those sexual problems of our time, which manifest deficiencies of the reality-sense and the denial of our greatest need in relationship.

The tone of Mellors' last letter remains that of a man who sees in a woman his comfort, his healing matrix, his source of meaning in life, but very much in terms of the comforting mother, rather than as an equal partner in creativity. There is no future for his child, because he both refuses to countenance the exigencies of the world:

> You can't insure against the future, except by really believing in the best bit of you, and in the power beyond it. So I believe in the little flame between us. For me now, it's the only thing in the world. I've got no friends, not inward friends. Only you. And now the little flame is all I care about in my life. There's the baby, but that is a side issue. It's my Pentecost, the forked flame between me and you. The old Pentecost isn't quite right. Me and God is a bit uppish, somehow. But the little forked flame between me and you: there you are! That's what I abide by, and will abide by, Cliffords and Berthas, colliery companies and governments and the money-mass of people all not-withstanding.

The religious symbolism is used not to express the mystery of creation in sex, but rather to seek to elevate sex to religiose dimensions, to disguise the unreality here. This religiose note deceived many well-meaning churchmen into accepting Lawrence's untruths.

The relationship he craves here is still a dependent and eventually narcissistic one – 'I have no friends in the world, only you. You are all I care about. Our flame is what I abide by.' The 'fucking oneself into peace' as Mellors puts it in his last letter, about 'the little flame', is but an attempt to exorcize anxiety. The flame is simply one of sensuality in coition conceived as a detensioning anodyne, rather than the flame as of Eastern erotic symbolism that creates the child, and expresses the continuous renewal of the Cosmos.

But this unreal love is as much as Mellors and Connie ever

manage to achieve despite all the idyllic heights of their loving: and the last letter is mostly wild propaganda about doing away with the industrial system altogether.

> It was not woman's fault, or even love's fault, nor the fault of sex. The fault lay out here, in those evil electric lights and diabolical rattling of engines. There, in the world of the mechanical greed, sparkling with lights and gushing hot metal and roaring with traffic, there lay the vast evil thing, ready to destroy whatever did not conform. Soon it would destroy the wood, and the bluebells would spring no more. All vulnerable things must perish under the rolling and fuming of iron.

Much has gone under since Lawrence's time, and much more will go. 'One England blots out another.' Yet in each new generation there is a gain in sincerity, and an ever-renewed hope. Life is in some ways more ugly, noisy, vacant, more dull and pointless than ever before, even as 'external' civilization advances. But there is also more discrimination abroad. Over all our world hangs the horror of the total destruction of everything by nuclear fission, the last obscene manifestation of the hate and greed in human nature. But this may also be our salvation, by terrifying us into peace, and towards more realism in diplomacy.

In many ways Lawrence is right. But there are other signs, too, – of the gradual removal of ignorance, the lessening of class privilege and poverty, and the ending of tedious, limited, poor lives among working people. Only beginnings. Of course, there are too many 'money-boys and money-girls' pursuing the false ideals of a culture, impelled by hallucinatory defences against the real. But there are also hundreds of thousands of people with a questing intelligence and a keen sense of values. There are many now pursuing a new sincerity and richness in personal relationships. There are many readers of Lawrence, seeking the true and beautiful by his lights: and the good life could come quickly – by force of gathered ideas, and even by the machine itself. It depends what you believe about human nature. Lawrence lost faith in everyone's but his own, in its enclosed narcissistic self-consumption.

Nowadays also there is growing an informed and intelligent creature care at the very places where Lawrence is weak – care for the growth of love, in family life, and for the child. In developing patterns of social organization, welfare care, and education, there is the basis of a new and better community. There is no true chance of sweeping the machine away, except by more machines: the impulse is not mere greed, but a desire that all may escape from tedium, as Lawrence escaped himself, into a life of leisure and creativity. But we shall not improve human life merely by episodes of 'warm-hearted fucking' in huts in the woods, irresponsible to the procreation between our loins, and to the realities of our social context. I am not saying that there should not be episodes in our lives such as this in Connie's. Such wild raptures come to all, and are beautiful; a youth without them would be lacking, but they are not incompatible with maturity, work, marriage, parenthood, nor with staying in one's context, and accepting one's inner and outer reality. A more real rapture, gladly accepting imperfect reality, can go on all one's life. It is true that we must accept the reality of the body and its needs. But in this book Lawrence's picture has half the reality missing, those realities of the civilized heart and other aspects of love.

The reasons are in Lawrence's fear. No sooner does the bird of Morelorence's passion fly, than the bird of fear flies with it, from the bastions of the industrial world that destroyed his father, and has made the women predatory:

> his penis began to stir like a live bird. At the same time an oppression, a dread of exposing himself and her to that Thing that sparkled viciously in the electric light ...

Sex must 'heal' this fear, and so alter the world. He must 'come right' with a woman – he must fuck warm-heartedly, *then the world will look all right to him*. This confusion of projection is then extended into a theory that if *we all* 'fucked warm-heartedly' *the world would come right*. But the fact is that the world's failure in sex, and its failures in social living and organization, in common humanity, courtesy, tenderness to one another are related in complex civilized ways, so that one is not dependent on the other, but each is an index of the other. 'Failure' in sex as we have seen, is a manifestation of a whole deficiency in reality sense, and in the growth of love. Means to the restoration of order are in a complex combination of healing medicine, healing love, public care, and the promotion of good feelings and by culture, all contributing to foster, by care, good concepts, and creative effort, the maximum security, for the potentialities and sanity of the next generation. In this it is important to keep concepts, derived from imaginative culture, – as of love – fresh and viable – to this Lawrence has made the biggest single contribution in our century – insisting as he did on the free flow of tender feelings, and at best, on mutual regard, as in the relationship between Ursula and Birkin. Lawrence has helped us to hold on to much. In education – which in this book he implicitly denies – we have the means to speed the dissemination of his best value as possessed concepts, in ways transcending the older forms of traditional wisdom – if education would only concern itself with *being* rather than knowing, by the nourishment of the sensibility and the intuitive faculties.

But the falsifications in this book are such that if taken over in the sense that we might try to live by them, they might make life more difficult and more insecure, and our attitudes more destructive. Lawrence's postulation of a direct connection between the inability to achieve orgasm and 'the industrial system' is ludicrously far-fetched even taken as symbolic. Ironically, it is a fallacy which appeals most to the mechanical-minded America Lawrence hated. The destruction of industry and the return to the woods as 'naturals' would by no means restore us to the easy 'natural coming' of the savage. Indeed, here we meet yet another modern myth – the savage in fact has no free rich happy sex, as Malinowski and others have shown. In some places in adolescence there is sexual freedom – but at a price, later. Most primitive people are deeply subjected to taboos, some with hideous painful rites, which they cling to in order to survive. In the savage world individual freedom of choice in love does not exist as we know it. There fulfilment and consciousness are limited by elaborate ceremonies, taboos, magic, and rigorous patterns of relationship. In primitive conditions it is impossible for men to develop the more complex forms of individual potentiality and that freedom of self-determination such as we value above everything in the Western world. The savage has solved his reality problems less well than we – or perhaps has not begun to solve them, or solves them by false solutions. Certainly they would be false solutions for us. It is true that Lawrence in Mellors dismisses native women – who 'come naturally' – as 'mud' – but his abandonment of 'the industrial system' can surely only imply a return to 'mud' savagery? Can we take this message from this idyllic and idealizing book seriously, however insistent Lawrence's solemnity? It is of course a mere romance, a Rousseauistic nostalgia for a primitive life that never existed. It merely symbolizes, in yet another way, a nostalgia for a hallucinated 'perfect Eden' of infancy. In truth, it implies a rejection of the high value which we set on individuality and personal 'disquality' in the west, such as Lawrence strove to uphold. Not even Lawrence would want to share his wife with his cousins, and he must have been aware of such things as the prevalence of sexual diseases spreading through the savage places of the world, in the pursuit of 'natural' sexual 'freedom'. There is no fulfilment in a flight to unreal 'bliss'. As he indicates so marvellously in Constance, happiness and reality are 'here in my bosom and at home' – not in Venice, or in the 'good time', but here at Wragby, in England, in an old hut or cottage, in bed. Here we find ourselves. But significantly, in his idyll he avoids the real diurnal domestic setting, the domestic tie, the meals together, the work together, the journey through time together – and such aspects of the whole reality of marriage and procreativity.

In this sense there is a fateful sense in which Lawrence did not *stay*. His flight from these things parallels his restless wanderings round the world. Unlike Christian he does not even stay on the true quest path. The future is black, doomed, Morelorence says. The English reality was unbearable – yet we, to whom he preached, have to bear it, and have had to bear worse. To explain the horrors of our time he projects, from his own psychic weakness, an explanation derived from an unconscious apprehension that his father failed to give his mother the love the son wished he could give her himself. This he projects on the machine world, destructively. His pronouncements on industry are for these reasons unreal Luddite nonsense of the mind – despairing, negative and destructive nonsense at that. The machine has enchained millions, but in a human hope that millions should be freed, from economic insecurity, from inequality of privilege, from poverty. If we learn how to subdue the machine, and its side-effects in terms of quantitative attitudes and acquisitiveness, then we may triumph over famine, over the inequality and uncertainty of food production in the world, over starvation, over too-early death, over discomfort and uncertainty, and free men from tedious lives and an environment deficient in culture. A humane leisured cultured life *could* arise which would justify, possibly, just, some of the horrors of the industrial era. There could be forms of living for all, at the quality of the life of the slave-owning classes of ancient Athens, *for all human beings*. But to reach this potential quality of life for all human beings – and to seek it is not merely a greedy impulse on the part of the machine-builders – we must cherish and form the next generation, our children, to give them the security that seeks to strive towards the good, and creative attitudes. The primary task is to make a good environment for the infant, which means learning to love and promote love. And, as we have seen, this means fostering a more adequate reality sense in all, by all the powers at our disposal.

Alas, this book, in so far as it does anything, is likely to reinforce the desperate sensuality, sexual irresponsibility, and sex-anxious mentality of our time, weakening our reality sense by adding yet another hallucination. The Mellors of whom Lawrence approves is virtually a vindication of the worst prevalent, sensual, unreal and irresponsible attitudes to sex. It is, alas, at times, Mellors whose 'spunk has gone dead', and who is 'carrion-bodied', 'without balls': for the balls are the mystic seat of the new child, in whom sexual togetherness is consummated, rather than a mere god's appendage, to be the subject of the lover-mother's adoration. Mellors is dissociated from reality to such an extent as to belong to that life-denial that, perhaps, destroyed the physical Lawrence.

Lawrence is here in the throes of his overinsistence of the body at the expense of the mind, and torn by accepting the fatal division between psyche and soma.[1]

The unreality of the 'body-life' is paralleled by an abysmal prostration of intelligence. There is much anti-intellectual prejudice in the book, which extends even to creative writing, science, art, and even 'thinking' about the social context of sex.

Compare, for instance, the way Lawrence approves Mellors' ridiculously prejudiced and uninformed attack on art, the art of Duncan Forbes. Forbes (characteristically) is also unfairly caricatured, with a 'yellow face' again, 'In another wave of hate the artist's face looked yellow . . .' A victory for Mellors!

> 'It's a pure bit of murder,' said Mellors at last; a speech Duncan by no means expected from a gamekeeper . . .
> . . . it murders all the bowels of compassion in a man . . .
> (Mellors gazes 'with a flickering detachment that was something like the dancing of a moth, at the pictures'.)
> 'I think all these tubes and corrugated vibrations are stupid enough for anything, and pretty sentimental. They show a lot of self-pity and an awful lot of nervous self-opinion, seems to me.'

'I'm not just my Lady's fucker, after all,' Mellors says, and Lawrence is anxious to make him more than that. But he is *not* more than that. A 'moth's vitality' is no grounds for art criticism, even if we may share Lawrence's contempt for the bogus art of metropolitan fashion. No wonder Hilda is pale with anger when Connie tells her defensively he 'understands tenderness' and 'she would be proud to bear his child'.

'The rest o' times' are but 'complication' to Mellors. But he is a reader, as well as an art-critic:

> . . . some from a circulating library. There were books about Bolshevist Russia, books of travel, a volume about the atom and the electron, another book about the composition of the earth's core, and the causes of earthquakes: then a few novels: then three books on India. So! He was a reader after all!

[1] In addition Lawrence refuses entirely to consider the reality of birth control honestly, of course. His inability to do so has no doubt some connection with his unconscious hostility to procreation, and the inevitable guilt and pain around such feelings.

– he has a mind! What a painful gesture this is! Some cultivation, apart from his business with horses! Even the mindless body which is to be her life's companion, the source of life she has discovered, has a mind! Remarkable discovery! The discovery that after all Mellors is not a performing animal, of extravagant potency, but a civilized being! Yet what he has, as 'mind', amounts to little more than a splenetic contempt for things of the mind. In this too, as well as in his sex, he is a vindicated recrudescence of the historically degraded working-class man, with nothing but a resentful contempt for the culture possessed by the 'bosses' and the refinements his wife tries to discover, and to give her children. Yet this is the 'phallus bearer', 'the son of god', the man whom we are to imitate, in restoring nature to human nature, and order to society, 'a really exceptional being'!

It is pathetic that such a man as Lawrence should have been driven by his inner psychic needs to make such travesties of human nature, of our sexual life in the whole being, of love, marriage and 'the creative act which is more than procreative'. Love is only creative because we are intelligent, and feeling, and divided into men and women, 'separate . . . separate', each with equal rights to respect, mutual understanding and the life of body, and intelligence. Far from finding the poet's 'liars' we need continual touch with art such as Lawrence's best, which enriches our capacity for 'union with body and soul'. Lawrence would, in this work, return us to the life of the ignorant savage.

This attitude of 'the world well lost' is given an earnest, prophetic, but utterly false, vindication in terms of social theory and protest. Society is not insane, a terrible monster: it is as sane as we can make it for ourselves, our loves and our children.

II
– AND LOVE?

The most that can be said about *Lady Chatterley's Lover* to justify its public availability is that at least it makes sexual experience explicit in an unfurtive way. There is perhaps less harm in what is nowadays called 'frankness' than in ignorance and taboo. Yet such 'realism' may still be very unreal. The influence of *Lady Chatterley* merges, we must not forget, with a mass of other influences, all tending towards mental self-conscious sex and unreal attitudes to life. When the *News of the World* recently sold an extra 250,000 copies because it printed the ghost-written 'confessions' of a woman whose reality sense was obviously gravely disturbed, and who was later established by legal trials as a prostitute and perjurer, even readers of *The Guardian* showed themselves capable of admiring this woman as 'a lovable Nell Gwynne' and as 'utterly feminine'. 'She can give herself in love' they wrote. Elements in our culture are reversing norms to a dangerous extent. Contributing to this are such features as the wide use of images of the 'all providing mother' – such as the 'generous'-looking photographer's model. We find it harder to distinguish between images of living that are damagingly unreal (at the play-boy level) and the picture of a true love-relationship. Indeed, the latter is not an ideal at all at the *Daily Express* level, or at that (not far removed) of Kingsley Amis' novels.

There is another kind of ignorance, worse than the ignorance of the facts of sex from which we are now supposed to be freed: *it is the ignorance of love*. What we need now are embodiments in imagination of the nature of love, concepts of what is worth striving and waiting for, and of adult satisfactions. Lawrence elsewhere is one of the greatest sources of such concepts – but, as I have tried to show, not in this work. This book merges into the implications that one finds in many sources of sex-mentality nowadays – advertisements, films, television 'love' plays, pulp books, popular songs and song-racket idols – that there is nothing worth 'waiting' for, nothing beyond indulgent sensuality. This, as Shakespeare knew, as appetite becomes a universal wolf, destroys the sense of significance, because it exacerbates our sense of Time, and undermines our sense of continuity won by 'spiritual struggle'. As Erich Fromm says in his book on Freud, the whole trend of our world, psychically, is infantile, seeking the immediate satisfaction rather than the more remote, deeper, more real, complex and mature satisfaction. It thrives on the unreal, and seeks to avoid the painful, but more satisfying, real. *Lady Chatterley's* concentration on sex at the expense of love is at one with this infantile limitation on our quest for love. In sex the mature satisfaction may be found in the security of marriage, marriage with sex firmly established in its natural complex, accepting gladly all the responsibilities of the place of that marriage in the world and society, and the creative responsibility of procreation. As D. W. Winnicott says, the arrival of each child enriches the parents' lives, while the parents' sexual love, unconsciously apprehended by their children, fills them with a deep sense of security, even though they are jealous. Even the jealousy (as in their Oedipal feelings) is a spur to their own growth and development. As things are we need all the help we can get to form positive creative concepts, ideals and illumination of the richer aspects of normal fulfilment. We are continually engaged in contest over the complicated organism of the family in the community, to help us hold it together against the assaults of coincidence, chance, sickness, time and death. We need to defend it against our own inward psychic treachery and failings, and against the destructive elements in both *avant-garde* and popular culture in an acquisitive and irresponsible society.

Lawrence pursued the quest for love all his life, and one strives to understand him. But *Lady Chatterley's Lover* does not really convey an impression of love at all, nor does it convey the complexity of the context in which love is created, as do Lawrence's great works, *The Rainbow* and *Women in Love*, so much better. The satisfactions Mellors seeks are the egocentric 'healing' infantile ones, our age's norms, and he disowns responsibilities as we tend too easily to disown them by denying the woman's needs – and the child's. Mellors does these things with Lawrence's complete approval. Only Connie, because Lawrence is perceptive enough to understand her with his acute perception of woman, persists in seeking the creative drive in love towards having a child and security for her child. But Mellors resents this, again with Lawrence's approval, to 'preserve his dignity and self-respect', and to 'defend' himself. Thus Connie, in her cringing, pleading submissiveness, humiliated, and denied all but sensuality, bears a significant resemblance to the 'sex-symbols' of our own time: whatever Lawrence and Mellors tell us, she *is* a bit of a Hollywood image herself – and it is not surprising that this book was the first of Lawrence's to be filmed, and is being filmed again.

Thus *Lady Chatterley* is one more contribution, as it happens, to our preoccupation, in mental terms, with the immediate sensual satisfactions, and with that sex which is but a distraction from the quest for love, and from reality as a whole. Mellors does not wait to consider what he is doing. He is driven by 'life'. It is good that we should be driven by life. But life also makes huge real demands, and we must learn to meet them if the life that comes of the crea-tive-procreative act is to fulfil itself truly and fully, in the child, and in ourselves as parents. Lawrence is not really concerned in this book to render the obligations, the exigencies, the claims of life: he turns instead to the immediate satisfactions of sensuality, seek-ing in this way to lay the ghosts of infantile anxiety: which is what too many are too much encouraged to do by our decadent culture that taboos tender feelings and denies the reality of love. Many people watching films of love-making, or reading books describ-ing acts of sex are not really concerned with real sensuality as they might suppose they are – they are committing an act of verbal or visual sex, of onanism, of mental sex only, to allay anxiety. They are looking the wrong way, or rather they are preoccupied only with a closed-circuit image, using the false images to fob them-selves off with a hallucination of an impossible and unreal 'perfect' relationship (see Lawrence's poem, *When I went to the Cinema*). They need to come to terms with 'co-operative mutuality': in fact they indulge in oral aggression and compulsive *voyeur*-craving merely: in thumb-suck. To read *Lady Chatterley's Lover*, though it set out to vindicate sex, normal sex, is *not* itself a sensual, normal, experience – it is a mental one, and a narcissistic one, with oral-aggressive and *voyeur* elements, short-circuited back to the self, not polarized with another creature, nor opening fresh awarenesses of reality. The hallucination makes insufficient claims on us to come to terms with our inward reality or the reality of the world: and it does not by such art release us to more acute and positive living. It lies. What it will not do is to add to our possessed understanding of love, to letting our 'fine discrimination flow', or lead us out to actual reality. Lawrence's short stories such as *Second Best*, for instance, a lovely tender story about young courtship, do this: so do his best poems: most of *Lady Chatterley* does not.

As Richard Hoggart said in the witness box at the *Lady Chatterley* trial, Lawrence is saying 'one fucks'. But there is a limited use in saying merely that, even as an acceptance of our reality: 'fucking' is nothing: it can be no more than evacuation. Love is nothing if not creative. The trouble is that Lawrence says so little else other than 'this is what lovers do, what lovers should do, in the body, to find fullness of creative living there': he does not go on to establish a reality of love 'beyond' the erotic – as Chaucer does, for instance, in his Debate on Marriage. In fact, as I have suggested, he is not even as 'real' about sex as the Wyf of Bath.

I find myself especially wanting to repudiate most Connie's remark and Lawrence's endorsement of it: 'The poets are wrong – all one wanted is this rather awful sensuality!' The poets, says Lawrence, said one wanted 'sentiment' – but this was wrong. The fact, he implies, is that we need sensuality. But, in fact, we need sensuality only to forget about it: just as we eat to forget about hunger. What we remember of a meal at best is with whom we shared it, and what it lent to our sense of being alive, as in an infant what sustains him is the concept of the mother's love and continuity. The gustation belongs to mortality, death and time: what triumphs is relationship. We certainly do not want persistent mental consciousness of sensuality, unless we are sick. Poetry needs to celebrate all that 'sentiment' in man and woman which transcends the sensual, which is larger than the mortality, though rooted in it, and conquers death, for the sake of the continuity of human life. This is the truth of love: love itself, happy, creative love is less aware, less mental, about its sensual depths, the more fulfilled it is. Sensuality merely moves from hunger to 'flop' (*post coitum contristus est animal*) – the sentient, conscious being needs to resolve all the other elements (aggression and desire) in a going out, in giving, to the other partner, and a sense of the other's reality and continuing existence.

It is no substitute for this built up, transcending, love reality, to drag the 'reality' of sex to the conscious surface as Lawrence does. Because he could not enter into sexual life without an overbearing sense of shame and doom, he endeavours by anxious over-insistence to exorcize fear by verbal ravishment. At the same time, because he was an artist, seeking his personal order and reality in words, he offers us at best some shared conquest of his terrible suffering: and there are lovely moments in this book, too. But only where he does not involve us in his own over-insistent mental verbalizing, the too private, too exhibitionist-narcissistic displays of his own self-ravishing.

One may make absolute objections to the awareness. To the lover there is no awareness: he is gone to body; entirely beyond self-consciousness or even 'rather awful sensuality', lost – at best. When lovers are most together in bodily love they are not watch-fully conscious of what they do. To be conscious is to restrict the flow of bodily love. Lawrence's characters are said to be 'lost', but, like Mellors, they never stop mentally verbalizing, sloganizing, and comparing, while we are watching all the time, aware. This is but a symptom of the failure to be able to 'give', 'lapse' or 'let go' in love. Thus, if one seeks the kind of coition Lawrence offers in the name of 'warm-hearted fucking', one is seeking something false, something too anxiously aware of itself and the 'whirlpools of sensation'. The lover who is gone into the act of creation is lost in what is happening to him: to describe such an act is to reduce its mystic 'now'. As in battle, or in some dangerous moment in wild country, or an accident, or storm, or in a strange place suddenly, in which body and mind together cry, 'Am I really here, in this extraordinary manifestation of life's possibilities – is this me?' On the top of a mountain, or in a storm of machine-gun fire, or fallen into a river, sudden awareness beyond the normal – there is something of this in the suspended mind, as in coition. One touches the pulse of life itself – the natural life to which one be-longs, and rides on in darkness. Lawrence grasps this in Connie as she goes to the wood in Spring, seeking life. The mind in coition is suspended, and the creativity which the body is living on its own is in all senses indescribable because consciousness has no grasp on it, as Lawrence sometimes shows he knew. 'On which no con-sciousness could seize' – then why try to seize it! To try is destruc-tive, and neurotic, because it brings us back out of the flux – as if we daren't 'let go' the inhibiting will.

But even if we accept the awareness, what is so dismally absent from Lawrence's book is a poetic rendering of the poetic aftermath of coition, from which we derive a deep sense of meaning as it flows into love. Nearly always his lovers begin to talk, anxiously, comparatively, despite the occasional tenderness. In coition, at best, the sensual experience, on which the mind had no grasp except to be awe-stricken by the sense of it happening, is forgotten as soon as ended: a loss of the self in togetherness, it is a death, a draught of Lethe, lethal to consciousness. Lawrence's lovers are so restless – always seeking renewal of the phallus, further satisfaction, more exploration of the 'deepest places of shame', and then the endless verbal post mortems. Love and peace are always missing: 'It was not love: it was not voluptuousness – only a rather awful sensuality.'

It seems to me, from an experience at least as tormented as Lawrence's, as full of imperfections, blocks, distrustings and misgivings, at times as remote from happiness as sexual experience could ever be, that in this book about lovers, Lawrence fails to render the one experience which makes love 'valid and precious'. He approaches it only once, where Connie reflects on her possible conception. It is that return, in the mind amazed by the tumult of passionate bodily life, which has been suspended by it and during it, to a post-coital sensibility of love. I call it sensibility – being sensible – because it is not mental consciousness, analytical, comparative. It is hardly verbal, and can only be expressed if at all in poetry or music or ballet, embodied informs of expression belonging to the intuitive level, but as emotion organized into pattern – in the very 'sentiment' which Lawrence shows his heroine here distrusting. It is the flux of an awareness of togetherness, beyond 'happiness', and having its richness chiefly in a great tenderness of gratitude, and in the contemplation of the creativity of love. The lover becomes aware, rather than conscious, of the whole being with which he has met together in life: aware of the woman's whole organic self, and her creative power, in gratitude for the gift of life to her, and to the lover. This awareness moves beyond the sense of her inward life – the anemone of the womb's mouth, that Lawrence describes, the secret life of the ova, the womb's

cycles, the energetic search by the sperm for fertility, the involve-
ment of the whole body in the search for mutual satisfaction, and
towards creative giving, the awakening and subsequent peace in
the breasts, lower centres and the whole body – to the contemplation of the children created or to be created, and the whole gamut
of experiences of sorrow, tenderness, childbirth, potential childbirth, the bony foetus in the belly, the birth pangs, the suckling,
the creation and growth of the family. The experience is only
complete if it includes awareness of procreation, even if procreation has been prevented. Even then, of course, there is no absolute
sureness, and in this is the germ of awe at creativity, always. All
this satisfies what D. W. Winnicott calls the 'body and soul longing for union with body and soul'.

That is, from the beginning, in a sexual relationship, there is a
constant return to the mind, after love-making, in post-coital
contemplation, in extreme happiness, of concepts which belong
to the consciousness, to the powers of intelligent contemplation
of the meaning of love, to philosophy, religion, poetry, values.
In this, love merges from bodily life into our bridge-building
between inner and outer reality. So it becomes a poetic apprehension of the meaning of life, at a moment when 'riotous appetite' is stilled, and the reckless search for sensual pleasure in the
body is fulfilled. Love is a poetic-philosophical activity, which
every creature may engage in, at the moment of closest touch
between a man and a woman. Not least the miners who have 'lost
their intuitive faculties', not least our advertive-seeking young,
even 'money boys' and 'money girls' can experience this philosophical, mystical state. Indeed their sensuality may even be a kind of
search not merely only for the allaying of anxiety, de-tensioning
or mere physical satisfaction, but for this very sense of significance
and creative meaning felt deeply in post-coital awareness. Alas,
the meaning is not fully there unless there is a love which can
transcend the sensuality. Only our 'finding of the object' and other-
than-erotic-awarenesses can transcend the anxiety of having
annihilated desire – in such sense of meaning, that is, *is* our escape
from post-coital depression.

The importance of this source of meaning in love is in its utter unlikeness to anything Lawrence portrays. It is quite remote from Mellors' mental consciousness, 'Thank God I've got a woman'. It is quite remote from Connie's mystical exclamations of awe: 'It was lovely!', 'The voice crying out in the innermost night. The Life!' It is not at all 'religiose' as are Lawrence's accounts of the feelings of Connie's 'adoration' in terms of 'phallus bearers', or of 'the sons of god with the daughters of men'. His lovers never escape from anxious preoccupation with the satisfaction of their sensual drive, and their anxiety about whether their bodily love is adequate or not, and on his part whether he has lost his 'dignity', or hers whether he 'really loves her'.

By contrast with the reality of love, what is offered by this book is an insult to the human mind and civilization, in its recommendation of a return to a pastoral state of drone-life (apart from the efforts of warm-hearted coition).

> If the men wore scarlet trousers as I said, they wouldn't think so much of money: if they could dance and hop and skip, and sing and swagger and be handsome, they could do with very little cash. And amuse the women themselves, and be amused by the women. They ought to learn to be naked and handsome, and to sing in a mass and dance the old group dances, and carve the stools they sit on, and embroider their own emblems. . . . That's the way to solve the industrial problem . . . the mass of the people oughtn't to try to think because they *can't*. They should be alive and frisky, and acknowledge the great God Pan . . .

Isn't this virtually a description of the life our more restless and aimless adolescents seek to lead, with their distractive dances, their 'cool' heroes, their exhibitionist, acquisitive sex, their self-conscious and uneasy eroticism? Of course, in adolescence a degree of such 'protest' against reality is acceptable – even necessary. But there is an adult reality, by which such an immature picture of life must be rejected as inadequate and unsatisfying.

The book lacks stamina, irony, intelligence: it is cranky and false. But these are not, as Leavis would have them, occasional weaknesses in a great creative intelligence which elsewhere gives an overall impression of sanity. They are related to central weaknesses in Lawrence's attitude to life, sex, and society. In this *Lady*

Chatterley's Lover, the most popular of his works, is a reversal of even the best values expressed in the masterly dramatic poems *The Rainbow* and *Women in Love*, but it also points to places and themes in those works which, in the end, do not reach the truth either, if we resist Lawrence's manic persuasions. Alas, the most widely read of Lawrence's books in his most uncreative – one in which the child fruit of sexual togetherness is not walking under the rainbow, but rejected as a 'side issue'. Meanwhile our children suffer from his book the disturbances caused by anxious accounts of sexual intercourse (which we and they can only receive from the book as aggressive and cruel), and an early introduction to that inhibiting mentality about sex which the best, creative, life-seeking Lawrence most abhorred.

And today, what have we but this? Almost inevitably we find in the child now an intense, precocious secret sexual preoccupation. The upper self is rapidly engaged in exploiting the lower self. A child and its own roused, inflamed sex, its own shame and masturbation, its own cruel, secret sexual excitement and sex *curiosity*, this is the greatest tragedy of our day. The child does not so much want to act as to *know*. The thought of actual sex connection is usually repulsive. There is an aversion from the normal coition act. But the craving to feel, to see, to taste, to *know*, mentally in the head, this is insatiable. Anything, so that the sensation and experience shall come through the upper channels. This is the secret of our introversion and our perversion today. Anything rather than spontaneous direct action from the sensual self. Anything rather than the merely normal passion. Introduce any trick, any idea, any mental element you can into sex, but make it an affair of the upper consciousness, the mind and eyes and mouth and fingers. This is our vice, our dirt, our disease.

Fantasia of the Unconscious, D. H. Lawrence

Alas – Lawrence's book itself has inevitably become part of the disease. Even by his own anger and guilty insistence here he betrays that his very impulse to write *Lady Chatterley* was at one with the most damaging dissociations of our time.

FIVE

We Never Come Through

Look! We Have Come Through!

She knew there was no leaving him, the darkness held them both and contained them, it was not to be surpassed. Besides, she had a full mystic knowledge of his suave loins of darkness, dark-clad and suave, and in this knowledge there was some of the inevitability and the beauty of fate, fate which one asks for, which one accepts in full. He sat still like an Egyptian Pharaoh, driving the car. He felt as if he were seated in immemorial potency, like the great carven statues of real Egypt, as real and fulfilled with subtle strength as these are, with a vague inscrutable smile on their lips. He knew what it was to have the strange and magical current of force in his back and loins, and down his legs, so perfect that it stayed him immobile, and left his face subtly mindlessly smiling, the deepest physical control, magical, mystical, a force in darkness, like electricity.

Women in Love

This is Birkin, reflecting on the satisfactions of sexual inter-course. As Leavis says, *Women in Love* is not, as Middleton Murry would have it, 'a working out' of a personal argument in the 'imaginary consummation of Birkin and Ursula' *only*. It *is* that, as any creative work of an artist must be spun out of the artist's own experience -- each creature in the novel being part of himself. But *Women in Love* transmutes the personal much more into dramatized art, and seeks to express the truth that Leavis quotes from *Psychoanalysis and the Unconscious*: 'Love is a thing to be learned, through centuries of patient effort.' But the insistent verbalism of the above manifests that same kind of anxiety which in *Lady Chatterley* becomes a total falsification, and in *Women in Love* (as W. W. Robson has pointed out in his excellent essay in *The Pelican Guide to Literature* Volume 7, *The Modern Age*)

led Lawrence to allow that novel – which was intended to be
about women in love – to become, in the end, not at all the book
he promises in the beginning.

In *Lady Chatterley's Lover* he set out, too, to make a further
quest in the 'patient effort', of learning love. But Lawrence's
animus against 'nonsense about love and unselfishness . . . more
crude and repugnant than savage fetish-worship' has in that work
run out of control – and love there becomes savage fetish-worship
and altruism is denied. Neither Mellors nor Connie (nor Lawrence
indeed) discovers the essential culmination of human fulfilment,
in giving, in the acceptance of procreation, and responsibility to
a reality greater than the self. 'Love,' says Lawrence in the same
statement, 'is the complex maintenance of individual integrity
throughout the incalculable processes of interhuman polarity.'
But Connie's 'individual integrity' is sacrificed in the end to
Mellors' (Lawrence's – Morelorence's) concern for male domination and his need to deny woman. While one accepts that the processes of polarity are 'incalculable', they do not benefit from
falsification.

Lawrence in such passages as that quoted from *Women in Love*
above is faking the meaning of sex to himself: and much of *Lady
Chatterley* is a fake in this way. Lawrence sought to make a work
which would stand as an artefact in 'immemorial potency'. We
are cowed. But the more we learn love, the more we discover
that it is in fact a much gentler, yet more exacting experience –
like those experiences dramatized in Lawrence's own work at
best – and not this dark, potent mystical cult, this sensual self-
ravishment, in body or words.

The more real process of 'patient effort' – close to the personal
quest in Lawrence's life – we can discover in *Look! We Have
Come Through!* In the poems Lawrence does a better thing than in
his novel. The 'Argument' of the series might in a sense be that of
Lady Chatterley's Lover: but in the poems he really follows the
argument:

After much struggling and loss in love and in the world of man, the
protagonist throws in his lot with a woman who is already married.
Together they go into another country, she perforce leaving her

children behind. The conflict of love and hate goes on between the man and woman, and between these two and the world around them, till it reaches some sort of conclusion.

There are notes of uncertainty here which reveal something of the reasons for the failure of *Lady Chatterley*. 'The protagonist' is not a detached, realized dramatic character in the poems, not even as 'placed' as is Mellors in the novel. Lawrence is closely identified with his protagonist and with Mellors, and in both fails to separate the man who suffers from the man who creates. Here the 'some sort of conclusion' is 'the measure of equanimity', which is as much as Mellors and Connie could attain. The title, as I have pointed out, contains a fatal idealizing impulse – that is to will a situation in which one can say 'I have come through' – when, in fact, we never 'come through' – we only go on going through, working and creating.

To elevate one's expectations from sex to the level of 'immemorial potency' is to court disaster. The dread which remains in spite of all efforts to exorcise it in Mellors, is with Lawrence throughout his poems:

> You are the call and I am the answer,
> You are the wish and I am the fulfilment,
> You are the night, and I the day.
> > What else? it is perfect enough.
> > It is perfectly complete,
> > You and I,
> > What more – ?
> Strange, how we suffer in spite of this!
> > > (*Bei Hennef*)

In this series of poems are many over-intimate revelations of Lawrence's sexual history in his marriage, released to the world with the courage of the 'broken-backed snake'. They are over-intimate in the sense in which we feel that the expression can do nothing for us, any more than the verbal utterance could do everything for Lawrence. We admire his striving, but he cannot *place* these experiences, because he cannot (unaided) gain insight into them. As in *Lady Chatterley* he virtually brings us to the borders of things into which only psychoanalysis could penetrate further:

          The night was a failure
             but why not – ?
       In the darkness
          with the pale dawn seething at the window
          through the black frame
          I could not be free,
          not free myself from the past, those others –
          and our love was a confusion,
          there was a horror,
          you recoiled away from me.
                              (*First Morning*)

It is this haunting, this horror, that Lawrence was still seeking to
exorcise verbally in *Lady Chatterley*. The escape is sought for, as an
oblivion, for peace: but only a fitful peace could come! In some
lines the peace yearned for seems almost to be death:

       I wish it would be completely dark everywhere,
       inside me and out, heavily dark
       utterly.
                          (And Oh – that the man
                          I am might cease to be)

   Judged in terms of poetic quality, only a few of the poems in
the series *Look! We Have Come Through!* have very great interest:
they are too personal, too little anything more than personal, as of
'a man speaking to men'. Their failure to be achieved as poems, to
order the experience itself, relates to the failure to allay the personal ghosts, such as Mellors experiences. Like Connie, 'she' thinks
of her procreativity, and Lawrence resists it:

       My hand withered in your hand.
       For you were straining with a wild heart, back, back again,
       Back to those children you have left behind, to all the
                                 aeons of the past . . .
       At last, as you stood, your white gown falling from
                                 your breasts,
       You looked into my eyes, and said: 'But this is joy!'
       I acquiesced again.

'Acquiesced' – the word reminds us of Mellors' unwillingness to open himself as if he fears to be hurt and humiliated. 'Threw in his lot', 'acquiesced' – the words come from one who cannot easily and gladly give himself! The creative woman is feared:

> But the shadow of lying was in your eyes,
> The mother in you, *fierce as a murderess*, glaring
> > to England,
> Yearning towards England, towards your young children,
> Insisting upon your motherhood, devastating
> *I have learned to curse your motherhood* . . .
> Therefore, even in the hour of my deepest, passionate,
> > *malediction*
> I try to remember it is also well between us.
> That you are with me in the end.
> > (My italics)

As with Connie and Mellors, the woman is 'there' – symbolized in *Lady Chatterley* by mutual orgasm – yet in him the fear and jealousy, and the malediction, remain. The feelings he describes about motherhood are probably not like that in *her* at all, but are in him, and projected over the woman he fears. Because of their love the world seems to become 'gone': Lawrence makes his quest for love with great energy and beauty:

> At last I can throw away the world without end, and
> > meet you
> Unsheathed and naked and narrow and white:
> At last you can throw immortality off, and I see you
> Glistening with all the moment and all your beauty.

But still a reserve is held:

> Out of *indifference* I love you . . .
> > (*Frohnleichnam*)

And there is still fear:

> 'There is something in you that destroys me – !'

She cries. There follow two poems which suggest how over-dependent Lawrence was in the relationship – dependent in an infantile sense, as Mellors is. These poems are significantly called

Mutilation and *Humiliation*. These are both things that Lawrence (as Morelorence) deeply feared unconsciously, and they associate, obviously, with Lawrence's dismay that at times possession of the desired woman led to an annihilation which brought pain even in satisfaction:

> Tonight I have left her alone.
> They would have it I left her for ever.
> Ah my God how it aches!
> Where she is cut off from me!
>
> A cripple!
> Oh God, to be mutilated!
> To be a cripple!
>
> And if I never see her again?
> I think if they told me so
> I could convulse the heavens with my horror.

I would not wish to deny that reality of love which seems 'as strong as death' or the capacity of a lover to proclaim 'let Rome in Tiber melt', or even to prefer death or the end of the world to the end of his love. But the terms here in which Lawrence puts the matter are strangely neurotic – in terms of bodily mutilation, rather than in terms of the nobility of a cosmic gesture as in, 'My heaven dissolved so . . .', of Donne. It was the same fear of mutilation that he punishes in Clifford, a fear of retributive castration. For Lawrence there is something in his fear of being deprived of relationship and suffering in consequence of a total loss of existence, *such as an infant fears if separated from the mother. Humiliation* goes on:

> Do not leave me, or I shall break.
> Do not leave me.
> What should I be, I myself,
> 'I'?
> What should I think of death?
> If I died, it would not be you:
> It would be simply the same
> Lack of you . . .
> And God that she is necessary!

That she is *'necessary'* (in a poem called *Humiliation*) is related to
the reason for seeking to humiliate the woman in *Lady Chatterley*.
An adult needs to accept that, though he might suffer terribly
from the ending of a relationship, he would not in fact die. Not to
accept this fact often goes with the need to make impossible demands on a relationship -- as, indeed Lawrence does and as Mellors
does – with his author's approval.

The relation of such things in these poems to *Lady Chatterley* is
obvious – the fears in each of the lovers, Clifford's being a cripple,
Connie's 'Don't leave me!' and his (Mellors') attitude to Connie –
'It heals me!' and his demands on her for immediate submissive
satisfaction.

In *Look! We Have Come Through!* at this point, from his fresh
honeymoon experience follow some lovely poems – among the
tenderest and most beautiful in all Lawrence's work: *A Young
Wife*:

> The pain of loving you
> Is almost more than I can bear.

Also *Green*:

> She opened her eyes, and green
> They shone, clear like flowers undone
> For the first time, now for the first time seen.

Then *River Roses*, *Gloire de Dijon*, and others – honeymoon
moments caught of great tenderness, having behind them a deep
sensuality, but one which is subdued, tacit and peaceful. The poems
catch from time the very touch of love, the sweet sense of togetherness, from the civilized experience of living together. The depth of
the poems comes from no over-insistence on sensuality, but from
the keen perceptions and joy in living that goes with post-coital
tenderness in love. In these poems of Lawrence, written just after
his marriage, with the bliss of honeymoon overcoming his sense
of fear and doom for a time, the 'continual sense of her' (a phrase
from a poem by Edgell Rickword) gives them a subtle beauty of
atmosphere, and a quality capturing the sweetness of love of a kind
one never finds in *Lady Chatterley's Lover*. 'She' is real, in a world

of real flowers, allowed her own identity, while he maintains his.
Here is one of the most beautiful of these poems:

> Just a few of the roses we gathered from the Isar
> Are fallen, and their mauve-red petals on the cloth
> Float like boats on a river, while other
> Roses are reluctant to fall, reluctant and loth.
>
> She laughs at me across the table, saying
> I am beautiful. I look at the rumpled young roses
> And suddenly realize, in them as me,
> How lovely is the self this day discloses.
>
> *Roses on the Breakfast Table*

How one would give the whole of *Lady Chatterley* for those eight
lines! I remember, when seeking through Lawrence for poems for
my anthology *Iron Honey Gold*, for poetic material to convey to
young people the experience in imagination of love, being by this
point in some despair: the poems in this volume were so tortured.
They were passionate, but they were not good poetry. They
lacked rhythm and clarity, because they were unrealized, and in-
sufficiently separated from 'the man' in terms of 'a man speaking
to men'. And then, to come across *Green*, and this poem – the
anxiety gone, and the true voice of love's gladness speaking! One
is directly moved, to read *Roses on the Breakfast Table*: it captures
so the evanescence of love, the small, touch-light, changeable
quality of love between two people which is the reality, rather
than the great phallus-worshipping, ghost-chasing sensuality of
Lady Chatterley, and 'immemorial potency' – all of which is a
great bore. Here *is* a man speaking to men, making the love-
experience universal to us – we recognize the mood as one we
have experienced: so much of *Lady Chatterley* seems alien to our
real experience. And here is a love which conquers Time. As the
lovers come down from their bed they see on the table roses they
have picked by the river – the river which flows (like Time). The
petals have 'fallen', the splash of colour (like blood, the blood of
passion and of mortal flesh) only enhancing their evanescence,
floating 'like boats' down the 'river' of Time. Other roses are
reluctant to drop their petals (notice he says the '*roses* are fallen' –

the rose here is a potent sexual symbol, and the substitution of
'roses' for 'petals' is made not only to avoid conventional expression
– the rose here is the self given in love – the reluctance of yielding
being given by enactment across the line break. There is a loss in
the falling. How deeply the image goes, how much more deeply
than any description of sexual intercourse!) She laughs at him (and
for Lawrence, how happily far from the fear of humiliation he
must have been to be glad of this!). And as she does so he sees in
the roses images of themselves: 'rumpled, young' – the rose, as in
Blake, relates to the 'bed of crimson joy' – they are the lovers' bed,
which was also 'rumpled' by the young lover:

> And suddenly realize, in them as me . . .
> How lovely is the self *this* day

There is no doubt that the sensual joy of love is behind this moment of small, petal-like rapture between Lawrence and his wife;
'this day' is 'our day' – there is a powerful concept of 'us' here –
and the moment is an acceptance by Lawrence of his own sexuality, and their bodily love as 'lovely' and a natural beauty, like the
roses, floating in the same river of Time. This is the kind of
moment in which the bodily life generates from its richness an
awareness which develops concepts of 'love'. The activity belonging to the intelligent civilized consciousness, and this apprehends
a love-reality that triumphs over Time in a sense of continuity.
The roots of the concepts are, like the sexual meaning of the roses,
in the unconscious and in the whole bodily being. But this is
implicit, not verbalized. To truly accept the reality and beauty of
sex is indivisibly bound up with *loving oneself* as Lawrence comes
to do here: he is happy to be a lover, and his guilty sense of doom
is for once absent, allowing him to be so. He has his identity ('she
laughs at me'), she has hers, and time and place are real. As the
next poem says, 'I am myself at last . . .'

But the fears remain still with Lawrence, the fears of annihilation and rejection, of being deprived of affection. Dissociation
follows: the bridges between inner and outer reality break down:

> The space of the world is immense, before me and around me
> If I turn quickly, I am terrified, feeling space surround me:

Like a man in a boat on very clear, deep water, frightens
                        and confounds me . . .
                Song of a Man who is Not Loved

And these fears associate with his fears of the multitude, over
whom (in *Lady Chatterley*) he projects his paranoia:

                        Ah, if only
There were no teeming
Swarms of mankind in the world, and we were less lonely!

And then, strangely enough, in the middle of the series of poems
of 'coming through' to adult love with a woman – or perhaps not
strangely, when we know what we do know about Lawrence's
relationship with his mother – there is a passionate poem to his
dead mother as 'little darling' (written at *Lago di Garda*). Even the
loveliness of self he has discovered belongs to his mother: it is as if
he is re-establishing her claim over him, even on honeymoon:

        . . . For what is loveliness my love,
                Save you have it with me!
        All the things that are lovely –
                The things you never knew –
        I wanted to gather them one by one
                And bring them to you.
        . . . I'll whisper the ghostly truth to you
                And tell you how
        I know you here in the darkness,
                How you sit in the throne of my eyes
        At peace, and look out of the windows
                In glad surprise.
                        Everlasting Flowers
                        (*For a dead mother*)

The second stanza quoted above might serve as a terrible motto
for *Lady Chatterley's Lover* – for Lawrence is obviously wishing
powerfully – and largely unbeknown to himself – to give his
mother the things he enjoys, both sexual beauty and the beauty of
the natural world, even though he apprehends them through his
love for Frieda. For the same reason he made his mother into
Connie Chatterley, and brought her his gifts as himself as Mellors:

the mode of bringing one creature to enter the experience of another is given in the last verse. The tender passion of his love is strangely poured out here on the dead mother, even in a sickly infantile rhythm, the jingling measure of a cheap greetings card – despite the beauties of the scene described, the poem is frighteningly indulged nostalgia: the man cannot escape from mother-love even in his marriage relationship. So his images become confused, and touch with the real recedes.

With the dissolution of the object, unpolarized aggression and destructiveness assert themselves. So, the mother-possessed man and the woman begin to fight. Lawrence, like Mellors, is sensually cruel:

> What? – your throat is bruised, bruised with my kisses?
> Ah, but if I am cruel what then are you?
> I am bruised right through
>
> *A Bad Beginning*

and he lays down conditions, as Mellors does – is 'provident'

> You would take me to your breast! but no,
> You should come to mine,
> It were better so . . .
> Not as a visitor either, nor a sweet
> And winsome child of innocence; nor
> As an insolent mistress . . .
> Come to me like a woman coming home
> To the man who is her husband . . .
>   Which way are you coming?
>
> *A Bad Beginning*

The poem is called A Bad Beginning: and it is – love wilts at such conditions, such constraints. As Chaucer said, 'Love will not be constrayned by maistrye. . . .' Lawrence wants Frieda to come to him as a Mrs Morel to Morel or Paul: yet when he makes Mrs Morel Constance, he forces her, as Mellors or Morelorence, to be submissive to such injunctions. Connie *is* a 'sweet and winsome child of innocence'. Is it compatible with being 'a woman' – 'he and she . . . joined together for ever' – to be told *how* she must come to his arms? This implies surely that the man has the right to

order her to? Lawrence still wants to control the woman he fears,
and so the inconsistency increases, with his hostile discrimination
against her. Note the phrase 'take me to your breast': love with a
woman for him is still the anxiety-allaying comfort, as from a
mother. He wants to be loved by being given to: he is less able to
love by giving. He needs, like the sick Paul Morel, to lie on his
mother's breast – as when 'He took ease of her'. Lawrence cannot
escape his relationship with his mother: it possesses him, and her
corpse-candle burns between him and Frieda, as in the revealing
All Souls:

> On your grave in England the weeds grow
> But I am your naked candle burning,
> And there is not your grave, in England,
> The world is your grave . . .
>
> I forget you, have forgotten you.
> I am busy at my burning,
> I am busy only at my life.
> But my feet are on your grave, planted . . .
>
> I am a naked candle burning off on your grave

Strange that Lawrence should have been so unaware of the sexual
meaning here to allow this poem, with all its implications, in the
phallic symbolism of the candle, even so as to add the word
'naked'. His feet are in her grave, and she is in his 'phallic' 'naked
self', 'standing' on her grave. Here are the roots of his anxiety, his
sense of doom, his narcissism – for if she is in him, looking out
from his eyes, and he

> my naked body standing on your grave
> Upright towards heaven is burning off to you
> Its flame of life, now and always, till the end . . .

'Naked candle', 'naked body', 'standing', 'burning off' – the intense erotic power of the words suggest a coition with the self, in
order to find the mother. His mother is present in his phallic
experience, too intensely. So, 'I stand for the resurrection of the
body' – and by self-coition Lawrence attempts to resurrect his

mother's body, so that she can look out of his eyes at the world, even be present in his own married sexual experience. Strange quality in Lawrence, that explains so much, not least the narcissistic intensity of *Lady Chatterley's Lover* and its life-denying elements! For Lawrence projects his search for the mother in intense passionate incestuous love of her, dead, over Frieda's desire to be with her own living children. Naturally this mixes with Lawrence's jealousy of her sexual experience with her former husband, and is reinforced in its hate. In *Lady Chatterley* it is distilled into the ferocious indifference to child bearing, procreativity, and the conception by Lady Chatterley of Mellors' child.

Thus the poems in *Look! We Have Come Through!* move, as does *Lady Chatterley's Lover*, into storm and recrimination from which turmoil there seems at times no escape. We hear the voice of Lawrence quarrelling with Frieda: we hear the dominating male, with his father's voice, Morelorence seeking to humiliate her, to reduce her to Connie's submissiveness. Frieda, however, was not the kind to be tipped up on the path – she demanded to be treated as an equal being:

> Listen, I have no use
>> For so rare a visit;
> Mine is a common devil's
>> Requisite.
>
> Rise up and go, I have no use for you
>> And your blithe, glad mien.
> No angels here, for me no goddesses,
>> Nor any Queen.

(Ah, the 'sons of gods with the daughters of men')

> Put ashes on your head, put sackcloth on
>> *And learn to serve!*

('She had to become his slave!')

> You have fed me with your sweetness, now I am sick
> As I deserve.
> Be common stuff

(She must be a 'nice bit of arse', a 'nice bit o' cunt')

What are you by yourself, do you think, and what
    The mere fruit of your womb?
Is it more than the apples of Sodom you scorn so, the men
    Who abound?

Bring forth the sons of your womb, then, and put them
    Into the fire
Of Sodom that covers the earth; bring them forth
    From the womb of your precious desire.

You woman most holy, you mother, you being beyond
    Question or diminution,
Add yourself up, and your seed, to the *nought*
    Of your last solution.

Lawrence hates the woman so much he must seek to destroy
her. By anal possession Mellors brings Constance to 'the nought
of her last solution', too.

These poems have little to offer, expressive as they are only of
neurotic states, aberrant attitudes, beyond the poet's power to
grapple with them. Their destructive implications – intensely
hostile to creativity – yield no insights. Down with the woman
and her fruit! The impulse to deny the woman and her creative
power, and her right to respect and finally to annihilate her to
nought culminates in the novel in Connie's death in the night of
'awful sensuality'. To take a woman anally is the ultimate denial
of her feminity, and, as I have suggested, a neurotic attempt to
prove her body is not full of hostile wounding forces: a similar
fear lies behind male homosexuality. The act of anal possession is
an expression of the man's wishes that the woman was not a
woman. 'Since I must serve and struggle with the immanent
mystery . . .' But the woman and the womb *are* the mystery: for
Lawrence the mystery was the apples of Sodom, the man the
phallus bearer. In fear, because of his attachment to his mother, he
feared vengeance from the father, even in the woman's secret
places. So the woman must be denied and brought to 'nought' and
her progency put to the fire. In this impulse Lawrence expresses a
destructive impulse not unrelated to that psychotic manifestation

that burned alive newborn Jewish children in concentration camps.[1]

In the poems *Both Sides of the Medal* and *Loggerheads* we have a voice as bitter and ironic as Ezra Pound's irony. But it has not the strength of intelligent self-knowledge: there is no developing grasp on personal reality, merely a sequence of impossible arguments for the denial of mutual regard in marriage. Among these are poems of desperate sensuality – of the throat bruised with kisses, the search for ways of bringing the woman to sacrifice, to humiliation and 'nought': 'You're a dove I have bought for sacrifice . . .'

There are, too, with these poems of strange lusts to tear a rabbit in, such as *Rabbit Snared in the Night*:

I must be reciprocating *your* vacuous, hideous passion . . .

The poetry here becomes at times adolescent in the ungoverned surges of its verbal intensity. It is devoid of any true interest of rhythm or texture. Lawrence himself symbolizes his quest as a search for 'the gate' of Paradise in *Paradise Re-Entered*: here is another motto-poem for *Lady Chatterley*:

> To the intoxication,
> The mind, fused like a bead,
> Flees in its agitation
> The flames' stiff speed:
>
> At last to calm incandescence,
>   Burned clean by remorseless hate,
> Now at the day's renascence
>
> We approach the gate . . .
> But we storm the angel-guarded
> Gates of the long discarded
> Garden, which God has hoarded
> Against our pain.

The first line is 'Through the strait gate of passion'. The quest is a sensual quest, for the possession of a plenty which it seems 'God' has 'hoarded' – the attitude revealed here seems to be one which is

[1] See *The Tragedy of Children under Nazi Rule*, by Kiryl Sosnowski, Zachodnia Agencia Prasowa, 1962.

depressive, as though 'God' were hostile. The poem is guilty, too, as though to open a hoard of plenty were wrong. Strangely, it is 'hate' which 'burns clean' – the ferocious urge to bring the woman to her 'nought'. The poem revels in the satisfactions of anger and cruelty, and it reveals the hostile and destructive side of Lawrence that was to thwart him in *Lady Chatterley* and lead him to become malevolent. The reality of love cannot be found, and do the 'aggressive components' are not resolved. The verse under the unreality becomes empty and false:

> Beautiful, candid lovers,
> Burnt out of our earthly covers,
> We might have nestled like plovers
> In the fields of eternity . . .

The poor verse goes with the frenetic sensuality, immature and yearning. The language becomes stilted and takes on the lifeless-ness of, say, the most morbid Swinburne and the air of *malaise* of the *fin de siècle* movement. We turn back to *Lady Chatterley* to see that it too belongs to this same *genre* of lifeless, over-literary and over-nervous writing. The search expressed in these bad poems is the same search for peace by sensuality. The oral aggres-sion is at one with the 'remorseless hate' that seeks to 'burn out shame', by a sensuality that consumes. It seeks to burn the mind to sleep, to cleave the consciousness, to allay the sense of doom. But it cannot find paradise, because it is a false solution. Without love, coition allays anxiety merely like an anodyne, leaving no sense of continuity to make the intervals of exhausted passion tolerable. So, annihilation is feared, and the poetic effort is a means to going on living.

> Worse, do not let me deceive myself . . .

is the last line of *Look! We Have Come Through!* But driven so by his neurotic self-deceptions, Lawrence had to be convincing, or, he felt, perish. In the end, defeated in the conflict between truth and lie, the tormented psyche-soma perished, and wanted the world to perish too.

The best Lawrentian rhythm and creativity, however, returned

like the Phoenix he is, to the series *Look! We Have Come Through,!*
with those poems which delineate 'a measure of equanimity'.
While here there are still failures of mutual regard and maturity
to record, it is obvious that the protagonists are as happy as they
could be, and that real state of relationship is one Lawrence is
really striving to accept. She is his 'little one' – and he exerts
towards her a tenderness such as Mellors is incapable of rendering
Connie.

> How I love all of you!
>> How lovely your round head, your arms...
>>> I feel that we
> Are a bonfire of oneness, me flame flung leaping
>>>> round you...
>> You the core of fire, crept into me...

This is tender and beautiful again, the great Lawrence of *Spring*,
Mountain Lion, and *Snake* – of those poems of wonder at Creation,
who can speak of our need to 'have the courage of our feelings'.
But he is yet over-dependent:

> How quaveringly I depend on you, to keep me alive . . .
> Supposing you didn't want me! I should sink down
> Like a light that has no sustenance . . .
>
> Nourish me, and endue me, I am only of you,
> *I am of your issue* . . .

He is her baby son, son of Lady Chatterley, of the 'little one', the
girl-mother:

> How I depend on you utterly,
>> My little one, my big one!

But mother and wife have become merged, and for a moment
Lawrence can even contemplate parenthood:

> And think, there will something come forth from us
> We two, folded small together,
> There will something come forth from us.
> Children, acts, utterance,
> Perhaps only happiness.
>>>>>>> *Wedlock*

The verse is most poignant, for perhaps the strange malevolence that speaks through Lady Chatterley is that of Lawrence having been denied the child he timidly here expresses his hope to have. It would have been a difficult experience for him to have a family but it was one which nobody more deserved. His understanding of children (as in *Aaron's Rod* and *The Rainbow*) was profound. Yet his whole psyche is polarized against procreation, too. This 'measure of equanimity' is a measure of a kind of security more appropriate to the infant than the adult lover:

> So I hope I shall spend eternity
> With my face down buried between her breasts
> And my still heart full of security,
> And my still hands full of her breasts.
>
> *Song of a Man who is loved*

Strange, however, that Lawrence of all people should have looked to a future of eternity 'buried', still, with a heart full of security, as if his woman was a matrix, a healing place of forgetfulness of the world. 'Security' here is too much the allaying of anxiety. But in the later poems there is even a reconciliation with the world, and adult reality, with a relaxation of fear of harm:

> What is the knocking?
> What is the knocking at the door in the night?
> It is somebody wants to do us harm.
> No, no, it is the three strange angels.
> Admit them, admit them.
>
> *Song of a Man who Has come Through*

> I could cry with joy, because I am in the new world . . .
> I was so weary of the world
> I was so sick of it
> It was all tainted with myself . . .

In '*She said as well to me*' and *New Heaven and Earth* we have the account of how, in learning to touch one another she learned awe – was told, at any rate, to have awe:

> Don't touch me and appreciate me.
> You would think twice before you touched a weasel . . .
> Nor the adder we saw . . .

The protagonist finds a new earth when all was destroyed.

The murdered bodies of youths and men in heaps –

The anxiety of the war, the war wound which lies so heavily behind *Lady Chatterley*, is grasped as an aspect of the reality of the twentieth century. As with all of us, the threat war brings seems to confirm our unconscious depressive attitudes, that the world is hostile and we have no resources to deal with it. In this state love can be the means to a touch with reality and to a gradual restitution of our faith in continuity and of our hope.

> I, in the sour black tomb, trodden to absolute death . . .
> I put out my hand in the night, one night, and my hand
> touched that which was verily not me . . .
>
> I am the discoverer!
>
> . . . whom I married years ago . . .
> Yet rising from the tomb . . .
>   I was carried by the current in death
> over to the new world, was climbing out on the shore . . .
>   . . . she too has strange green eyes!
>
> White sand and fruits unknown and perfumes that never
> can blow across the dark seas to our usual world!
> And land that beats with a pulse!
> And valleys that draw close in love!
> And strange ways where I fall into oblivion of uttermost
>   living!
> And she who is the other has strange-mounded breasts
>   and strange sheer slopes and white levels.

This is a very beautiful poem in its sense of renewal and of awed discovery in the familiar life, imbued with a sense of gentle triumphing, creative love. It is as though Lawrence suddenly found not the mother, nor himself, in his wife – but a sudden disclosure of her real otherness as a creature. There are passages, lovely passages, of bodily contemplation in *Lady Chatterley's Lover* which echo this, but they are more often anxious and insistent, more sensual, more tractarian. They lack the essential rhythm as here of a mystical but domestic love-experience. Here

is the achievement of the apprehension of the reality of being
'separate, separate'.

This sense of her real 'otherness' Lawrence found terrible, but
yet a source of great self-realization and harmony between himself and his wife. It gives him a greater sense of his own reality, and
of that of the world. The philosophical perception of separateness
in togetherness is achieved here in a poem *Manifesto*, and it sums
up the best truth of *Women in Love*.

> When she has put her hand on my secret, darkest
>   sources, the darkest outgoings,
> when it has struck home to her, like a death,
>   'this is *him*!'
> she has no part in it, no part whatever,
> it is the terrible other,
>
> I shall be cleared, distinct, single as if burnished
>   in silver . . .
>
> One clear, burnished, isolated being, unique,
> and she also, pure, isolated, complete,
> two of us, utterably distinguished, and in
>   unutterable conjunction.
>
> Then we shall be free, freer than angels, ah
>   perfect . . .
> After that, there will only remain that all men
>   detach themselves and become unique . . .
>
> Every human being
>
> We shall love, we shall hate,
> But it will be like music, sheer utterance . . .
> like lightning and the rainbow . . .
> We shall not look before and after.
> We shall *be*, *now*.
> We shall know in full
> We, the mystic NOW.

This Manifesto is acceptable – and how different from the manifesto in Mellors' mind during his final act of coition with Connie
in the novel, or the Manifesto of his letter at the end of *Lady*

Chatterley, or the recommendation in *Lady Chatterley* that 'warm-hearted fucking' will cure human woe! Here Lawrence's love, his sense of tender togetherness takes him beyond selfishness into the mutual regard between lovers, and the at-one-ness with creation, through love, that has affinities with the Eastern concepts such as I have quoted of creative sex as a reflection of the Divine Creativity, or Shakespeare's perception of love and continuity. Here we have a vision of civilized love – not enclosed in mere eroticism. The love-problem is solved not by sensuality, but by a better sense of the 'not-me'. How different is this dealing with 'touch' from what is symbolized in *Lady Chatterley* by Connie's touch on Mellors' 'balls', and her being 'a little terrified' by his penis. Here, as in the poem above about his wife's flank, the word 'touch' has another significance than the sensual caress – it means to touch the other being's reality and existence, and become aware of its separateness, its separate right to *be*, to be both in separateness and in conjunction, its 'disquality'. It is true that if we could reach this 'touch' (cf. the conversation between Connie and Mrs Bolton), and were freed from our clinging ghosts, our infantile dependence, our attempts to possess and dominate – if we could achieve balanced separateness in togetherness, as Birkin and Ursula do, then the 'rainbow' would be ours – for the children of the next generations to walk beneath. It *would* put the world right indeed.

If we could all accept this separateness, accept ourselves as separate, mysterious parts of created life each with its own 'mystic NOW', living now, without caring for progress, or being haunted by the past, 'knowing ('within and without') in full' *now*, then indeed, as Lawrence says here, the world would be like music, and human life like the flower, the lightning, the rainbow. It is a magnificent passage: and true, because it is a vision of the reality of each our separate existence, mysterious and unique, and the truth of togetherness in love, with its values of mutual regard by which we can try to live.

How different from the recommendation of 'warm-hearted fucking' for a solution for the world's ills! 'Too much cold-blooded fucking' – yes – but too much mere 'fucking' and 'fucking' talk and not enough love in truth. Too much anxious talk, writing, sensual questing, looking and enquiring about sex. How much more real in the best poems here is the philosophical concept derived from the history of the personal love and the record of its rhythms and forms. These rhythms and forms are not sensual, but belong to intelligent apprehensions, rooted in passion, but becoming concepts – concepts of the nature of human nature, of love, of marriage, of courteous regard, of separateness in togetherness. Here the aggressive and destructive impulses are fused with the erotic. Rooted in the sensual, their civilized experience of love yet counts most in areas far remote from the sensual.

Lady Chatterley's Lover denies mind and love: the poet's are 'liars'. *Look! We Have Come Through! is* a definition of love and marriage, however little truly remarkable poetry is to be found in it. And it shows that the poets are not liars: we need them more than 'rather awful sensuality', to help us find reality and love.

The reasons for the falsification in the novel, however, are confirmed in the personal history. Even at the end, there is a flaw. – the flaw which makes Lawrence still anxious, even at the end of all his work. It is that he still feels that his wife does not accept their separateness in togetherness:

> I want her though, to take the same from me.
> She touches me as if I were herself, her own.
> She has not realized yet, that fearful thing, that
> I am the other,
> She thinks we are all of one piece.
> It is painfully untrue.
>
> *Manifesto*

Lawrence still wants to *teach* Frieda something – he is still discriminating against her. He still attributes to her impulses his fears. What he is anxious to dispel in her is projected from himself – by his own fear that he is not 'separate', not separate from her nor from the ghosts of the past. Essentially it is a problem of his sense of his own identity, and of loving himself. The very activity of discriminating is a denial of the philosophical conclusion of the poems, for if she is 'separate' then she is entitled to her own conclusions about separateness. But Lawrence, because he is not separated enough from his mother, will not have his wife exerting her essential woman's right to be 'clear', apart, distinct, single 'as if burnished in silver' – that right to be healed and cleared belongs to the man, the sons of gods. She as 'the daughter of men' can only be 'pure', 'isolated', 'complete' – but must make no demands on him! She must give, suckle, heal, allay, submit. She must be the 'mother' such as an infant 'makes'. It is a subtle difference, and in the end a failure to accept his own conclusions. For such reasons Lawrence was forced to invent the Mellors who was to teach Connie – to teach woman, as he wishes to 'teach' Frieda – her 'place'. In the end, as we have seen, this fear of the loss of the self in 'horrible mingling' became a denial of the 'other' that develops into an attack on all humanity and all reality, in destructive animus.

F. R. Leavis commends Lawrence for his enactment in Birkin of the prophetic preaching in which Birkin indulges – or in which Lawrence indulges through Birkin:

> There is now to come the new day, when we are beings each of us, fulfilled in difference. The man is pure man, the woman pure woman, and they are perfectly polarized. But there is no longer any of the horrible merging mingling self-abnegation of love. There is only the pure duality of polarization, each one free from any contamination of the other. In each, the individual is primal, sex is subordinate, but perfectly perfectly polarized. Each has a single separate being, with its own laws. The man has his pure freedom, the woman hers. Each recognizes the perfection of the polarized sex-circuit. Each admits the different nature in the other.

This perception of a relationship between man and woman, as Leavis points out, is the obverse of that between Gerald and Gudrun, which is mutually destructive. But it is realized neither in *Lady Chatterley* nor in *Look! We Have Come Through!* Nor is it, to tell the truth, found anywhere in Lawrence's work. Yet the reality of an actual relationship behind the poems makes less possible the kind of falsification made in the novel, and gives us a half-dozen quiet poems which are of far greater value than the notorious book, in the quest for love.

Appendix A

Few readers, I think, feel anything but irritation with Aaron in *Aaron's Rod*, who leaves his family and wanders aimlessly among 'artistic' people and aristocrats in Europe. The irritation is but exacerbated by the interminable conversations by which Lawrence, who is both Aaron and Lilly (Llaaronce, as it were), seeks to justify the hero. Most of these conversations, despite their occasional fleeting felicities, are crude attempts to vindicate Lawrence's fear of woman, and the realities of femininity and love which include procreation. In his denial of the reality of the woman's sexual needs – to be aroused, to be given security, to be *courted* – Lawrence invents the most ridiculous nonsense about historical precedents, as if to deny the reality of this present life altogether:

'It is love itself which gnaws us inside, like a cancer,' said the Italian . . . 'there is for both of us, I know it, something which bites us, which eats us within, and drives us, drives us, somewhere, we don't know where. But it drives us, and eats away the life – and yet we love each other and we must not be separate . . .'

'Why is it?'

'Because a woman, she now first wants the man, and he must go to her because he is wanted. Do you understand? You know – supposing I go to a woman – supposing she is my wife – and I go to her, yes, with my blood all ready, because it is I who want. Then she puts me off. Then she says, not now, not now, I am tired, I am not well. I do not feel like it. She puts me off – till I am angry or sorry or whatever I am – but till my blood has gone down again, you understand, and I don't want her any more. And then she puts her arms round me, and caresses me, and makes love to me – till she rouses me once more. So, and so she rouses me – and so I come to her. And I love her, it is very good, very good. But it is she who began, it was her initiative, you know. I do not think, in all my life, my wife has loved me from *my* initiative, you know. . . . Then she says all she wants is that I should desire her, that I should love her and desire her. But even that is putting *her* will first . . .'

The feelings here (obviously this is Lawrence speaking) are more to be explained in some such terms as I use above, in discussing the reactions of the baby to the mother in feeding, than adult sexuality. Lawrence could not tolerate being 'turned down' by a woman – it obviously filled him with fear. But so, too, does the erotic approach of the woman, and her desires, in which he fears domination. It is likely that behind such a strong fear lies some trouble in Lawrence's own formation of relationship with the mother in infancy, because here he shows that in sex he wants to 'create' the object of desire before it comes: that is, he cannot bear the woman to make the first approach. It is possible that if, when he was a baby, his food was forced on him before he was ready, because of some theory of his mother's, or because of working class methods, he would have such a fear. To be, as a man, so appalled by feminine domination, as a threat of extinction suggests such an early cause – particularly since the reality sense is so deeply affected, and feminine advance regarded with terror, as if it was a feed coming before he was 'ready'. A contributing element may have been the intense sensitivity of Lawrence's acute phantasy power in infancy itself.

The terror of the woman's sexual approach is so deep that the Marchese can cry,

> 'It matters life or death. It used to be that desire started in the man, and the woman answered. It used to be so for a long time in Italy. For this reason the women were kept away from the men. For this reason the Catholic religion tried to keep the girls in convents, and innocent, before marriage. So that with their minds they should not know, and should not start this terrible thing, the woman's desire over a man, beforehand....'

There is a good deal more ridiculous sexual history to follow: but, of course, Lawrence may be talking about infancy as an unconsciously remembered state, rather than any historical facts of which he was aware. The repulsion at the feminine 'will' is soon linked with Lawrence's loathing of the procreative family:

> 'Eve.... Ah, I hate Eve ... the bourgeois husband he goes on being the same, he is the horse, and she the driver. And when she says gee-up, you know – then he comes ready, like a hired maquereau. Only

he feels so good, *like a good little boy at her breast.* And then there are the nice little children, And so they keep the world going – But for me – ' he spat suddenly and with frenzy on the floor.

'You are quite right, my boy,' said Argyle. 'You are quite right. They've got the start of us, the women: and we've got to canter when they say gee-up. I – oh, I went through it all. But then I broke the shafts and smashed the matrimonial cart, I can tell you, and I didn't care whether I smashed her up along with it or not.'

'She is dead and buried these dozen years . . .'

(My italics)

This cruelty and hatred is fully endorsed by Lawrence, and he is far from seeing, in any of these characters, the inadequacy they betray in their capacities to be men, and to cope with feminine reality, with marriage, family life, and to maintain self-respect. Though Argyle cries about 'a man with a drop of spunk in him' – and we suspect Lawrence desperately wanted to show himself that – we feel that none of these are such men – otherwise there would be no need for them to exert in such ways their splenetic hatred of women, 'She will . . . harry you into submission . . . make a dog of you . . . cuckold you . . . you'll submit . . . your only chance is to smash the shafts . . . uncanny hellish strength . . . she-bear . . . wolf . . . knuckling under . . .': the language is deeply charged with hate – and fear.

As with his unrealities about sex in *Lady Chatterley,* Lawrence tries to enlist us into accepting this nonsense, by making his characters agree that 'their experience' was similar in a crudely mechanical way:

'What was yours?' asked Lilly.
'Mine was the same. Mine was the same, if ever it was,' said Argyle with a grimace.
'And yours, Lilly?' asked the Marchese anxiously.
'Not very different,' said Lilly.

But despite this attempt to universalize his own fears, by attributing them to a bunch of self-like characters, Lawrence must also express his sense of the alternative to accepting woman's reality:

'Does he seek another woman? Do you, Aaron?'

'I don't *want* to,' said Aaron, 'But – I can't stand by myself in the middle of the world and in the middle of people, and know I am quite by myself, and nowhere to go, and nothing to hold on to. I can for a day or two – But then it becomes unbearable as well . . .'

The denial of woman is a denial of relationship, and of reality. So Lawrence knows he would be left with 'nothing to hold on to'. For him a relationship with a woman is 'the core' as with Aaron and Mellors: but yet he cannot accept the reality of any actual relationship. For this reason he gravitates towards that fascist-like domination which is a fear of being dominated (see p. 204 above) and so the unsatisfactory end of *Aaron's Rod* is in Lawrentian bunkum about 'let them in their souls submit to some greater soul than theirs . . . submission to the heroic soul in a greater man. . . . It is life-submission.' Lilly (who is Lawrence) has a face like 'a Byzantine eikon', and Aaron (who is also Lawrence) looks into it:

'And whom shall I submit to?' he said.

'Your soul will tell you,' replied the other.

Here we almost have an expression of that reversion to magic and denial of reality in favour of modes of infantile omnipotence such as found expression in Nazism. Though Lawrence saw Fascism as 'evil', there was a strong impulse in him to be fascinated by the mystic domination exerted by one man over others (as in *Kangaroo*), by incantation (as in *The Plumed Serpent*), and by the way adult responsibility could be forfeited in submission to a 'greater soul'. This recurrent latter theme is a 'false solution' elsewhere in his work. While in general Lawrence asserts the reality of individual life against political crudities, it is not enough to describe him as standing for 'sanity', for there is much that is destructive and even sinister in Lawrence's preoccupation with 'life-submission', where he means not 'submission to life', but 'submission of one's individual life'.

Appendix B

Gerald in *Women in Love* represents that exertion of will over the whole creature which Lawrence associates with the industrial world: thus he bears an obvious relationship to Morelorence, or, rather, more particularly, to Lawrence's father. As we have seen, Lawrence identifies himself with horses, in particular with St Mawr: but here, I think, because the horse is a mare, we may consider that the horse is a symbol of the mother. The 'disgusting dream' that is re-enacted here – although one accepts its poetic symbolism as F. R. Leavis interprets it – gains its especially disturbing force by being a phantasy of sadistic sexual intercourse between father and mother. Certainly there is no mistaking the sexual undertones:

> . . . a glistening, half-smiling look came into Gerald's face. He brought her back again, inevitably . . .
> It seemed as if he sank into her, magnetically, and could thrust her back against herself . . .

Such violence is how sexual intercourse between parents would seem to a child.

> . . . she convulsed herself utterly away from the horror . . . but he leaned forward, his face shining with fixed amusement, and at last he brought her down, sank her down, and was bearing her back to the mark.
> . . . It made Gudrun faint with poignant dizziness, which seemed to penetrate her to the heart . . .

Gerald is, of course, showing the girls how to make a female submit, as Lawrence shows us in *Lady Chatterley* how a 'real man' gets across 'a lady':

> He bit himself down on the mare like a keen edge biting home, and forced her round. She roared as she breathed, her nostrils were two wide, hot, holes, her mouth was apart, her eyes frenzied. It was a repulsive sight. But he held on her unrelaxed, with an almost mechanical relentlessness, keen as a sword pressing into her . . .

There are many phrases here which associate with the descriptions of sexual intercourse of a slightly sadistic kind in *Lady Chatterley*. Lawrence is here, I think, impelled to recreate in this act of cruel domination a phantasy memory of parental sexual intercourse:

> the man closed round her, and brought her down, almost as if she were part of his own physique.

– which is just as a child would see the physical one-ness of man and woman in its phantasies of 'horrible mingling'.

Appendix C

One of the most marvellous passages in Lawrence occurs in the Chapter '*Excurse*' (XXIII) in *Women in Love* – and it is marvellous because the protagonist is a real woman. For once Lawrence happily embraces a woman's needs, her reality, and her 'separate, separate' existence. The dialogue breaks, in its realization, away from the Lawrentian mouthings such as we find in *Aaron's Rod*. The complex sexual and fertility symbolism of the girl's unconscious plucking at berries is a lovely touch, and a means by which Lawrence keeps the scene authentic:

> . . . in the stress of her violent emotion, she got down from the car and went to the hedgerow, picking unconsciously some flesh-pink spindleberries, some of which were burst, showing their orange seeds.
>
> 'Ah, you are a fool,' he cried, bitterly, with some contempt.
>
> 'Yes, I am. I *am* a fool. And thank God for it. I'm too big a fool to swallow your cleverness . . .'

Note how 'flesh-pink' makes the caress by poetic symbolism erotic, yet inexplicit, while conveying beauty, creativity, awe and even fear (cf. 'burst'). Lawrence realizes the woman's *nous*, that rumbles his attempts to cloak his special pleading with weighted arguments:

> 'Go to your spiritual brides – but don't come to me as well, because I'm not having any, thank you. You're not satisfied, are you? Your spiritual brides can't give you what you want, they aren't common and fleshy enough for you, aren't they? . . . You will marry me for daily use . . . I know your dirty little game . . .'

Wonderful to hear the rhythms of a real woman's anger and pride, with their roots in real bodily jealousy, from a Lawrence who feared that womanly reality so!

> He stood in silence. A wonderful tenderness burned in him, at the sight of her quivering, so sensitive fingers: and at the same time he was full of rage and callousness.

The experience is delineated with great accuracy – the reality of this woman bringing Birkin-Lawrence to respect her and thus to love her more deeply, because she has established and is exerting her right to challenge in him:

'This is a degrading exhibition,' he said coolly.

'Yes, degrading indeed,' she said. 'But more degrading to you.'

'*You*', she cried. 'You! You truth-lover! You purity-monger! It *stinks,* your truth and your purity . . .

'You, and love! You may well say you don't want love. No, you want *yourself,* and dirt and death – that's what you want. You are so *perverse,* so death-eating. And then – '

'There's a bicycle coming,' he said, writhing under her loud denunciation.

She glanced down the road.

'I don't care,' she said.

Nevertheless, she was silent. The cyclist, having heard the voices raised in altercation, glanced curiously at the man, and the woman, and at the standing motorcar as he passed.

' – Afternoon,' he said, cheerfully.

– Wonderful comic touch! How much this passage restores one's faith in the great Lawrence, who can register and record life, without untruth, and be honest. Here Ursula makes the kind of exposure of Lawrence's narcissism I have tried to do in this book: if only Connie had tackled Mellors so! Ursula speaks in a real, hot-blooded way – and Lawrence is so glad of the truth that he can allow that comic and touching passage of the bicycle, the moment of breach, and touch with the outer world – a touch such as never comes into *Lady Chatterley.*

The whole scene should be read: it is one of great beauty. Ursula leaves Birkin after flinging down the rings:

He felt tired and weak. Yet he also was relieved. . . . No doubt Ursula was right . . .

This marks a great spiritual moment in Lawrence – here is no fear of female domination that must be 'broken': but a recognition of the woman's right to express truths with her intelligence, and that one should be prepared to accept her estimation of experiences in life. Here we follow the development of a relationship that is deeply sexual – but the growth of love is in the whole complex of being, not least the intelligence.

> He knew that his spirituality was a concomitant of a process of depravity, a sort of pleasure in self-destruction. . . . But . . . was not Ursula's way of emotional intimacy, emotional and physical, was it not just as dangerous, as Hermione's abstract spiritual intimacy? Fusion, fusion, this horrible fusion of two beings . . .

But here, instead of special pleading, or recording the kind of sloganizing that goes on in Mellors' head, we have a repulsion and fear *placed* as being in Birkin's mind, as Ursula leaves him stunned by the energy of that rage which goes with love. How we possess the scene as the delineation of what happens between a woman and man! We feel it as our experience, as universal experience – as we do hardly anything in *Lady Chatterley*! The lie is given to Birkin's recoil from 'horrible merging' by his immediately bending down to pick up the rings – though he does it from a sense that it is a pity they should lie there, rather than as an acceptance of her love. Yet . . .

> He could not bear to see the rings lying in the pale mud of the road. He picked them up, and wiped them unconsciously on his hands. They were the little tokens of the reality of beauty, the reality of happiness in warm creation. But he had made his hands all dirty and gritty . . .

The phrase 'happiness in warm creation' is significant: this is the Lawrence of truly creative attitudes to writing and life, even in a muddy moment. The passage is as deeply moving as *Green* and *Roses on the Breakfast Table* – it holds on to *reality*, and has great economy. The rings make Birkin's hands dirty – this symbolizes the down-to-earth quality of the real marriage, and the 'messiness' of the bodily reality that Birkin fears about love. In picking the rings up he comes to take up the reality of beauty and of bonds – so much more powerfully real than his fear. So he is overcome:

> There was a darkness over his mind. . . There was a point of anxiety in his heart now. He wanted her to come back. . . . He breathed lightly and regularly like an infant, that breathes innocently, beyond the touch of responsibility . . .

The anxiety is that she will not come back: he accepts that he cannot live without her. He recaptures in this moment the innocence of the infant whose joy is that of being beyond the acceptance of the 'responsibility' of disillusion. He wants now to take up Ursula as an adult woman. The pain is the pain of accepting reality. The moment is grave, tender and lovely – and no one can read it without tears who can respond to the art of words:

> She was coming back. He saw her drifting desultorily under the high hedge, advancing towards him slowly. He did not move, he did not look again. He was as if asleep, at peace, slumbering and utterly relaxed.
>
> She came up before him, hanging her head.
>
> 'See what a flower I found you,' she said, wistfully holding a piece of purple bell-heather under his face.
>
> . . . Everything had become simple again. . . . It was peace . . .

Yes! we cry! It is like that – not the whirlpools, the insistency, the fear, the breaking down of domination. Here is no controlled, half-conscious woman. Let the woman bring her reality and her claim to equal, disequal, life to you, and accept! 'He stood up and looked into her face. It was new and oh, so delicate in its luminous wonder and fear.' The most moving thing about this passage of very great writing is that Lawrence is able to see that the woman, in her real identity, fears too, and in both the anxieties and disturbances aroused by love are tenderly met, side by side, in simplicity and mutual regard, compassion, and *love*.

Index